27/6

Depression in Mentally Retarded Children and Adults

An Update for Clinical Practice

Anton Dosen,
Frank J. Menolascino,
Editors

Logon Publications
Leiden - the Netherlands

D1492773

CIP-GEGEVENS KONINKLIJKE BIBLIOTHEEK, DEN HAAG

Depression

Depression in mentally retarded children and adults /
(ed. by Anton Dosen ... et al.) - Leiden: Logon Publications
Met lit. opg.
ISBN 90-73197-01-5
SISO 606.3   UDC 616.89-056.36
Trefw.: depressiviteit: geestelijk gehandicapten.

Cover illustration: Samotnosc (Loneliness) by Leszek Kucz (Poland)
private collection

Printed in the Netherlands by ICG Printing bv, Dordrecht

Table of Contents

page

Introduction   6

About the authors   8

Section 1: Overview

1. Mental retardation and the risk, nature and types of
   mental illness
   F.J. Menolascino   11

2. The phenomenon of depression: general state of the art
   G.J. Zwanikken   35

3. The prevalence and specific aspects of depression
   in mentally retarded individuals
   M.H. Fleisher and M.A. Weiler   51

Section 2: Etiology

4. Developmental and biological factors in the mentally
   retarded and vulnerability to depression
   A. Dosen and S. Bojanin   63

5. Psychological characteristics of mentally retarded persons
   and the risk of depression
   A. Dosen and J.J.M. Gielen   81

6. Depression in persons with mental retardation:
   toward an existential analysis
   J.J. McGee and F.J. Menolascino   95

Section 3: Phenomenology

7. Depression in mentally retarded children
   A. Dosen   113

8. Depression in mildly and moderately retarded adults
   K.A. Day   129

9. Depression in severely and profoundly retarded adults
    F.J. Menolascino and M.A. Weiler   155

10. Bipolar disorder in persons with developmental disorder:
    an overview
    R. Sovner   175

Section 4: Diagnosis

11. Diagnostic instruments to aid depressed mentally
    retarded individuals
    S.R. Love and J.L. Matson   199

12. Biochemical findings in depressed mentally retarded
    individuals
    S.L. Ruedrich   219

Section 5: Treatment

13. Treatment, care and management
    K.A. Day   235

14. Psychotherapeutic approaches in the treatment of
    depressive mentally retarded children
    A. Dosen   255

15. Treatment of depression in mentally retarded children:
    a developmental approach
    S. Bojanin and V. Ispanovic-Radojkovic   265

16. Psychotherapeutic approaches in the treatment of depression
    in   mentally retarded adults
    G. Prouty and M. Cronwall   281

17. Symbolic interactional therapy: a treatment intervention
    for depression in adults with mental retardation
    J.B. Caton   295

page

18. Behavioral treatment of depression
    B.A. Benson   309

19. Psychopharmacological approaches in treatment of
    depression in the mentally retarded
    J. Lund   331

Section 6: Services

20. Caring for the mental health for the mentally retarded
    population
    A. Dosen and F.J. Menolascino   341

Conclusion
A. Dosen and F.J. Menolascino   351

Subject index   355

Introduction

In recent years, scientists and researchers from a number of fields have demonstrated a growing interest in the occurrence of mental illness in the mentally retarded population. Although psychiatric diagnostic categories are now recognized for all levels of mental retardation, the prevalence of depression within these varying levels remains a challenging issue.

When one considers the unique biopsychosocial aspects of the lives of the mentally retarded in a world where intellectual ability is rewarded, it seems clear that depression would occur at a higher rate than in the population generally. Still, for a variety of reasons, the diagnosis of depression is established with distinct infrequency in the mentally handicapped.

One of the reasons for this diagnostic blindspot is that a certain unfamiliarity with the concept of depression in the mentally retarded continues. And, to some extent, the difference in the symptomatology of depressed mentally retarded individuals, when compared to that of depressed nonretarded individuals, adds unfocused confusion to the clinical pictures that emerge. Nevertheless, experienced diagnosticians continue to report that behind a facade of severe and persistent behavioral difficulties, underlying depression can often be found. In order to recognize it, however, one has to look for it, and, considering the scant number of publications and scientific conferences which have addressed this issue, many clinicians simply do not know what to look for.

In 1988, an International Scientific Symposium on Depression was organized in which scientists from around the world presented their work and shared their ideas concerning mental health care for the mentally retarded. Supported by the success of this symposium and by the enthusiastic willingness of its participants to cooperate, the existing knowledge on depression in the mentally retarded has been gathered into one book, the first of its kind on this issue.

In this volume, depression is approached as a conceptually broad phenomenon, theoretically as well as practically. We hope that the collection of expertise and insight gathered here will contribute to an enhanced understanding of the psychiatric disorders found in the mentally retarded and that, in this way, professionals from both mental retardation and mental health fields will be brought together in an effort to serve more effectively the needs of this deserving population.

Anton Dosen, M.D.
Frank Menolascino, M.D.

About the authors

Betsey A. Benson, Ph.D., Institute for the Study of Developmental Disabilities, University of Illinois at Chicago, Chicago, Illinois, U.S.A.

Svetomir Bojanin, M.D., Professor of Neuropsychology, University of Belgrade, Head of Institute for Mental Health of Children and Youth, Belgrade, Yugoslavia

Julie B. Caton, M.S., Mental Health Clinical Therapist, Department of Counseling and Educational Psychology, State University of New York at Buffalo, Buffalo, New York, U.S.A.

Melinda Cronwall, M.A., Mental Health Counselor, Pre-Therapy Institute, Matteson, Illinois, U.S.A.

Kenneth A. Day, M.D., Consultant Psychiatrist, Northgate Hospital Morpeth, Senior Lecturer, Department of Psychiatry, University of Newcastle-upon-Tyne, United Kingdom.

Anton Dosen, M.D., Consultant Psychiatrist and Director of Treatment, Clinic for Psychiatric and Behavioral Disorders in the Mentally Retarded "Nieuw Spraeland", Oostrum, The Netherlands.

Mark H. Fleisher, M.D., Instructor, University of Nebraska/Creighton University, Combined Department of Psychiatry, Omaha, Nebraska, U.S.A.

Jan J.M. Gielen, Ph.D., Clinical Psychologist, Institute for the Mentally Retarded "Eckartdal", Eindhoven, The Netherlands.

Veronika Ispanovic-Radojkovic, M.D., Associate Professor of Child Neurology and Psychiatry, Institute for Mental Health and University of Belgrade, Yugoslavia.

Steven R. Love, M.A., Doctoral Student in Clinical Psychology, Louisiana State University, Baton Rouge, Louisiana, U.S.A.

Jens Lund, M.D., Institute of Psychiatric Demography, Aarhus Psychiatric Hospital, Risskov, Denmark.

Johnny L. Matson, Ph.D., Professor, Department of Psychology, Louisiana State University, Baton Rouge, Louisiana, U.S.A.

John J. McGee, Ph.D., Associate Professor of Psychiatry, Creighton University, Omaha, Nebraska, U.S.A.

Frank J. Menolascino, M.D., Chairman and Professor, University of Nebraska/Creighton University, combined Department of Psychiatry, Omaha, Nebraska, U.S.A.

Garry Prouty, M.D., Professor of Mental Health, Prairie State College, Chicago Heights, Illinois, U.S.A.

Stephen L. Ruedrich, M.D., Associate Professor of Psychiatry, Residency Training Director in Psychiatry, Case Western Reserve University, School of Medicine, Cleveland, Ohio, U.S.A.

Robert Sovner, M.D., Consultant Psychiatrist and Medical Director, Lutheran Center for Mental Health and Mental Retardation, Brighton, Massachusetts, U.S.A.

Martin A. Weiler, M.D., Associate Professor, University of Nebraska/Creighton University, combined Department of Psychiatry, Omaha, Nebraska, U.S.A.

Gosewijn J. Zwanikken, M.D., Professor of Psychiatry, Chairman Department of Psychiatry, Catholic University, Nijmegen, the Netherlands.

Anton Dosen and Frank J. Menolascino (Eds.) (1990). Depression in mentally retarded children and adults. Leiden, the Netherlands: Logon Publications. ISBN 90-73197-01-5

Chapter 1

Mental retardation and the risk, nature and types of mental illness

Frank J. Menolascino, M.D.

Introduction

The definition of mental retardation as found in the diagnostic system of the American Association on Mental Deficiency (Grossman, 1983) posits the presence of sub-average intellectual functioning and associated deficits in social-adaptive behavior. The majority of disorders listed as capable of producing the symptom of mental retardation, however, are more descriptive of syndromes rather than specifically understood diagnostic entities (particularly AAMD categories VII and VIII; see Table 1.1). It should be noted that the definition or description of the causes of mental retardation says little about expected behaviors beyond rough guidelines regarding social-adaptive accomplishments at differing levels of retardation.

Similar perplexity may exist in the delineation of the causes and manifestations of mental illness in a given individual. The widely accepted diagnostic classification of mental illness found in DSM-III-R (American Psychiatric Association, 1987) notes a number of mental illnesses which can (1) embody the symptom of mental retardation (e.g., the organic mental disorders); (2) include mental retardation as a transitory finding in the clinical picture (e.g., in the regression often noted in schizophrenia); or (3) involve pervasive developmental delays, separated only with great difficulty from similar manifestations of mental retardation (e.g., infantile autism). Thus, when the uncertainty of primary causes in mental retardation is combined with the problems of clinical description in mental illness, an area of possible confusion can arise; similar symptomatic behaviors can have different fundamental causes.

11

Table 1.1
Classification of the causes of mental retardation*

0. **Infections and intoxications**
    (e.g., prenatal and postnatal infections)

I. **Trauma or physical agent**
    (e.g., inborn errors of metabolism)

II. **Metabolism or nutrition**
    (e.g., inborn errors of metabolism)

III. **Gross brain disease (postnasal)**
    (e.g., neurocutaneous dysplasia)

IV. **Unknown prenatal influence**
    (e.g., malformations of the brain)

V. **Chromosomal abnormality**
    (e.g., Down's Syndrome)

VI. **Gestational disorder**
    (e.g., prematurity)

VII. **Following psychiatric disorder**
    (e.g., childhood schizophrenia)

VIII. **Environmental influences**
    (e.g., psychosocial disadvantages)

IX. **Other conditions**
    (e.g., defects of special senses)

* American Association on Mental Deficiency (Grossman, 1983).

For example, the origins of a retarded child's hyperactivity may range from motor expressions of anxiety to manifestations of cerebral dysfunction, or it may be due to both. Similarly, a shortened attention span may be the end product of determinants ranging from inadequate parenting relationships in infancy (suggesting that the parents were unable to operate as a selective stimulation barrier for the child) to impaired (i.e., neurologic) midbrain screening of incoming stimuli. The moderately retarded adult can surely have a seizure disorder and may also display schizophrenia, along with his or her "old" symptoms of mental retardation. Failure to describe and/or delineate these multiple disorders in the same individual sharply limits both professional understanding and effective treatment.

A valuable concept in assessing mental illness in mentally retarded persons (particularly children) is that of developmental contingency. This concept stresses both timing and interaction of the extrinsic and intrinsic elements which may be major determining factors in symptom production at different neuroanatomical, physiologic, and/or developmental states of physical or personality development. A careful review of personal and clinical histories should be conducted for each patient, with an overriding concern for capturing the dynamic flow of developmental events that produces the present set of symptoms of mental illness. Such considerations underscore the dynamic interplay of constitutional factors, validated cerebral trauma, and the quality and quantity of parenting. Figure 1.1 illustrates the complexity of evaluating the impact of different developmental contingencies that clinicians may assess and attempt to alter therapeutically in any given child or adult (Menolascino & Dosen, 1990). Indeed, many of the factors listed in Figure 1.1 have become key points in the translation from theoretical domain to clinical setting for mental health professionals.

Influences of the levels of mental retardation

Individuals with mental retardation are, in general, nearly twice as likely as the nonretarded to demonstrate severe behavioral problems or mental illness (Eaton & Menolascino, 1982; May & May, 1979; Menolascino & McCann, 1983; Menolascino & Stark, 1984). This risk may result, in part, from the retarded person's difficulty with the processing of information; their allied medical, physical, or special sensory handicaps; cultural and familial factors; society's nonacceptance of retarded persons, as well as elements of raw prejudice against them.

13

Figure 1.1
Developmental contingencies of personality functioning

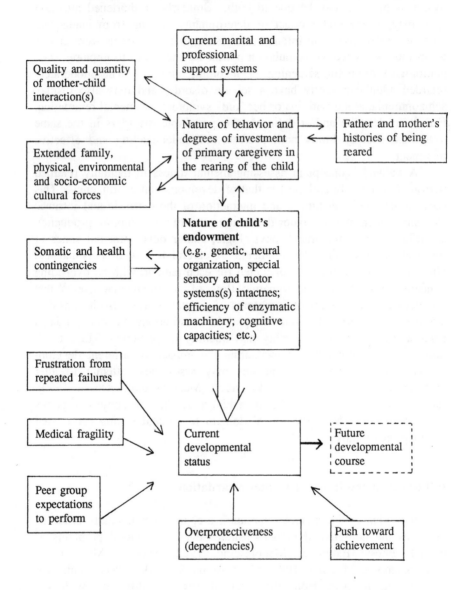

Other factors include the inability of the more severely retarded to communicate their feelings. Even those who appear to have superficially adequate language skills for their level of retardation, have extreme difficulty in the processing of abstract feelings and emotions. Exploration of the at-risk nature of the mentally retarded has made it abundantly clear that any condition which renders one less capable of handling reality-based demands make one more susceptible to mental illness.

The factors which make retarded individuals particularly vulnerable to mental illness include:

1. Delayed language development, with particular reference to a delayed ability to express appropriate needs, and a decreased exploration of the world. Lack of ability to understand the interpersonal world around them leads to a very concrete cause-and-effect understanding of that world.

2. Constricted emotional and personality growth secondary to delayed self-concept (i.e., differentiating the self from the non-self). Allied components are sensory and motor handicaps, and delayed integrative functions. These include poor reality perceptions and retained primitive thinking (e.g., problems in handling aggression, difficulty in pinpointing sources of frustration, magical thinking, confusion of reality/fantasy).

3. Major handicaps secondary to central nervous system impairments. These often lead to secondary behavior manifestations (e.g., self-stimulation as an external replacement for impaired inner resources).

4. Low self-esteem fostered by early attendance at special schools. This leads to a sense of "differentness" and, eventually, a self-image of deviancy. These children perceive that they have failed their parents, which leads to an increased need for praise and approval. Ongoing lack of approval from peers leads to an increasing sense of incompetence and ineffectiveness. Peer rejection and lowered family and group expectations are reflected in lowered individual motivation.

5. Relative inability to understand the demands of culture secondary to the presence of intellectual and social-adaptive limitations.

6. Impaired memory and transfer of learning. This leads to lowered inner control and decreased ability to delay responses and plan alternative methods of action. Thinking tends to be concrete and rigid, leading to poor responses to external and internal stress.

7. Atypical personality defenses include increased obsessional behaviors which help to control new situations and/or cope with the environment. Fears, however, are retained longer and defenses are more

15

fixed, leading to rigidity of lifestyle and increased utilization of nonadaptive defenses (e.g., denial, compulsive rigidity, withdrawal, regression, projection, etc.).

8. Vulnerability in adulthood. Continuation of the previously noted factors in childhood and adolescence leads directly to longer dependence, social and vocational limitations, and interference with heterosexual experiences. Failure to master key adaptational tasks at developmentally appropriate milestones in childhood and adolescence, when coupled with lowered global intelligence, culminates in poor judgment.

Severe retardation

The risk factors outlined above are further augmented by the level of mental retardation present. In the severely retarded, for example, the presence of major central nervous system impairment tends to greatly diminish the ability to access or participate in social transactions. Many of these individuals have sensory handicaps, such as deafness and blindness, and severe motor and physical disabilities, such as cerebral palsy and associated seizure disorders. All such conditions render the individual far more likely to experience difficulty in dealing with stress, and even with what might generally be regarded as minor changes in daily routine (Rutter & Schopler, 1978). Severe language delay, which is usually present, hinders the development of complex personality development, thereby enhancing vulnerability to emotional under- or overreaction. In many severely retarded people, the lack of expressive language can lead to "primitive" communication in the form of self-injurious, aggressive, or self-stimulatory behaviors, which are often attempts to respond to, interact with, or otherwise master an overly complex or unresponsive world. Without gentle and stable interpersonal support systems, the severely retarded tend to react adversely to interpersonal stress and can easily withdraw from the world through stereotyped and out-of-contact behaviors that mimic autism (e.g., arm waving, rocking, etc.).

Moderate retardation

The personality characteristics of the moderately retarded can either be programmed for maximal developmental growth or become the focal point for mental illness. Benign autism, non-obsessive repetitiousness, relative inflexibility, passivity, and simplicity of emotional life (Webster, 1971) are all fertile ground for both the initiation of a mental illness (if a highly supportive family or necessary program services are not provided) and misdiagnosis. Regarding the latter, one must be careful not to view the personality characteristics of the moderately retarded as signs or symptoms of mental illness. The few available autobiographies of moderately retarded individuals, in which basic personality features are noted without the presence of symptoms or signs of allied mental illness, are helpful in this regard (e.g., Hunt, 1967).

While moderately retarded persons can easily manage the basic parameters of language, daily living skills, and simple vocational tasks, their functionally adaptive and communicative abilities are often a facade. It is too often assumed that these individuals are successfully assimilating information and dealing with complex situations, such as the death of a loved one, the loss of a friend, or a serious somatic illness, when these experiences can actually be overwhelming. If moderately retarded persons in situational crises are not fully understood, enabled to express themselves, or actively supported in times of stress, they may quickly succumb to a structured mental illness, such as an adjustment disorder, as a stepping stone to a more serious mental illness, such as an affective disorder.

Mild retardation

More often than not, the mildly mentally retarded are cognizant of their behaviors and understand the consequences of their actions. Through naivete, misdirection, exploitation, or pressure of societal prejudice, however, some interpersonal activities remain outside their adaptive range of control and can lead to severe behavioral problems, marginal identities, or mental illness far more easily than in the population at large. The often nearly normal appearance of the mildly retarded tends to preclude their clear identification by others as being handicapped, leading to unrealistic expectations and major interpersonal failures. Emotional disturbances often result when the mildly retarded individual is labeled as deviant and becomes enmeshed in a dynamic interplay of disturbed family transactions. Society's devaluation of retarded individuals often results in segregation, leading to the subsequent development of a subculture of deviancy. Raw prejudice can lead to increased deviancy which, in turn, can lead to a greater number of socially unacceptable behaviors. In our experience with mildly retarded individuals, it is not uncommon to encounter severe psychosexual disorders, suicide attempts, and legal transgressions.

Low self-esteem is very frequent in the mildly retarded; the stigma of attending special classes and the adverse encounters within their social-interpersonal environments tends to make them feel ineffective and different (Menolascino & McCann, 1983). This may be compounded by the individual's inability to integrate the normal developmental sequences at appropriate times. For example, during the late childhood period of personality integration, the mildly retarded person has considerable difficulty in understanding the symbolic abstractions of schoolwork and the ongoing complexities of social-adaptive expectations from both family and peer groups. It is at this stage that they often gain some understanding of their limitations. Unfortunately, the mildly retarded are not likely to be buffered or redirected by loved ones into new interpersonal coping styles, and remain at risk for the development of marginal identities or mental illness.

Concerns about heightened sexual activity and/or aggressive proclivities in the mildly retarded have been greatly clarified. Rather than the old view of greater or less than normal sexual-aggressive drives (Barr, 1904), it has become clear that the strength of these drives is not as important as the ability to manage them. Successful personal management depends upon the nature of the individual's personality growth, defenses, social opportunities to express these drives, and specific training in modulating or redirecting them. All of these considerations are recognized areas of conflict that are very amenable to psychotherapeutic approaches. Needless to say, the mildly retarded are prime candidates for such treatment.

A lingering professional bias does, however, occasionally emerge; the symptom of mental retardation may be viewed as a signal not to treat the retarded person's accompanying mental illness. This bias was clearly identified almost two decades ago by Woodward, Jaffe, and Brown (1970) when they noted that:

> There are two prevalent attitudes on the part of many practicing child psychiatrists in the New York area with which we differ strongly; 1) There is the attitude that a psychiatric diagnosis must be made in terms of either "organicity" or "non-organicity." Those holding this view seem unable to conceive of a mixed picture. Our experience would suggest that a mixed picture is common. To us it is irrational to say that a child with brain damage can have only one form of pathology, and this explains everything. Why can't a child have mixed brain damage and a psychoneurosis? 2) There is an attitude that a child who has any evidence of brain damage at all, even an isolated abnormal electroencephalogram without other evidence of central nervous system involvement, should not be offered

18

psychotherapy. This attitude exists in spite of the known fact that many disturbed children respond poorly to psychotherapeutic programs, and have no evidence of organic lesions. We believe that the decision whether a child should have psychotherapy depends on the estimate of his ability to profit by it, regardless of the presence of organic pathology (p. 290).

This pair of attitudinal biases may have added unduly to the paucity of evidence regarding effective efforts to treat mental illness in these individuals. Indeed, such professional blind spots may have incorrectly pushed some retarded citizens into institutional patienthood as "chronically disturbed retarded persons."

Emotional adjustment problems related to different models of care

An alternative way to view the emotional adjustment challenges of the mentally retarded is to consider how such challenges are related to the various types of care given to these individuals during their formative years. Providing optimal care for the retarded at home, in the community, or in an institutional setting is extremely difficult because there is no average retarded person. Although some grouping can be done based on the level of retardation, as outlined above, the great variation of abilities often seen within each of these persons remains a striking component. This variability, plus the difficulty that primary caregivers have in fully understanding the retarded, seems to be the basis for a number of emotional problems. The most common types of caregiver errors involve either overly limited or excessive expectations. Errors in either direction can contribute significantly to a great many emotional problems.

Limited expectations

Many mentally retarded people experience too few expectations and, when combined with too little effort on the part of caregivers, tend to show a pattern of underachievement and a syndrome of detachment. One characteristic problem involves profound and often indiscriminately expressed affect hunger. For example, moderately and mildly retarded persons often have no extended experiences with significant or meaningful object relations and, as a result, their indiscriminate approaches to strangers can become a serious problem. A variant of this detachment syndrome is more often seen in the severely retarded. Instead of exhibiting indiscriminate approach behaviors, this group often withdraws,

19

developing a pattern of primitive and self-stimulating behaviors similar to those seen in infantile autism.

Another variant in this model of care involves caregivers who actually do too much instead of too little. Such overprotection fosters dependence and smothers initiative and learning. In areas lacking community-based programs, parents faced with the singularly unhappy decision of sending their children to an institution, sometimes feel that the only acceptable solution is to care for the afflicted family member at home. All too often this is done in an isolated part of the house away from external social contacts. Here the devoted parents tend to the child's every need, thus increasing the child's dependency and almost eliminating any capacity for the development of effective social-adaptive functions. Whereas the detached mildly or moderately retarded person is at risk to develop the counterpart of a character disorder, the overprotected retarded person is more likely to show symptoms of inflexibility, autistic thinking, and separation anxiety. Stereotypical behavior may also emerge as a pattern of self-stimulation. As might be expected, the detached individual is at risk to show active but indiscriminate behavior in community placement efforts, whereas the retarded person with a history of over-protective isolation is more likely to respond to the social and self-help demands of the community with anxiety and anger.

Excessive expectations

At the other end of the spectrum are the caregivers with unrealistically high expectations. One of the most common problems in very young moderately retarded children, who do not have physical stigmata, is the parents' failure to recognize their child's intellectual limitations before the time of normal language acquisition. It is not unusual for an autistic-like psychosis to occur in a sensitive, seemingly intelligent (but nevertheless retarded) child when his or her conscientious parents do all the "right" things during the second year of life to facilitate language skills. Verbal demands to name objects often cause the moderately retarded child to react with increasing anxiety and a variety of avoidance behaviors, reflecting language disability and lack of pleasure in verbal interaction. Conversely, if retardation is detected early (by the age of 2 or 3) and if ways are found to communicate with these children that do not depend unduly upon verbal productions, their autistic-like behavior is frequently abandoned.

Similar examples of the effects of excessive expectations are occasionally seen in innovative institutional or community programs in which more severely retarded children may be subjected to overly intense

20

efforts to maximize their capabilities. In some cases, this has resulted in an increasing number of seizures or patterns of autistic withdrawal. One of the most distressing problems involves the outburst of violent behavior that can occur when excessive expectations have been maintained for too long. Unfortunately, such children are frequently placed on high dosages of medication in an effort to control aggression that is actually reactive in nature and not a symptom of psychosis.

Information concerning models of care appropriate to the management of mentally retarded people can provide valuable guidelines for maximizing their developmental potential. Expectations based on observed behavior (rather than expected behavior), level of retardation, and the typically beneficial role of early educational and socialization programs help define the principal model programs that the mentally retarded need. Conversely, inappropriate expectations and lack of early developmentally oriented programs will only heighten the vulnerability of retarded individuals to mental illness.

Frequency and types of mental illness in the mentally retarded

Failure to assess clearly all parameters of a mentally retarded individual's behavior can result in major diagnostic errors. The mental status examination of a mentally retarded individual cannot be accomplished in isolation from general diagnostic procedures (Szymanski & Tanguay, 1980). In short, the mental health professional should ideally carry out his or her own physical and neurologic examinations, and should be prepared to interpret pediatric, internal medicine, and neurologic consultations, as well as psychological evaluations and electroencephalograms. By following this process, the mental health professional is in a much better position to see the whole person, and thereby piece together the diagnostic puzzle that mental illness can present in the mentally retarded individual.

A series of reports on mentally retarded individuals who live with their primary families and/or in their primary communities (Eaton & Menolascino, 1982; Edgerton, Bollinger & Herr, 1984; Halldin, 1984; Menolascino & McCann, 1983; Reid, Ballinger, Heather & Melvin, 1984) have noted that the mentally retarded do fall prey to the same types of mental illness that befall people with normal intellectual abilities. The full range of psychoses, neuroses, personality disorders, behavior disorders, and adjustment reactions are in evidence. Even if mentally retarded persons are emotionally well adjusted, they will experience some difficulty

21

functioning independently or semi-independently in their respective communities. If their lives are complicated by mental illness, their adjustment difficulties are obviously compounded. Recent studies rather consistently report a 20% to 35% frequency rate of emotional disturbances among this population (Eaton & Menolascino, 1982; Groden, Dominque & Pueschel, 1982) and strongly suggest that clinical focus is to be placed on the diagnosis and subsequent treatment of combined findings.

A community-based study

In attempting to determine the frequency and types of mental illness in the mentally retarded, studies conducted prior to 1960 assessed only institutionalized patients. Yet these individuals typically experience a higher prevalence of mental illness and more severe levels of mental retardation than are usually noted. Similarly, previous studies of community-based individuals often narrowly focused on a single age group. A more recent clinical study (Menolascino, Levitas & Greiner, 1986), however, was conducted over a five-year period in a community-based population of both mentally retarded children and adults. The setting for this study, the Eastern Nebraska Community Office of Retardation (ENCOR), has been operational for over 20 years, serving a five-county region with a population base of 482,000, 80% of which is urban. A total of 543 mentally retarded persons, who had been referred for assessment, were determined by the psychiatric consultant to be both mentally retarded and mentally ill. These individuals represent the study group illustrated in Table 1.2 and are discussed in the sections which follow.

Table 1.2
Psychiatric disorders in a community-based sample
of 543 mentally retarded persons

Psychiatric diagnosis	Ages					Total
	1-15	16-20	21-30	31-35	36+	
Schizophrenia						
catatonic	1	4	3		2	10
paranoid		8	8	4	10	30
undifferentiated		15	18	5	15	45
residual			17	13	15	45
						138

22

Psychiatric diagnosis	Ages					Total
	1-15	16-20	21-30	31-35	36+	
Organic brain disorders						
behavioral reaction	15	7	19	8	6	55
psychotic reaction	4	2	24	8	5	43
presenile dementia					7	7
						105
Adjustment disorders						
childhood & adolescent	19	25				44
disturbance of conduct	8	10				18
adulthood			27	9	5	41
						103
Personality disorders						
schizoid		2	4			6
paranoid			2	1		3
narcissistic			2	4	1	7
avoidant		1	3	1	2	7
passive aggressive		5	6	5	6	22
antisocial		1	15	2	5	23
						68
Affective disorders						
unipolar manic disorder			4	3		7
bipolar affective			2		3	5
major depression, recurrent	5	4	15	5	5	32
cyclothymic disorder			1			1
						45
Psychosexual disorders						
fetishism		1				1
transvestism		2				4
zoophilia	1					1
pedophilia	1	1	6	1	3	12
exhibitionism	1	1	3		1	6
ego-dystonic homosexuality	1	1				2
not classified		3	3	1	1	8
						34
Anxiety disorders						
generalized	2	3	2	2		9
post traumatic stress		2	3	2	3	10
obsessive compulsive					1	1
						20
Other mental disorders						
pervasive developmental	14	2				16
anorexia nervosa	3	2	1			6
oppositional disorder		2				2
substance use			3	1	2	6
						30

Schizophrenia

Instances of paranoid schizophrenia were noted in both the verbal and nonverbal patients in our study, and, in the entire group of individuals with combined diagnoses of mental retardation and schizophrenia, the altered affective responses, bizarre rituals, and utilization of interpersonal distancing clearly marked the observed behaviors as schizophrenic. Although some clinicians have seriously questioned whether the markedly primitive behaviors noted at certain levels of mental retardation can be separated from schizophrenia, this was not our experience. On the contrary, these individuals displayed very clear developmental indices of prof-schizophrenia; schizophrenia which had been engrafted upon distinct earlier indices of mental retardation. Because the psychotic child, however, frequently functions at a mentally retarded level, psychotic reactions of childhood present a major challenge to the clinician. The presence of bizarre behavior, persistent withdrawal, echolalic speech, and affective unavailability of some of the adolescents in the study outlined in Table 1.2, who had clearly regressed from a higher level of functioning, was particularly striking.

It is important to note that treatment guidelines may differ for youngsters with autistic reactions from those recommended for children with the combined mental retardation-childhood schizophrenia syndrome noted above. The mentally retarded child who develops schizophrenia will primarily require mental health services, with mental retardation services utilized in a secondary role until functional psychosis subsides. Conversely, the vast majority of autistic youngsters seem to profit primarily from mental retardation services and secondarily from mental health consultations (Rutter and Schopler, 1978).

Personality disorders

The personality disorders found in this study were characterized by chronically maladaptive patterns of behavior which were qualitatively different from either the psychotic or anxiety disorders delineated in DSM-III-R (American Psychiatric Association, 1987). Although the schizoid personality in particular is only rarely reported in the mentally retarded population, we noted it in 6 of our study patients. Generally, the personality disorders noted in Table 1.2 were based primarily upon extrinsic factors; none had causal relationships to the symptom of mental retardation.

Anxiety disorders

Recent reviews of the occurrence of psychoneurotic disorders in the mentally retarded (May & May, 1979; Parsons, May & Menolascino, 1984) dispute the earlier concept of incompatibility between neurosis and mental retardation. Interestingly, such disorders seem to be more commonly observed in individuals who fall within the high-moderate and mild levels of mental retardation, which has prompted some speculation that the complexity of psychoneurotic transactions is beyond the adaptive limits of more severely mentally retarded people. Alternatively, the manifestations of psychoneuroses may not be as obvious, or may present differently, in the supervised and regimented lives of the more severely retarded.

In our study, neurotic phenomena was attributable to factors associated with atypical developmental patterns involved in disturbed family functioning. For example, anxiety disorders in mentally retarded children clearly connected the symptoms of anxiety, such as fear of failure and insecurity, to exogenous factors, such as chronic frustration, unrealistic family expectations, and persistent interpersonal deprivations.

Adjustment disorders

Because mentally retarded individuals have a predisposition to overreact to stimuli and a limited understanding of social-interpersonal expectations, they are more likely to exhibit personality disorganization after minimal interpersonal stress. Viewed within a diagnostic context, the clinician must be alert to the Brief Reactive Psychosis caused by continuing inappropriate social-adaptive expectations or unexpected and frequent changes in externally imposed life patterns.

Such disorders respond rapidly to environmental adjustment, realignment of parental, residential, and educational expectations, brief utilization of psychopharmacologic adjuncts, and/or supportive psycho-therapy.

Affective disorders

Although scant attention had previously been paid to the appearance and recognition of depression in individuals with mental retardation, when one considers the language and communication deficits of this group, their lack of social skills and social networks, it becomes obvious that all of the hallmarks of loneliness are present, and that the mentally retarded are certainly at risk for the development of affective disorders (Matson, 1982a, 1982b; Schloss, 1982; Wells & Duncan, 1980).

Retarded individuals often develop severe behavioral or depressive reactions to what may appear to be far less stressful situations, losses, or environmental changes than caregivers would tend to expect. Consequently, such transitional behavioral-adjustment problems tend to be misunderstood by caregivers who are not fully appreciative of the difficulty mentally retarded people have in dealing with abstract phenomena. In addition, the retarded individual may display clinical signs of depression which differ from those observed in the nonretarded population. Vegetative signs will be found, however, as will a high frequency of family histories and biochemical parameters compatible with, and indicative of, affective disorders. A total of 32 mentally retarded people in the study illustrated in Table 1.2 were noted to suffer from recurrent major depression.

Depression remains the most frequent affective disorder noted in the elderly who are, in fact, the most prone to develop it (Schloss, 1982; Kazdin, Matson & Senatore, 1983). In the general population of nonretarded individuals over 65 years of age, suicide has been rather consistently reported to be the cause of 17% of recorded deaths -- although this group composes only 11% of the total population of the United States. Blazer, Bachar, and Manton (1986) have projected that this suicide rate will increase four-fold during the next four decades due to increased social stress, alienation of the current "baby boomers," and elevated recent rates of suicide in middle age. The mentally retarded elderly, with the enhanced at-risk factors previously noted, would appear to be even more vulnerable than the elderly population at large. Early diagnostic prevention issues for these individuals are in need of attention in the fields of both psychiatry and, particularly, mental retardation.

Dementia

Progressive deterioration of mental functioning that does not conform to a particular psychiatric diagnosis may represent dementia. It appears that the symptoms of dementia, as carefully defined by Wells and Duncan (1980), will become much more commonplace as the population increases in age. From a psychiatric and neurologic standpoint, dementia is of great interest because its multiple possible causes require the establishment of a rigorous differential diagnosis. It is for this reason, among others, that the broad designation "organic brain syndrome" does not suffice, either for the benefit of the patient or the advancement of research.

Table 1.3
**Psychiatric disorders in a community-based sample
of 67 elderly mentally retarded persons**

Age			Diagnosis	Sex		Level of retardation		
55-64	65-70	70+		M	F	Mild	Moderate	Severe
6	8	7	295.60 Chronic schizophrenia (with acute acerbation)	11	10	12	8	1
3			295.40 Acute schizophrenic episode (paraphrenia)	3		2	1	
4	3		290.10 Presenile dementia of the Alzheimer type	4	3	2	5	
	2	1	Senile dementia	3	3			
	4	2	294.9 Organic brain syndrome secondary to senile dementia	4	2	4	2	
3	3		Unipolar affective disorder (depression)	4	2	3	2	1
2	2		Chronic bipolar affective disorder	3	1	2	2	
1	2		Brief reactive psychosis	3		2	1	
3	4	2	Adjustment disorder	6	3	8	1	
2	1		Personality disorder	2	1	3		
1	1		Anxiety disorder		2	2		
25	30	12	**Totals**	40	27	43	22	2

We know that decline in cognitive function may result from normal-pressure hydrocephalus; multiple cerebral infarcts; central nervous system syphilis; thyroid disorders; kidney, liver, heart or lung failure; iatrogenic drug combinations; exposure to organic mercury or bromides; Creutzfeld-Jakob disease; the spongioform encephalopathies; atypical infectious agents such as kuru, etc. Similarly, a dementing process may constitute part of the clinical complex in pernicious anemia, Whipple's disease, and chronic alcoholism. The commonest cause of irreversible cognitive decline in old age is Alzheimer's disease.

The psychiatrist who is present with a patient displaying or complaining of progressive deterioration of mental functioning, must be aware of some of the foregoing specific causes of dementia, both treatable and non-treatable. It is important to make a confident diagnosis of presently non-treatable dementia, as a modern management approach regarding the patient and the family will greatly depend upon this key differential diagnostic point.

Table 1.3 summarizes the types of mental illness found in a review of diagnostic data derived from a sample of 67 middle-aged and elderly mentally retarded individuals who were admitted to the Nebraska Psychiatric Institute for evaluation and/or treatment. Review of this table clearly reveals that these individuals can, and do, fall prey to many of the major psychiatric syndromes.

A suggested framework for viewing mental illness in the mentally retarded

The conceptual framework which follows has proved to be quite helpful when employed as an approach to everyday clinical challenges in both diagnosis and, particularly, treatment and management of individuals with mental illness and mental retardation (Menolascino & McCann, 1983). It is based on the author's extended clinical experiences with three general types of mentally retarded individuals suffering from associated mental illnesses: those with primitive, atypical, and abnormal patterns of behavior.

Primitive behavior

Primitive behavior is usually manifested by severely or profoundly retarded individuals who additionally display gross delays in their behavioral repertoires. Such behaviors involve extremely rudimentary utilization of special sensory modalities; particularly touch, position, oral exploratory activity, and externally directed verbalizations. In diagnostic interviews, certain primitive behaviors such as the mouthing and licking of objects, excessive tactile stimulation, autistic hand movements, skin picking, and body rocking, are frequently noted.

For children, the very primitiveness of overall behavior, in conjunction with much stereotyping, may initially suggest a psychotic disorder of childhood. Such youngsters will, however, make eye contact and interact with the examiner quite readily, despite their minimal behavioral repertoire. Similarly, one might form the initial impression that the level and persistence of primitive behaviors are actually secondary to intrinsic and/or extrinsic deprivation factors. Yet upon further investigation, these children will display concurrent multiple indices of developmental arrest of either primary or congenital origin. Clarifying the diagnosis, realigning parental and professional expectations, and focusing upon specific treatment modalities are the keys to providing effective help to retarded individuals who display primitive behaviors.

Atypical behavior

Atypical behaviors include poor emotional control (as evidenced by emotional outbursts), impulsiveness, sullenness, obstinacy, mild legal transgressions, and generally poor adaptation to prevocational or vocational training programs. For example, a retarded adolescent may be committed to an institution because of ongoing adjustment difficulties within his or her home community, but it is important to note that such difficulties may not necessarily be experienced within the primary family structure. Instances of atypical behavior are only atypical for the institutional settings in which these individuals find themselves -- they are really quite typical within the primary family subculture. Etiologic diagnosis is usually in the realm of "cultural-familial mental retardation" or "idiopathic mental retardation."

When the individual with atypical behavior arrives at an institution, psychiatric consultation is most commonly requested because the patient refuses to cooperate with the training or social expectations of the institutional setting, or because continual abrasive comments and/or contact from the family belittles the institution's ability to help their family member. The family may actually deny the reality of any social-adaptive problems, or harass the institutional staff for focusing upon and attempting to modify problem behaviors.

It would seem that formerly institutionalized mentally retarded individuals with atypical behavior are increasingly "flunking out" of community-based service programs and continue their persistently atypical behavior within a social system other than the primary family. Management is difficult unless very close coordination exists between the administrative segments of institutional treatment teams. Nevertheless, the total environment of an institution can help to modify motivational potential, effect changes in the individual's value system, and help him or her to achieve more positive social-adaptive approaches to interpersonal transactions and to the world of work.

Abnormal behavior

Most of the clearly abnormal behavioral challenges encountered in institutionalized or community-based samples of retarded individuals encompass instances of psychotic behavior. It is truly remarkable that one still sees psychotic patients who have literally been dumped into institutions for the mentally retarded because of the absence of specific treatment programs in their home communities. Treatment nihilism is also a major problem. One typically notes a clinical history of great enthusiasm when treatment is initiated, but slowness of response is often disillusioning and the patient is referred as non-treatable. A broad view of developmental potentials and psychotic characteristics must be wedded to specific treatment goals if this type of treatment failure is to be avoided.

In the clinical interview, persons with psychotic disorders will present the following behavioral dimensions:
1) bizarreness of manner, gesture, and posture;
2) uncommunicative speech;
3) little or no discrimination between animate and inanimate objects;
4) identification with most inanimate objects;
5) displays of deviant affective expression;
6) few, if any, relationships with peers;
7) passive compliance to external demands or stimuli; and
8) marked negativism.

Many institutions for the retarded have built up large backlogs of psychotic patients whose definitive treatment needs have never been appropriately addressed. Such patients are typically referred elsewhere during acute episodes, and returned in a sub-acute remission state. Because institutional staff frequently view these individuals as "odd" or "dangerous," the psychotic process is often refueled by apprehensive personnel until the patient is pushed once again into an acute state.

30

Professional postures

Professionals need to review and re-define their approaches toward the mentally retarded-mentally ill in an effort to attain a posture built on developmental hopefulness, gentleness, and warmth; often an artful blend of the "active" role taken in pediatrics with the role of "mutual participation" adapted in psychiatry. It is also helpful to consider the initial creation of a passively dependent, or at least physically tolerant, relationship with each person. In the beginning, most profoundly retarded people with severe behavioral problems need to develop a passive-aggressive relationship with their professional caregivers, a relationship that tends to evolve into an increasingly dynamic interaction. In addition to the relationship itself, a secondary purpose involves the leading of that individual into a variety of learning-readiness opportunities; a state we refer to as the threshold of learning. This initial receptivity to developmental interactions will gradually, but invariably, lead to control over maladaptive behaviors and expanded opportunities for advanced interactions (McGee, Menolascino, Hobbs & Menousek, 1987; Menolascino & Dosen, 1990).

During the initial week of treatment intervention, the professional needs to create a series of sequential developmental interactions, from obtaining eye contact to focusing on directional tasks which progress from simple to more complex operations. In the beginning, however, mentally retarded individuals will tend to "win" or control most interpersonal transactions through obstinacy, screaming, hitting, refusing to sit, indiscriminately throwing objects, or running away. They will initially attempt to maintain, or even increase, the barriers which exist between themselves and their caregivers, who may represent the intrusions of a chaotic external world. The professional must attempt to understand this individualistic, initial stage of rebellion and isolation, and energetically continue to attempt to engage the patient in a series of concrete, specific developmental activities. At the same time, one needs to tolerate an initial barrage of heightened inappropriate behaviors in a passive, yet supportive and firm manner. Meaningful contact can best be achieved through constant and sincere displays of warmth, tolerance, and uncritical acceptance (Greenspan, 1980; McGee, Menolascino, Hobbs & Menousek, 1987).

31

Conclusion

The diagnostic considerations and management plans reviewed in this chapter strongly suggest that a variety of treatment approaches must be utilized if we are to effectively help the mentally retarded-mentally ill. For example, a mentally retarded person with a psychotic disorder may need a specific type of milieu setting, psychoactive drugs to reduce excessive motor activity and mood fluctuations, ongoing citizen advocate contacts, behavior shaping to stimulate positive reinforcement of specific adaptive behaviors, and active involvement of a family support system. Due to the complexity of these treatment ingredients, the team approach is a prime pathway for providing a wide spectrum of individualized services for our mentally retarded-mentally ill citizens.

Retarded persons are subject to the same basic types of mental illness as the general population (Menolascino & McCann, 1983; Menolascino & Stark, 1984). Because of their tendency toward central nervous system impairment and diminished overall coping ability, they present somewhat greater than average risks for psychosis, long-term behavioral disturbances, and transient adjustment disorders. Understanding the nature and underlying causes of mental illness in the mentally retarded is only the beginning, yet it provides the caregiver with insight into the patient's problems and an indication of appropriate treatment and ongoing care.

Regardless of the types or intensities of behavior, the caregiver's fundamental goal should be to break through whatever avoidant, self-injurious, disruptive, or destructive behaviors might exist, and to respectfully and gently move the individual from such a state to one of human interdependence. Clearly, persons with a dual diagnosis of mental retardation and mental illness present a persistent challenge to the clinician and require specialized service models if their needs are to be appropriately met. It is hoped that the recent renaissance of involvement of mental health personnel worldwide will aid greatly in helping our mentally retarded citizens to live, work, and socialize in the mainstreams of society through the provision of services which are both highly sophisticated and readily available.

References

American Psychiatric Association (1987). Diagnostic and Statistical Manual of Mental Disorders (3rd Ed., Revised). Washington, DC: American Psychiatric Association.

Barr, W. (1904). Mental Defectives: Their History, Treatment and Training. Philadelphia: Blakiston's Son & Co.

Blazer, D.G., Bachar, J.R. & Manton, K.G. (1986). Suicide in late life: Review and commentary. Journal of the American Geriatrics Society, 34, 7, 519-525.

Edgerton, R.B., Bollinger, M. & Herr, B. (1984). The cloak of competence: After two decades. American Journal of Mental Deficiency, 88, 345-351.

Eaton, L. & Menolascino, F. (1982). Psychiatric disorders in the mentally retarded: Types, problems and challenges. American Journal of Psychiatry, 139, 1297-1303.

Greenspan, S. (1980). A unifying framework for educating caregivers about discipline. Omaha: Boystown Center for the Study of Youth Development.

Groden, G., Dominque, D. & Pueschel, S. (1982). Behavioral/emotional problems in mentally retarded children and youth. Psychology Reports, 51, 143-146.

Grossman, H. J. (1983). Manual of terminology and classification in mental retardation. Washington, DC: American Association on Mental Deficiency.

Halldin, J. (1984). Prevalence of mental disorder in an urban population in central Sweden. Acta Psychiatrica Scandinavica, 17, 159-163.

Hunt, N. (1967). The world of Nigel Hunt. New York: Talinger.

Kazdin, A.E., Matson, J.L. & Senatore, V. (1983). Assessment of depression in mentally retarded adults. American Journal of Psychiatry, 140, 8, 1040-1043.

Matson, J.L. (1982a). Depression in the mentally retarded: A review. Education and Training of the Mentally Retarded, 17, 159-163.

Matson, J.L. (1982b). The treatment of behavioral characteristics of depression in the mentally retarded. Behavior Therapy, 13, 209-218.

May, J., & May, J. (1979). Overview of emotional disturbances in mentally retarded individuals. Presented at the Annual Convention of the National Association for Retarded Citizens, Atlanta.

McGee, J.J., Menolascino, F.J., Hobbs, D.C. & Menousek, P.E. (1987). Gentle Teaching: A Non-Aversive Approach to Helping Persons with Mental Retardation. New York: Human Sciences Press.

Menolascino, F.J. & McCann, B.M. (1983). Mental health and mental retardation: Bridging the gap. Baltimore MD: University Park Press.

Menolascino, F.J. & Stark, J.A. (1984). Handbook of mental illness in the mentally retarded. New York: Plenum Press.

Menolascino, F.J., Levitas, A. & Greiner, C. (1986). The nature and types of mental illness in the mentally retarded. Psychopharmacology Bulletin, 22, 4, 1060-1071.

Menolascino, F.J. & Dosen, A. (1990). Developmental Aspects of Mental Retardation (in press).

Parsons, J.A., May, J.G. & Menolascino, F.J. (1984). The nature and incidence of mental illness in mentally retarded individuals. In: F. Menolascino & J. Stark (Eds.), Handbook of mental illness in the mentally retarded. New York: Plenum Press.

Reid, A.H., Ballinger, B.H., Heather B.B. & Melvin, S.J. (1984). The natural history of behavioral symptoms among severely and profoundly mentally retarded patients. British Journal of Psychiatry, 145, 289-293.

Rutter, M. & Schopler, E. (1978). Autism: A Reappraisal of concepts and treatments. New York: Plenum Press.

Schloss, P.J. (1982). Verbal interaction patterns of depressed and non-depressed institutionalized mentally retarded adults. Applied Research in Mental Retardation, 3, 1-12.

Szymanski, L. & Tanguay, P. (1980). Emotional disorders of mentally retarded persons. Baltimore: University Park Press.

Webster, T. (1971). Unique aspects of emotional development in mentally retarded children. In: F. Menolascino (Ed.), Psychiatric aspects of the diagnosis and treatment of mental retardation. Seattle: Special Child Publications.

Wells, C.E. & Duncan, G.W. (1980). Neurology for psychiatrists. Philadelphia: F.A. Davis Co.

Woodward, K., Jaffe, N. & Brown, D. (1970). Early psychiatric intervention for young mentally retarded children. In: F. Menolascino (Ed.), Psychiatric approaches to mental retardation. New York: Basic Books.

Anton Dosen and Frank J. Menolascino (Eds.) (1990). Depression in mentally retarded children and adults. Leiden, the Netherlands: Logon Publications. ISBN 90-73197-01-5

Chapter 2

The phenomenon of depression: general state of the art

Gosewijn J. Zwanikken, M.D.

Introduction

The human being is in many ways similar to the other animals; struggling to attain a feeling of well-being in an optimal environment, and retreating from troubles and threats. The affective state of depression, or as I prefer to characterize it, the change of mood that we call depression, is a condition we experience as discomfort. When we are feeling low, therefore, we will attempt to change our mental state for the better, be it through the aid of laymen or professionals.

Yet depression is not an unequivocal concept; it is an omnibus term (Angst, 1987; Klerman, Endicott, Spitzer et al., 1979; Rutter, 1986). And since our rich Western culture provides numerous facilities and a wide range of professionals who attempt to relieve this human distress, the use of many different concepts, sometimes with identical labels, has become rather common. Depression may, for example, indicate a feeling tone, a set of cognitions, or some pathological state. In nosological terms, depression can be a symptom, a syndrome, a number of linked symptoms, or a disease. Considering this wide variety of connotations, it is essential that we attain a fuller clarity of what the term "depression" actually denotes.

The shifting concept of depression

For many decades, physicians and psychiatrists have tried unremittingly to define the disease of depression sharply. The intention was, and still is, to explore the cause of the disease and to find ways of treating it as effectively as possible. The general point of departure begins with Emil Kraepelin (1913) who, while working in a mental hospital with very seriously, predominantly suicidal, depressive patients, grouped deviations of mood into the family of manic-depressive psychosis; a conception that has retained its worth until the present day. According to this concept, depression resembles a disease inasmuch as it can be identified through diagnostic procedures by employing appropriate diagnostic tools -- the practice of medicine in the Aristotelian tradition.

Now, some 100 years after Kraepelin, impressive social and cultural developments with far-reaching consequences have occurred, defining the psychiatry of today's mental hospital as definitely different from that practiced in institutions of the same name a century ago. Outside the mental hospital, a still-developing field of residential and semi-residential mental health care has emerged. Governments and professional workers have made energetic attempts -- not always correctly, or even fairly, in my opinion -- to reduce the contribution of the mental hospital to mental health care. As a result, the population of patients treated for depressive signs and symptoms is now radically different from what it was for Kraepelin.

One of the consequences of this shift in patient population has been the delimitation of the clinical picture of what we refer to as typical depression. Previously, this image was one which met our professional prototype; the brain model. A picture that did not match this prototype we referred to as atypical, particularly when referring to differing races, cultures, sub-cultures, income levels, age groups, and, above all, people with below average cognitive capacities and a retarded progress of development. Social and cultural contexts have, therefore, become increasingly important to our understanding and assessment of the concept or concepts of depression.

It is also difficult to underestimate the influence of government officials on the various shifts in our conceptions of depression. Political decisions about the limits of our willingness to pay for treatment from public resources cannot be avoided. The Dutch government, for example, currently curtails spending on health care which includes mental health aspects by drawing a distinction between "pathology" and "problem," between psychiatric disease and psychosocial distress. A designation of "disease" allows access to a psychiatrist and is funded. Psychosocial problems, however, are constructed to be non-medical in nature and amenable to resolution through the aid of friends, neighbors, relatives, clergymen, self-help groups or social welfare -- all of which cost far less than the aid rendered by a medical institution. Thus, a psychotic depression is allowed to be classified as a disease, a slight depression with vital signs and symptoms is not. Such conceptualization and classification has resulted in a Babylonian multiplicity of diagnostic distinctions that, at best, helps us only very little.

The classification of depression

We have many classifications of depressive states at our disposal. Within these classifications we are confronted with both multiple criteria and multiple meanings, all of which aim at appropriateness of prognosis and effectiveness of therapy. Classifications based on a single factor have proved to be too simple. And the multi-causal, multi-conditional, or multidimensional approaches do not bring anything essentially new to light; they only serve as aids in the avoidance of error. None of these classification schemes, however, goes beyond the level of description. Of course, we are not dealing with natural objects classifiable in a system by the Swedish botanist Carl Linne. But as long as we are insufficiently acquainted with the causes of depression, which is what prevails at the moment, we can only try to formulate a method of classification which optimally serves our aims. In doing so, we should attempt to delimit our codification as such to 1) assist in the determination of treatment regimens (e.g., psychopharmacological); 2) appropriately assess short-term and long-term prognoses; and 3) effectively communicate at national and international levels.

In addition to the World Health Organization's (1977) International Classification of Diseases, Injuries and Causes of Death (ICD-9), the American Psychiatric Association's Diagnostic and Statistical Manual of Mental Disorders (DSM-III-R; 1987) is the most widely used system of classification, drawing distinctions between major and minor mood disorders, bipolar and unipolar mood disorders, and between depression with or without psychotic features and "melancholic" characteristics. The validity of these nosological distinctions, however, remains dubious.

When we speak of depression, what we usually have in mind are such phenomena as feelings (e.g., guilt, self-reproach, inferiority) and cognitions (e.g., of worthlessness, self-depreciation). The depressed individual experiences hopelessness, feels unworthy, sees nothing that can be done to change the situation, and remains convinced that things will not improve. As Beck formulated in 1976, depression is tantamount to negativism toward the self, toward the present situation, and toward the future.

37

Epidemiology

Results from recently completed studies (Bland, Newman & Arn, 1986; Gastpar & Kielholz, 1983; Murphy et al., 1984; Weissman, 1987) indicate that major depression is a highly prevalent disorder. I would even venture to say that depression is the most common of psychiatric disorders. Its expectancy rate for the general population is from 3% to 8%, and transcultural differences are small. Its diagnosis can be established in adults as well as in children, although the rate of incidence is higher in younger people, and the average age of onset is young adulthood. Established risk factors for developing depression are:
1. female gender;
2. birth after World War II;
3. personal history of depression;
4. family history of a major depressive disorder; and
5. being separated, divorced or unhappily married.

It could be argued that most population surveys identify too many cases of depression by scoring false positives, although it is equally probable that the general physician and medical specialist quite frequently miss the diagnosis altogether. The specificity of case definition in psychiatric practice is high, but the sensitivity is low, particularly in reference to light or "neurotic" depression. This also holds true for certain disorders connected with age (Rutter, 1986), sex, race, and intelligence. We are in need, therefore, of better diagnostic strategies and improved personality topology.

A systems approach to etiology and pathogenesis

We have so many models of etiology and pathogenic process that the hypothesis of depression as a "final common pathway" actually does help in unifying a real variety of explanatory directions. Yet the concept of behavioral disorders as multiply determined is outdated, even in the way DSM-III-R suggests in its multidimensional layout. The greatest drawback of DSM-III-R classification is that it was designed for research objectives, and compiling as homogeneous a population as possible for the sake of research is not the same as the mental health care of individuals. DSM-III-R reduces both psychogenesis and sociogenesis to points on an axis of a classification system -- an insurmountable handicap when a diagnostic formulation of an individual case is required. We are in need of a more encompassing approach; in short, a systems approach.

General Systems Theory (Miller, 1978) provides us with the best tool for organizing our knowledge and skills in handling and managing patients with depressive disorders. The most relevant levels of analysis are:

1. social and cultural context;
2. the relational network;
3. the inner world of experience (in connection with external stressors); and
4. somatic levels (i.e., general health, endocrine regulatory circuits, neurophysiology, chromosomes, molecular neurobiochemistry).

Social and cultural context

Culture plays a crucial role in determining the ways in which feelings of depression are perceived, processed, reacted to and communicated, both verbally and nonverbally. Culture also determines the variance of experience and expression of such feelings between children and adults, rich and poor, women and men. The manner in which an individual is permitted or expected to experience both the self and the context is also, to a great extent, dependent upon one's culture.

An additional aspect of any culture involves its professional subculture. For example, the classical notion of disease has been of little use to the mental health professional; it has proved to be much too limited in scope. Phenomenology, a manner of thought and practice that is superannuated in Europe, seems to be making a comeback based on the assumption that it will support theoretical classification. Yet for the benefit of the individual patient, the professional needs a frame of reference that takes into account the creation and maintenance of a relationship, the importance of context, and the many variations of experience. Sociogenesis and psychogenesis are not axes but distinct domains, levels of abstraction and levels of analysis that, in DSM-III-R, are spatially and conceptually reduced to an axis and, in some cases, to a point on a line. A positivistic and objectivistic view of mankind and science obscures the specific human dimensions of life and experience.

During the last century we have learned to pay closer attention to the individual and to create more room for individualism. The same holds true for minority groups which, not long ago, were just as neglected as the mentally handicapped and mentally retarded. Nevertheless, with increased individualism comes the risk of amplified loneliness and depression.

39

The relational network

The first-degree relatives of patients with an affective disorder run increased risks of suffering from the same affective disorder, and knowledge of such a risk can permit early diagnosis and intervention. In addition, however, members of the same family not only share genetic potential, they also share physical surroundings and, most importantly, they share an emotional climate.

For emotional well-being, we are dependent on family and friends. This is as true for the very young child who would die without parenting as it is for the adult who lives in relational contexts. If the physical needs of the child are insufficiently provided for, it can languish, suffer retarded physical growth, and ultimately perish. Failure to meet the emotional needs of a child for a warm, secure, and stable relationship with at least one parental figure can lead to a depressive state even among the very young. Separation from the mother can also result in anaclitic depression, a condition most likely to occur between the age of 6 months and 4 years. In this state, both the susceptibility to infectious disease and the risk of death are increased.

All human beings remain dependent on others for emotional and relational nourishment during their life span, some more than others, but all of us to some extent. The loss of a loved one will always be followed by a mourning reaction. This reaction will usually remain within the limits of what we call normal, but in a number of cases pathological reactions will occur. Other losses can have the same consequence: loss of honor, bodily integrity, and, for some, even the loss of money or other possessions, should these be perceived by the individual as central to his or her vision of the future.

Some individuals, like those with personality disorders, run above average risks for vulnerability to loss. This also holds true for persons who are mentally subnormal. Because of the inadequacy of their information-processing capacities, the mentally retarded are less able to detach themselves from the immediate situation in order to view it from a long-range perspective. They lack what might be referred to as "the helicopter talent".

Men and women also differ in their information processing capacities and strategies. The striking difference in the incidence of depressive states among women when compared to men is not necessarily a fundamental consequence of upbringing or environmental influences. Biological differences are probably involved, differences that can already be perceived in the very young. Culture and education can modify the differences between men and women by either accentuating or blurring them. Yet there can be no disagreement over the fact that, in contrast to men, women are more able to sense and share their own moods and affects, particularly with members of the same sex. In a clinical situation, women are also better able to reveal and articulate their emotions, while men are more inclined to employ rational and intellectual problem solving strategies. Still, optimal adaptation calls for the use of both abilities in combinations appropriate to changing situations.

Based on the above perspective, it is understandable that the female occupies a central position in both the nuclear and extended family. When she is in a low mood, the whole family can become depressive. Because men are more inclined to move in the peripheral regions of the family, it is always useful to scrutinize if a married woman's depression is an expression of emotional neglect. That is of the utmost importance when a women has young children and is confined to the home, since depression can also be an expression of emotional deprivation and stimulus hunger. If one of the children is depressed, it can indicate that something is fundamentally wrong with the relationship between the parents or among the family members.

Depression can also be understood as a consequence of aggression turned against the self. In identifying with the aggressor, the individual is self-victimized. It is a mental strategy often observed in people who were not allowed as children to defend themselves against parents or siblings, and who have thus learned to avoid conflict and confrontation. They prefer suffering and depression to turning against the aggressive and frustrating party.

Another potentially pathogenic interactive process is scapegoating, in which members of the relational network conspire -- usually unconsciously, but in some cases consciously -- to attribute all evil and inferiority to one of its members; the scapegoat. The individual so determined can react in different ways. One of the possibilities is to become depressive under the hostile pressure of important others, who can then continue to express their aggression by delivering the scapegoat to the mental healthcare system rather than comforting, supporting, and encouraging him or her, which is what is essentially needed. Any member of a family runs the risk of being singled out as a scapegoat, but this is particularly true for the child who is developmentally retarded.

The inner world of experience

Selecting, processing, storing, retrieving, and using information are terms derived from the computer world which are also, within limits,

41

appropriate for describing our cognitive capacities. The human being is an animal with an enormously developed cerebrum and, accordingly, great information-processing potential. We select our data out of that which has meaning for us, that which has value and relevance for the attainment of pleasure and the avoidance of displeasure.

While psychogenesis is sometimes compared with computer software as opposed to hardware, medicine and psychiatry are presumed to concern themselves with the hardware rather than the software of an individual. This, however, is an erroneous conceptualization. The computer parallel is inaccurately drawn. As an information processing system, the human being is a computer with **flexible** hardware.

In synchrony with variations of nature and vehemence of basic needs, the bodily organization changes, and with it the hardware of the cerebral information processing system. Thus, changes will occur in the data itself, acquiring stimulus character as a consequence of altered input and processing. The behavioral aspect of the changed bodily organization we call temperament. Its most important aspects are sensitivity to stimuli, excitability of affect and, last but not least, basic mood.

In 1930, the German psychiatrist Erwin Straus (1930) wrote a little book that still is of great value, *Geschehnis und Erlebnis*, or *Life Event and Experience*, in which he pleaded against a purely objectivistic and positivistic evaluation of human vicissitudes. Significance cannot be found in the event itself, but in the experience of the event. It is extremely difficult to determine in an objective way the significance of an event for a particular individual. This is only possible via an exploration of subjectivity; a path requiring accurate empathy, unconditional regard, and congruence between conversational partners (e.g., patient and doctor or researcher). Only by entering into, building, and maintaining a sufficiently safe situation and relationship will it become possible to disclose the individual world of experience that runs through the inner self. Verbal language with its symbols and figures is an important tool. But symbols and figures are partially, if not totally, specific to the individual -- a vision which contradicts the organic-biological laws, as well as the laws of conditioning and learning theory.

The hardware of the information-processing human organism is not only flexible and changeable in synchrony with the organizational state of the body (e.g., as a consequence of low glucose or high adrenaline levels), it can also be changed by the data which reach the cerebrum, the program employed, and the outcome of processing. In effect, the software changes the hardware. Such changes can be augmented if the organism is younger or more vulnerable, yet as the organism matures, vulnerability to some noxious influences decreases, while vulnerability to others increases. For example, a baby is more vulnerable to super-cooling than an adult, but less vulnerable to pictures of cruelty, as long as the intensity of light and sound does not trespass the infant's threshold of tolerance.

The somatic levels

It has not yet been possible to find a fundamental and unequivocal biological disturbance that can sufficiently explain the etiology and pathogenesis of depression. Only state-dependent biological characteristics have been identified in some depressive subgroups, but these may simply be co-variations or secondary changes. Bonnhoeffer (1910) has pointed out that a depressive mood can also be symptomatic of an organic disease; the behavioral consequence of a malignant tumor, cerebral disorder, chronic infectious disease, metabolic or endocrine disorder (e.g., of thyroid or adrenal glands), hepatic or renal failure. Alcohol is an important depressant as well, as are drugs prescribed by physicians, including antihypertensives (e.g., reserpine is a classic example of an amine-depleter), corticosteroids, contraceptives, fenfluramine, and antihistamines.

Research into cerebral organization, particularly with regard to the functions of the left and right hemispheres, has not led to results of obvious practical use (Gianotti, 1972; Otto, Yeo, & Dougher, 1987; Wexler, 1980). The same applies to what we have learned about neurophysiological processes in neuronal networks. For example, in patients with major affective disorders the latency period prior to the initial REM phase is shortened, while REM activity during the night is found to be higher than normal. Antidepressants retard or suppress REM sleep and the effectiveness of sleep deprivation is explained by this suppression, a phenomenon which is, again, state-dependent.

The greatest, though for psychiatry still moderate, progress has been made at the level of molecular processes and genetics. Depression will cluster in families, for example, with monozygotic twins demonstrating greater concordance than dizygotic twins. Adoption studies (Cadoret, 1978; Mendelewics & Rainer, 1977; Weissman, Gershon, Kidd et al., 1984) make it clear that genetic factors explain this incidence better than do factors of milieu. Unipolar depression can be explained genetically less well than bipolar mood disorders, thus providing a reason to hypothesize polygenetic transmission. Yet polygenesis is, for the time being, a hypothesis promulgated out of ignorance and sustained by our inability to demonstrate the existence of separate factors. Although the X chromosome and chromosome 21 have been suspected, a satisfactory

43

genetic marker is not yet available. Nor are we as yet in a position to know the mechanism of action. It could be a problem of production, transport, distribution, or changing sensitivity receptors. We need, therefore, a more reliable sub-typing of depressive states in our search for stable, inheritable, trait-specific, and state-independent markers.

The search for biochemical markers of depression (Asberg, Martensson & Wagner, 1986; Kielholz & Poldinger, 1986; Matussek, 1986; Whybrow, Akiskal & McKinney, 1984) have attracted particular attention, yet most turn out to be markers of state and not of trait -- they are abnormal during depressive episodes but return to normal upon recovery. The depletion theory (Sitaram, Nurnberger, Gershon, & Gillin, 1982; Whybrow, Akiskal, & McKinney, 1984) of monoamine nor-adrenaline as a cause of depression is almost certainly oversimplified. Data supporting a deficiency of 5-HT in depression are meager and inconsistent. The overall clinical evidence favoring an amine deficiency hypothesis is weak. Tipped markers have shown only moderate sensitivity and specificity (APA Task Force, 1987; Miller & Nelson, 1987).

A substantial body of research into the biochemical correlates of depression in adult life has also been accumulated (Kielholz & Poldinger, 1986; Matusek, 1986; Whybrow, Akiskal & McKinney, 1984), yet it is difficult to maintain an overall view of this broad field, and the relevant pharmacological literature is both extensive and complex. The search for effective short-term treatment and prevention through the use of antide-pressants and MAO-inhibitors has yielded interesting heuristic hypotheses amenable to experimental testing. The possibilities of cholinergic hypersensitivity, disturbance in the metabolism of GABA, or hypofunction of the serotonin system in a subgroup of depressive patients are still open. The roles of growth hormones, thyroid-stimulating hormones, and prolactin remain uncertain as well. Currently, most researchers believe that depression reflects a down- regulation of post-synaptic neurons due to a reduction in the number of receptors, the outcome of which is a decrease in post-synaptic function as a stable correlate of the remedial action of antidepressive drugs. Nevertheless, the majority of studies conducted at the biochemical level have been carried out with hospitalized patients, even though most individuals with depression have not been and never will be hospitalized.

In one subgroup of depressive patients, the secretion of cortisol by the adrenal cortex is increased, a phenomenon upon which the Dexa-methasone Suppression Test (DST) is based. The American Psychiatric Association considers it to be one of the first laboratory tests to hold promise for more meaningful classifications, more efficient treatment selections, and more accurate prognoses (APA Task Force, 1987). However, the DST results in many false positives and has only limited power in differentiating major depressive disorders from other acute and severe illnesses. In addition, it provides merely marginal differentiation among a range of depressive disorders. It does, however, produce a greater reliability of descriptive diagnosis and promotes the homogenization of groups for the purpose of research. In the case of a negative DST, some researchers will venture to state that a diagnosis of an affective disorder is almost certainly incorrect.

Diagnosis and treatment

Although a diagnosis of depression requires a subjective reporting of mood and ideation, young children and retarded persons may not be able to articulate such experience. Yet on the psychological level, depression can be inferred not so much from feelings of sadness as from anhedonia; the impairment of the capacity to experience pleasure or to respond to the anticipation of pleasure. Accompanying symptoms include a lack of responsiveness to ongoing activities, emotional emptiness, a feeling of flatness or distance, and psychomotor retardation or agitation. Of course, the concepts of affects and mood, the awareness of emotion in oneself and others, and the appreciation of emotional connotations in social situations will vary with culture, age, and mental development. Associated phenomena, such as anxiety, irritability, forgetfulness, tension, and inability to concentrate, can put the clinician on the right track. The most important data can be derived from a complete medical history and an investigation into the nuclear family and family tree.

Any diagnosis of depression needs to be differentiated from normal grief reactions, distress due to acute illness, or demoralization. An accurate and complete medical history as well as physical and psychiatric examinations can exclude depressive syndromes in schizophrenia, anxiety disorders, personality disorders, anorexia nervosa, and alcoholism. So-called secondary depression differs little from primary depression in terms of course, familial clustering, or reaction to treatment. In difficult cases, response to a long-term course of treatment with antidepressants or ECT can help in differentiating between depression with and without a biological etiology.

Since useful antidepressive drugs are now available, we need to know who might be expected to respond optimally to them. Effective treatment with antidepressants requires the recognition of well-defined

45

clinical features, the presence or absence of which may easily be determined. The most suitable of these features include the so-called vital symptoms: lack of pleasure in eating and sex, obstipation, sleep disturbances, and typical fluctuations of symptoms during the day. Hallucinations and delusions are of minor importance as long as their content can be understood in reference to basic mood. For the purpose of research, one can resort to questionnaires and rating scales such as the Beck Depression Inventory (Beck, Ward, Mendelson et al., 1961), the Hamilton Depression Scale (Hamilton, 1967), and the Montgomery-Asberg Depression Rating Scale (Montgomery & Asberg, 1979). In general, however, the reliability of such rating scales is low, producing high prevalence rates and large numbers of false positives; any unhealthy or unhappy person may score high (Snaith, 1987) and individuals with identical scores can prove to be totally different in terms of required treatment.

Therapy for depression has to be adapted to the etiological factors that seem to be involved in the individual case. Appropriate treatment can consist of family therapy, individual psychotherapy, behavior therapy, supportive psychotherapy, pharmacotherapy, ECT, sleep deprivation, and therapy for any other somatic or mental disorders diagnosed. The most effective treatment for major depression is ECT followed by the administration of tricyclic antidepressants. Criteria for the choice of a specific antidepressant are lacking since differential effectiveness has not yet been demonstrated. Claims of greater efficacy, shorter latency of onset of action, or more favorable profiles of side-effects remain unsubstantiated, although overdoses involving some are less lethal than overdoses involving others. A good clue to making an appropriate choice, however, can consist of a favorable response by the patient to an earlier depressive episode or a prior favorable response by a family member. The likelihood of positive response is greatest in endogenomorph depression with so-called vital symptoms and an autonomous, biological etiology. A lack of response, however, does not prove that the disorder is not depressive in origin.

The most frequent causes of ineffectiveness in drug therapy involve doses that are too low, treatment duration that is too short, and noncompliance. When we do not succeed in getting a therapeutic response, we too often change our diagnosis -- a strategy that poses some problems. Of all patients with a depressive disorder, 30% do not react to the first antidepressant prescribed (Gelzer, 1986; Insel & Murphy, 1984). The same holds true for reaction to a second, chemically different antidepressant. A practical solution to this situation is to employ the phrase "therapy-resistant depression" when only there is an absence of therapeutic response after adequate treatment with two antidepressants, a MAO inhibitor, and ECT, as well as a persistence of the disorder for a period of at least one year.

The side-effects of antidepressants are many. Among the definite risks, which can assist us in determining which drug to administer, are prostatism, anti-cholinergic activity in hypermetropia, and disorders of conduction in the heart muscle. Determination of blood levels is indicated in cases of toxic symptoms, lack of therapeutic response, or high intoxication risks as may occur among cardiac patients and the elderly.

Most patients suffering from depressive disorders recover completely within a period ranging from several months to one year. A major depressive disorder may last for years and ultimately ebb away. According to Angst (1987), 10% to 20% of depressed patients become chronic, 15% die by suicide. Apart from death by suicide, the overall mortality is higher than average. During the intervals between depressive episodes, patients may display many residual symptoms as a consequence of incomplete remission, leading to social damage and deterioration.

It is obvious that depression remains a serious health problem and that all of our efforts are needed to combat this potentially deadly illness.

Conclusion

Because the human race is confronted with much unhappiness, the professional who sets to the task of helping others will frequently meet with people who are "pressed down," since depression is one of the more frequent, if not the most frequent, discomforting states of mood and mind. At a fundamental level, a depressive state can be conceived of as a strategy in conservation -- stepping back, as it were, in order to better proceed. But an overall explanation of this disorder has to take into account many levels of investigation, from the most concrete to the very abstract, for depression can be the expression of:
1) a defect of one or more genes;
2) a disturbance in the biochemical interactions of the synaptic cleft;
3) a disturbance in the conduction and distribution of stimuli in neuronal circuits;
4) a disturbed function on the cerebral level, particularly, perhaps, involving cooperation between the left and right hemispheres;

5) the loss of a loving relationship or anything else that is highly valued;
6) the turning of aggression against the self in order to avoid conflict or coping with loss;
7) a process of scapegoating within a family or social network;
8) a way of thinking and operating within a professional group, a society, or a culture.

One, some, or all of these levels of analysis can be useful -- simultaneously, sequentially or in different combinations. It should be clear from the foregoing that a solid diagnosis of depression calls for an all-encompassing investigation of the patient within his or her social and cultural contexts.

References

American Psychiatric Association. (1987). Diagnostic and statistical manual of mental disorders (3rd Ed.-Revised). Washington: APA.

Angst, J. (1987). Begriff der Affektieven Erkrankunger. In K. Kisker, H. Lauter, J. Meyer, C. Muller & E. Stromgren (eds.), Affektieve Psychosen. Berlin: Springer.

APA Task Force on Laboratory Tests in Psychiatry (1987). The dexamethasone suppression test: An overview of its current status in psychiatry. American Journal of Psychiatry, 144, 1253-1262.

Asberg, M., Martensson, B., & Wagner, A. (1986). Biochemical markers of serotonin functions in depression and suicidal behaviors. In H. Hippius, G. Klerman & N. Matussek (eds.), New results in depression research. Berlin: Springer.

Beck, A.T. (1976). Cognitive therapy and the emotional disorders. New York: International University Press.

Beck, A.T., Ward, G.H., Mendelson, M. et al. (1976). An inventory for measuring depression. Archives of General Psychiatry, 4, 561-571.

Bonnhoeffer, K. (1910). Die symptomatischen Psychosen im Gefolge von Akuten Infektionen und inneren Erkrankungen. Leipzig/Wien: Deuticke.

Cadoret, R.J. (1978). Psychopathology in adopted-away offspring of biologic parents with antisocial behavior. Archives of General Psychiatry, 35, 176-184.

Gastpar, M., & Kielholz, P. (1983). Depressionsdiagnostik in der all-gemeinpraxis unter besonderer Berucksichtigung der larvierten De-pression. In W. Poldinger (ed.), Aktuelle Aspekte der Depressionsbehandlung. Bern: Huber.

Gelzer, J. (1986). Limits to chemotherapy of depression. Psychopathol-ogy, 19, supp. 2, 108-117.

Gianotti, G. (1972). Emotional behavior and hemispheric side of the lesion. Cortex, 8, 41-55.

Hamilton, M. (1967). Development of a rating scale for primary de-pressive illness. British Journal of Social and Clinical Psyhology, 6, 278-296.

Insel, T.K., Murphy, D.L. (1984). Pharmacologic response and subgroups of patients with affective illness. In R.M. Post & J.C. Ballenger (eds.), Neurobiology of mood disorder. Baltimore: Williams and Wilkins.

Kielholz, P., Poldinger, W. (1986). Latest findings in the aetiology and therapy of depression. International Commemorative Symposium organised in collaboration with the WHO and WPA. Psycho-pathology, 19, suppl. 2.

Klerman, G.L., Endicott, J., Spitzer, R. et al. (1979). Neurotic depress-ions: A systematic analysis of multiple criteria and meanings. American Journal of Psychiatry, 136, 57-61.

Kraepelin, E. (1913). Psychiatrie. Ein Lehrbuch fur Studierende und Arzte. Achte, vollstandig umgearbeitete Auflage, bd III, II, II. Leipzig: Verlag von Johann Ambrosius Barth.

Matussek, N. (1986). Biological aspects of depression. Psychopathology, 19, suppl. 2, 66-71.

Mendelewics, J., & Rainer, J. D. (1977). Adoption study supporting genetic transmission in manic depressive illness. Lancet, 268, 327-329.

Miller, J.P. (1978). Living systems. New York: McGraw-Hill.

Miller, K.B., & Nelson, J.C. (1987). Does the dexamethasone suppression test relate to subtypes, factors, symptoms of severity? Archives of General Psychiatry, 44, 769-774.

Montgomery, S.A., & Asberg, M. (1979). A new depression scale designed to be sensitive to change. British Journal of Psychiatry, 134, 382-389.

Murphy, J.M. et al. (1984). Stability of prevalence. Depression and anxiety disorders. Archives of General Psychiatry, 44, 990-997.

Otto, M.W., Yeo, R.A., & Dougher, M.J. (1987). Right hemisphere involvement in depression: Toward a neuropsychological theory of negative affective experiences. Biological Psychiatry, 22, 1201-1215.

Rutter, M. (1986). Depressive feelings, cognitions and disorders: A research postscript. In: M. Rutter, C. Izard & P. Read (eds.), Depression in young people: Developmental and clinical perspectives. New York: Guilford Press.

Sitaram, N., Nurnberger, J.I., Gershon, E.S., & Gillin, C. (1982). Cholinergic regulation of mood and REM-sleep: potential model and marker of vulnerability to affective disorder. American Journal of Psychiatry, 139, 571-576.

Snaith, R.P. (1987). The concepts of mild depression. British Journal of Psychiatry, 150, 387-393.

Straus, E. (1930). Geschehnis und Erlebnis. Berlin: Springer.

Weissman, M.M., Gershon, E.S., Kidd, K.K. et al. (1987). Psychiatric disorder in the relatives of probands with affective disorder. Archives of General Psychiatry, 41, 13-21.

Weissman, M.M. (1987). Advances in psychiatric epidemiology: Rates and risks for major depression. American Journal of Public Health, 77, 445-451.

Wexler, B.E. (1980). Cerebral laterality and psychiatry: A review of literature. American Journal of Psychiatry, 137, 279-291.

Whybrow, P.C., Akiskal, H.S., & McKinney, W.T. (1984). Mood disorder. Toward a new psychobiology. New York/London: Plenum Press.

World Health Organization. (1977). International classification of diseases: 9th revision (ICD-9). Washington, D.C.

Anton Dosen and Frank J. Menolascino (Eds.) (1990). Depression in mentally retarded children and adults. Leiden, the Netherlands: Logon Publications. ISBN 90-73197-01-5

Chapter 3

The prevalence and specific aspects of depression in mentally retarded individuals

Mark H. Fleisher, M.D.
Martin A. Weiler, M.D.

Introduction

In writing this chapter, several problems were present from the outset. Many of the studies we reviewed had been performed with what we felt were inadequate methodologies. Even studies that offered useful data were often difficult to interpret because of their wide varieties of terminology and diagnostic formulations. This is not a problem peculiar to researchers in the field of dual diagnosis, however; it is a problem common to virtually all who study mental illness. Nevertheless, the importance of depression among the mentally retarded cannot be realized without arriving at some estimate of the general scope of the problem. In this chapter we will offer some measure of understanding concerning the diagnosis of depression as found in the literature that deals with its prevalence and discuss the symptoms of depression as diagnostic dilemmas for those who serve the dually diagnosed.

Accepting affective disorders in the mentally retarded

After decades of study, there can be little doubt that mentally retarded persons can and do suffer from affective disorders, although questions do remain concerning their susceptibility to the full range of mood disorders found within the general population. As the affective disorders become, in general, more clearly understood, the challenge will then be to apply that understanding to the specialized population of the mentally handicapped.

The broad acceptance of depression and other affective disorders as diagnosable entities in the mentally retarded is relatively recent. As late as 1967, William Gardner published a brief review article that addressed the possible causes of severe depressive reactions in this population. Following psychodynamic theories, Gardner proposed that one reason why we might expect to find lower rates of depression among the "subculture" of the mentally retarded was due to their "difference in moral standards." A lack of high moral standards among the mentally handicapped, he reasoned, translated into less guilt over failure. He continued by referencing Penrose's 1963 book *The Biology of Mental Defect* in which Penrose referred to the "concepts of Freud" in stating that the ego and, thus, the superego were weak in those of subnormal intelligence, the consequence of which was that the conscious and subconscious could not generate the feelings of guilt and worthlessness that produce affective disorders. By current thinking, however, one would have to consider whether the emotions of guilt and worthlessness produce or are a result of an affective disturbance. It is possible that the lack of ego and superego development could merely alter the presentation and cognitive elaboration of depressive symptoms. Another important ability serving ego function is linguistic competence, which may require substantial development before an individual can understand and answer questions related to guilt and worthlessness. If one assumes that the relatively complicated feelings of guilt and worthlessness are necessary components of affective disorders, it would follow that those without the capacity to elaborate such emotions could not become depressed. This assumption may account for the low rates and lesser intensity of affective upset described by Penrose.

While Freudian theory continues to have a greater or lesser influence on psychiatric analysis depending on one's educational background, the biological models continue to progress. Many believe that these receptor-transmitter models can illuminate the genesis and expression of affective disorders in those of less than normal intelligence or development. A number of investigators have come to the conclusion that, for a variety of biological, psychological, and sociological reasons, the mentally retarded are at an even greater risk for developing affective disorders than the general population (Benson, 1985; Dosen, 1984; Kazdin, Matson & Senatore, 1983; Lund, 1985; Reiss, 1985; Simmons, 1968). Indeed, the same intrinsic and extrinsic factors that can be so important to the presentation of depression in the mentally retarded, may contribute to the findings that mental illness is generally twice as common among the mentally retarded as it is among the nonretarded population (Menolascino, Levitas & Greiner, 1986).

The most common themes present in the arguments for biological and psychosocial contributors are remarkably similar. For example, an early paper written by Simmons (1968), which reviews the work of Phillips in the 1960s, described maladaptive behaviors as typically characterized by poor coping skills, inferior self-image, social isolation, and antisocial acting out. Additionally, regardless of the level of retardation present, parental reactions to their retarded children can contribute to their own social isolation and worsen the state of their children's mental health. In an investigation conducted at the University of Illinois at Chicago concerning the specific correlations between social competence and depression in mildly retarded adults (Benson, Reiss, Smith & Laman; 1985), depression was again found to be associated with informant ratings of poor social abilities. Deficient social skills were also reported in review articles to be crucial to affective disturbances (Reiss, 1985). Primary among these were poor social problem-solving skills, which present as an inability to easily or thoughtfully generate solutions to the most common social difficulties.

Some authors express their arguments so gracefully that one is left with very little doubt about the importance of biological, psychological, and social contributions to emotional health. For example, Steven Reiss (1985) writes convincingly about the lack of social support, rejection, ultimate stigmatization, and disruption that contributes to the development of psychopathology among the mildly and moderately retarded. It is easy enough for us to appreciate the changes in ourselves when denied the support we need at home, work, or play to extrapolate the effects to the mentally retarded. Inappropriate assertiveness and inadequate leisure skills are additional repeated themes. Both may cause a greater number of chronic emotional problems in the mentally retarded than in the general population. In fact, one becomes hard pressed to explain how the emotional, social, and cognitive weight of these combined deficiencies could *not* contribute to higher rates of depressive symptoms among the mentally handicapped.

Depression and depressive symptoms

The central issue of psychiatric diagnosis is the ability to define a manifested set of behaviors or test results and to label those behaviors and results in a manner that can be applicable to all patients with a high degree of statistical certainty. The American Psychiatric Association's Diagnostic and Statistical Manual of Mental Disorders-Third Edition-Revised (DSM-III-R; American Psychiatric Association, 1987) is the latest effort in an ongoing attempt to systematize psychiatric diagnoses with a maximum of clarity and accuracy and a minimum of contradiction. Unfortunately, this and other works, such as the International Classification of Diseases-9 (ICD-9; World Health Organization, 1988), were constructed for patients of normal intelligence. Since no biological markers are currently available to make a diagnosis of depression with a high degree of confidence and no standard definition of depression exists for the mentally retarded population, many researchers have tried to work within alternative definitions and presentations. A redefinition of depression to include acts of anger and aversive behaviors as a defensive method of dealing with feelings of helplessness and hopelessness has been suggested by Berman (1967). Physically able, institutionalized mentally retarded patients are seen as externalizing their anger by releasing aversive acts upon the staff. Berman references several dynamically oriented authors and describes behaviors that could cross levels of retardation, but does not establish criteria for either depression or other affective disorders for any specific levels of developmental disability.

Somewhat different conclusions are reached by researchers who find it useful to divide the mentally retarded into groups for the purpose of diagnosing depression and manic-depressive disorder. After reviewing twenty-five published reports that dealt with occurrences of affective symptoms, Sovner & Hurley (1982) concluded that mildly and moderately retarded individuals could be diagnosed according to the criteria set forth in DSM-III (American Psychiatric Association, 1980). For the severely and profoundly retarded, the authors found that affective diagnoses could be made on the basis of clinically observable changes in behavior, vegetative signs, and a positive family history. The various studies that the authors reviewed used a variety of diagnostic criteria, including those of DSM-II (American Psychiatric Association, 1968) and the ICD-8 (World Health Organization, 1967). Based on the original reports of case studies whose subject numbers ranged from one to nine, Sovner and Hurley grouped the likelihood of a correct affective diagnosis into four categories; definite, probable, possible, and doubtful. Although some cases were not given a diagnosis because the behaviors described were too vague, the authors were convinced that affective disorders should be considered whenever behavioral changes were noted, even in the severely and profoundly retarded.

In a wide-ranging review article published in 1983, Matson stressed the importance of considering both behavioral changes and the reports of third parties in making a diagnosis of depression in the mentally retarded. His earliest report is of a 24-year-old woman, described in 1888 by Hurd, who exhibited occasionally violent behavioral changes, the presentation of which was clearly that of an affective disorder. Yet while several valid observations of patients spanning approximately one hundred years of studies have been made, we are still left without a definite, proven set of criteria for depression or other affective disorders in the mentally retarded.

Four nonspecific factors associated with mental retardation which influence and confuse the diagnostic process were reported by Sovner in 1986. These factors include (1) intellectual distortion, wherein concrete and reduced communication skills lead to the inability of patients to label and report their own experiences; (2) psychosocial masking, which diminishes social skills and life experiences to such a degree that symptoms are either missed or erroneously attributed as important psychiatric indicators when, in fact, they are not; (3) cognitive disintegration, which is a stress-induced disruption of basic and advanced information processing, leading to psychotic presentations likely to be misdiagnosed as schizophreniform disorders; and (4) baseline exaggeration, which involves an increase in the cognitive deficiencies or maladaptive, stereotypic behaviors that were present beforehand, thus confusing diagnoses, symptoms, and outcomes after treatment.

The studies reviewed in this section have, in their own ways, advanced our understanding of the difficulties inherent in diagnosis, but, as we shall see, we are not yet at a point where we have standardized symptoms and behaviors with which to accurately report the prevalence of affective disorders in the mentally retarded population.

Reports on the prevalence of major depression

There have been a number of published reports on the prevalence of major depression among the mentally retarded, the conclusions of which fall into three categories. The first category, represented primarily by early investigators, demonstrates generally low rates of depression or severe depression among the groups studied. The second category offers data that confirms affective disorders but uses terminology or methodology that is difficult to interpret or utilize. The third category will be represented by the results of one large study that is relatively recent and has been vigorously referenced in other articles. This paper finds the prevalence rate to be much higher than the numbers reported by earlier investigators and closer to the rates published for the general population in the United States. In addition to reviewing these papers, we will briefly look at the most recently published prevalence rates for the general population of the United States for major depression in Epidemiologic Catchment Areas.

Category I

An early review article (Gardner, 1967) that commented on four studies conducted during the 1930's through the 1960's generally supported the argument for low prevalence rates. L.S. Penrose's 1938 study of 1,280 institutionalized mentally retarded patients found that "few persons demonstrated affective disorders." Interestingly, insufficient statistics were included in the original report, although Gardner did reference a personal communication between Penrose and Craft that revealed only one patient out of 1,280 to demonstrate "strong depressive trends." One could easily argue that this report should be taken with a certain amount of caution due to the lack of statistical support and the fact that the 1938 study group was totally composed of institutionalized patients. Gardner next references Pollock's 1945 study which supported Penrose's earlier finding of low rates for depressive reactions. Of 444 mentally retarded individuals, only 1.6% were found to be manic-depressive and only a limited number of these were found to demonstrate predominately depressive symptoms. A 1959 study by Craft of 314 hospitalized mentally retarded adults was also reviewed, revealing no reportable cases of manic-depressive disorder and only one diagnosis of depressive illness. Gardner relates some of Craft's descriptive findings and reports that the single diagnosis of depression was evidently a mild case that occurred during menses. Finally, Gardner relates the findings of an unpublished paper by Davis covering a five-year period of mentally retarded patient admissions to a New York State hospital for the mentally ill. The sample population consisted of 268 individuals, 131 of whom were male. The range of ages was from 18 to "over 65". All patients were diagnosed as having psychotic reactions. Of these 268 patients, 1.1% were further diagnosed as having severe depressive disturbances. Gardner reports this rate as being significantly lower than rates for nonretarded admissions.

What is striking about these reports is not just the variety of methodology and the lack of corroborating evidence, but the validity that was assigned to them. It is also noteworthy that these were the only articles on the prevalence of depression in mentally retarded individuals that could be found at the time. Gardner's natural conclusion was that significantly more work needed to be performed in order to support or refute these early, epidemiologically vague studies.

Category II

Two papers in particular offer striking examples of the second grouping referred to above. The first reports on a computerized study of admissions to the psychiatric hospitals of Denmark (Lund, 1985). All patients admitted to psychiatric facilities with a determination of mental retardation were automatically registered. The central theme of the work was not to document prevalence as such, but to report on a perceived increase of dually diagnosed patients and to suggest that alternate treatment approaches be found. While some might argue that this was not a broadly representative study, in that all subjects were drawn from an inpatient setting, there is some benefit to the inclusiveness of the study group. After all, an entire nation's psychiatric admissions were systematically screened, and the percentage found to be mentally retarded were assigned diagnoses by mental health workers. While the author does offer percentages for the psychiatric categories of 5,107 patient admissions over a thirteen-year period, the classification system employed is that of ICD-8 (World Health Organization, 1967), which does not contain a category for major depression.

The second paper has been referred to previously (Sovner and Hurley, 1982). The authors reviewed all the pertinent English language publications in the behavioral sciences literature that discussed mental retardation and affective disorders. The total number of papers reviewed was twenty-five. From this, the authors concluded that the mentally retarded could suffer from the full range of affective disorders described at that time and that even the severely and profoundly retarded could be diagnosed with affective disorders by employing a case review format which is, by its nature, subjective.

Category III

The last paper we will review described a large study that has been frequently referenced as offering valid diagnoses of major depression among the mentally retarded. Jacobsen (1982) reported on an epidemiological study of over 30,000 recipients of services for the developmentally disabled in the state of New York. His data was based on the New York Developmental Disabilities Information Survey, which allows research of up to three problem behaviors, drawn from a list of 29, that could influence placement decisions for the State of New York service agency.

Behaviors were grouped into four categories -- major, minor, cognitive, and affective -- and span a broad range of potential behaviors seen in individuals with developmental disabilities. Jacobsen's results suggested that 47.7% of the mentally retarded individuals studied displayed some problem behavior and that 17.1% had concomitant psychiatric impairment. Under the grouping of affect-related problems, the following percentages were noted: extreme mood changes, 5.6%; appropriate affect not displayed, 4.9%; lack of interpersonal responsiveness, 12.3%; suicidal threats/attempts, 0.4%; depression, 2.9%; and extreme irritability, 2.9%. Under minor behaviors, crying and temper tantrums were recorded in 13.7% of the total population.

Jacobson also reported on the incidence of behaviors when the total study population of 30,578 was broken down into two groups; those with psychiatric and developmental disabilities (3,555) and those with developmental disabilities alone (27,023). Although problem behaviors were much higher in the group with psychiatric and developmental disabilities, 13.5% of the group with developmental disabilities alone showed crying and temper tantrums, and 9.9% showed a lack of interpersonal responsiveness. This is, at best, suggestive of the possibility that substantial numbers of recipients were experiencing symptoms of depression that were not prominent enough to come to the attention of the psychiatric assessment and treatment systems. An important consideration in this study is that depression was rated as a behavior in contrast to a syndrome. Several other behaviors related to potential depression could have competed with the three allowed in the recording. Crying, temper tantrums, and lack of interpersonal responsiveness were the behaviors most frequently noted in this study and suggest the possibility of high rates of major depression. This study did not, however, investigate all or even most of the symptoms associated with major depressive disorder as a syndrome. The behaviors noted above are also, of course, not pathonomic for a major depressive disorder. Firm conclusions can, therefore, not be drawn.

Epidemiologic Catchment Area statistics

At this point it may be useful to examine the data obtained from a five-site Epidemiologic Catchment Area (ECA) study recently published in the United States (Regier et al, 1988). One-month prevalence rates from five research sites covered the major psychiatric diagnoses and were compared to previously published six-month and lifetime prevalence rates. The ECA findings were based on 18,571 individuals who were interviewed using verifiable testing instruments. The following rates are standardized according to the age, sex, and race distribution of the 1980 noninstitution-alized population of the United States aged 18 years or more (1980 was the last year that nationwide census information was gathered). When diagnostic categories are restricted to those also covered in international studies using the Present State Examination, the combined standardized results are within the ranges reported for Europe and Australia as well:

* The one-month combined site prevalence rate for major depressive episodes was 2.2%.
* The six-month combined site prevalence rate for major depressive episodes was 3.0%.
* The lifetime combined site prevalence rate for major depressive episodes was 5.8%.

This study represents one of the most thorough done to date in determining prevalence rates over time for specific psychiatric disorders. The diagnoses were clearly defined according to DSM-III (American Psychiatric Association, 1980) criteria, the patient selection process seemed well planned and representative of the population, and the results were standardized to the best and latest population data. That the ECA results are similar to European and Australian data is an encouraging example of a study that can adapt its results to other international standards, although it would certainly be easier if there were no need to adapt data to data and method to method.

Conclusion

First and foremost, we believe that no study has yet been accom-plished that describes the prevalence of major depression among the mentally retarded in a methodologically supportable manner, despite the amount of effort invested and the useful information obtained. Problems inherent in diagnostic criteria and nomenclature from nation to nation remain to be solved. What we have been able to conclude is that the developmentally disabled do suffer from affective disorders and that for a variety of social, biological, and psychological reasons, it is likely that their prevalence rates are probably higher than for the general population. Without reliable data that would be useful in planning community programs, allocating resources, and diagnosing and treating the dually diagnosed, we will continue to rely on assumptions that are, at best, incomplete.

59

References

American Psychiatric Association (1968). Diagnostic and Statistical Manual of Mental Disorders. Washington, D.C.:APA.

American Psychiatric Association (1980). Diagnostic and Statistical Manual of Mental Disorders -Third Edition. Washington, D.C.: APA.

American Psychiatric Association (1987). Diagnostic and Statistical Manual of Mental Disorders -Third Edition-Revised. Washington, D.C.: APA.

Benson, B.A. (1985). Behavior disorders and mental retardation: Associations with age, sex, and level of functioning in an outpatient clinic sample. Applied Research in Mental Retardation, 6, 79-85.

Benson, B.A., Reiss, S., Smith, D. & Laman, D. (1985). Psychosocial correlates of depression in mentally retarded adults II: Poor social skills. American Journal of Mental Deficiency, 89, 657-659.

Berman, M.I. (1967). Mental retardation and depression. Mental Retardation, 12, 19-21.

Dosen, A. (1984). Depressive conditions in mentally handicapped children. Acta Paedopsychiatrica, 50, 29-40.

Gardner, W.I. (1967). Occurrence of severe depressive reactions in the mentally retarded. American Journal of Psychiatry, 124, 386-388.

Jacobson, J. (1982). Problem behavior and psychiatric impairment within a developmentally disabled population I: Behavior frequency. Applied Research in Mental Retardation, 3, 121-139.

Kazdin, A.E., Matson, J.L. & Senatore, V. (1983). Assessment of depression in mentally retarded adults. American Journal of Psychiatry, 140, 1040-1043.

Lund, J. (1985). Mentally retarded admitted to psychiatric hospitals in Denmark. Acta Psychiatrica Scandinavica, 72, 202-205.

Matson, J.L. (1983). Depression in the mentally retarded: Toward a conceptual analysis of diagnosis. Progress in Behavior Modification, 15, 57-79.

Menolascino F.J., Levitas, A., Greiner, C. (1986). The nature and types of mental illness in the mentally retarded. Psychopharmacology Bulletin, 22, 1060-1071.

Penrose, L.S. (1963). The Biology of Mental Defect-Third Edition. New York: Grune & Stratton.

Regier, D., Boyd, J. Burke, J. Rae, D., Meyers, J., Kramer, M., Robins, L., George, L., Karno, M. & Locke, B. (1988). One month prevalence of mental disorders in the United States. Archives of General Psychiatry, 45, 977-986.

Reiss, S. (1985). The mentally retarded, emotionally disturbed adult. Children with Emotional Disorders and Developmental Disabilities, 9, 171-190.

Simmons, J.Q. (1968). Emotional problems in mental retardation: Utilization of psychiatric services. Psychiatric Clinics of North America, 15, 957-967.

Sovner, R. (1986). Limiting factors in the use of DSM-III criteria with mentally ill/mentally retarded persons. Psychopharmacology Update, 22, 1055-1059.

Sovner, R. & Hurley, A. (1982). Do the mentally retarded suffer from affective illness? Archives of General Psychiatry, 40, 61-67.

World Health Organization (1967). International Classification of Diseases - Volume 8. Washington, D.C.: The United States Government Printing Office.

World Health Organization (1988). International Classification of Diseases - Volume 9. Washington, D.C.: The United States Government Printing Office.

Anton Dosen and Frank J. Menolascino (Eds.) (1990). Depression in mentally retarded children and adults. Leiden, the Netherlands: Logon Publications. ISBN 90-73197-01-5

Chapter 4

Developmental and biological factors in the mentally retarded and vulnerability to depression

Anton Dosen, M.D.,
Svetomir Bojanin, M.D.

Introduction

The theoretical postulates about depression are changing. Early psychoanalysts (Abraham, 1927; Freud, 1927 (1957)) argued that the superego had to be developed for depression to occur and, thus, could not occur in younger children. Later, psychodynamically oriented authors (Spitz, 1946; Bowlby, 1973) hypothesized that depression could indeed be caused early in childhood due to the loss of a "love object". Early experience of loss, such as a long lasting separation of the child from the mother, may predispose the child to depression later in life. Other authors (Sandler & Joffee, 1965) considered depression as the loss of a previous state of self, meaning the loss of a sense of happiness and other attributes needed for an awareness of the integrity of the self.

Some learning theorists (Brown, Harris & Copeland, 1977; Seligman, 1975) suggest that if a person comes to believe that his or her actions will not initiate or terminate a gratifying or aversive experience, they learn to become helpless, the consequence of which is depressive behavior. Early loss of affection or other uncontrollable negative events might initiate this learned helplessness and induce a feeling of incapacity, withdrawal, and self-depreciation. Such an individual would respond to further losses and stressful events with depression.

Besides psychological factors, there is an additional hypothesis that depression could be caused by specific neurobiological conditions or changes. This hypothesis is receiving increasing attention from researchers. Genetic (possibly X-linked) factors, biogenic amine abnormalities, endocrinological and neurophysiological disorders may play a role in the occurrence of depression. However, from a clinical perspective it should be stressed that the combination of psychological and biological factors and a predisposition to depression can often be found in the very early stages of development. It is strongly felt that not only biological factors influence the psychological condition, but that psychological and environmental factors may also cause changes in the biological substrate.

Despite the lack of scientific research, we believe that, from the developmental point of view, there should be no doubt about the existence of depression in the mentally retarded. Yet because of the specific biological substrate determining mental retardation, as well as the developmental course and environmental circumstances of this population (Dosen, 1989), the appearance, course, and frequency of this disorder may be different from that of the nonretarded population. Such differences are the reason for diagnostic and treatment difficulties.

In an effort to provide an overview of the various factors which determine the occurrence and symptomatology of depression in the mentally retarded, we will begin to form a foundation of the neurophysiological and neuropsychological development of a retarded child, comparing a retarded and nonretarded child within the framework of the psychosocial developmental model. This should be helpful in understanding the differences in development and serve as a basis for better diagnostic insight (Dosen, 1987).

Psycho-social development

The psychosocial development of a child begins before the birth (Bojanin, 1985) and continues through characteristic phases into adulthood. The characteristic stages of psychosocial development are principally determined by chronological age (Piaget, 1955; Mahler, Pine & Bergman, 1975).

The first schemata of emotional life are made during intrauterine period. The infant reacts with relaxation or excitement to particular visceral and external stimuli, accepting or rejecting them and developing in this manner the basic schemata for pleasure or displeasure. These reactions emerge parallel with the beginning of myelinization (maturation) of primary sensory and motor areas of the cortex and some parts of the limbic system (Luria, 1973, Yacovlev & Lecours, 1967). Further development and differentiation of psychic functions depends on the maturation of secondary and tertiary areas of the cerebral cortex during the first and second year of life (secondary areas), in the third year and, later, by 7 and 12 years of age (tertiary areas).

Schematically, the functions of these three cortex areas could be illustrated by the following example: When hearing the word "fire," the reaction of a person will be dependent upon the context of the situation. Through the primary areas of the cortex, the person has received an acoustic stimulus of a particular intensity and duration. Through the secondary areas, he or she has perceived that the acoustic stimulus was a human voice and that it was a word with a particular meaning. Via the tertiary areas, the person can recognize the real message within the real situation and can organize his or her own reaction (behavior-output).

Maturation has a hierarchical course; myelinization of the tertiary areas take place after particular secondary areas have reached a certain level of maturation. Sensory stimulation of the infant by the environment is inevitable for the growing, differentiation, and maturation of the cortex tissue. Through the maturation of cerebral tissue, the child gradually develops more and more complex cognitive and emotional schemata. "Perceiving" goes together with "feeling" and both are possible on the basis of sufficiently developed cerebral tissue. Maturation of particular areas moved parallel with the phasic development of cognitive, emotional, and social abilities of the child. For example, due to the growing function of the tertiary areas of the cortex, by the end of the first year and into the second the child is building up a notion of object permanence. She or he has learned that a particular object exists even though it can be neither seen nor felt at the moment. Due to this cognitive ability, the child learns to be sure of the mother's love and protection even though she is absent. Basic emotional security grows, making the child able to tolerate separation from the mother and to establish individuation.

From neurophysiological findings and theories regarding cognitive (Piaget, 1955) emotional, and social development (Bowlby, 1973; Mahler, Pine & Bergman, 1975) a model of socio-emotional development can be drawn:

1. First adaptation phase (0 - 6 months)
   a) integration of sensoric stimuli
   b) integration of the structure of place, time and persons.
2. First socialization phase (6 - 18 months)
   a) bonding
   b) creating a secure base.
3. First individuation phase (18 - 36 months)
   a) separation
   b) individuation

c) development of a unique personality

During the first adaptation phase the child adapts to the outside world by integrating sensoric stimuli and becoming confident about the rhythm of activity of the spaces and the persons in his or her environment. Wallon (1969) considered this period to be the biological phase of life, or a phase of biological symbiosis between the child and the mother. The period after six months he regarded as social symbiosis. We believe, however, that not only the first six months but even the period preceding birth cannot be seen as biological only. Outside factors consisting of social elements also have an important influence on development during this early stage. The initial affects of pleasurable excitement and unpleasurable protest are being experienced in this phase as well. Anxiety is usually global and disorganizing. Underlying pre-representational concerns are hypothesized to be related to themes of annihilation (Greenspan, 1985). This kind of basic anxiety we will refer to as "existential anxiety".

During the second phase (first socialization phase), bonding and creating a secure emotional base take a central place. A number of new functions in communication emerge during this phase (e.g., the use of distal senses; Spitz, 1946), motor coordination in standing and walking, control of sphincters, the beginning of speech, etc. These abilities are the result of increasing maturation in the secondary cortex system and the activation of tertiary areas, preparing the child for establishing physical distance from the mother and experiencing independence.

These are the first practo-gnostic constructs ("morphosinthesis" according to Denny-Brown & Baker, 1944) by which the child becomes able to recognize its own existence within its own social space. In this phase, the affects of pleasure and displeasure become further differentiated. The child can demonstrate love and anger toward others. Clinging and organized negativism are also present. Anxiety is related to the loss of a love object and annihilation of an emerging somatic self (existential anxiety).

The third phase (first individuation phase) is characterized by more complex cognitive and emotional functions which precipitate the awareness of personal existence. In this period, the myelinization of the tertiary areas of the cortex proceeds rapidly. Hearing improves, complex verbal communications are begun, and hearing and sight are combined into new cognitive structures. Parallel to increased motor control, growing cognitive abilities, and awareness of the ego, the child can begin to differentiate new emotions, such as love, unhappiness, and envy, at both preverbal and emerging verbal levels (Greenspan, 1985). Anxiety is still related to the loss of a loved person but also to the loss of approval and acceptance. However, this sort of anxiety can be better tolerated. This is not existential anxiety anymore, but another quality which could be named "social anxiety".

The development in the first three years of life is, from the neurophysiological as well as from the psychological point of view, of a determinable importance for further development of personality. It may be underlined that within the first three years of life the basis for personality is created. Adverse influences during this period may have biological, psychological, and sociological consequences leading to the emergence of different forms of psychopathology. During further personality development, parallel with increasing cognitive abilities, further differentiation of emotions takes place. Between the age of four and seven the child experiences pride and joy in the psychological and bodily self, but feelings of shame and humiliation emerge. Empathy and tenderness are additionally in evidence but are of a fragile nature and easily lost if competitive strivings are enhanced. Anxiety and fears are related to bodily injury and loss of respect and love. Self-esteem emerges as well as feelings of guilt. For the professional, such knowledge of development and differentiation of emotional life is important for recognizing the symptoms of affective disorders at different levels of psychic development.

The expression of depression at different developmental stages

We have tried to accentuate that the socio-emotional development of a child in the first three years is characterized by the gradual differentiation of the qualities of affect. It is to be expected that a disturbance in affect at different developmental stages will result in different symptoms. However, it is important to underscore that an affective disorder, such as depression, involves not only a disturbance of mood (i.e., an observable state of affective condition) but also a disorder in psychomotor functioning, vitality and manners of thought. Knowledge of the development of these various developmental aspects is needed in order to recognize a disorder. According to the phenomenological concept of depression, a full appraisal of unhappiness, a lowering of vigor and energy, a sense of rejection, and a negative self-image is only possible when a person is able to view himself or herself in these terms and to describe such feelings to others. Most preschool children, as well as severely mentally retarded persons are not able to do so. Nevertheless, various studies strongly suggest that depression may be experienced as early as the second year of life or even younger. Spitz (1946) described withdrawal into a state of apathy in infants in the second half of the first year after separation from their mothers. Here he used the term "anaclitic depression," suggesting that the behavior of these children was an infantile form of depression. Engel and Reichsman (1956) described a "conversation withdrawal" reaction in a child neglected by the mother during the first year of life. The girl reacted to strangers by withdrawal, detachment, and falling into a state of sleep. The authors believed that to be a basic biological pattern underlying the later "giving up" syndrome of depression. Reite, Short, Seiler & Pauley (1980) reported physiological and behavioral changes in infant monkeys after separation from their mothers. Anthony (1975) describes depression and anxiety in childhood as "basic psycho-biological affective reactions" during the adaptation of the child to its surroundings. These findings and many other studies in human and animal infants suggest that reactions to a loss of affective bonding may be experienced as catastrophic (existential anxiety), having implications not only for behavior, but also for physiological changes suggestive of general impairment in the autonomic homeostatic regulatory process. Disorders in sleeping, eating, and motor activities and failure to thrive are involved as well. Similar states can be produced by the lack of cognitive stimulation, nutritional or organic deficiency diseases.

Some authors (Bemporad & Wilson, 1978) hesitate to classify these infantile reactions to loss as depression in the classic sense. They rather look at this condition as "developmental deprivation," an unpleasant global experience of the underdeveloped psyche precipitated by the absence of external stimulation and bearing a relationship to the later onset of depression. These studies suggest that the loss of an affective bond as well as understimulation and excessive or inappropriate stimulation may cause disengagement from active interaction with the environment at both motor and perceptual levels and possibly metabolic rearrangement as well. Neurobiochemical changes in the central nervous system (CNS) are also possible but, unfortunately not very well researched until recently.

From the developmental point of view, these reactions can be understood as representing a depressive state at a low level of development. In the first developmental phase (0-6 months), this condition can occur by inappropriate stimulation and loss of achieved structures in space, time, and persons. In the second developmental stage (6-18 months), the loss of an established affective bond could provoke the onset of depression. Bowlby (1973) has argued that separation from the mother causes a feeling of hopelessness and despair in a child. Other authors (Reite,

Short, Seiler & Pauley, 1980) suggest that any disturbance in attachment may have implications in the neurobiological substrate and the regulations of affective behavior in the infant.

During the third developmental phase (18-36 months) and further personality development, because of a differentiation in emotional life other symptoms of adverse circumstances emerge. By experiencing ego development and the need to become less dependent on important others, the child becomes involved in a struggle for its own independence. Horney (1950) argues that this situation may cause "basic anxiety" in the child. This is a sort of social anxiety characterized by disappointment, sorrow, shame, and guilt. In pathological cases, this can lead to a low self-esteem, depressed mood, motor retardation, and disorders of vegetative functions. On this developmental level, symptoms of depression are more characteristic those found in school-age children.

From the developmental point of view, the definition of depression as the loss of previous state of self (Sandler & Joffee, 1965) deserves to be underlined. A very early experience of self is related not only to bonding, but to experiences associated with one's surroundings as well as cognitive and emotional schemata related to adaptation and survival. Obviously, reactions of the child to changes in personal and material surroundings at a very early age (first adaptation phase) are more global than at later ages. The quality of change is usually less important than the quantity. The child reacts in the same way whether due to special changes in the environment, separation from the mother, or somatic illness. In all cases, he or she reacts through disturbances in psychomotor and vegetative functions (vitality).

In the first socialization phase, however, the quality of change does make a difference. Separation from the mother upsets the child, while a change of environment, if the mother is present, does not. At a higher level of socioemotional development, the child becomes more resilient in adverse environmental influences and reacts more selectively change. However, disorders at this level are also manifested by disturbances in vegetative and motor functions.

At the third socioemotional level and beyond the child may even tolerate separation from the mother if he or she can find comfort with others. Adverse events cause fewer global reactions. Initially, the child will react with personality disturbance symptoms, and, if the adverse situation lasts longer or becomes more severe, symptoms of vegetative and motor disturbance emerge.

It might be concluded from this schema that a child on a lower developmental level is more prone to react to adverse situations with very basic (vital or existential) symptoms, while children on higher levels react first with disturbances in their personal qualities. This conclusion is important for discussing the phenomenon of depression at different levels of mental retardation.

Characteristics of a mentally retarded person

According to most investigators, retarded psychosocial development has been viewed as being a combinatorial result of genetic, organic, social, biochemical, and various other factors. They agree that, in most cases, there is no single major cause of mental retardation. Nevertheless, diagnosticians often demonstrate a tendency to look for an isolated instance of brain tissue damage in the search for brain dysfunction.

That brain damage in most retarded children occurs during the prenatal (51%) and perinatal (12%) periods (Iivanainen, 1981), that there are various pathways of reaction to this damage, as well as great plasticity in the developing brain (Chess & Hassibi, 1978), are facts which are often overlooked. Some investigators (Ebels, 1980; Shaffer, 1977) believe that brain damage in early childhood has a tendency to generalize. For example, damage which could cause neurological dropout in an adult, results in broad impairment of psychological functioning in a young child. Ebels (1980) distinguishes two categories of developmental damage; primary damage to systems in very early states (e.g., proliferating matrices), and secondary damage to relatively established structures (e.g., the cerebral or cerebellar cortex). Primary damage affects not only the structure directly involved, but others with which it is in some way connected. Experiments with rats, for example, demonstrate that early destruction of immature elements of the cerebellum results in a severely hypoplastic cerebellum.

From a developmental viewpoint, the slow rate of motor skill acquisition and other functional abilities in a retarded child could indicate that the maturation of all cortex areas is delayed (secondary damage). We have, however, often found there to be normal development in motor abilities, particularly in mildly and moderately retarded children; the parents of these children notice retardation only in the second or third year. We explain this phenomenon as a discrepancy in maturation between the primary and secondary brain systems, and the tertiary system. Delayed development and maturation of tertiary cortex areas seem to be a common feature in retarded children (Luria, 1973) and, due to delay in the maturation of this system, such children cannot organize or accommodate their new experiences into cognitive and emotional schemata.

As a rule, these children show disharmonious motor behavior. They have axial and imitation synkinesis, cannot relax their muscles (paratonia), and are not lateralized. These features usually disappear in nonretarded children by the age of six, while in retarded children they may last longer. Furthermore, gnostic functions such as recognition of form, colors, distances, and interactions are insufficient in these children. Concerning speech development, in the best cases, they may be able to describe their own perceptions, but are unable to use speech in expressing the meanings of these events -- "interactions communication" according to Luria (1982). Interactions communication becomes possible through the maturation of tertiary cortex areas, a part of the brain in the mentally retarded that dysfunctions and causes a lack of simultaneous synthesis of personal experiences in a formal, thoughtful manner (Luria, 1982).

From the Piagetian point of view, the cognitive development of a mentally retarded child is characterized by slower progression through the normal cognitive stages, and by the lower limits of full development. Due to slower maturation of the primary and secondary bran systems, one would expect that the child's motor activity would be less intense, the consequence of which would be delayed learning. Based on experience, however, we know that most retarded children during their first months of life remain entirely passive and uninterested in their surroundings. It is, therefore, probable that children with delayed brain development begin to suffer under a second handicap at an early stage; understimulation caused by delayed interaction with their surroundings. Such children do not activate their environment like normal children. They seek no attention and do not, therefore, receive it. Their developmental stages usually last longer than those of normal children; each progressive stage becoming increasingly long. At last, these children remain in one stage and progress no further.

The Piagetian model has been applied to the classification of mental retardation (Bojanin, 1985; Grossman, 1983; Piaget & Inhelder, 1947). According to this model, profoundly retarded people do not advance beyond the sensorimotor level. They can acquire skills in grasping, manipulating, and exploring objects, they may reach an understanding of the constancy of objects, they may also establish basic social relationships with important people in their lives, but their functioning and reactions remain on the level of children no older than two. Severe mental retardation is comparable to the developmental level reached by the general population within two to four years of life; a pre-operational level in which speech is used to communicate. Such communication remains extremely simple, lacking in both generalization and symbolism. Individuals with this degree of retardation are also deficient in the cognitive concepts required to predict new events. Moderate mental retardation is comparable to a range in age of four to seven years; the stage of pre-logical thinking. These people are able to create useful, non-abstract concepts of their experiences, but perceptions predominate and problems are solved mainly by trial and error. The mildly retarded population approximates the general population of between seven and eleven years of age; the stage of concrete thinking operations. Although problems are solved through logical thought, these individuals are unable to manipulate purely abstract terms. Thus, according to the theory of Piaget, retarded person simply do not reach the formal operations stage (i.e., eleven years through adulthood) in which symbolic and abstract forms of thought predominate.

The growth of a stable personality requires that cognitive, emotional, and social development maintain a parallel course; the level of cognitive development can be used as milestone for appropriate social and emotional growth. For profoundly retarded children, however, the highest level that can be reached in our developmental model is the first socialization phase. The severely retarded can reach the first individuation phase, but do not follow though with further personality development. A portion of the moderately retarded remain in the third phase as well.

Such differentiation may leave the impression of oversimplication. However, while it is true that the social behavior of a severely retarded adult with a high level of functioning in a constant environment may be better than that of a child of three, if that adult were to be confronted with difficult problems, he or she would regress to the toddler level. In practice, therefore, emotional and social levels may rise above the cognitive level, but it would be a mistake to judge the social skills and responsibilities of such a person on the basis of social functioning achieved by special training in a stable environment, rather than on the basis of an ability to adapt to new circumstances through inherent cognitive competence. In unfavorable circumstances (e.g., inadequate stimulation, affective neglect, etc.), cognitive, emotional, and social development pursue discrepant courses. Very often, emotional development will lag behind cognitive and social development, and this discrepancy is especially striking in children with psychiatric disorders (Dosen, 1989).

Due to neurophysiological problems, mentally retarded children may be confronted with severe difficulties as early as the first adaptation phase.

Sensory integration and structure in space, time, and persons demands more time in retarded than in nonretarded children. Bonding during the second developmental phase may pursue a difficult course and the establishment of a secure emotional base may be insufficient. The consolidation of personality during the first individuation phase and beyond may proceed in a manner different from nonretarded children. While individuation of a normal child leads to creation of an independent person, mentally retarded individuals will remain dependent upon others.

In summary, the development of a mentally retarded person is characterized by insufficient integration of functions of the CNS, the striking feature of which is the lack of dominance of the cortex as the highest integrative neural structure. The result of this dysfunction is immaturity of neuro-muscular structures, a weak differentiation of gnostic functions, and shortages of emotional and social development which lead to disharmonious personality development. All of these factors may lie behind the hightened risk for behavioral difficulties and psychiatric disorders.

Depression in mentally retarded persons

For various reasons, mentally retarded children are often confronted with unfavorable circumstances during their development. During the first developmental phase, such circumstances may already be the reason for inadequate stimulation or erroneous appraisals of the child's needs, the consequence of which may be difficulties in adaptation and problems in the process of bonding.

Case history #1

A severely mentally retarded three-year-old girl was admitted to the clinic because of self-injurious behavior and stagnation of development. Because of serious somatic problems during her two first years, she was frequently hospitalized for weeks or months at a time. The parents described their daughter as withdrawn, refusing bodily contact, changing from very irritated to passive and apathetic, and displaying difficulties in sleeping, eating, and gaining weight. At the age of two, she had been examined by a child psychiatrist and diagnosed as autistic.

Taking into account her developmental course and symptomatology, we saw the child as depressed, rather than autistic, because of a disturbed adaptation to her surroundings. By constantly changing

73

her surroundings due to somatic illnesses and frequent hospitaliz-ations, the child was unable to find her psychophysiological homeostasis, the consequence of which was an exhaustion of her biological compensatory apparatus, like much chronic stress. In our opinion, this had caused biochemical imbalance in the CNS, resulting in disorders of psychomotor and vegetative functions (vitality).

Difficulties in the first and second phase of socioemotional development and problems in attachment behavior have often been reported by parents of mentally retarded children who were later diagnosed as suffering from depression. According to the parents, preschool age problems of attachment usually diminished or disappeared, but in stressful circumstances these children were inclined to react with depressive symptoms. Frequent problems of individuation, especially those related to a weak emotional security base and separation anxiety, can be expected in the mentally retarded for reasons already mentioned. We are inclined to speak about a "developmental depression" in these persons.

Case history #2

A 10-year-old girl was admitted because of self-injurious behavior and a number of additional symptoms suggesting a depressive condition. Her depression began simultaneously with the onset of a severe relationship conflict between her parents. Becasue of the threatened breakdown of her marriage, the girl's mother became upset and desperate, and was unable to give as much attention as she previously had to her child. The girl experienced this desperation and lack of attention as a loss of her mother's love and, not being able to compensate for this threat to her existence, fell into a depressive state, exhibiting symptoms of disorders in vitality, motor functions, and general behavior. The reason for her lack of compensatory ability probably lay in unfinished individuation. Psychotherapeutic treatment directed toward improving of her relationship with the environment provided good results (See Chapter 14).

Based on our clinical experience, developmental difficulties during the first three years of life, which result in an insecure emotional base and individuation problems, may lead to depressive states if one is confronted with unsolvable problems or stress. Apparently, these children are emotionally too weak to bear their burdens. Similar developmental problems probably play a role in the onset of depression in mentally retarded adolescents and adults after leaving their parents' homes for lives in group homes and institutions. However, other factors may also play a role in the onset of this sort of depression. Besides shortcomings in emotional development, so-called "learned helplessness" may also precipitate a depressive state (Rutter, 1985). Due to frequent experiences of failure, incompetence, and dependence on other people, mentally retarded persons are inclined to feel helpless in an unfamiliar situation and are thus prone to develop low self-esteem along with other symptoms of depression.

For the mentally retarded at lower cognitive levels, withdrawal and passivity are often found to be characteristic. Although these behaviors are not necessarily symptoms of depression, the diagnostician has to be aware of the fact that due to lack of activity and interaction with the environment, these individuals gradually become understimulated and socially deprived, causing a decrease in need for or interest in sensations from the outside world and an increase in awareness of visceral or vegetative sensations. Actually, visceral sensations are a part of the first cognitive schemata of existence at a very early stage of psychosocial development. However, the organization of sensoric stimuli from the outside world and voluntary motor and visceral sensations are still unconsciously present. In the socially deprived mentally retarded, the old cognitive schemata of visceral sensation may be actuated and become conscious. In these persons, tension, displeasure, and probably pain may be remarkable, leading to restlessness, despair, and self-injurious activities (Bojanin, 1985). Additional symptoms of depression may also be found.

In the adolescent and adult mentally retarded, a disturbed awareness of time may be one of the factors precipitating depression. This mechanism can be explained as follows: Being unable to develop a formal manner of thinking (in the sense of Piaget), mentally retarded individuals lack the ability to create a concept of the future. Retarded persons on a higher level of functioning may create near-future expectations on the grounds of existing indications, but are unable to plan the future according to experiences in the past or to control their present feelings and actions according to their expectations (Bojanin, 1985). This means that a mentally retarded person is more dependent upon the situation "here and now" than a nonretarded individual. It is difficult to decrease present discomfort by asking for patience concerning future rewards. This is the reason why displacement from a familiar location or separation from a dependable person may make these persons extremely vulnerable to painful or anxious experiences. In losing sustaining

75

surroundings and support, retarded persons are more prone to react with helplessness and despair.

Conclusion

Although workers in the field of mental retardation recognize the importance of developmental aspects in the forming of personality, in their practical work with the behaviorally disturbed mentally retarded it is striking to see how often developmental factors are underestimated in psychiatric diagnosis and treatment. Undoubtedly, the reason for this lies in the shortage of scientific research in this field.

Some researchers highlight the relationship between the organic-biological basis of mental retardation and certain forms of depression. Particularly in the severely mentally retarded, the organic brian pathology underlying mental deficiency might indeed foster the occurrence of an affective disorder (Reid & Naylor, 1976). Metabolic disorders, like PKU, are also described as possible factors in the onset of depression (Realmuto et al, 1986). Some authors have found a relatively high prevalence of depression in particular genetic disorders such as Fragile X (Reiss et al, 1986) and Down syndrome (Szymanski & Biederman, 1984). Others have found correlations among dysfunction of the right hemisphere, learning difficulties, and depression (Brumback & Staton, 1982)

From studies such as these, one could assume that mentally retarded persons, because of their frequent developmental and biological anomalies, are highly at risk for the onset of depressive illnesses. However, this presumption lacks support from broader epidemiological investigations. At this time we have reason to expect that, due to specific biological substrates and developmental processes, the mentally retarded may be more vulnerable to the psychopathological agents which cause depression, but further scientific investigation in this area is needed to draw any solid scientific conclusion.

References

Abraham, K. (1927). Notes on the psychoanalytic investigation and treatment of manic-depressive insanity and allied conditions. In E. Jones (ed.), Selected Papers. Lodon: Hogerth Press.

Anthony, J.E. (1975). Childhood depression. In J. Anthony & T. Benedek (eds.), Depression and human existence. Boston: Little Brown.

Bemporad, J.R., Wilson, A. (1978). A developmental approach to depression in childhood and adolescence. J Am Psychoanal, 6(3), 325-352.

Bojanin S. (1985). Neuropsihologija razvojnog doba. Beograd: Univerzitet u Beogradu.

Bowlby, J.V. (1973). Attachment and loss. Vol 2.- Separation. New York: Basic Books.

Brown, G., Harris, T., Copeland, S. (1977). Depression and loss. Brit. J. Psychiat., 130, 1-18.

Brumback, R.A., Staton, R.D. (1982). A hypothesis regarding the commonality of right hemisphere involvement in learning disability, attentional disorder, and childhood major depressive disorder. Percept and Motor Skills, 55, 1091-1097.

Chess S., Hassibi, C. (1978). Behavioral deviations in mentally retarded children. In: S. Chess & A. Thomas (eds.), Annual Progress in Child Psychiatry and Child Development. New York: Brunner/Mazel.

Denny-Brown, D., Baker, B. (1944). Amorophosinthesis from left parietal lesion. Arch neurol psychiat, 71, 302-313.

Dosen, A. (1987). Razvojno-dinamicki pristup dijagnostici psihickih poremecaja kod mentalno retardirane djece. Psihijatrija Danas, 4, 383-388.

Dosen, A. (1989). Diagnosis and treatment of mental illness in mentally retarded children: A developmental model. Child Psych & Human Dev, 20(1), 73-84.

Freud, S. (1957). Mourning and Melancholia. London: Hogarth Press. (First edition, 1927).

Ebels, E.I. (1980). Maturation of the central nervous system. In: M. Rutter (ed.), Scientific foundations of developmental psychiatry. London: W. Heinemann Medical Books.

Engel, G.L. and Schmale, A.H. (1972). Conservation-withdrawal. A primary regularly process for organismic homeostasis. In Ciba Foundation Symposium 8; Psychology, Emotions and Psychosomatic Illness. Amsterdam: Elsevier Press.

Engel, G.L. and Reichsman, F. (1956). Spontaneous and experimentally induced depressions in an infant with a gastric fistula. J Am Psychoanal Ass, 4, 428-452.

Greenspan, S.J. (1985). Normal child development. In: A. Freedman, H. Kaplan (eds.), Comprehensive Textbook of Psychiatry. Baltimore: William & Wilkins.

Grossman, H.J. (1983). Classification in mental retardation. Washington, D.C.: American Association on Mental Deficiency.

Horney, K. (1950). Neurosis and human growth. New York: W.W. Norton.

Iivanainen, M. (1981). Neurological examination of the mentally retarded child. Evidence of central nervous system abnormality. In: B. Cooper (ed.), Assessing the handicaps and needs of mentally retarded children. London: Academic Press.

Kerr, F.W.L. (1975). Structural and functional evidence of plasticity in the central nervous system. Experimental Neurology, 48, 16.

Luria, A.R. (1973). The working brain. London: Penguin Press.

Luria, A.R. (1982). Osnovi neurolingvistike. Beogrand: Nolit.

Mahler, M.S., Pine, F., Bergman A. (1975). The psychological birth of the human infant. New York: Basic Books.

Piaget, J. (1955). The childs construction of reality. London: Routledge & Kegan.

Piaget, J., Inhelder, B. (1947). Diagnosis of mental operations and theory of intelligence. Amer J Ment Defic, 57, 401-406.

Realmuto, G.M., Garfinkel, B.D., Tuchman, M., Tsai, M.Y., Chang, P., Fisch, R.O., Shapiro, S. (1986). Psychiatric diagnosis and behavioral characteristics of phenylketonuric children. J Nerv Ment Dis, 9, 536-540.

Reid, A.H., Naylor, G.J. (1976). Short cycle manic-depressive psychosis in mental defectives; a clinical and psychological study. J Ment Def Research, 20, 67-76.

Reiss, A.L., Feinstein, C., Toomey, K.E., Goldsmith, B., Rosenbaum, K., Caruso, M.A. (1986). Psychiatric disability associated with the fragile X chromosome. Am J Med Gen, 23, 393-401.

Reite, M., Short, R., Seiler, C., Pauley, D. (1980). Attachment, loss and depression. J Child Psychiat & Psychology, 22, 141-169.

Rutter, M. (1985). Psychopathology and development: links between childhood and adult life. In: M. Rutter, L. Hersov (eds.), Child and Adolescent Psychiatry: A Modern Approach. Oxford: Blackwell Scientific Publications.

Sandler, A., Joffee, W.G. (1965). Notes on childhood depression. Int J Psychoanal, 46, 89-96.

Seligman, M. (1975). Helplessness. San Francisco: Freeman & Co.

Shaffer, D. (1977). Brain injury. In: M. Rutter, L. Hersov (eds.), Child Psychiatry: Modern Approaches. London: Blackwell Scientific Publishers.

Spitz, R. (1946). Anaclitic depression. Psychoanal Study Child, 2, 113-117.

Szymanski, L.S., Biederman, J. (1984). Depression and anorexia nervosa of persons with Down syndrome. Am J Ment Def, 89, 246-251.

Wallon, H. (1965). Les etapes de la sociabilite chez l'enfant. Enfance, 4, 305-323.

Yakovlev, P., Lecours, A. (1967). Regional development of the brain in early life. Oxford: Blackwell Scientific Publications.

Anton Dosen and Frank J. Menolascino (Eds.) (1990). Depression in mentally retarded children and adults. Leiden, the Netherlands: Logon Publications. ISBN 90-73197-01-5

Chapter 5

Psychosocial characteristics of mentally retarded persons and the risk of depression

Anton Dosen, M.D.
Jan J.M. Gielen, Ph.D.

Introduction

Historically, the relationship between personality attributes and vulnerability to depression has attracted considerable attention. The concept of personality implies a relatively stable inborn temperament as well as developmentally acquired characteristics and determinants. A personality vulnerable to depression would thus have developmentally acquired components or a specific biological substrate by which to become depression-prone. Recent investigations in this field tend to support the classic notion that cyclothymic, hyperthymic and, to some extent, dysthymic personalities represent genetically attenuated expressions of the major affective disorders (Akiskal, Hirschfeld and Yerevanian, 1983). On the other hand, authors in both the psychodynamic and behavioral traditions generally assume that particular developmental disturbances and maladaptive self-attributions provide a framework for vulnerability to depression (Arieti and Bemporad, 1980; Beck and Rush, 1979). However, from clinical practice we know that depression may also arise out of personality structures that are not remarkable or sufficiently deviant to warrant a personality disorder diagnosis.

Based on the psychodynamic approach, we will focus in this chapter on how specific circumstances and relationships within which mentally retarded persons are reared may interact with specific personality characteristics to predispose these individuals to develop depressive illnesses.

The depressive personality

Before we start with the specific problems of the mentally retarded, it is necessary to report the findings of some investigators concerning the qualities of "depressive personality" in nonretarded persons. Bowlby (1977) discussed "compulsively self-reliant" and "anxiously attached" personalities and their predisposition toward depression. A compulsively self-reliant person disavows any interest in close interpersonal contact, but is actually ambiguous towards it. On the other hand, when an anxiously attached person establishes relationships, he or she becomes excessively dependent on attachment figures.

Arieti and Bemporad (1980) discussed the depressed patient's need for either a "dominant other" or "dominant goal." In order to maintain their own self-regard, such individuals are highly dependent on narcissistic supplies from others. The roots of such a personality are found in early unsatisfactory attachment experiences which lead to vulnerable self-esteem.

Chodoff (1972) found that a mixture of obsessional and dependent traits was the hallmark of the depressed personality, while Pilkonis and Frank (1988) pointed out that in patients with recurrent depression, the most common personality features were avoidance, compulsiveness, and dependency. Akiskal et al. (1983), in a review of the literature, found the following to be attributive to the depression-prone personality; introversion, lack of self-confidence, tendency to worry, obsessionalism, and pessimism. However, the authors also questioned whether these attributes were always characteristic of a premorbid personality, or if they occured as a post-depressive personality disturbance.

Beck and Rush (1979) determined that unipolar depression is not only an affective disorder, but a cognitive disorder as well. Characteristic is the cognitive triad of negative image of the self, negative image of the world, and negative image of the future. The typical cognitive disorder is closely related to the concept of learned helplessness (Seligman, 1975) as a potential etiological variable in depression (Reynolds and Miller, 1985), and the theory describes depressives as reacting passively to a wide variety of noxious stimuli.

Hirschfeld, Klerman, Clayton and Keller (1983) found that women who had recovered from primary non-bipolar depression were strikingly introverted, hesitant, and restrained with low sociability, gregariousness, and self-confidence, and increased interpersonal dependency. Akiskal et al. (1983) tentatively concluded that of all the personality attributes hypothesized to predispose one to non-bipolar conditions, introversion

82

appears to be the trait for which there is the strongest evidence. Other attributes, such as dependency and negative self-attributions, may largely reflect state effects on a postdepressive personality.

Dependent personality of the mentally retarded

Webster (1970) has postulated a primary psychopathology of mental retardation consisting of intellectual deficit, slow rate of development, immature personality, self-absorption, repetitiousness, inflexibility, and passivity. Studies reveal that children of this type run a very high risk of being overwhelmed by the anticipating and correcting behaviors of the mother (Field, 1978). Instead of being responsive and sensitive, the mother who perceives her child as inert feels a strong tendency to direct the child in communication. It seems as if the mother is continuously repelling her anxiety concerning her abnormal baby and trying to cope with these emotions by constantly determining the baby's responses. It is thus impossible for her to let communication depend on the baby's social rhythms. By demonstrating such anticipatory behavior, the mother also hopes to redirect the baby's inertia into a more responsive pattern of behavior. However, by initiating all communication, she deprives the child of its autonomy in the long run, the result of which will be a breakdown in communication. Brinich (1980) stated it this way: "When communication breaks down, the powerful take over."

In our opinion, this overwhelming maternal attitude may form an important sociogenetic factor in the development of a dependent personality in the retarded child, in whom a low grade of autonomy is characteristic in any case. If this unbalanced pattern of communication continues, the child will linger in a relationship of dependency, initially with its mother, later with family, educators, etc., insofar as these individuals are inclined toward a censorious manner of communication. This state of dependency will leave its influence on the child's developing sense of self. Instead of developing a true autonomous self, the communication-dependent child will construct a sense of self which includes "having-functions-that-must-be-performed-by-or-with-others" (Levitas & Gilson, 1988). The child will experience himself or herself as containing a piece of "outer" or, rather, containing a void which must always be filled by someone from the outer world, some caregiver. For such a child there will be no experience of the full spectrum of independent skill and he or she will lack any emotional repayment for abandoning closeness with the mother. Thus retarded children lack the pride and self-esteem of accomplishment, as well as the security of knowing that they can face the world alone. Cognitive, emotional, and social developmental factors all combine to blunt the individuation process (Levitas & Gilson, 1988).

As time progresses, mentally retarded children may become even more intensely aware of their helplessness. They may need to react with greater grandiosity and omnipotent fantasy than their nonretarded peers. The resultant behavior can provoke increasingly protective parental reactions, resulting in an even greater loss of self-esteem and compensating fantasy. When these children enter pre-adolescence, the role of the initial caregiver is taken over by other caregivers. The relationships mentally retarded children build with these persons are relatively undifferentiated; such children treat all adults similarly as caregivers, regardless of age, kinship, or sex, seeking to please caregivers so as never to be without one. The pre-adolescent retarded child seldom, if ever, tolerates being alone for long. Otherwise, the sense of self would never be complete, the experience of the self would be defective or broken. Sometimes this sense of broken self-image is compensated for with its counterpart; the mentally retarded child imagines himself or herself to be the "perfect" adult. Idealization of models takes place, is reflected in the omnipotence of the caretakers, and an unmodified omnipotent superego emerges. Nevertheless, the non-autonomous sense of self will result in a failure to develop a stable and integrated process of self-regulation. Self-regulation for the retarded adolescent is based upon the constant presence of supervision and his or her activities are regulated by continuous reference to the wishes of others. When the retarded adolescent reaches adulthood, the conditions for what Gilson and Levitas (1988) call "a secondary psychosocial deficit" have been established which may account for the frequency, presentation, and types of psychopathology observed in retarded people.

Apparently, this state of dependency is pre-figured by patterns of behavior which are established in early childhood in rudimentary forms. It emerges from the parent's perceptions that their child's inert temperament must be dealt with by overpowering his or her initiations. As the years go by, other caregivers become the "outer" part of the self to which the mentally retarded person must continuously refer for security. However, such a state of dependency, however, will immediately affect the well-being of the retarded individual. The investigations of Reynolds and Miller (1985) indicate that educable mentally retarded adolescents manifest a significantly greater degree of depressive symptomatology than their nonretarded peers. The authors hypothesize that such adolescents are particularly vulnerable to depression because of a higher probability of long term exposure to social and environmental stressors, intensified by learned helplessness. Others (Benson, Reiss, Smith and Laman, 1985; Reiss & Benson, 1985) have delineated a number of negative social conditions which contribute to the development and maintenance of emotional problems in mentally retarded adults, among them are low levels of social support and poor social skills. To compound these problems, the findings of Laman and Reiss (1987) show that depressed mildly retarded adults are withdrawn, interact less with others, tend to be occupied with themselves, and demonstrate antisocial behavior.

Most investigators into the pre-existent vulnerability to depression refer to increased interpersonal dependency. Arieti (1962) has hypothesized that depression-prone adults have invested too much of their self-esteem in an external source, which he termed "the dominant other". He pointed out that this "other" need not be a flesh and blood individual, but may also be an organization, social circle, etc. In our opinion, the same state of dependency causes a specific risk in the development of depressive symptomatology in the mentally retarded person when he or she is forced, after a prolonged period of attachment, to abandon the "invested" social group.

Case History #1

Maria is a 58-year-old mildly retarded woman with Down syndrome who has been living in a group of twelve patients at an institution for the mentally retarded for one year. At the age of 17, Maria became a helper in a nunnery where she stayed for the following 35 years. In reports from the nunnery, she was described as a gay, somewhat childish and talkative woman who liked to be the center of attention. She had no firm relationships except with one girlfriend to whom she grew very attached. After the death of her girlfriend 7 years ago, Maria became isolated and only a great deal of affective and social support could prevent a relapse. Four years later, Maria's mother, with whom she had a very close relationship, died. Soon afterwards, Maria had to leave the cloister because of rennovation. Finally, she was placed in a short-stay home because the cloister had been sold.

Reports from the short-stay home showed that Maria cried a great deal during the first weeks following admission, expressing a strong desire to return to the nunnery, and frequently calling her mother. Family visits proved to be an important social support for her since she was extremely anxious about being left alone. Going to bed caused problems since she always wanted someone to be nearby. After three weeks, Maria found a girlfriend in the home who coddled her, gave affection to her, and cheered her up. Such support prevented Maria from having a further relapse.

One year ago Maria was brought into the living-group she stays with presently. After admission she frequently reproached the staff with, "They all have me left alone". She refused to take off her overcoat and sat waiting for someone to come pick her up. She cried frequently for her mother, whose death was denied, and frequent changes of mood. Her father, siblings, and sisters from the nunnery are called on to help, but Maria remained outside the front door continually ready for departure. There were no social contacts with the other patients.

After four months, the situation grew worse. Maria displayed physical resistance and acting-out behaviors with outrageous yells and crying. She also showed intense apathetic grief. She refused to eat, complained of aches and pains, and seemed both physically and psychologically exhausted. Administration of antidepressant medication resulted in paradoxal effects and was discontinued after two weeks.

Six months after admission, the decision was made that Maria would be nursed in bed for 24 hours a day, with full care, feeding, and coddling. At first she permitted no social or physical contact and remained passively apathetic, but her appetite increased and she remained fairly quiet. After about two weeks of nursing, Mariaa began to amuse herself with puzzles and picture books. She is grew more active and would occasionally leave her bed without protest, but refused to be left alone afterward. During the following two weeks, she moved about freely and even made physical contact with both nurses and patients. Whereas Maria once only spoke of leaving the group, she began to speak of other things and tolerated being left alone.

Eight months following admission, Maria's fits of temper and crying were rarely heard, her gaiety had returned, and her apathy had disappeared. If she became tearful, she could find comfort in her bed. After ten months, Maria could say, "Now I live here." Yet she retains a strong hunger for social and

affective support, a dependency which could become dangerous
if her current relationships are broken once more.

Difficult temperament of the mentally retarded

In an investigation by Blok (1989), difficult temperament in the
mentally retarded consisted of high reaction intensity, stubbornness, low
adaptability, and low mood level, which he found in approximately 40%
of the residents of institutions for the mentally retarded in Holland. Such
characteristics make the mentally retarded person prone to environmental
conflicts and behavioral problems which can lead to interactional and
emotional difficulties. While mothers often report that their mentally
retarded babies are extremely easy to care for, during the second or third
year, these mothers note a change in their children's behavior involving
hyperactivity and irritability demanding maximal care. Another type of
retarded child, less often reported, is initially irritable and hyperactive, and
does not demonstrate any change in behavior during his or her later years.
In our opinion, these children might be placed within a group labeled
"difficult temperament." Characteristics of difficult temperament are:
irregularity in biological functions, predominance of withdrawal responses
to new stimuli, slowness in adapting to changes in the environment,
frequent expressions of negative mood, and predominance of intense
reactions (Thomas, Chess & Burch, 1968; Thomas & Chess, 1977). Such
children generally attract attention by the rapid building up of emotion to
a peak of negative excitement (Brazelton, 1973). Babies of this type are
very active and quickly startled and irritated by lights, murmurs, and
normal movements.

Attachment studies indicate that these irritable babies run a high risk
of forming an anxious attachment to the caregiver (Crockenberg, 1981).
The most irritable actually run the risk of their mothers detaching from
the relationship altogether (Van den Boom, 1988). Many mothers of
persistently crying babies are considerably less sensitive in their interactions, particularly when they are unfamiliar with how to manage a
newborn. Nevertheless, the mother generally receives little support for her
problem, and the combination of irritability in the child and weak social
support for the mother results in a serious threat to the quality of the
caregiver-child relationship (Crockenberg, 1981). One can easily imagine
that the irritability of the baby becomes an enormous frustration when the
mother finally learns that her child is mentally retarded as well.
Depending on the amount of social support she receives at this point, she

may suffer from feelings of guilt and worthlessness, build upon a negative self-image, and develop a depressive reaction, processes which are seriously frustrating to the establishment of stable social communication with the child. The steady exchange of communicative signals will fade away and the child's confidence in its environment will be reduced. As the mother protects herself from disappointing contact with her child, or if she succombs to a depressive episode, a point of genuine maternal deprivation is reached. This phenomenon may provoke separation-anxiety and real object-loss for the mentally retarded child.

The risk of depression in the mentally retarded

Various authors emphasize that a certain sense of separateness is needed before a child can establish distance from an important other, and that episodes of separation lead to feelings of anxiety and helplessness (Arieti, 1962; Bowlby, 1973; Mahler, Pine & Bergman, 1975). If we keep in mind that the mentally retarded child will generally reach his or her individuation phase much later than the normal child, we can imagine that efforts toward separation by the caregiver come too early; the retarded child, although he or she may well have attained the appropriate chronological age, may not yet have adequately delt with mentally left the rapprochement subphase toward autonomy. Thus, a significant reduction in attachment behavior by the caregiver may cause significant separation anxiety. Sometimes, a mentally retarded child will never psychologically outgrow the bonding phase with the mother and, in some sense, will always have a kind of symbiotic dependency on caregivers, relying heavily on their proximity for security and as a defense against separation-anxiety. When detached, the child may react with distress and apathy similar to that described in nonretarded children by Spitz and Bowlby (see Chapter 4, this volume).

However, it is not only the bonding-figure who may retreat too early from the bonded relationship, the child may do so as well. Unequal maturation of different regions of the brain may provoke a situation in which the more mature areas trigger a detachment which is incompatible with the current psychosocial phase of development. Particularly during puberty there is a risk that the child will be urged to meet expectations normally reserved for nonretarded peers. Often, under pressure from an omnipotent self-image, the child will force himself or herself to meet those expectations, even if it means ignoring the real psychological need of proximity to a caregiver. When omnipotent feelings break down,

88

however, the child is confronted with an extreme sense of helplessness and separation-anxiety, the possible consequence of which is a depressive condition.

In short, the quantity and quality of mothering during the bonding and individuation phases, the ability of imaginary representation of the bonding figure, the level of self/object representation, the intensity of separation-anxiety as a consequence of detachment episodes, all play a role in the formation of a remarkably dependent personality. In our opinion it is not the secondary psychosocial deficit per se, nor is it the sense of broken self-image or low self-esteem that set the stage for depression. Rather, it seems to be the accentuated dependency, the perpetuating feeling of helplessness, and the threatening loss of the significant other that poses a heavy burden on the preservation of the self.

The same holds true for the concept of maternal deprivation, which is hypothesized to be a crucial etiological variable in the genesis of childhood and infant depression, often extending into adulthood (Trad, 1986). Results of studies into the genesis of infant depression indicate that one isolated incident seldom provokes prolonged displays of depressive symptomatology. Thus, while depressive-like phenomena generally erupt immediately following the separation experience, such phenomena seem to disappear or recede if the caregiver relationship is resumed. However, this does not necessarily mean that the underlying sense of loss provoking the symptomatology has been resolved. Symptoms may go into remission. Early separation experiences may be overshadowed by later developmental trends and cognitive growth, yet it is doubtful whether further psychological and physical development can make the distress of early separation anxiety disappear entirely. The work of Field et al. (in Trad, 1986) does suggest that once evocative memory is present, as it is at a very early age, the experience of separation, along with its affective correlates, is retained. Early experiences of genuine object-loss are evoked immediately, and responded to with depressive symptomatology. Thus, evocative memory may be regarded as a trigger in the development of depression during adulthood, and depression-prone individuals will lean heavily on important others, who have come to take the place of the early bonding-figure. Obviously, the mentally retarded run a high risk in this regard.

Every separation from a well-known environment or person can provoke a renewed depressive reaction. Too many separation experiences may result in an enduring state of depression. The mentally retarded who live in institutions may be subjected to many losses of attachment-figures.

Too many traumatic experiences of separation will result in a kind of self-protection and the mentally retarded person will no longer enter into any relationships at all.

Case History #2

Marc is a mildly mentally retarded boy of 29 years. Because of psychiatric illness, his mother was unable to rear him and he was immediately transferred to a foster home. At the age of six, because of incapabilities within the foster-family, Marc was transferred to an institution. At the age of 20, Marc moved into a new foster home. Yet after 8 years, he had to leave because the foster mother was expecting her fourth child. Finally, at the age of 28, Marc was admitted to a special unit for the mentally retarded-mentally ill.

Soon after admission it was noted that Marc had no self-confidence and could not tolerate any criticism, contradiction, or confrontation regarding his behavior. He was very meddlesome and anxious, and liked to provoke patients and staff alike. Although Marc signaled great affective sensitivity, he kept a large affective distance and tolerated no physical or affective proximity. His behavior was described as hyperactive, impulsive, and chaotic. His sleep was disturbed and his mood swung from cheerfulness to sadness and irritability. Depression was suspected and antidepressant medication was prescribed.

Two months following admission, Marc began to run away. Several times he wandered off and was brought back by the police, haggered and emaciated. Although he was placed under 24-hour supervision, he showed great inventiveness and continued to escape. His room was full of all kinds of rubbish and knives and he began to speak of "voices" that ordered him to run away or set fire to something. In his diary he described dialogues with a fictitious twin brother. Supervision was increased and antipsychotic medication initiated.

About one month later, the "voices" faded away. Although Marc continued to look for ways to escape, he began to tolerate physical contact and he was sometimes inclined to participate in group games. His behavior became more generally restful and his weight increased. His antipsychotic medication was decreased and withdrawn. Today he no longer tries to escape and maintains a special position within the group where he is appreciated because of his jokes and laughter.

Consequences for practice

Keeping in mind the high risk run by the mentally retarded of developing a dependent personality, one can expect the incidence of depressive states in this population to be greater than in the nonretarded population. In reality, however, the diagnosis of depression in the mentally retarded is not particularly frequent; it may often go unrecognized. The fact is that most professionals in the field of mental retardation are more attentive to the behavioral features of a retarded person than to the emotional and interactional causes of behavior. In our daily practice we are often confronted with depressive states which have lasted for a long time and were previously treated as behavioral problems, conduct disorders, or adjustment disorders. Earlier intervention and better care for these persons must be made available and the following preventive measures should be routinely undertaken:
- Early support and counseling should be provided to the family of the retarded child.
- Continuity of environment should be maintained.
- Continuity of important persons should be established.
- Confidence in the external environment, in peers, and in unfamiliar people should be instilled and maintained.
- Overprotection should be prevented.
- Individuation should be supported by teaching social skills and activities, and by developing motivation and initiative.
- A cognitive approach to the learned helplessness should be taken.
- Future care should be planned according to the concepts of normalization and social integration.

Conclusion

Studies into the relationship between personality attributes and depression have brought to light some typical characteristics which may make any individual vulnerable to depression. Interpersonal dependency and social introversion are associated with the depression-prone personality, and may be seen as risk-factors contributing to the development of depressive disorders. Negative cognitive interpretations of reality may also be closely related to this scenario.

Mentally retarded children and adults run an even greater risk. For example, the passivity, repetitiousness, and inflexibility of the retarded child makes him or her affectively and socially dependent on caregivers.

Because of a characteristic low level of autonomy, the cessation of a dependent relationship may cause feelings of learned helplessness, worthlessness, and depressive symptomatology. In addition, the mentally retarded child with a difficult temperament runs the risk of either maternal overprotection or maternal deprivation. Early experiences of helplessness, separation, and anxiety easily endure into adulthood and repetitive episodes of loss can be catastrophic. It is vital, therefore, the practical mental health care measures be initiated early in the lives of the mentally retarded as well as their families and caregivers.

References

Akiskal, H.S., Hirschfeld, R.M.A & Yerevanian, B.I. (1983). The relationship of personality to affective disorders: a critical review. Archives of General Psychiatry, 40, 801-810.

Arieti, S. (1962). The psychotherapeutic approach to depression. American Journal of Psychotherapy, 16, 397-406.

Arieti, S. & Bemporad, J.R. (1980). The psychological organization of depression. American Journal of Psychiatry, 137, 1360-1365.

Beck, A.T. & Rush, A.J. (1979). Cognitive therapy of depression. New York: John Wiley.

Benson, B.A., Reiss, S., Smith, D.C. & Laman, D.S. (1985). Psychosocial correlates of depression in mentally retarded adults II: poor social skills and difficult life goals. American Journal of Mental Deficiency, 89, 657-659.

Blok, J.B. (1989): Temperament bij zwakzinngen, constructie van een meet-instrument: Doctoral dissertation, de Vrije Universiteit, Amsterdam.

Bowlby, J. (1973). Attachment and loss II: separation, anxiety and anger. London: The Hogarth Press.

Bowlby, J. (1977). The making and breaking of affectional bonds I: aetiology and psychopathology in the light of attachment theory. British Journal of Psychiatry, 130, 201-210.

Brazelton, T.B. (1973). Neonatal Behavioral Assessment Scale. Philadelphia: Lippincott.

Brinich, P.M. (1980) Childhood deafness and maternal control. Journal of Communication Disorder, 13, 75-81.

Chodoff, P. (1972). The depressive personality: a critical review. Archives of General Psychiatry, 27, 666-673.

Crockenberg, S.G. (1981). Infant irritability, mother responsiveness, and social support influences on the security of infant-mother attachment. Child Development, 52, 857-865.

Field, T.M. (1978). The three Rs of infant-adult interactions: rhythms, repertoires and responsivity. Journal of Pediatric Psychology, 3, 131-136.

Gilson, S.F. & Levitas, A.S. (1988). Normalization: a biopsychosocial approach. In: F. Menolascino & J. McGee (eds.), Three populations of primary focus. Omaha, Nebraska: University of Nebraska Medical Center/Creighton University School of Medicine Departments of Psychiatry.

Hirschfeld, R.M., Klerman, G.L., Clayton, P.J. & Keller, M.B. (1983). Personality and depression: empirical findings. Archives of General Psychiatry, 40, 993-998.

Laman, D.S. & Reiss, S. (1987). Social skill deficiencies associated with depressed mood of mentally retarded adults. American Journal of Mental Deficiency, 92, 2, 224-229.

Levitas, A.S. & Gilson, S. (1988). Emotional and developmental needs of mentally retarded people. In: F. Menolascino & J. McGee (eds.), Three populations of primary focus. Omaha, Nebraska: University of Nebraska Medical Center/Creighton University School of Medicine Departments of Psychiatry.

Mahler, M.F., Pine, A., & Bergman, F. (1975). The psychological birth of the human infant. New York: Basic Books.

Pilkonis, P.A., & Frank, E. (1988). Personality pathology in recurrent depression: nature, prevalence and relationship to treatment response. American Journal of Psychiatry, 145, 4, 435-441.

Reiss, S. & Benson, B.A. (1985). Psychosocial correlates of depression in mentally retarded adults I: minimal social support and stigmatization. American Journal of Mental Deficiency, 89, 331-337.

Reynolds, W.M. & Miller, K.L. (1985). Depression and learned helplessness in mentally retarded and nonmentally retarded adolescents: an initial investigation. Applied Research in Mental Retardation, 6, 295-306.

Seligman, M. (1975). Helplessness. San Francisco: W.M. Freeman.

Thomas, A., Chess, A., & Birch, H.G. (1968). Temperament and behavior disorders in children. New York: University Press.

Thomas, A. & Chess, A. (1977). Temperament and development. New York: Brunner/Mazel.

Trad, P.V. (1986). Infant depression, paradigms and paradoxes. New York: Springer.

Van den Boom, D.C. (1988). Neonatal irritability and the development of attachment: observation and intervention. Unpublished Master's Thesis, University of Leiden, Holland.

Webster, T.G. (1970). Unique aspects and emotional development in mentally retarded children. In: F.J. Menolascino (ed.), Psychiatric Approaches to Mental Retardation. New York: Basic Books.

Anton Dosen and Frank J. Menolascino (Eds.) (1990). Depression in mentally retarded children and adults. Leiden, the Netherlands: Logon Publications. ISBN 90-73197-01-5

Chapter 6

Depression in persons with mental retardation: toward an existential analysis

John J. McGee, Ph.D.
Frank J. Menolascino, M.D.

Introduction

This chapter deals with depression in persons with mental retardation from an existential perspective. Its purpose is to provide insight into the confrontation these individuals have with ultimate concerns related to existence, their struggle with anxiety, and the impact that the external world has on their inner life. It identifies and analyzes the life conditions of several persons with depression in order to delineate their reality and the interactive factors that led to their depression.

Literature review

Webster (1970) examined the emotional vulnerabilities inherent in persons with mental retardation and found a number of primary psychological characteristics: difficulty in interacting with and relating to others, repetitiousness of the familiar, inflexibility, lack of self-assertion, and difficulty in processing abstract thoughts and feelings. He also reported secondary influences that commonly complicate their emotional development: a broad range of sensory and perceptual deprivations from various causes, difficulty in mediating external stimuli, confused parental or other caregiver expectations which alternate between expecting too much and too little, excessive shyness, fears and inhibitions, moderate to severe reactions to the loss or withdrawal of significant others, and exaggerated negativism and compulsiveness. The global impact of these vulnerabilities results in an underlying dissipation of existential responsibility and an attraction to learned helplessness.

Research related to psychosocial factors in the development of emotional disturbances in persons with mental retardation has offered few additional insights (Reiss, 1985). Indeed, it has been noted that some studies disregard the possible presence of depression in persons with mental retardation (Reiss, Levitan, & Szyzko, 1982). Since these individuals do not typically complain of mood changes or express depressive symptoms, diagnosis often has to be made based on the appearance of sadness or changes in appetite, sleep, or behavior (Gelder, Gath, & Mayou, 1989).

Matson (1983) identified eight target behaviors related to depression in persons with mild mental retardation: decreased number of words spoken, irritability, somatic complaints, poor grooming, negative self-statements, poor eye contact, lack of emotional tone, and speech latency. McGee (1987) noted that communication difficulties in themselves often result in depressive symptoms such as aggression and active or passive withdrawal. In more severe forms of mental retardation, its expression is more subtle and can be observed in self-stimulation, self-injury, hyper-activity, and ruptures in bonded relationships.

Initial hypotheses into the causes of depression in persons with mental retardation have centered on the impact of poor or inadequate relationships. Simmons (1968) posited negative parental reactions to the experience of raising a child with mental retardation and the resultant negative self-concept, social isolation, and antisocial behavior. Bryan (1980) cited the adolescent period as being difficult for persons with handicaps due to the realization of permanent differences with peers, the inability to participate in leisure activities, and conflict and confusion about sexual maturity. Dosen (1984) noted a number of interactive phenomena as possible causative factors in the depression of children with mental retardation: basic psychobiological affective reactions related to the surrounding environment; noxious environmental influences which trigger the condition in individuals with weak self-concepts; chronic deprivation of affective stimuli; loss of a love-object ending in existential calamity; inadequate or anxious attachment bonds between mother or caregiver and child; sudden loss or change in an existing affective relationship; and chronic feelings of not being accepted and appreciated. O'Neil (1982) cited several other factors: parental overprotection or excessive control, intrusive caregivers, and deficient social skills on the part of the mentally retarded individual. Brady (1984) also hypothesized that deficiencies in social skills were important in the etiology of depression. Benson, Smith, Reiss, and Laman (1985) reported that depression was associated with informant ratings of poor social skills. Laman and Reiss (1987) analyzed the relationship between poor social skills and low levels of social support and found that these phenomena were associated with mild mental retardation. Reiss and Benson (1985) found negative correlations between depression and social support and positive correlations with perceived stigmatization. Reiss (1985) proposed three broad psychosocial factors in the development of depression: negative social conditions such as prejudice and stigmatization, inadequate social support such as inadequate access to support networks, and deficient social skills such as the ability to converse, express feelings, and act assertively.

The existential paradigm

The existential paradigm of psychopathology rests on the assumption that depression represents an inefficient mode of coping with anxiety. Two broad defense strategies can deal with this existential anxiety: the belief in personal specialness and inviolability that enables one to feel responsible and in control, and the belief that one is protected by an ultimate rescuer. These form a coping-collapse continuum and constitute the existential dialectic--two extreme modes of facing the human situation--by either totally separating oneself from others or fusing with others as omnipotent intercessors.

Yalom (1980) defines depression as the collapse of an ultimate rescuer, that is, the individual becomes overwhelmed with fear and anxiety when confronted with the actual or perceived loss of the force or being that has loved, watched over, and protected him or her. Arieti (1977) describes depression as the breakdown of defenses and the loss of resources with which to counteract overwhelming feelings of self-depletion and self-condemnation. Depression ensues when one's own life-meaning fails or when the belief in a perceived protector or dispenser of life-meaning is ruptured through death, abandonment, or withdrawal of love and attention. Rotter (1960) reported that individuals with an external locus of control depend more on others for answers, support, and guidance than on themselves, and Abramson & Sackeim (1977) report a strong relationship between an external locus of control and depression. The loss of an ultimate rescuer is accompanied by a sense of powerlessness, low self-regard, and unworthiness. Persons with mental retardation are inherently more vulnerable to depression due to their emotional fragility and their propensity toward that which is external for emotional well-being.

An existential understanding of depression in persons with mental retardation is based on critical questions related to one's life-situation: meaninglessness, aloneness, lack of choice, and death (Yalom, 1985) or feelings of homelessness and friendlessness (Fowler, 1977). Although often unable to verbally communicate such feelings, persons with mental retardation pass through this questioning process and, indeed, feel inner anguish as deeply and perhaps more acutely than others. Their meta-communication can speak forcefully of meaning or meaninglessness, friendship or separateness, and interdependence or dependence; these expressions are apparent not only in their words, but in their movements, gestures, tone, and gazes.

Due to emotional vulnerabilities and life-situations, which make mentally retarded persons more dependent on others than on self-responsibility, these existential questions and their ongoing understanding take on a vital significance. Although these individuals are able to live, work, and play in the confluence of community life, the condition of mental retardation heightens their dependence upon others for the definition of life-meaning, the assurance of companionship, help in choice-making, and coping with loss. Significant others play an important role in the creation, deepening, and stabilization of feelings of self-worth and being at-home through an ongoing matrix of dependable, unconditional affection in relationships where one can feel safe, free, and cherished. However, any onslaught against these feelings, their absence or loss, leaves the individual feeling alone and unable to encounter love, empathy, warmth, or uncalculated generosity. Once sundered, anguish occurs; a state in which there is no emotional place to return to, no one to share burdens with, and no sense of security.

Questions about the meaning of life pose profound challenges to all persons. Those with mental retardation, although perhaps not processing such questions in the same cognitive depth or in the same manner, feel and respond to them with equal or greater acuity than most since society tends to exacerbate the vulnerabilities and emotional fragility of the mentally retarded through marginalizing institutions, alienating segregation, and depersonalizing controls. Depression emerges from the overwhelming feeling of one's inability to cope with such general questions as well as those generated by specific experiences, such as the death of a parent or close friend, the loss of a job, dissatisfaction with relationships, illness in the family, siblings moving from home, changes in residence, or changes in caregivers. Supposedly insignificant routine changes can leave the mentally retarded person with feelings of confusion and fear, often inexpressible feelings of meaninglessness, uselessness, and aloneness.

Interpersonal relationships are central to the life of all persons and depression is a reflection of the lack of feeling at-home with significant others. Such éxternal causes of depression are generally traced to particular factors and dealt with separately, but often the causative history is much more complex than the uncovering of any singular experience or the remediation of any target behavior. Such events are typically the final assault in an ascending spiral of negative social interactions such as unstable, overprotective, or sterile caregiving relationships, institutional segregation, societal prejudice, rejection, stigmatization, and oppression with their resultant gnawing feelings of hopelessness.

Case studies

An analysis of the life histories and conditions of 12 persons with mental retardation and depression was conducted at the Creighton University-University of Nebraska Department of Psychiatry Dual Diagnosis Service through a random selection of individuals treated in 1988-1989 in order to analyze the social patterns which precede the depression as well as the triggering factors which led to the collapse of coping mechanisms (see Table 6.1). The presence and level of mental retardation was arrived at through standard psychometric procedures. Diagnosis was based on the use of inventories such as the Beck scale, clinical interviews, and observations. The historical relationships and triggering causes were defined through an interdisciplinary process and clinical interviews with significant others as well as the individuals themselves. Four distinct patterns of caregiving relationships were identified. *Overprotective relationships* were defined as those in which the parent or other consistent caregiver demonstrated love and affection toward the individual, but in a suffocating and restrictive manner with low expectations for the individual's developmental capacities. *Authoritarian relationships* were defined as cold, depersonalized, and controlling, based on management by reward and punishment. *Aloneness* was defined as the absence of any significant relationship in the mentally retarded individual's life; perhaps they were living "independently," but they were incapable of reaching out to others and were therefore left alone. *Well nurtured* social patterns were defined as those in which significant others had historically provided dependable and unconditional affection, safety, and support until their disappearance through, for example, death or illness. The triggering mechanisms clustered around feelings of profound loss derived from stressful experiences such as the death of a parent or

99

relative, frequent staff turn-over, distanced relationships, and even the loss of a favorite object. Life dissatisfaction was also identified as a central theme wherein an interface between lonely living and meaningless work mobilized to effectuate feelings of powerlessness and apathy. Although these are broad categorizations, they appeared to describe predominant experiences.

Table 6.1
Case studies of depression in persons with mental retardation

Patient	Age	MR	Historic Relationships	Social Pattern Triggering Cause
B.W.	29	Moderate	Overprotection	Death of Parents
D.M.	25	Moderate	Well Nurtured	Death of Grandmother
S.M.	17	Severe	Well Nurtured	Death of Father
K.B.	32	Mild	Authoritarian	Dissatisfaction with Sheltered Work
D.E.	49	Mild	Aloneness	Job Dissatisfaction
M.B.	27	Severe	Well Nurtured	Residential Placement
J.H.	28	Mild	Aloneness	Multiple Residential Placement
J.J.	32	Profound	Aloneness	Distanced Care Givers
S.C.	41	Mild	Authoritarian	Distanced Care Givers
A.S.	4	Moderate	Overprotection	Divorce
S.D.	22	Mild	Well Nurtured	Residential Placement
D.G.	25	Severe	Authoritarian	Loss of Favorite Object

Death

B.W. was a 29-year-old man who was well integrated in the community. He had a close but overprotected relationship with his parents. He stayed at home after having graduated from special education classes and chose not to become involved in a local sheltered workshop. His parents provided for his daily needs and he was content to pass his days with them and his older brother. However, due to tragic circumstances, both his parents died within a year of one another, leaving B.W. with deep feelings of confusion, emptiness, and isolation. His alcoholic brother was unable to fill the role of the parents and left B.W. floundering alone at home. He lost thirty pounds during the following year, suffered from poor sleep patterns, refused to leave the apartment, and rejected outside help. He also developed a pattern of nearly constant fear, sought constant reassurance, and distrusted relationships with others. He often stated that he only had two meaningful relationships left in his life, namely, his brother and his cat. Three years after his parents' death, with a confused look and his hand pointed upward, B.W. could only describe their death as, "Mom and Dad, all gone." His view of the world had been emptied of meaning and filled with despair in the absence of his ultimate rescuers.

D.M. was a 25-year-old man with Down's Syndrome. He lived a very satisfying life at home with his parents and three younger siblings. He also had a close relationship with his grandmother. He attended a local sheltered workshop and enjoyed interacting with others. One day as he was sitting at home, his grandmother walked in front of him, collapsed, and died from a stroke. He was shattered by the belief that he had caused her death. Nothing could convince him otherwise. Over the next three months, he lost his ability to speak, refused to go to work, withdrew into his room, and communicated through blinking his eyes. His posture became poor, his head bowed, and his arms were held close to his chest. His parents and siblings continued to provide uncalculated love and support, but were frustrated in their attempts to bring him back around. They visited several psychiatrists and were told that he was "just retarded" and "non-compliant" and should that they institutionalize him. D.M.'s response to death was to seek

101

refuge in his inner being, occasionally mumbling, "Killed grandmother..." The concrete world of his mental retardation made him assume responsibility for her death and, thereby, overwhelmed his being.

S.M. was a 17-year-old boy with two older siblings. He had been diagnosed as having severe mental retardation and a pervasive developmental disorder. He had a well-nurtured and reciprocal relationship with his parents and deeply admired his father. He attended a local high school and spent a large percentage of his time with non-handicapped students. He especially enjoyed his part-time employment in a local restaurant because it reminded him of his father's work. He had a history of minor behavioral difficulties such as mumbling to himself, stereotypical hand movements, and occasional aggression. However, his parents tolerated these and provided him with a normalized life style. His father died after a protracted illness. S.M. and his mother had received counseling during the course of this illness and were prepared to confront his difficulty in dealing with the father's death. S.M. had a reactive depression subsequent to the father's death: withdrawing into his bedroom, listening to records that his father had bought for him, murmuring to himself more, occasionally crying, and withdrawing from his peers. S.M.'s understanding of his father's death was made concrete through psychotherapy that focused on the meaning of his father's death, that he still loved his child, and that S.M. now needed to help his mother.

These three individuals speak of the sentient nature of persons with mental retardation related to the existential confusion surrounding the question of death. Each had a history of warm familial relationships, although B.W.'s situation was excessively overprotected. Additionally, his lack of a social network subsequent to the death of his parents left him in a protracted and near-hopeless situation. D.M.'s severe depressive episode was exacerbated by the lack of sensitive and competent psychotherapy. In spite of affectionate familial relations, he withdrew into a near-catatonic state. S.M.'s depression was lessened due to increased psychotherapeutic support after his father's death.

Meaninglessness

Two of the cases reviewed in our study were triggered by all-encompassing feelings of meaninglessness and lack of choice due to caregivers who played an omnipotent role in governing where and how these individuals could act, work, and live.

K.B. was a 32-year-old woman with mild mental retardation and a history of familial neglect and abuse. She had been placed in a series of community residences, was generally bored, and did not have any close relationships. One day she was told by her residential staff that she had to go to the sheltered workshop whether she liked it or not. She then began to work less, complained of poor treatment, and spent her days at home alone. She was judged to be "just a complainer." After several months, she resorted to locking herself in her apartment and refused to allow anyone to enter, although her social worker was occasionally able to gain entrance. She lost weight, her appearance became disheveled, and she began to express suicidal ideations. She was placed on a "token" program, but increasingly spoke of life as "not worth living." Her countenance became deeply sad, her head was cast down, and her voice was flat and whining. She felt that her life was meaningless and she was overwhelmed by her lack of warm relationships, devalued work, and infantile treatment.

D.E. was a 49-year-old man with mild mental retardation who had worked at the same job for fifteen years. However, over a two month period he became increasingly dissatisfied with his work. He stayed at home, withdrew from social contacts, and engaged in frequent bouts of crying. He also started to have frequent aggressive outbursts, and suffered from insomnia and hypersensitivity to noise. He was unable to specify the reasons for his apparently sudden dislike for his work. Like K.B., however, he had lost hope and felt hemmed in by forces and circumstances beyond his control. His vocational "independence" had left him unable to reach out to others.

Aloneness

Seven of the mentally retarded persons in our review felt disconnected from others due to the sudden loss or long-term lack of stable, consistent, and nurturing relationships in their lives.

M.B. was a 27-year-old man with severe mental retardation, a severe hearing disorder, and a visual handicap. He had had a well-nurtured relationship with his widowed father, but due to his father's ill health had been placed in a community group home. He was devastated by the loss of daily contact with his father and experienced it as death. Within four months, he had lost forty pounds and had almost completely withdrawn from social interactions. His expressive language and ability to care for himself decreased significantly. He spent much of the time seated, waving his arms back and forth in self-isolation.

J.H. was a 27-year-old man with mild mental retardation. Due to parental abuse and neglect, he had been placed in a foster home at the age of four followed by twelve other foster homes, two institutions, and two group homes. The accumulated effect of these changes and his pre-existent disabilities had left him in a chronic state of despair--poor appetite, low energy, hyper-somnia, frequent self-injury, and clinging onto anyone or restraining his arms inside his shirt. His facial expression was almost always melancholic. His life-history represented abandonment to his own solitude in the absence of any nurturing relationship.

J.J. was a 32-year-old man with profound mental retardation who was also nonambulatory and blind. He had resided in a large public institution since the age of 24 and his contacts with his parents and siblings had been minimal. His self-stimulatory behaviors increased substantially in this setting; he developed a flat affect, a wailing scream, aggression, self-injury, frequent bouts of crying, and withdrawal. His caregivers had a distanced relationship with him characterized by perfunctory "programs;" the use of reward and punishment and frequent verbal reprimands and restraint. J.J.'s responses to his alone-ness were increased "behavioral problems."

S.C., a 41-year-old man with mild mental retardation, had been active at home, enjoyed being in the community, and worked on a part-time basis. Due to his parents advanced age and inability to care for him, however, he had been placed in an institutional setting at the age of thirty-eight. In this setting, he recognized that he was "different" from those with whom he lived and also from those who cared for him. He was completely dissatisfied with his life, expressing irritability toward his caregivers, running away, isolating himself, yelling and complaining. He found no joy in his life and refused to participate in almost all activities. He felt separated from others, unable to relate to them, and powerless to change his situation. These feelings left him emotionally homeless.

A.S. was a four-year-old child with moderate mental retardation who had a severe reactive depression as a result of his parent's divorce. Upon his father's departure, he refused to eat and subsequently lost significant body weight. Any attempt to feed him resulted in severe temper tantrums. His naturally over-protective mother employed a series of behavioral techniques but, due to their failure, she resorted to force-feeding him by wrapping his torso in a sheet at meal time in order to prevent his flailing about. He frequently cried out, "Daddy!" and was unable to reconcile himself to this loss.

S.D. was a twenty-two-year-old woman with Down's Syndrome who resided with her parents and three older siblings. She had been well integrated into community life and her parents had a nurturing and supportive relationship with her. They attempted to totally disregard her disability and at times had unrealistically high expectations; she was expected to be like her siblings. However, when her siblings left home, she began to talk to herself, complain, and withdraw into her bedroom. She also experimented with adult sexual relationships "like her sister" which were unfortunately, exploitative in nature and left her even more confused and anxious. She refused to attend a local sheltered workshop and developed poor eating and sleeping habits. After six months, she created an imaginary "friend" and only would interact with him--as if her feelings of aloneness could be replaced only by the friendship found in an invented world.

Loss of objects
D.G. was a woman with severe mental retardation who had a history of stereotypical movements and self-injurious picking at her arms. Although caregiver relationships were authoritar-ian, these problems were controlled in her group home and

workshop settings. Over a three-week period, however, she began to withdraw from others, cried frequently, lost weight, and significantly increased her self-injury and stereotypy. Her caregivers continued to manage her deteriorating behaviors through a series of programs based on verbal praise for the absence of these behaviors and verbal reprimands for their occurrence. Her perplexed caregivers finally discovered that she was upset due to the fact that they had taken her favorite chair away for repairs. Once the chair was returned, the depressive symptoms began to disappear. Her life and its meaning were centered on this rocking chair in the absence of warm and valuing relationships.

Discussion

Based on these experiences and others, we have found that the loss of a loved one can trigger feelings of aloneness and emptiness in spite of warm, although sometimes overprotective, relationships. A mentally retarded individual's dependent nature makes him or her exceedingly vulnerable to such loss and, when it occurs, the result can be an upheaval of emotional balance. It is not merely a problem of grief and understanding, it also signifies the global breakdown of meaning, stability and security, and the subsequent feelings of fear and homelessness. It raises the existential question: "If my loved one is no longer with me, who will save me?"

Other forms of loss or transition can elicit a similar process--whether the change involves teachers or other caregivers, the moving of siblings, change in residential or vocational placement, or the loss of a seemingly insignificant object. Caregivers often suddenly or routinely initiate such transitions or alterations while disregarding the impact they can have on the lives of those in their care.

Yet for persons with mental retardation, such events can take on a profound meaning which is often the equivalent of death.

Another element which can exacerbate vulnerability in the mentally retarded is the feeling of lack of self-agency within one's quotidian situation--monotonous sheltered workshop tasks, cold and sterile relationships with caregivers, depersonalizing and demeaning rules and regulations, and programs fixated on compliance. An individual can develop feelings of hopelessness while seated in a sheltered workshop day after day performing robot-like tasks with only authoritarian interactions from distanced caregivers. Even when given the opportunity to make decisions in modern interdisciplinary team processes, one can still feel overcome by a sense of purposelessness.

Table 6.2
Inner and outer vulnerabilities

Person-related	Situation-related
* Disabling conditions -- Physical, sensorial, and biological factors	* Settings -- Segregated living, schooling, working, playing
* Communication -- Difficulty in receptive and expressive language -- Difficulty in absorbing, integrating, and transforming alienating conditions	* Cultural impact -- Prejudice -- Marginalization -- Reification -- Lack of acceptance and support by others
* Emotionality -- Difficulty in tolerating anxiety -- Heightened feelings of insecurity -- Difficulty in feeling at-home -- Difficulty in reaching out and creating warm personal relationships	* Modes of interacting -- Difficulty in expressing warm unconditional valuing -- Focus on independence -- Difficulty in reaching out and initiating unconditional valuing

Existential vulnerabilities
The case studies presented in this chapter have illustrated an existential and social understanding of the inner and outer dimensions that can lead to or exacerbate vulnerabilities inherent in persons with mental retardation (See Table 6.2).

The very nature of mental retardation, as well as a host of allied developmental disabilities, makes it more difficult for the affected individuals to develop a sense of empowerment, understand their roles in the world, and reach out to others. At the same time, society often aggravates these difficulties through marginalizing responses such as segregated schools, congregate living, devaluing work, and depersonalizing interventions that reify the individual. Although these inner and outer dimensions are inherent in the reality of mental retardation, they are generally subtle and often seemingly insignificant, yet they gnaw at the human spirit. The inability to communicate, to fully understand one's reality, to absorb, integrate, and transform complex events makes it critical for caregivers to reach out and provide stable and consistent feelings of trust, affection, and companionship.

The central paradigm revolves around unconditional valuing, the expression of dialogue, and the bringing of potentially significant others into the psychotherapeutic process in order to create or re-create feelings of security, companionship, and being at-home in the world (McGee, 1989).

Interventions

The twelve individuals represented in this chapter demonstrated varying types of existential dilemmas and each required an intricate interplay of various guided human experiences. Each person's life-condition necessitated both an individualized approach with a psychotherapist as well as a family approach involving significant others, whether actual parents, siblings, or primary caregivers such as group home staff. The therapeutic experiences involved factors such as: 1) instillation of hope; 2) the corrective recapitulation of a "family" group; 3) imparting information; 4) the development of socializing techniques; 5) interpersonal learning; 6) catharsis; and 7) dialogue related to existential factors (Yalom, 1985). The therapist must necessarily play a directive role in this process since mental retardation and its accompanying vulnerabilities make it difficult to effectuate self-agency. Thus, the therapist assumes an exceptional responsibility in relation to the individual, the "family" of caregivers, and social action.

The therapeutic process centers on ways to help the individual reconstruct a world reflective of meaning, companionship, choice, and the creation of specific opportunities to effectuate these. The primary therapeutic strategy is to enter into a dialogue that centers on reflecting both the feelings and the content of the person's dilemma and its conflicts. The therapist has to enable the individual to feel secure by building up a trusting relationship based on a recognition of the fullness of that person and unconditional valuing.

Conclusion

Both in terms of diagnosis and intervention, the study of depression needs to account for a mutuality between the individual and therapist as well as the "family" of caregivers. This can be done through the development of an existential paradigm capable of dealing with ultimate concerns in the struggle with anxiety. As tragic as depression is, its presence in persons with mental retardation demonstrates their full sentient nature, their hunger for meaning and companionship, and their interdependence with others. A singular focus on observable behaviors fails to consider the inner world or deal with life-concerns. The challenge is not only to effectuate modified behaviors, but rather to enhance the meaning of life, to re-establish feelings of self-esteem and union with others, to encourage self-empowerment, and to expand meaningful relationships in order to counteract death, loss, and existential aloneness.

References

Abramson, L. & Sackeim, H. (1977). A paradox in depression: Uncontrollability and self-blame. Psychology Bulletin, 84, 838-852.

Arieti, S. (1977). Psychotherapy of severe depression. American Journal of Psychiatry, 134, 864-868.

Benson, A., Reiss, S., Smith, D.C. & Laman, D.S. (1985). Psychosocial correlates of depression in mentally retarded adults: II. Poor social skills. American Journal of Mental Deficiency, 89, 687-659.

Brady, J.P. (1984). Social skills training for psychiatric patients: II. Clinical outcome studies. American Journal of Psychiatry, 141, 491-498.

Bryan, D.P. (1980). Depression and suicide among adolescents and young adults with selective handicapping conditions. Exceptional Children Quarterly, 1, 57-65.

Dosen, A. (1984). Depression conditions in mentally handicapped children. Acta Paedopsychiatrica, 50, 29-40.

Fowler, J.W. (1977). Alienation as a human experience. In: F.A. Eigo (ed.), From alienation to at-one-ness. Villanova, PN: Villanova University Press.

Gelder, M., Gath, D. & Mayou, R. (1989). Oxford textbook of psychiatry. Oxford: Oxford University Press.

Laman, D.S. & Reiss, S. (1987). Social skills deficiencies associated with depressed mood of mentally retarded adults. American Journal of Mental Deficiency, 92, 224-229.

Matson, J. (1983). Depression in the mentally retarded: Toward a conceptual analysis of diagnosis. In: M. Hersen, R. Eisler, & P. Miller (eds.), Progress in behavior modification. New York: Academic Press.

McGee, J.J., Menolascino, F.J., Hobbs, D. & Menousek, P. (1987). Gentle teaching: a nonaversive approach for helping persons with mental retardation. New York : Human Sciences Press.

McGee, J.J. (1989). Being with others: Toward a psychology of interdependence. Omaha: Creighton University Department of Psychiatry.

O'Neil, M.A. (1982). Depression and mental retardation. 90th Annual Convention of the American Psychological Association, Washington, D.C. (Unpublished document).

Reiss, S. (1985). The mentally retarded, emotionally disturbed adult. In: M. Sigman (ed.), Children with emotional disorders and developmental disabilities. New York: Grune and Stratton.

Reiss, S. & Benson, B.A. (1985). Psychosocial correlates of depression in mentally retarded adults: I. Minimal social support and stigmatization. American Journal of Mental Deficiency, 89, 331-337.

Reiss, S., Levitan, G., & Szyzko, J. (1982). Emotionally disturbed, mentally retarded people: An undeserved population. American Psychologist, 37, 361-367.

Rotter, J. (1960). Some implications of social learning theory for the prediction of goal-directed behavior from testing procedures. Psychology Review, 67, 301-316.

Simmons, J.Q. (1968). Emotional problems in mental retardation: Utilization of psychiatric services. Pediatric Clinics of North America, 15, 957-967.

Webster, T. (1970). Unique aspects of emotional development in mentally retarded children. In: F. Menolascino (ed.), Psychiatric approaches to mental retardation. New York: Basic Books.

Yalom, I. (1980). Existential psychotherapy. New York: Basic Books.

Yalom, I. (1985). The theory and practice of group psychotherapy. New York: Basic Books.

Anton Dosen and Frank J. Menolascino (Eds.) (1990). Depression in mentally retarded children and adults. Leiden, the Netherlands: Logon Publications. ISBN 90-73197-01-5

Chapter 7

Depression in mentally retarded children and adults

Anton Dosen, M.D.

Introduction

Depression in mentally retarded children is a little known phenomenon. Although there is some recognition that depression does occur in this population, there is as yet no agreement among scientists on three questions of fundamental diagnostic importance:
1. Does depression in mentally retarded children exist?
2. Do depressed retarded children show the same symptoms as non-retarded depressed children?
3. Is depression in the mentally retarded caused by the same factors as in the nonretarded?

Similar questions were actually raised two decades ago when the existence of depression in nonretarded children was discussed. Currently, most psychiatrists entertain no doubt that depression in nonretarded children does occur. The frequency of its prevalence is approximately 2.5% among those of school age (Kashani, Ray & Charles, 1984). The fact that depression among retarded children is still questioned by some professionals reflects an insufficiency of knowledge regarding this phenomenon. During the last ten years, some efforts have been made by various authors to disseminate information and to focus the attention of workers in the field of mental retardation to the fact that mentally retarded children do suffer of depression and that they need to receive treatment for this specific condition.

A brief review of the literature

Corbett (1979) was actually speaking of depression in his description of mentally retarded children who showed aggressive and destructive behaviour, since these children were predominantly anxious, fearful, and suffering from misery and unhappiness. Problems involving sleeping and eating were also usually present. From the data in his sample, which consisted of non-institutionalized children with an IQ under 50, Corbett concluded that a depressed state might be diagnosed in approximately 8% of these children.

Reid (1980, 1985) described several cases of manic-depressive psychosis in severely and profoundly retarded school-age children. Symptoms included periodic changes in mood and psychomotor activities, yet according to Reid, manic-depressive psychosis occurs only occasionally in childhood. Way (1983) reported depressive states of a neurotic or reactive type in approximately 16% of the children referred for psychiatric service, while psychotic depressive illness was found in approximately 2%. Striking symptoms included crying, sleeping and eating disorders, withdrawal, regression, and psychomotor retardation. Benson (1985) reported an anxious-depressed withdrawal disorder in 15% of the children and adolescents referred to an out-patient mental health clinic. The characteristics of these patients were depressed affect, low self-esteem, social withdrawal, and crying.

Gillberg, Persson, Grufman & Themoner (1986) noted a depressive syndrome in 4% of the mildly retarded children they studied and a 1.5% prevalence in the more severely retarded. The samples consisted of children involved in an epidemiological investigation of psychiatric disorders in the mentally retarded and diagnostic criteria were the same as those used in DSM-III (APA, 1980). Dosen (1984b) found a depressive condition in 16% of the children referred to an observation center for retarded children with behavioral problems.

Obviously, some of the authors cited were inclined to report the most striking forms of depression, such as depressive psychosis or endogenous manic-depressive illness. Other authors had different forms of depression in mind, such as neurotic or reactive depression, or dysthymic disorders. Most authors, however, did not use standardized diagnostic criteria; the diagnoses were established by clinical examination. In addition, the children under study varied widely in age and intellectual profiles and were selected according to a variety of criteria (e.g., psychiatric in-patients, psychiatric out-patients, a general population of retarded children, etc.). In spite of these shortcomings, it is safe to surmise from these investigations that depression of differing forms does occur in mentally retarded children of varying cognitive levels. This conclusion, however, calls for a more satisfactory formulation of the multiple determinants needed for diagnosis and treatment.

Table 7.1
Children with A psychiatric type of illness
(Major Affective Disorder)

I.
Symptoms found in all children:

dysphoria and sadness
(observed or verbalized)
change of vegetative
functions
(e.g. disorders of sleeping,
eating, etc.)
change of motor activity
irritability

II.
Symptoms found only in the severely and profoundly retarded children:

auto-aggression
stereotypy
constipation

III.
Symptoms found in school-aged mildly retarded children:

death wishes
low self-esteem
hallucinations
delusions
somatic complaints

IV.
Other symptoms (not in all children):

periodicity of illness
withdrawal
agitation
hyperactivity
anxiety
aggression
auto-aggression
destructiveness
stereotypy
constipation
death wishes
low self-esteem
hallucinations
delusions
somatic complaints

Table 7.2

Symptoms in nonretarded pre-school children with Major Affective Disorder	Symptoms based on DSM-III, Weinberg, and RDC for depression in school children
1. Dysphoria, sadness (observed or verbalized)	1. Dysphoria, sadness (verbalized)
2. Withdrawal	2. Anhedonia
3. Anhedonia	3. Sleep disorders
4. Sleep disorders	4. Poor appetite
5. Irritability	5. Cognitive impairment
6. Aggressiveness	6. Agitation
7. Anxiety	7. Loss of energy
8. Periodic changes of mood and vitality	8. Low self-esteem
9. Low self-esteem	9. Death wishes
10. Poor appetite	10. Withdrawal
11. Hyperactivity	11. Somatic complaints
12. Hypoactivity	12. Irritability
13. Destructiveness	13. Psychomotor retardation
14. Agitation	
15. Death wishes	
16. Hallucinations and delusions	
17. Somatic complaints	

Two forms of depression have been distinguished in the course of our clinical work:
1) Manic-depressive illness of the endogenous type (identical to Major Affective Disorder, DSM-III)
2) Depressive condition of neurotic or reactive type (comparable to Dysthymic Disorder, DSM-III).

Children with a psychotic type of illness

In 11 out of the 700 cases we studied (1.6%), a clinical diagnosis of depression of the endogenous type, manic-depressive psychosis, or major affective disorder was established. Diagnostic work was performed by a multi-disciplinary team consisting of a child psychiatrist, psychologist, pediatrician, social worker, and teacher. The diagnostic process was coordinated by a child psychiatrist and included the history of the child, a somatic and psychological examination, and clinical observation of the child's behavior. In several cases, a diagnosis was established after some initial explorative treatment, but diagnoses were predominantly based on phenomenological characteristics involving episodes of change in vegetative functions and mood.

For the purpose of a retrospective study, an inventory of strikingly common symptoms in all children was compiled and clustered according to developmental age and level of verbal communication (Table 7.1). This index of symptoms was compared to the lists of symptoms of depression found in nonretarded school and pre-school children, which was based on a combination of three standard checklists for depression: DSM-III, Research Diagnostic Criteria (Spitzer, Endicott and Robins, 1977) and Weinberg Criteria (Weinberg, Ruttman, Sullivan, Penick and Dietz, 1973) (see Table 7.2).

With regard to the symptom itemization of nonretarded pre-schoolers, the difficulties we encountered were largely due to the unavailability of standard lists for depressive pre-schoolers on the one hand, and the reluctance of using the lists utilized for the older group on the other. Consequently, the researchers resorted to compiling a new combined inventory of symptoms on the basis of case descriptions culled from the scientific literature (Feinstein & Wolpert, 1973; Giancotti & Vinci, 1986; Kashani, Ray & Charles, 1984; Kashani & Ray, 1987; Kerstenbaum, 1979; Poznanski & Zrull, 1970; Poznanski, Israel & Grossman, 1984). Fourteen case descriptions of these authors were analyzed in our study, yielding the symptoms listed in Table 7.2.

The children involved in our study were between 4 and 16 years of age, and their intelligence ranged from profound retardation to border normal level. In all, the sample consisted of 700 mentally retarded children admitted to our observation clinic because of their behavioral and functional problems. The results of our analysis are presented in Tables 7.3 and 7.4.

117

Table 7.3
Common symptoms in nonretarded preschool and school children and frequency in retarded children

Symptoms found in 70-100% of retarded children	Symptoms found in 25-70% of retarded children	Symptoms found in less than 25% of retarded children
dysphoria (observed or verbalized)	withdrawal	death wishes
sleep disorders	hypoactivity	low self-esteem
anhedonia	agitation	somatic complaints
change of appetite		hallucinations
irritability		delusions

Table 7.4
Other Symptoms in Retarded Children Found in More than 50% of Cases

Mildly/Moderately Retarded	Severely/Profoundly Retarded	Verbal Children	Non-Verbal Children
Aggression+	Aggression+	Anxiety+	Aggression+
Anxiety	Periodic changes of mood & vitality	Aggression+	Auto-aggression
Periodic changes of mood & vitality	Auto-aggression	Periodic changes	Stereotypic movements
Destructiveness+	Stereotypic movements	Hyperactivity+	Periodic changes+
Hyperactivity+	Constipation		Constipation

Symptoms with + have been also reported in nonretarded pre-school children

It appears that certain symptoms were frequently represented in our sample, independent of the age or cognitive level of the child. However, these same indications are also common in nonretarded children independent of their ages. These symptoms are dysphoria and sadness (observed or verbalized), anhedonia, sleep disorders, irritability, and change of appetite. Less frequently, the symptoms involved withdrawal, agitation, and hyperactivity. There were also symptoms which occur quite often in retarded pre-schoolers and school-age children and in some nonretarded pre-schoolers, but not in nonretarded school-age children. These symptoms include hyperactivity, anxiety, aggression, destructiveness, and periodic changes of mood and vitality.

Some symptoms were found only in severely retarded, profoundly retarded, and non-verbal children: auto-aggression, stereotypic movements, and constipation. Finally, there were a number of symptoms found to occur mainly in nonretarded children. Among these are death wishes, low self-esteem, hallucinations, delusions, and somatic complaints. No connection between symptoms and brain pathology was noted. Nevertheless, in a number of children a disturbance of tryptophan resorption was indicated. This might be of some importance, possibly indicating a disorder of biochemical balance in the central nervous system (Chouinard, Young, Annable & Sourkes, 1979). A familial prevalence of affective disorder was not found as frequently in retarded children as it was in nonretarded children.

In general, after the diagnosis of depression of the psychotic type had been established, medications were prescribed for most children. Two children received tricyclic antidepressants, only one of whom reacted favorably. Three children received lithium carbonate; positive results were noted for two children and negative results for the third. Three children also received carbamazepine with good results in two of the children and an unconvincing outcome in the third. In two cases, tryptophan and nicotinamide were prescribed with positive results (see Table 7.5). Several weeks after the medications had been initiated, their effects were evaluated and, whenever considered advisable, secondary treatment, such as psychotherapy, was begun. Several children were treated by a combination of medication and relationship therapy (Dosen, 1984a; see also Chapters 4 and 14).

Table 7.5
Effects of medication

Medication	Number of children	Positive result	Negative result
Tricyclic antidepressants	2	1	1
Lithium Carbonate	3	2	1
Carbamazepine	3*	2	1
Tryptophan & Nicotinamide	3*	2	1
No medication	2	2	-

Total number of children: 11
* In 2 children, one medication was replaced by another.

It is interesting to note that during the diagnostic phase, sponta-neous recovery occurred in two children. Obviously, the acceptance, social support, and simulation they received within the therapeutic milieu had a curative influence on them.

Depression of the neurotic type

Of the 194 retarded children who were admitted to our clinic for behavioral and functional problems, 31 (16%) displayed a depression-like disorder (Dosen, 1984b). This condition was comparable to neurotic or reactive depression, or to the Dysthymic Disorder in DSM-III (APA, 1980). The children were between 5 and 16 years of age and their intelligence varied from severely retarded to border normal levels.

Table 7.6
Atypical depression-like states
in mentally retarded children
aged 5 to 16 years

Of 194 children, 31 (16%) showed 4 or more of the following symptoms:

Symptoms	Number of Children	
	N	%
1. Behavioral disorders (hyperactivity, aggression, passivity, inhibition)	31	100
2. Marked "affective hunger"	31	100
3. Fear of failure	31	100
4. Somber or indifferent mood	31	100
5. Arrest or regression of cognitive development	23	74
6. Disorders of sleep, appetite, constipation, encopresis, enuresis	11	35
7. Somatic complaints	5	16

All children diagnosed as depressive came to our clinic from their homes. They all attended special kindergartens or schools for retarded children. For most of the children, the reasons for admission were serious behavioral problems such as aggressiveness, restlessness, destructiveness, passivity, withdrawal, poor performance at school, or delay in development of social skills or speech. Apart from their

121

behavioral and academic problems, clinical observation also disclosed a striking degree of fear of failure when these children were asked to perform tasks. Many children had somatic complaints such as vomiting, encopresis, enuresis, or constipation. In some, the mood was depressive and dysphoric, in others it was one of indifference or apathy. Some of the children seemed to have superficial moods, scarcely responsive to the environmental situation. In communicating with adults they showed a certain insecurity and ambivalence and had no apparent interest in their peers.

During psychotherapeutic treatment, a particularly striking feature was that all children developed a strong affective bond with the therapist and showed a seemingly insatiable hunger for affection. They often tended to regress behaviorally to an earlier phase of emotional development in which they enjoyed more primitive communication and received more attention from the therapist. Symptoms are summarized in Table 7.6.

In most of the children, the onset of depression was not acute but had progressed slowly from an early age. Very often the mothers had already become aware of their child's behavioral problems, difficulties in social contact, hyperactivity, and negativism when the child was only a toddler. In some cases, the depression began after a somatic illness, separation from the mother, or removal from the home. Our treatment, the results of which were predominantly good, consisted of psychotherapeutic intervention and the simulation of development. In particular cases, this treatment was supported by antidepressant drugs.

Discussion

Most scientists who are concerned with psychiatric disorders of the mentally retarded agree that specific biological and social relationship factors in mentally retarded children might play an important role in the prevalence of depression. To say the least, multiple organic physical and functional failures, developmental difficulties, social inadequacies and, not infrequently, chronically low self-esteem are predisposing factors.

In general, psychopathology affects four dimensions of life: vitality, behavior, mood, and thought content. Symptomatology may depend on the degree of severity of the disorder, rather than on its etiology, and while the disorder occurs independently of age or IQ, its appearance could well be colored by these two variables.

Different types of depression, from the psychotic to the neurotic form, can be readily distinguished. In its psychotic form, symptoms along the vegetative dimension are more accentuated, while in a neurotic form behavioral disorders are more striking. Our experience, as well as reports of other investigators, indicate that a neurotic type of depression may take the form of a psychotic disorder if it endures too long or is exacerbated by negative life events.

Beck, Carlson, Russell & Brownfield (1987) are of the opinion that the symptoms of depression in mildly retarded, verbally able adolescents may be detected by the same rating scale for depression used with nonretarded adolescents. Some authors (Gillberg, Persson, Grufman & Themoner, 1986; Benson, 1985) advocate application of scales standardized for retarded youngsters. The diagnosis of depression in children of lower levels is, however, much more problematic (Gillberg, Persson, Grufman & Themoner, 1986).

In severely/profoundly retarded children and in retarded pre-school children, other symptoms, such as hyperactivity, self-injurious and stereotypic behavior, may be strikingly apparent. However, since these behavior patterns can be found in other types of mental illness among such children, it is judicious to consider these behavioral characteristics as aspecific, primitive reactions to stress, rather than manifestations of depression. Available literature and personal experience strongly suggest that in depressed mentally retarded children, the symptoms of vegetative and psychomotor disorders are more constant than the symptoms of mood and thought disorders. Obviously, disorders of mood and thought are relative since they are intimately tied to the introspective and expressive abilities of a particular child. Also the severity of depression may contribute to mood pattern.

Based on our experience, periodic changes in mood, such as weeping and apathy, are more striking in psychotic forms of depression than in milder syndromes. Apparently, neurotic depressive children have a limited ability to comprehend their own depression. A good observer, however, can notice the rapid swing from an unhappy face with downcast eyes to fleeting smiles. Some authors (Nissen, 1971) speak of a "poverty of affect" in these depressed children. In our sample, we found children with a superficial mood who were affect-empty rather than sad; they could not really cry or laugh. Often after successful treatment, these children began to cry and laugh spontaneously. Delayed emergence of self-esteem, feelings of guilt, and suicidal ideations were found in our sample only in older children of higher cognitive levels. These findings are congruent with those of other

123

authors (McConville & Brace, 1985) regarding the development of self-concept and awareness of higher social feelings in nonretarded depressed children. According to these authors, negative self-esteem becomes more common in depressed nonretarded children at the age of 8 to 12, while guilt feelings are found in most depressed children at the age of 10. Suicidal ideation increases in nonretarded children after the age of 10 and becomes ten times more frequent at the age of 15 (Shaffer, 1987). These findings might serve to clarify the fact that such symptoms occur less frequently among children having an IQ lower than 50.

As to the etiology of depression in the retarded, it is believed that endocrinologic, metabolic, genetic, and other biological abnormalities may play a part. Further, a specific developmental pattern of the mentally retarded may predispose them to prolonged stress, which depresses them and exhausts their psychological ability for compensation. This developmental pattern may indeed be a reason for such a child's chronic depressive state and impaired cognitive and social growth. Similar conditions have been reported in nonretarded children whose parents were chronically mentally ill. Since parents of the subjects in our sample often reported that their children, who had a prolonged history of the neurotic type of depression, had begun to show disturbed social contact when they were toddlers, it is reasonable to presume that the roots of depression might well lie in the child's attachment development very early in life. This sort of depression in the mentally retarded we prefer to call "developmental depression."

Consequently, it could be hypothesized that a number of specific factors, biological and developmental as well, are usually involved in the occurrence of depression in mentally retarded children and that the etiology of the disorder in this specific population is seemingly very complex. It is especially important to keep the complexity of this disturbance in mind during treatment. This means that biochemical remedies, developmentally-oriented psychotherapy, and other treatments strategies aimed at fostering the emotional and social growth of the child ought to be articulated in such a way as to meet the particular needs of each child. In our experience, we have produced good results through the application of relationship therapy (Dosen, 1984a), which is a psychotherapeutic method based on a developmental model, and antidepressant medication when necessary.

Conclusion

It is this author's view that depression in mentally retarded children has the same neurobiological and psychological basis as in nonretarded children. The disorder can occur independently of sex, age, or IQ. However, its appearance of can be affected or modified by age or IQ. Literature in this area offers a basis for launching several hypotheses:

-- Symptoms of vegetative (vital) and psychomotor disorders of depression in the mentally retarded are more constant than the verbal expression of dysphoria.

-- Mood changes are observable, but the child's verbal expression of changed mood is dependent on IQ and verbal abilities.

-- Thought content and suicidal behavior are often largely a function of developmental age.

-- Other, more specific symptoms, such as self-injurious behavior, aggression, etc., may be viewed as primitive reaction patterns to stress, usually displayed by children at a low level of emotional development.

The fact that depression is seldom diagnosed in mentally retarded children does not mean that this disorder does not occur in this population; it is simply not recognized. For recognition to take place, the diagnostician should first be aware of the possibility that this disorder *can* be expected in this population and probably with a higher frequency than in nonretarded patients.

A developmental approach toward evolving a diagnostic framework may be very useful, and in further scientific research, priority should be given to:

-- establishing diagnostic criteria for the development of checklists for different developmental levels of mentally retarded children;

-- determining the prevalence of disorder;

-- uncovering specific psychosocial factors which affect susceptibility to depression;

-- delineating the effects of specific drug treatments on depression;

-- creating psychotherapeutic and other approaches for use in the treatment of depressed mentally retarded children.

References

American Psychiatric Association (1980). Diagnostic and Statistical Manual of Mental Disorders Third Edition. Washington, D.C.: The Association.

Beck, D. C., Carlson, G. A., Russell, A. T., & Brownfield, F. E. (1987). Use of depression rating scales in developmentally and educationally delayed adolescents. Journal of the American Academy of Child Psychiatry, 26, 97-100.

Benson, B. A. (1985). Behavior disorder and mental retardation. Association with age, sex and level of functioning in an outpatient clinic sample. Applied Research in Mental Retardation, 6, 79-88.

Chouinard, G., Young, S. N., Annable, L., & Sourkes, T. L. (1979). Tryptophan-nicotinamide, imipramine and their combination in depression. Acta Psychiatrica Scandanavia, 59, 395-414.

Corbett, J.A. (1979). Psychiatric morbidity and mental retardation. In F. James & R. Snaith (eds.), Psychiatric illness and mental handicap. London: Gaskol Press.

Dosen, A. (1984a). Experiences with individual relationship therapy within a therapeutic milieu for retarded children with severe emotional disorders. In J. M. Berg (Ed.), Perspectives and progress in mental retardation (Vol. II). Baltimore, MD: University Park Press.

Dosen, A. (1984b). Depressive conditions in mentally retarded children. Acta Paedopsychiatrica, 50, 29-40.

Feinstein, S. C., & Wolpert, E. A. (1973). Juvenile manic-depressive illness. Journal of the American Academy of Child Psychiatry, 12, 123-136.

Giancotti, A., & Vinci, G. (1986). A major depression of psychogenic origin in a five-year old. American Journal of Orthopsychiatry, 56(4), 617-621.

Gillberg, C., Persson, E., Grufman, M., & Themoner, V. (1986). Psychiatric disorders in mildly and severely mentally retarded urban children and adolescents: Epidemiological aspects. British Journal of Psychiatry, 149, 68-74.

Kashani, J. H., & Carlson, F. A. (1987). Seriously depressed preschoolers. American Journal of Psychiatry, 194(3), 348-350.

Kashani, J. H., & Ray, J. S. (1987). Major depression with delusional features in a preschooler. Journal of the American Academy of Child Psychiatry, 26(2), 110-113.

Kashani, J. H., Ray, J. S., & Charles, G. A. (1984). Depression and depressive-like states in preschool-age children in a child development unit. American Journal of Psychiatry, 141, 1397-1402.

Kerstenbaum, C. J. (1979). Children at risk for manic-depressive illness, possible predictors. American Journal of Psychiatry, 136(9), 1206-1208.

McConville, B. J., & Brace, R. T. (1985). Depressive illnesses in children and adolescents: A review of current concepts. Canadian Journal of Psychiatry, 30, 119-129.

Nissen, G. (1971). Depressive syndrome im kindes- und jugendalter. Berlin: Springer-Verlag.

Poznanski, E., & Zrull, J. P. (1970). Childhood depression. Acta Psychiatrica, 23(80), 15.

Poznanski, E., Israel, M. C., & Grossmann, J. (1984). Hypomania in a four-year-old. Journal of the American Academy of Child Psychiatry, 23, 105-110.

Reid, A. H. (1980). Psychiatric disorders in mentally handicapped children, a clinical and follow-up study. Journal of Mental Deficiency Research, 18, 287-298.

Reid, A. (1985). Psychiatry and mental handicap. In M. Craft, J. Bicknell, & S. Hollins (Eds.), Mental handicap: A multi-disciplinary approach. London: Bailliere.

Shaffer, D. (1987). Depression, mania and suicidal acts. In M. Rutter & L. Hersov (Eds.), Child and adolescent psychiatry. Modern approaches. Oxford: Blackwell Scientific Publishers.

Spitzer, R.L., Endicott, J., Robins, E. (1977). Research Diagnostic Criteria, Third Edition. New York State Psychiatric Institute.

Way, M. C. (1983). The symptoms of affective disorder in severely retarded children. Paper presented at IASSMD congress - Toronto, Canada.

Weinberg, W., Ruttman, J., Sullivan, L., Penick, E., Dietz, S.G. (1973). Depression in children referred to an educational center: diagnosis and treatment. J. Pediatr., 83, 1065-1072.

Anton Dosen and Frank J. Menolascino (Eds.) (1990). Depression in mentally retarded children and adults. Leiden, the Netherlands: Logon Publications. ISBN 90-73197-01-5

Chapter 8

Depression in moderately and mildly mentally handicapped people

Kenneth A. Day, M.D.

Introduction

This chapter is concerned with depression in adults with moderate, mild, and borderline mental handicap and focuses on phenomenology and diagnosis. Treatment is only touched on as this is covered in detail in other contributions. The intention is to provide a practical guide for the practicing physician and no claim of a comprehensive literature review is made.

Although the nature and classification of depressive illness remains a subject of debate (Kendell, 1976), the traditional dichotomy between psychotic and neurotic depression is adhered to as research evidence seems to validate the concept of psychotic depression, even though the evidence for a separate entity of neurotic depression is less strong. The bulk of research in the mentally handicapped has, in fact, been concerned with the more severe forms of depression.

Psychotic depression

Psychotic depression is characterized by severe depressed mood, marked psychomotor retardation or agitation, severe vegetative symptoms including sleep disturbance, loss of appetite often with accompanying significant weight loss, diurnal variation of mood, a high risk of suicide, paranoia and delusions of guilt, a tendency to recur, an association with mania, a tendency to occur in middle age and later life, and a familial predisposition. It is variously known as manic depressive psychosis, affective psychosis, endogenous depression, vital depression, retarded depression, and melancholia.

Table 8.1
Prevalence studies of affective psychoses in the mentally handicapped

Author	Population Studied	No.	Prevalence Rate Affective Psychoses
Penrose 1938	Hospital Inpatients Adults	1280	1.9%
Pollack 1945	1 years Hospital Admission Adults	444	1.6%
Leck et al. 1967	Hospital Inpatients All Ages	1652	1.8%
Reid 1972	Hospital Inpatients Adults	500	1.2%
Heaton-Ward 1977	Hospital Inpatients Adults	1251	1.2%
Corbett 1979	Total Population	402	1.5%
Wright 1982	Hospital Inpatients Adults	1507	2.8%
Lund 1985	Total Population Sample	302	1.7%

Prevalence and aetiology

Affective psychoses, that is both mania and depression, occur in the mentally handicapped with the same frequency as they do in the general population. Despite the different populations studied and the problems of definition, diagnosis, and methodology, the results of epidemiological studies show a remarkable consistency (see Table 1).

As in the general population, the illness is more common in females, with a female to male ratio of around 2:1 (Day, 1985; Hucker, Day, George, & Roth, 1979; Reid, 1972; Wright, 1982).

There have been a number of reports of affective psychosis occurring in Down's syndrome (Cook & Leventhal, 1987; Keegan, Pettigrew, & Parker, 1974; McLaughlin, 1987; Menolascino, 1964; Roith, 1961; Sovner, Hurley, & Labrie, 1985; Warren, Holroyd, & Folstein, 1989) and Jancar (1979) has reported individual cases associated with intermittent porphyria, ichthyosis, and other physical conditions. But no specific links have been established between the syndromes causing mental handicap or the physical abnormalities associated with mental handicap.

The familial tendency, particularly for bipolar illnesses, found in the general population is also seen in the mentally handicapped. In Carlson's study (1979), of the 14 cases with bipolar illness, one half (5 definitely and 2 possibly) had a positive family history. A positive family history was present in 11 of Hucker et al.'s 16 patients and the morbidity risk for families was 13.3%, but there were no differences between the unipolar and bipolar groups (Hucker et al, 1979). However, only two of Berney and Jones' (1988) cases of early onset bipolar affective disorder had a positive family history and, after reviewing the evidence from other studies, they hypothesized organic cerebral dysfunction as a possible predisposing factor (Jones & Berney, 1987; Berney & Jones, 1988). Reid and his colleagues (1987) have recently described five patients with congenital mental handicap in whom bipolar manic depressive psychosis was associated with flexion deformities of the fingers, but failed to establish any clear genetic links.

Clinical features

The presentation of psychotic depression in the mentally handicapped varies greatly. Atypical presentations are common, but classical features can usually be found on careful examination and inquiry. Because of impaired intellectual and verbal skills mentally handicapped people often have difficulty in conceptualizing and communicating their feelings and experiences so that the behavioral components of the illness, like sleep or

131

Table 8.2
Clinical features in psychotic and neurotic depression
(Figures represent numbers of patients showing each feature)

Symptom	Psychotic* Depression n = 11	Neurotic Depression n = 26
Depressed mood (observed)	10 (91%)	21 (81%)
Depressed mood (complaint patient)	7 (63%)	18 (69%)
Social withdrawal	10 (91%)	9 (35%)
Reduced interest	10 (91%)	5 (19%)
Reduced concentration	8 (73%)	0
Deterioration in personal habits	7 (63%)	4 (15%)
Retardation of movement/speech	9 (82%)	0
Diurnal variation	3 (27%)	0
Reactivity (mood)	0	14 (54%)
Reduced libido	0	4 (15%)
Suicidal thoughts	6 (55%)	16 (62%)
Suicidal threats	0	4 (15%)
Suicidal attempts	0	11 (42%)
Reduced appetite	10 (91%)	12 (46%)
Weight loss	9 (82%)	8 (31%)
Early morning awakening	9 (82%)	3 (12%)
Other sleep disturbance	0	16 (62%)
Weeping/crying	4 (36%)	15 (58%)
Agitation	8 (73%)	8 (31%)
Irritability	4 (36%)	8 (31%)
Delusions (depressive)	5 (45%)	0
Paranoid delusions	4 (36%)	0
Ideas of reference	2 (18%)	0
Hallucinations	1 (9%)	0
Self reproach/guilt	3 (27%)	0
Poor self-image	0	3 (12%)
Reassurance seeking	7 (63%)	0
Anxiety symptoms	0	16 (62%)
Obsessional behavior	0	3 (12%)
Hypochondriasis	4 (36%)	7 (27%)
Hysterical symptoms	1 (9%)	5 (19%)
Aggression/temper tantrums	0	7 (27%)

*From Hucker et al., 1979

132

appetite disturbance and withdrawal, are usually diagnostically more important than symptomatic complaints--especially so in the more severely handicapped.

Table 2, which shows the symptom frequency in 11 psychotically depressed patients with an IQ range of 45-70, is fairly typical of the findings of all other major studies. The most common **presenting features** are depressed mood, reduced appetite with weight loss, sleep disturbance with early morning awakening, social withdrawal, and psychomotor retardation or agitation--all of which are readily observable by relatives or care staff and should alert to the possibility of an underlying depressive illness. **Symptomatic complaint of depression** is not invariable; only two-thirds of Hucker et al.'s (1979) cases complained of sadness or depressed mood, whilst Reid (1972) found that direct complaints of depression were rare and that his patients were more likely to complain of anxiety or feeling fed up. A depressed mood, however, can usually be inferred from facial expression, general demeanor, or tearfulness. Diurnal variation is uncommon and mood change sometimes poorly sustained (Reid, 1972) and there may be premenstrual exacerbation of symptoms in women (Wright, 1982).

Social withdrawal and **loss of interest** in normal activities invariably occurs and is an early presenting symptom. Profound **psychomotor retardation** with depressive stupor and mutism is not uncommon and the sudden occurrence of these symptoms may be the dramatic presenting feature of the illness. Alternatively, **irritability** and **agitation** - often to a marked degree and sometimes expressed as aggressivity and temper tantrums - may occur (Reid, 1972; Wright, 1982). Delusions of bodily dysfunction and **somatic complaints** are common and if the underlying depressive illness goes unrecognized, may result in extensive and unnecessary physical investigations or be dismissed as hypochondriasis (Hucker et al., 1979). Headaches and abdominal pain are the commonest complaints, but sometimes symptoms may take a bizarre form as in a case described by Reid and Leonard (1977) in which severe life-threatening vomiting was the principal feature.

Delusions of guilt and persecution also occur and may be accompanied by **auditory hallucinations** which threaten, frighten, are critical, or warn of disaster. Delusions tend to be vivid and dramatic involving fears of having legs and arms cut off, for example, but can also be banal, reflecting the limited horizons and cognitive functioning of the patient, and easily missed. Systematization rarely occurs and behavioral responses, like persistent hiding under the bedclothes in the case of a self-reproachful woman with marked paranoid feelings who thought her room was bugged, are sometimes the first evidence of delusions and hallucinations.

Feelings of hopelessness, self-blame, and thoughts of death and suicide, although often not readily apparent, can usually be elicited by careful inquiry or inferred from general demeanor and the content of delusional material. In Reid's series one patient made a false confession in order to be "put away," whilst others, although not directly referring to a desire to kill themselves, wished for "a long sleep" or to be "doped out of the world." **Suicidal attempts** are not uncommon. In over half of Hucker et al.'s (1979) series and a quarter of Reid's (1972), suicidal thoughts could be elicited, and a quarter of the patients in both series had made suicidal attempts, indicating the need for constant vigilance. Overdosing, attempted gassing, attempted self-strangulation, self-immolation, pouring boiling water over the head, and jumping from heights have all be reported (Benson & Laman, 1988; Hucker et al., 1979; Reid, 1972; Sternlicht, Pustel & Deutsch, 1970), indicating the seriousness of the intent, but consummated suicide is extremely rare (Sovner & Hurley 1982), poor planning and execution being the principal reasons for lack of success. Reid (1972) also described two cases in which self-injurious behavior in severely mentally handicapped patients occurred in association with marked depressive symptoms which he suggests could be interpreted as suicidal equivalents.

Atypical features occur frequently and may be the most striking presenting feature, masking other symptoms and creating diagnostic difficulties. Regression with attention-seeking and childish clinging behavior, a return of incontinence--sometimes with faecal smearing, deterioration in personal habits, and loss of previously held social skills are particularly common. Hysterical symptoms, including disturbance of gait, hysterical fits and aggressive acting-out behaviors are also seen. Negativism, robot-like responsiveness, elective mutism, and waxy flexibility sometimes occur, providing further evidence for the view that catatonia is more usually a sign of affective disorder than schizophrenia (Reis, 1985).

Affective psychosis may be precipitated in the mentally handicapped, as in the non-handicapped, by a range of psychosocial and physical stresses. A precipitant was noted in 7 of the 19 cases described by Reid, (1972) and 2 of the 16 cases reported by Hucker et al. (1979). These included termination of pregnancy and sterilization, hepatitis, deep vein thrombosis, prostatectomy, acute labrynthitis, treatment with corticosteroids, and separation from relatives or friends. McLoughlin and Bhate (1987) have reported a case of severe psychotic depression in a middle aged moderately mentally handicapped woman following the death of her parents.

Unusual and rare forms

No consideration of psychotic depression in the mentally handicapped would be complete without reference to **mixed states** and **schizoaffective psychosis**. Whilst it is beyond the scope of this chapter to enter into the contentious issue of the nature and status of these states, it has to be recorded that they do occur in mentally handicapped people and can pose considerable diagnostic problems. In an analysis of 23 case studies drawn from the literature, Carlson (1979) found 3 (13%) who simultaneously showed the features of mania and depression. A mixed picture was present in a third of Reid's (1972) cases and he described them as exhibiting perplexity, lability, and irritability, a curious dissociation between motor and mental over-activity, and a mixture of grandiose and depressive delusions. Although there are no specific studies, patients are sometimes encountered in clinical practice who show a mix of both schizophrenic and affective symptoms or, who over the course of a number of illnesses, may present on one occasion with a pure affective illness and on another with a mixed picture (see case history 3 below). The not infrequent coexistence of catatonic phenomena has already been mentioned.

Occasionally, cases of **rapid cycling psychosis** are encountered in which the illness follows a regular cyclical pattern with periods of elation and depression occurring at intervals of a few weeks to a few days: the author has under his care a young man with a 24 hour cycle. This condition has been described in severely and mildly mentally handicapped adults and children, tends to have an onset in adolescence and to be sustained over many years, and is often resistant to Lithium and other treatment measures (Berney & Jones, 1988; Hucker, 1975; Jones & Berney, 1987; Reid & Naylor, 1976). Naylor and his colleagues (1976) have demonstrated certain cyclical biochemical changes accompanying clinical symptoms in four mentally handicapped patients with rapid cycling psychosis, but these differed from patient to patient and they urge caution in interpreting their findings.

Diagnosis

The difficulties of diagnosing mental illness in the mentally handicapped have been well summarized by Sovner (1986). He identified four factors which impact on the diagnosis process: **intellectual distortion** - concrete thinking and impaired communication skills which

135

impair the patient's ability to conceptualize and describe his or her feelings; **psychosocial masking** - the limited life experiences of mentally handicapped people resulting in a blandness of symptomatology and the danger of missed symptoms; **cognitive disintegration** - the tendency of a mentally handicapped person to become disorganized under emotional stress with resulting regressive behavior and atypical symptoms; and **baseline exaggeration** - an increase in other maladaptive behaviors as a consequence of illness; for example, a sudden increase in the severity or frequency of self-injurious behavior.

Accurate diagnosis requires a **full and detailed history**, careful **examination and observation** of the patient, a close **study of the natural history** of the illness, and, above all, **alertness to the possibility**. A positive family history, positive Dexamethasone Suppression Test, and positive response to treatment all provide important confirmatory evidence - particularly where it is difficult to find a sufficient number of diagnosis-specific symptoms.

History and examination

The value and importance of a skilled clinical interview and examination cannot be over-stressed. The general paucity of subjective complaints means that much greater reliance has to be placed on **objective data** obtained by observing the patient and from the reports of relatives and care staff. Particularly important are the **biological or vegetative features** of sleep and appetite disturbance, weight loss, psychomotor retardation, and reported differences from the patient's normal behavior (Rivinus & Harmatz, 1979). A period of **inpatient observation** without treatment may be required before the diagnosis can be made and, in some cases, this can only be firmly established over the course of several illnesses on the basis of a clear periodicity with intervening "normal periods" and/or a clear response to ECT or antidepressant medication (Day, 1985). **Atypical symptoms** may mask or obscure the picture; deterioration from a previous level of functioning or the occurrence of new and unusual behaviors should always alert to the possibility of an underlying psychotic depression.

Whilst there are problems for even the experienced psychiatrist, a more fundamental problem is the frequent failure of the immediate carers and other professionals to consider the possibility of depression in the first instance, as in the following example - one of many known to the author.

A young man with Down's syndrome had stopped eating, suffered marked weight loss, and was in imminent danger of

136

dying from severe dehydration when his desperate parents sought psychiatric help. His symptoms had been considered to be behavioral in origin and he was undergoing a behavior modification program under the direction of a psychologist at his day center. Careful inquiry quickly revealed other features of depression and he responded well to antidepressant medication. Six months later he suffered an attack of renal colic due to renal calculi, probably caused by his earlier dehydration, which, interestingly, was again misdiagnosed by the primary care team as a behavior problem.

An almost identical case has been reported by Szymanski and Biederman (1984). Reiss and Szyszko (1983) have termed this **diagnostic overshadowing** and in a series of elegant laboratory experiments demonstrated that the diagnosis of psychiatric illness is less likely to be made when the observer knows that a person is mentally handicapped. It is the author's firm conviction that all mentally handicapped people displaying behavioral problems should have a full psychiatric screening before embarking on behavior modification programs and, where appropriate, continued psychiatric monitoring.

Rating scales

In an attempt to improve diagnostic accuracy and reliability at clinical level, a number of workers have used rating scales developed primarily as research instruments. Successes have been reported in the use of the Beck Depression Inventory, Zung Self Rating Depression Scale, MMPI Depression Scale, and the Hamilton Rating Scale for Depression (Kazdin, Matson, & Senatore, 1983; Sireling, 1986), and Reid and his colleagues have standardized the Goldberg Clinical Interview Schedule for use with mentally handicapped patients (Ballinger, Armstrong, Presly, & Reid, 1975). However, a major weakness of these scales, which have been designed for the non-handicapped, is that they rely significantly upon the ability of the patient to describe subjective feelings. It is generally agreed that in the mentally handicapped diagnostic scales should, as far as possible, reflect the behavioral rather than the subjective components of the illness. To this end the author and his colleagues (Hucker et al., 1979) have published diagnostic criteria for depression based upon the research criteria of Feighner and his associates (1972), but adapted for use with mentally handicapped people (Table 3).

Table 8.3
Diagnostic criteria for psychotic depression
in the mentally handicapped

Hucker et al., 1979	Sovner, 1986
A. Depressed mood (complaint or observation)	I. A disturbance of mood characterized by sadness, withdrawal or agitation
B. At least 4 of the following:	II. Any 4* of the following symptoms:
agitation or retardation	change in sleep
reduced sleep	change in appetite and/or weight
loss of appetite or weight loss of more than 7 lb.	onset or increase in severity of self-injurious behaviour
loss of energy (interest) or libido	apathy
self reproach/guilt	psychomotor retardation
loss of concentration	loss of activity of daily living skills, e.g. onset of urinary incontinence
suicidal ruminations/attempt	
diurnal mood variation (mornings worse)	catatonic stupor and/or rigidity
depressive delusions	spontaneous crying
	fearfulness
C. No symptoms of schizophrenia	

A, B, and C required and patient must be different from his/her normal self

* Only 3 symptoms needed if there is a positive history of depression in a first degree relative.

Sovner (1986) pointed out that this still contains some items dependent upon adequate communication and self-assessment skills and proposed his own list of 'distortion free diagnostic criteria for affective disorders' (see also Table 3).

Neither scale has so far been validated, but both are useful at the clinical level, particularly with the moderately and severely mentally handicapped. Senatore and his colleagues (1985) have recently developed and piloted a Psychopathology Inventory for Mentally Retarded Adults (self-report and informant versions) based on DSM-III criteria.

Biological markers

Recent years have seen an increasing search for biological markers in psychotic depression (Joyce, 1985). Whilst research is still in its infancy, this is an area with enormous potential for improving diagnostic reliability in the mentally handicapped, if and when techniques can be adequately refined.

The **Dexamethasone Suppression Test** (DST) introduced in the late 1970s is the best researched of the possible techniques (Oei, 1988; Rubin, 1985). Studies have shown that between 40-70% of endogenously depressed patients fail to suppress plasma cortisol following an intramuscular dose of 1 mg. of Dexamethasone as compared to only 5% of controls and that this is reversed during treatment and after clinical improvement. Non-suppression has also been reported in other psychiatric conditions. So far there have been few studies of the DST in the mentally handicapped. Pirodsky, Gibbs, Hesse, Hsieh, Krause, and Rodriguez (1985), Beckwith, Parker, Pawlarczyk, Couk, Schumacher, and Yearwood (1985), and Ruedrich, Wadle, Sallach, Hahn, and Menolascino (1987) all found that a high percentage of mentally handicapped people diagnosed as having, or suspected clinically to be suffering from, depression showed non-suppression as compared to a non-depressed mentally handicapped control group. However, in another study (Sireling, 1986) only one of four mentally handicapped patients with a major depressive disorder failed to suppress cortisol production. More work is needed both in non-handicapped and handicapped populations, but in the meantime the DST used carefully with due regard to its limitations, and taken together with the clinical picture and family history, can provide a useful adjunct to diagnosis, helping to increase reliability and perhaps swinging the balance where there is uncertainty and atypical presentations (Pirodsky et al., 1985).

Other potentially diagnostically valuable biological markers, so far only explored in a preliminary fashion in non-handicapped depressives, are blunted TSH (thyroid stimulating hormone) response and the EEG sleep abnormality of shortened REM (rapid eye movement) latency which have been found to be associated with endogenous depression. Some researchers have suggested that combining EEG with the DST test would further increase the diagnostic reliability.

Treatment response

In difficult cases an empirical diagnosis based upon all available information has to be made and tested by the response to treatment. In these situations a systematic approach is essential, with the use of only one treatment method, e.g. ECT or antidepressant medication, at a time. Only one antidepressant drug should be used at a time, the dosage should be adequate (up to the therapeutic maximum provided there are no serious side effects), and an adequate duration should be allowed for a treatment response before moving on to another drug or ECT or reviewing the diagnosis. This approach has led some writers to refer to 'drug responsive' or 'antidepressant responsive depression' in the mentally handicapped (Sovner, 1986).

Differential diagnosis

Psychotic depression in the mentally handicapped must be differentiated from other forms of psychiatric disorder. This can sometimes be difficult because of atypical presentations and the paucity of classical symptoms. Misdiagnosis in the early stages of the illness is not uncommon (Hucker et al., 1979). **Reactive depression** can usually be distinguished by a less severe level of mood change, the absence of biological features and an associated and obvious precipitating factor, although precipitating factors have been described in psychotic depression (Hucker et al., 1979; McLoughlin & Bhate, 1987; Reid, 1972) and there is sometimes a confusing overlap of symptomatology. When paranoid features are prominent the illness may be confused with **paranoid psychosis** or **paraphrenia** - especially in the over 40s. Mixed states, where the symptoms of mania and depression are closely intertwined, can lead to a mistaken diagnosis of **schizophrenia** (Hasan & Mooney, 1979; Kadambari, 1986) or a toxic confusional state (Reid, 1972). The possibility of an underlying depression as the cause of **behavioral change** must always be considered, particularly where this is of recent onset or where existing behavior has shown an increase in severity. Hypochondriacal symptoms may be mistaken for **physical illness** and rigorously investigated before the true diagnosis is made (Hucker et al., 1979).

Hypothyroidism and **early dementia** must also be considered, particularly in the older age groups and Down's individual (Warren et al., 1989).

Natural history and prognosis

The affective psychoses are generally regarded as illnesses of the middle years. Slater and Roth (1977) give the mean age of onset in males as 53 years and in females as 51 years, and point out that an episode before the age of 20 years is very rare, although cases have been reported (Hassenyeh & Davison, 1980). Age at first episode appears to be substantially lower in the mentally handicapped, and an onset in adolescence not uncommon. Reid (1972) gives means of 32 years for females and 27 years for males, and Hucker et al. (1979) 34 years for females and 26 years for males. In the latter series, 4 of the 16 cases had suffered their first illness in adolescence. Berney and Jones (1988) have recently reported 8 cases of early onset bipolar affective disorder in mentally handicapped adolescents.

As in the non-handicapped, the illness tends to follow a recurring course and bipolar illnesses appear to be common. In a study of 24 cases in mentally handicapped people aged 40 years and over, the author (Day, 1985) found that 21 (88%) had suffered recurrent illnesses with up to 8 major episodes during a 10 year period, and that in 15 (63%) the illness was bipolar, including 5 cases of rapid short cycle psychosis. Carlson (1979), in her review of 23 cases histories collected from the literature, found that 14 (60%) suffered a bipolar illness. Further examination of Hucker et al.'s (1979) 16 cases showed that in 14 (88%) the illness was recurrent with up to 10 episodes (average 5) over a period of 11-20 years, and that in 7 (44%) the illness was bipolar.

Most studies (Carlson, 1979; Heaton-Ward, 1977; Hucker et al., 1979; Reid, 1972) report a good response to treatment with an illness duration of around two months and periods of up to ten years between discrete illnesses. In some cases the illness may prove unresponsive to treatment and run a prolonged course of up to 2-3 years. Rapid cycling illnesses seem particularly resistant to all forms of treatment (Jones & Berney, 1987; Hucker, 1975; Reid & Naylor, 1976).

Illustrative case histories

The following case histories are fairly typical examples of the presentation of the illness in clinical practice.

141

Case history #1

F. is 37 years old and moderately mentally handicapped, the consequence of brain damage at birth and meningococcal meningitis at the age of 4 years. He has a slight squint, dysarthric speech and an ataxic gait, but is capable, self-confident, and sociable. He suffered his first attack of psychotic depression at the age of 20 years when he became increasingly agitated and depressed over a period of five weeks, staying in the house, showing no interest in his usual activities, hardly speaking, was off his food, wouldn't leave his mother alone, became suspicious saying something was wrong and things were missing, and was generally tearful and unhappy. He was restored to health after six weeks on antidepressant medication, but quickly relapsed when this was stopped, improving on the reintroduction of the drug. He suffered further episodes, 3, 7, 10, and 12 years later, all characterized by marked psychomotor retardation with mutism, prominent vegetative and paranoid features, acute onset, and rapid progression. On three occasions there were a possible precipitant: a brother in the army going into a war zone, an attack and some mickey-taking by local youths, and the return home of a physically disabled brother who rather stole the limelight. Each episode responded rapidly to either antidepressant medication or ECT, and in between illnesses F. was his usual cheerful and sociable self. There was no family history of psychiatric illness. As the illnesses came on suddenly and presented so dramatically, there were no diagnostic problems. The initial presentation of the first illness raised the possibility of an anxiety state, but once the true diagnosis was established there was no difficulty on either the part of the professionals or his parents in quickly recognizing the onset of subsequent illnesses and referring rapidly for treatment.

Case history #2

M. is a 47-year woman with mild mental handicap who lives with her parents and is an only child. Her first psychiatric illness was at the age of 28 years when she was hospitalized with difficult, demanding, and aggressive behavior which responded to tranquilizing medication. Over the next decade she exhibited regular episodes of disturbed behavior which appeared to occur premenstrually. A further hospital admission was necessary at the age of 40 years when the clinical picture was one of noisiness, incessant talking, sleeplessness, and restlessness, which responded to tranquilizing medication. Three years later she required a prolonged period in the hospital following a further period of aggressive, noisy, and overactive behavior, this time with marked grandiosity. There followed a period of tearfulness, mutism, inappropriate behavior, and confusion, and this cyclical pattern of depressed periods followed by excitable spells continued for some months. A diagnosis of bipolar manic depressive psychosis was made and Lithium therapy commenced. There was a further excitable spell a year later, followed by a severe depressive episode two years later characterized by severe psychomotor retardation, mutism, and catatonic features. This illness made a good response to antidepressant medication, but she quickly moved into a state of mild elation and at the time of writing has been an inpatient for over six months and continues to show frequent mood swings. Between illnesses she is a sociable, cheerful person with a pleasant, equable temperament who enjoys life and presents no management problems. Her first two illnesses were diagnosed as behavior disorders, but in retrospect were clearly hypomanic episodes. The possibility of the premenstrual syndrome was pursued for nearly a decade despite the failure of hormonal treatment. The true diagnosis was only made after a prolonged period of hospitalization which enabled close observation of her symptomatology and response to treatment. The Dexamethasone Suppression Test was positive during each of the two episodes of severe depression. Interestingly, there is no family history of manic depressive disorder.

Case history #3

MT. is a 47-year old woman of borderline intelligence (IQ 74), married with three children. She suffered her first psychotic breakdown at the age of 28 years and has sub-sequently had 17 illnesses over a period of 16 years. These have varied in clinical presentation from pure depressive illness (5 episodes) pure schizophrenic illness (4 episodes) to mixed states in which both schizophrenic and depressive features were present (9 episodes) and one episode of mild elation. During the depressive episodes she shows classical features with psychomotor retardation, diurnal variation, early morning wakening, and guilt feelings--on one occasion she confessed to the police a minor misdemeanor committed 14 years previously. During the schizophrenic episodes she is hallucinated and deluded, has difficulty in putting her thoughts together, and becomes markedly paranoid, believing that attempts are being made to kill her and that her husband is being unfaithful. In some of the mixed states schizophrenic symptoms predominated, in others, depressive. Four episodes (3 mixed and 1 schizophrenic) were associated with major life events--marriage, hysterectomy, problems with her son, and the death of her father. All of the illnesses were discrete and responded well to either antipsychotic medication, antidepressant medication, or ECT. In between illnesses she is bright, cheerful, capable and coping, and shows no evidence of personality deterioration.

Neurotic depression

Neurotic depression is characterized by a mild depth of depression, the absence of psychotic features, minimal vegetative symptoms, the coexistence of other symptoms of neurosis such as anxiety, hypochondriasis, and obsessions, occurring in the context of social stresses or precipitants and represents a psychologically understandable reaction to stress in individuals with varying degrees of characterological vulnerability (Akiskal, Bitar, Puzantian, Rosenthal, & Walker, 1978). There is no history of elated mood or family predisposition. Understandably, the disorder is often termed reactive depression.

Prevalence

Neurotic disorder has not been well studied in the mentally handicapped and earlier epidemiological studies have generally shown a low prevalence (Forrest, 1979). However, clinical experience and more recent studies (Day, 1985; Lund, 1985; Richardson, Katz, Koller, McLaren, & Rubinstein, 1979) indicate that neurotic disorder is, in fact, quite common and a prominent reason for hospitalization. In a study of psychiatric disorder in mentally handicapped people aged 40 years and over, the author found that neurotic disorder was the diagnostic category in 33% of 43 patients admitted to a psychiatric unit for mentally handicapped adults, but had a low prevalence (3.7%) in 109 long stay residents with psychiatric problems. Eighteen of the total of 19 cases identified were neurotic depression (Day, 1985). In a further analysis of 215 consecutive admissions to the psychiatric unit, neurotic disorder was the cause of admission in 23% of cases, two-thirds of whom were suffering from neurotic depression (Day, in preparation). In no cases was the diagnosis made in a severely mentally handicapped person, and over 80% of cases were functioning in the mild to borderline intellectual range. The expected female preponderance was found, the female to male ratios being 2:1 and 3:1, respectively.

Clinical features

In the absence of any published studies, the author made a detailed study of 26 cases with a diagnosis of neurotic depression admitted to his unit over a period of eight years. Seventeen (65%) were aged between 20 and 40 years at the time of admission, only two were over 60 years and the average age at onset of the first neurotic illness was 35.4 years (range 16-66 years). Symptom frequency is shown in Table 2. The clinical picture presented is similar to that found in non-handicapped populations. **Depressed mood** was very noticeable and evidenced through bouts of weepiness, looking miserable, and frequent complaints of feeling depressed. Mood disorder was usually poorly sustained, fluctuating, labile and reactive, rapidly lifting with a change of environment: in over half of the cases depressive and other symptoms cleared almost immediately following removal from the precipitating circumstances, and admission to the more supportive environment of the hospital. Suicidal ideation occurred in two-thirds and **suicidal attempts** through overdosing or the superficial slashing of wrists were common and, as in the non-handicapped, were sometimes the first event to draw attention to the illness. They were rarely life-threatening and often accompanied by suicidal threats - one man phoned the police and the samaritans to announce his intentions--and often seem to be a "cry for help." Vegetative symptoms were uncommon, with the exception of reduced appetite which occurred in nearly a one-half of the cases. **Anxiety and other neurotic symptoms** were a prominent feature and occurred in two-thirds. Tension, panicky feelings, over-breathing, sweating, pallor, shakiness, and collapse were all common, as were concerns about physical health, headaches, and other bodily aches and pains. In those with markedly obsessional personalities, an increase in repetitive rituals, rumination, and other obsessional behaviors occurred and usually dominated the clinical picture. **Initial insomnia** and **general sleep disturbance,** sometimes with disturbing nightmares, but not early morning wakening was also very common. Although **behavioral problems,** like aggressivity, temper tantrums, and irritability, occurred in a quarter of the cases, they never dominated the clinical picture or caused diagnostic difficulties.

Precipitating factors

One or more precipitating factors were identified in each case and these are listed in Table 4. In nearly one-third of the cases precipitating factors were multiple, as in the example of a young woman who was experiencing marital problems, having difficulty controlling her three children, and whose grandmother with whom she had had an extremely close and supportive relationship had recently died.

Table 8.4
Precipitating events in 26 cases of neurotic depression

Precipitant	No.	%
Death or serious illness remaining caring relative	8	31%
Marital problems	7	27%
Family problems	4	15%
Other domestic problems	3	12%
Ill health	2	8%
Financial	1	4%
Unrequited love	1	4%
Single precipitant	17	65%
Multiple precipitants	9	35%

Sometimes the depressive episode was precipitated by an acute event occurring in a setting of chronic problems - acute financial problems in the presence of chronic marital disharmony and social inadequacy, for example. In yet others, it followed a chain of events as in the case of a middle-aged man, who, after the death of his mother, remained in the parental home by himself with little support, was unable to cope, lost the job he had held for 20 years as a consequence, became socially isolated, ran into financial problems, and had his gas supply cut off.

In one third, the illness followed the **death or serious illness** of a caring relative and a consequent dramatic change in the life situations of previously stable individuals without a past history of psychiatric break-down. This scenario is particularly common in the older age groups and accounted for over half the cases of reactive depression in a study of psychiatric disorder in the middle aged and elderly mentally handicapped (Day, 1985). Potentially preventable, these illnesses highlight the need for good forward planning, to avoid as far as possible a crisis situation, bereavement counseling, and better education of care staff. Cochran, Sran, and Varano (1977) have described a related condition precipitated by a move from one residential facility to another which they term the "Relocation Syndrome."

Relationship and interpersonal problems were the precipitant in over half the cases. A surprisingly large number of patients in the series were married (three men and nine women) and marital disputes were considered to be the precipitating factor in nearly 60% of this age group. Case histories revealed not only chronic marital disharmony, but also chronic coping problems with social inadequacy, mounting debts, and difficulties in dealing with the children. Often the problem was com-pounded by personality problems in the spouse or critical attitudes on the part of a non-handicapped spouse. Although this is not a representative sample, the frequency with which these couples experienced significant problems is noteworthy. Quarrelling within the family, particularly between the handicapped individual and one or other parent, and domestic disputes with neighbors or other hostel residents made up the rest of this group. **Financial and health worries** were uncommon precipitants and there was one case in which a depressive episode in a young man was the consequence of unrequited love.

Diagnosis and differential diagnosis

Diagnosis rarely presents any difficulty. The onset of the illness is usually acute, the patient complains quite openly of depression, has insight into its cause, and there is usually an obvious precipitating event. Atypical presentations are uncommon. Differentiation from **psychotic depression** is usually easy on the basis of reactivity of mood, the presence of other neurotic features, the absence of psychotic and veg-

147

etative features, evidence of a clear precipitant, and absence of a family history. In doubtful cases a negative DST can be helpful. Only one case in the author's series was misdiagnosed initially as psychotic depression. **Anxiety symptoms** and **obsessional behavior** may dominate the clinical picture in some cases and the possibility of an underlying depression in the presence of these symptoms should always be carefully considered.

Natural history and prognosis

A **predisposing personality** was present in all but four of the patients in the study. One third showed clear **neurotic traits** - being described as anxiety prone, shy, and obsessional, and an equal proportion displayed predominantly **hysterical traits** - being attention-seeking, histrionic, emotionally unstable, and touchy, with three showing a mixture of neurotic and hysterical traits. This constitutional predisposition was further evidenced by the finding that two-thirds had a past history and over three-quarters a subsequent history of neurotic illness--in most cases depression, but in some an anxiety neurosis. Two-thirds of the middle-aged and elderly mentally handicapped with neurotic disorder studied by the author also had either a past or subsequent history of neurotic breakdown (Day, 1985).

In the majority of cases the illness was discrete, related to a specific stress, and responded rapidly to treatment, but there were a few individuals in whom neurotic symptoms frequently surfaced or became chronic and who seemed to fall into the category of "characterological depression" described by Akiskal et al (1980). This group were characterized by a high frequency of behavioral problems and overdosing, an early age of onset, and the presence of hysterical traits in the personality. One man under chronic unremitting stress began to use alcohol to relive his symptoms, and eventually became alcohol dependent.

Illustrative case histories

Case history #4

R. is 39, illiterate, and has a full scale IQ of 58. Despite his intellectual limitations he attended normal school and had always managed to obtain employment in a laboring capacity, having held a regular job as a "dustman" for the five years prior to his illness. He had been married for ten years to a woman of average intelligence and they had a 9-year old daughter. He presented with a six month history of depressed mood, irritability, suicidal threats, and a recent overdose triggered by organizational changes at work which required him to fill in time sheets and coincided with the retirement of a friend who had helped him with this. Pre-existing marital problems emerged and his wife became increasingly resentful and critical of his inadequacies, revealing that she had long felt that his job reflected badly on herself and their daughter, and used his illness as an excuse to persuade him to give it up. Serious sexual difficulties developed and R. became impotent for long periods. His depression lifted quickly on admission to hospital where he became calm and relaxed but still lacked self-confidence and had difficulty mixing socially. Efforts directed at improving the marital situation were not particularly success-ful and he showed little inclination to return home, developing hysterical fits when pressed. Eventually after six months in hospital he did return, but the problems continued. His wife, who by now had obtained work and was fulfilling the dual role of housewife and breadwinner, continued to be critical and resentful in her attitude towards him. He remained moody and irritable, taking further overdoses, and on several occasions left her for brief periods. Four years later, however, they were still together, have a second child, his wife appears to have accepted his limitations and he is happily settled in sheltered work.

Case history #5

M. is a moderately mentally handicapped woman with a full scale IQ of 46. She had lived all her life at home with her Jewish parents whose unrealistic views about her capabil-ities contrasted markedly with their over-protective and over-restrictive attitudes towards her care and upbringing. A sensitive girl and easily upset, she was subject to bouts of depression and anxiety for which she received psychiatric outpatient treatment over a number of years. When she was in her early 30s her father suffered a hypertensive stroke and her mother a cardiac arrest during a gynaecological operation, and concern about M's future care led them to explore possible long-term placements for her. She was sent on an introductory basis to a number of private establishments throughout the country, often many miles from her home. She didn't under-stand the real purpose of these visits, which she was told were holidays, and became increasingly unsettled, depressed, and

149

agitated, constantly seeking reassurances that she would not be sent away again. Her sleep pattern was disturbed, her appetite depressed, and she lost weight. She constantly complained of headaches, exhibited marked anxiety symptoms with palpitations, expressed concern about her heart, refused to leave the house, and showed an increase in childish, demanding behavior. She required a lengthy hospital admission during which she was treated with antidepressants and anxiolytics, and her parents were counseled about their handling of the situation. On return home no further pressure was put on her to move and she remained well until the death of her father six months later when her symptoms returned in full. Initially she was treated at home at her mother's request, but soon had to be readmitted in a very depressed state and was eventually permanently placed in a private home where she settled well.

Conclusion

Psychotic and neurotic depression both occur commonly in the mentally handicapped. Psychotic depression occurs with a similar frequency to that in the general population, and neurotic depression is on the increase as mentally handicapped people are increasingly exposed to the normal stresses and strains of everyday life. Both illnesses are easily missed in clinical practice, particularly psychotic depression which may present atypically. Identification depends upon alertness to the possibility, a detailed history, and careful examination and observation.

References

Akiskal, H.S., Bitar, A.H., Puzantian, U.R., Rosenthal, T.L., & Walker, P.W. (1978). The nosological status of neurotic depression. Archives of General Psychiatry, 35, 756-766.

Akiskal, H.S., Rosenthal, T., Haykal, R., Lemmi, H., Rosenthal, R., & Scott-Strauss, A. (1980). Characterological depressions. Archives of General Psychiatry, 37, 777-783.

Ballinger, B.R., Armstrong, J., Presly, A.S., & Reid, A.H. (1975). Use of a standardised psychiatric interview in mentally handicapped patients. British Journal of Psychiatry, 127, 540-544.

Beckwith, B.E., Parker, L., Pawlarczyk, D., Couk, D.I., Schumacher, K.S., & Yearwood, K. (1985). The Dexamethasone Suppression Test in depressed retarded adults. Biological Psychiatry, 20, 825-831.

Benson, B.A., & Laman, D.S. (1988). Suicidal tendencies of mentally retarded adults in community settings. Australia and New Zealand Journal of Developmental Disabilities, 14, 49-54.

Berney, T.P., & Jones, P.M. (1988). Manic depressive disorder in the mentally handicapped. Australia and New Zealand Journal of Developmental Disabilities, 14, 219-225.

Carlson, G. (1979). Affective psychosis in mental retardates. Psychiatric Clinics of North America, 2, 499-510.

Cochran, W.E., Sran, P.K., & Varano, G.A. (1977). The relocation syndrome in mentally retarded individuals. Mental Retardation, 15, 10-12.

Cook, E.G., & Leventhal, B.L. (1987). Down's syndrome with mania. British Journal of Psychiatry, 150, 249-250.

Corbett, J.A. (1979). Psychiatric morbidity and mental retardation. In: James, F.E., Snaith, R.P. (Eds): Psychiatric Illness and mental handicap. Gaskell Press, London.

Day, K.A. (1985). Psychiatric disorder in the middle-aged and elderly mentally handicapped. British Journal of Psychiatry, 147, 660-667.

Feighner, J., Robins, E., Guze, S.B., Woodruff, R.A., Winokur, G., & Munoz, R. (1972). Diagnostic criteria for use in psychiatric research. Archives of General Psychiatry, 26, 57-63.

Forrest, A.D. (1979). Neurosis in the mentally handicapped. In: F.E. James & R.P. Snaith (Eds.), Psychiatric illness and mental handicap. Gaskell Press, London.

Hasan, M.K., & Mooney, R.P. (1979). Three cases of manic depressive illness in mentally retarded adults. American Journal of Psychiatry, 136, 1069-1071.

Hassenyeh, F., & Davison, K. (1980). Bipolar affective psychosis with onset before age of 16 years. Report of 10 cases. British Journal of Psychiatry, 137, 530-539.

Heaton-Ward, A. (1977). Psychosis in mental handicap. British Journal of Psychiatry, 130, 525-533.

Hucker, S.J. (1975). Pubertal manic-depressive psychosis and mental subnormality. British Journal of Mental Subnormality, 21, 34-37.

Hucker, S.J., Day, K.A., George, S., & Roth, M. (1979). Psychosis in mentally handicapped adults. In: F.E. James & R.P. Snaith (Eds.), Psychiatric illness and mental handicap. Gaskell Press, London.

151

Jancar, J. (1979). Organic causes of mental illness in the mentally handicapped. In: F.E. James & R.P. Snaith (Eds.), Psychiatric illness and mental handicap. Gaskell Press, London.

Jones, P., & Berney, T.P. (1987). Early onset rapid cycling bipolar affective disorder. Journal of Child Psychology and Psychiatry, 28(5), 731-738.

Joyce, P.R. (1985). Neuroendocrine changes in depression, a review. Australian and New Zealand Journal of Psychiatry, 19, 120-127.

Kadambari, S.R. (1986). Manic depressive psychosis in a mentally handicapped person: Diagnosis and management. British Journal of Psychiatry, 148, 595-596.

Kazdin, A.E., Matson, J.K., & Senatore, V. (1983). Assessment of depression in mentally retarded adults. American Journal of Psychiatry, 140, 1040-1043.

Keegan, D.L., Pettigrew, A., & Parker, Z. (1974). Psychosis in Down's syndrome treated with Amitriptyline. Canadian Medical Association Journal, 110, 1128-1129.

Kendell, R.E. (1976). The classification of depressions: A review of contemporary confusion. British Journal of Psychiatry, 129, 15-28.

Leck, I., Gordon, W.L., & McKeown, T. (1967). Medical and social needs of patients in hospitals for the mentally subnormal. British Journal of Preventive and Social Medicine, 21, 115-121.

Lund, J. (1985). The prevalence of psychiatric morbidity in mentally retarded adults. Acta Psychiatrica Scandanavica, 72, 563-570.

McLaughlin, M. (1987). Bipolar affective disorder in Down's syndrome. British Journal of Psychiatry, 151, 116-117.

McLoughlin, L.J., & Bhate, M.S. (1987). A case of affective psychosis following bereavement in a mentally handicapped woman. British Journal of Psychiatry, 151, 552-554.

Naylor, G.J., Reid, A.H., Dick, D.A.T., & Dick, E.G. (1976). A biochemical study of short cycle manic depressive psychosis in mental defectives. British Journal of Psychiatry, 128, 169-180.

Oei, T.I. (1988). The Dexamethasone Suppression Test as a variable in clinical diagnosis and research: A review. Journal of the Royal Society of Medicine, 81, 31-33.

Penrose, L.S., (1938). A clinical and genetic study of 1280 cases of mental defect. Special Report Series, Medical Reseach Council no. 229. London: HMSO.

Pirodsky, D.M., Gibbs, J.W., Hesse, R.A., Hsieh, M.C., Krause, R.B., & Rodriguez, W.H. (1985). Use of the Dexamethasone Suppression Test to detect depressive disorders of mentally retarded individuals. American Journal of Mental Deficiency, 90, 254-256.

Pollack, H.M. (1945). Mental disease among mental defectives. American Journal of Mental Deficiency, 49, 447-480.

Reid, A.H. (1972). Psychoses in adult mental defectives. 1. Manic depressive psychosis. British Journal of Psychiatry, 120, 205-212.

Reid, A.H., & Naylor, G.J. (1976). Short cycle manic depressive psychosis in mental defectives: A clinical and physiological study. Journal of Mental Deficiency Research, 20, 67-76.

Reid, A.H., & Leonard, A. (1977). Lithium treatment of cyclical vomiting in a mentally defective patient. British Journal of Psychiatry, 130, 316.

Reid, A.H., Swanson, A.J.S., Jain, A.S., Spowart, G., & Wright, A.F. (1987). Manic depressive psychosis with mental retardation and flexion deformities. British Journal of Psychiatry, 150, 92-97.

Reis, R.K. (1985). DSM-III implications of the diagnosis of catatonia and bipolar disorder. American Journal of Psychiatry, 142, 1471-1474.

Reiss, S., & Szyszko, J. (1983). Diagnostic overshadowing and professional experience with mentally retarded persons. American Journal of Mental Deficiency, 87, 396-402.

Richardson, S.A., Katz, M., Koller, H., McLaren, L., & Rubinstein, B. (1979). Some characteristics of a population of mentally retarded young adults in a British city: A basis for estimating some service needs. Journal of Mental Deficiency Research, 23, 275-283.

Rivinus, T.M., & Harmatz, J.S. (1979). Diagnosis and lithium treatment of affective disorder in the retarded: Five case studies. American Journal of Psychiatry, 136, 551-554.

Roith, A.I. (1961). Psychotic depression in a mongol. Journal of Mental Subnormality, 1, 45-57.

Rubin, R.T. (1985). The prospects for clinical psychoneuroendocrinology: Has the curtain been drawn across the neuroendocrine window? Psychological Medicine, 15, 451-454.

Ruedrich, S.L., Wadle, C.V., Sallach, H.S., Hahn, R.K., & Menolascino, F.J. (1987). Adrenocortical function and depressive illness in mentally retarded patients. American Journal of Psychiatry, 144, 597-602.

Senatore, V., Matson, J.L., & Kazdin, A.E. (1985). An inventory to assess psychopathology of mentally retarded adults. American Journal of Mental Deficiency, 89, 459-466.

Sireling, L. (1986). Depression in mentally handicapped patients: Diagnostic and neuroendocrine evaluation. British Journal of Psychiatry, 149, 274-278.

Slater, E., & Roth, M. (1977). Clinical psychiatry (3rd Ed.). London: Balliere Tindall and Cassell.

Sovner, R. (1986). Limiting factors in the use of DSM-III with mentally ill/mentally retarded persons. Psychopharmacology Bulletin, 22, 1055-1059.

Sovner, R., & Hurley, A. (1982). Suicidal behaviour in mentally retarded persons. Psychiatric Aspects of Mental Retardation Newsletter, 1(10).

Sovner, R., Hurley, A., & Labrie, R. (1985). Is mania incompatible with Down's syndrome? British Journal of Psychiatry, 146, 319-320.

Sternlicht, M., Pustel, G., & Deutsch, M.R. (1970). Suicidal tendencies among institutionalised retardates. Journal of Mental Subnormality, 16, 93-102.

Szymanski, L.S., & Biederman, J. (1984). Depression and anorexia nervosa of persons with Down's syndrome. American Journal of Mental Deficiency, 89, 246-251.

Warren, A.C., Holroyd, S., & Folstein, F. (1989). Major depression in Down's syndrome. British Journal of psychiatry, 155, 202-205.

Wright, E.C. (1982). The presentation of mental illness in mentally retarded adults. British Journal of Psychiatry, 141, 496-502.

Anton Dosen and Frank J. Menolascino (Eds.) (1990). Depression in mentally retarded children and adults. Leiden, the Netherlands: Logon Publications. ISBN 90-73197-01-5

Chapter 9

The challenge of depression and suicide in severely mentally retarded adults

Frank J. Menolascino, M.D.
Martin A. Weiler, M.D.

Introduction

Although standard DSM-III-R (1987) criteria are typically used to diagnose depression, presenting symptomatology in retarded adults will often differ from normal IQ groups due to the reduced cognitive abilities of the mentally handicapped as well as the inability of many to verbally express themselves. As in all diagnostic transactions, uncertainty will increase when language is poor, when there is a general lack of direct personal information (particularly of subjective states), and when more reliance has to be placed upon overt behavior of equivocal diagnostic significance. For example, rather than verbally expressing an emotion of hopelessness, the more severely retarded person will often express such feelings by withdrawing, behaving aggressively, or through a manifestation of atypical somatic signs (Berman, 1967; Hasan & Mooney, 1979). In addition, clinical histories are often shaped by caretakers' behavioral observations rather than by the subjective declarations of the individual patient. Thus, there is an increased risk that the clinician may stray from focusing on symptom clusters suggestive of known psychiatric disorders, and concentrate instead on what is seen to be "self-injurious" or "non-compliant" behavior (Menolascino, Levitas & Gilson, 1986). To further complicate matters, Ross and Rush (1981) have noted that some depressed individuals with right hemisphere vascular lesions simply do not exhibit depressed mood since this defect exists in brain areas which mediate emotional expression. Still, psychotic symptoms or psychotic-like functional impairments remain commonly observed manifestations of depression in the mentally retarded, leaving open the possibility that one may misdiagnose such symptoms as "organic psychosis" or "schizophrenia" and allow the affective disorders to remain untreated. Clearly, the presence of an affective illness in a mentally retarded individual poses major differential diagnostic challenges.

Differential diagnosis of psychiatric disorders in mentally retarded adults

Affective disorders and schizophrenia

A diagnosis of schizophrenia in the severely retarded adult is extremely difficult to establish since it is so heavily dependent upon criteria derived from verbal and social interactions; aspects not typical of this group. If schizophrenia is suspected, however, it is important to base such a diagnosis upon **all** DSM-III-R criteria since many mentally retarded people experience, as a part of their normal functioning, extreme wariness in new situations, avoidance of eye contact, and auditorization of thought. It is additionally important to secure a complete history from all available sources so as to document any episodes of exacerbation, remission, and stepwise deterioration of functioning (Parsons, May & Menolascino, 1984).

In an effort to distinguish between the manifestations of schizophrenia and those of depression in the non-verbal retarded adult, Sovner (1986) has suggested that the affective disorders can serve as a foundation for diagnoses not based on verbal criteria. Neuro-vegetative features and specific responses to anti-manic therapy, for example, can make the affective disorders relatively easy to diagnose, even in the severely retarded. Table 9.1 illustrates this distortion-free approach to both the major affective disorders (i.e., bipolar and major depression) and schizophrenia (Menolascino, 1988).

Because clinical presentation is often confounded by cognitive disintegration, it may be difficult to find four diagnosis-specific symptoms even when an affective disorder is strongly suspected. A positive history for an affective disorder in a first-degree relative can, therefore, be utilized to reduce the number of symptoms required. In these instances, it is proposed that only **three** of the symptoms listed in Table 9.1 are needed to confirm a diagnosis of depression in the severely retarded patient. The strong genetic component reported in affective disorders (Winokur, 1978) and the presence of such disorders in first-degree family members of many symptomatic mentally retarded persons (Carlson, 1979) underscores the value of a positive family history for increased sensitivity to this diagnostic challenge.

156

Table 9.1
Diagnosis of major affective disorders and schizophrenia in the mentally retarded

Mania (Sovner, 1986)	Schizophrenia (Menolascino, 1988)	Major depression (Sovner, 1986)
I.	I.	I.
A disturbance of mood characterized by elation, irritability, or excitability	Disturbance of thought and feeling(s) characterized by personality disorganization, bizarre behaviors and social/ adaptive regression	A disturbance of mood characterized by sadness, withdrawal, or agitation
II.	II.	II.
Any 4* of the following 7 symptoms:	Any 4* of the following 8 symptoms:	Any 4* of the following 9 symptoms:
- decreased sleep - overactivity - biphasic course - onset of distractibility - increase in severity of distractibility - onset of non-compliance - increase in severity of non-compliance * Only 3 symptoms needed if there is a positive history of bipolar disorder in a first-degree relative	- flat, blunted or incongruous affect - marked personal/ interpersonal withdrawal - regression in self-care, social and work skills - behaves as if hallucinated - prodromal of marked isolation, withdrawal, or anergia - markedly suspicious/ paranoid (failure to attend; non-compliant) - schizo-affective, unipolar depression, and bipolar affective disturbance have been ruled out - duration of 6 months (R/O reactive psychosis) * Only 3 symptoms needed if there is a positive history of schizophrenia in a first-degree relative	- change in sleep - change in appetite and/or weight - onset or increase in severity of self-injurious behavior - apathy - psychomotor retardation - loss of activity of daily living skills, e.g. onset of urinary incontinence - catatonic stupor and/or rigidity - spontaneous crying - fearfulness * Only 3 symptoms needed if there is a positive history of depression in a first-degree relative.

157

There have been a number of clinical reports over the years which have noted an association between catatonia and mental retardation (Earl, 1934; Keegan, Pettigrew & Parker, 1974; Rollin, 1946; Zlotlow & Kleiner, 1965), and there is a preponderance of recent evidence that catatonia is often a sign of an affective disorder as opposed to schizophrenia (Reis, 1985).In addition, it has been reported that many mentally retarded persons exhibit catatonic signs which are directly related to an antidepressant-responsive affective illness (Sovner, 1986). Accordingly, catatonia can also be utilized as a sign of the presence of a significant depressive illness in the mentally retarded.

As Table 9.1 makes clear, the confident differentiation between a bipolar disorder and schizophrenia in the mentally retarded demands that one carefully delineate the clinical significance of all presenting symptoms of psychosis. For example, isolated symptoms of schizophrenia (i.e., auditory hallucinations and delusions) occur in about 20% of well-validated cases of bipolar affective disorders (Pope & Lipinski, 1978). Thus, the presence of "schizophrenic" symptoms in a mentally retarded adult should caution the clinician to further explore whether any of the following associated components were present at onset:

1) euphoria or increased irritability coupled with motor overactivity;
2) pressure of speech;
3) a distinct sleep disorder; or
4) relevant biological markers, such as an altered EEG sleep analysis or Dexamethasone Suppression Test (Ruedrich, Wadle, Sallach, Hahn & Menolascino, 1987).

Accordingly, the differential diagnosis of a psychotic disorder in a severely retarded individual should embrace a close review of both the apparent and the possible clinical picture(s) of depression. Biphasic course is a classic sign of bipolar illness and one that can be observed in mentally retarded persons irrespective of the severity of their disabilities (Reid, 1976; Wallace, 1983).

Although the features of major depression which follow also apply directly to bipolar disorders in the mentally retarded, the regimentation and restrictions placed upon the lives of retarded people can serve to effectively camouflage mania. For example, sexual promiscuity may simply consist of visits to topless bars or single episodes with strangers or friends. Grandiosity will often take the form of an insistence that one is not retarded, or that one can do something clearly beyond one's capabilities or training. Unfortunately, such grandiosity may be erroneously attributed to poor judgement due to retardation, and the irritability which often follows these episodes may simply be dismissed as "non-compliant" behavior. The clinician should, therefore, be alert to sudden increases in sociability, productivity, energy, and interest in unattainable goals, all of which additionally risk misinterpretation as gratifying responses to recently initiated program interventions (Menolascino, Levitas & Gilson, 1986).

Major depression and the risk of suicide

The following guidelines have been suggested by the *Psychiatric Aspects of Mental Retardation Newsletter* (1982) as methods for increasing sensitivity to the actual risk of suicide among the mentally retarded:
1) differentiation between suicidal gestures and self-injurious behavior, which often has its roots in self-stimulation or attention-seeking;
2) description of suicide attempts in terms of intent and lethality;
3) determination of the future risk for suicide based on past personal and clinical histories of the individual being evaluated; and
4) analysis and treatment of the underlying psychiatric diagnosis.

For the mentally retarded adult, the emotions of guilt, despair, and helplessness may be expressed in terms of fears that one's family and friends no longer care or feel affection for the individual. Often, however, the withdrawal and quieting associated with depression may be entirely missed by caretakers or, worse, viewed as desireable. Sadness may be misinterpreted as an inevitable or appropriate response to mental retardation or to some loss of self-esteem. In addition, the vegetative signs, like the symptoms of mania in bipolar disorders, may be submerged in a regimented lifestyle. For example, the retarded adult may come to all meals and be put to bed or sent to work at the usual times, but changes in appetite, energy levels, sleep patterns, and recreational interests can clearly emerge and may be confirmed by the patient, caretakers, or family. Suicidal ideation may take the form of increased fearfulness, clinging dependence, mimicry of a suicidal act, or drawings suggestive of death and burial (Menolascino et al., 1986 - see Figure 9.1). Still, very little has been reported about suicidal behavior when it presents as a distinct sign of affective illness in the mentally retarded. Only two studies have explored this problem (Kaminer, Feinstein & Barett, 1987; Sternlicht, Pustel & Deutsch, 1970), one of which involved 45 mentally retarded persons who had attempted suicide at the Willowbrook State Developmental Center in Staten Island, New York.

Table 9.2
Overview of case vignettes

Patient	Psychiatric Diagnosis	Level of Mental Retardation	Presenting Problems
1	Depressive disorder; Chronic paranoid with schizophrenia.	Severe	Self-inflicted wounds. Drawings with suicidal themes. Reacts to stress with explosive and runaway behavior.
2	Major unipolar depression.	Severe	Attention-seeking. Property destruction. Self-abuse. Self-inflicted wounds.
3	Adjustment reaction of adulthood; Severe depression.	Severe	Temper tantrums. Suicidal ideations.
4	Bipolar affective disorder.	Severe	Destruction of property. Suicidal gestures. Drug overdose.
5	Depressive disorder; Chronic paranoid schizophrenia.	Severe	Crying spells. Auditory hallucinations.
6	Major unipolar depression.	Severe	Manipulative behaviors. Weight loss. Suicidal actions and ideations.

The mean IQ of the individuals studied was 55, with a range extending from 16 to 79. There were no completed suicide attempts in this study group, and the causes were reported as non-specific (Sternlicht, Pustel & Deutsch, 1970). Consequently, this chapter will focus on the experiences we have had with depressive disorders in severely retarded individuals who also presented with suicide manifestations.

Table 9.2 displays a brief summary of six severely retarded individuals (drawn from a sample of 105 mentally retarded-mentally ill persons who were examined and treated in an inpatient psychiatric facility during a twelve-month period) who received active psychiatric care for affective disorders. These individuals ranged from 25 to 48 years of age, some of whom had histories of psychiatric difficulties within the realm of major affective disorders. Most of these individuals had made documented suicide attempts involving self-inflicted wounds, proprietary drug overdoses, or ingestion of toxic materials. The average length of inpatient treatment was 28 days.

Case vignette 1

Cheryl was a 32-year-old severely retarded woman who was employed in a sheltered workshop and lived in a nearby group home. She had attended special education classes until the age of 21. Upon graduation, her parents, who had frequently given in to her demands, opted for community placement. Family history was negative for any affective disorders.

Cheryl was admitted for acute psychiatric care following a third unsuccessful suicide attempt. Her two previous attempts had involved chewing on a connected electrical cord and drinking a large can of cleaning fluid. She had had two prior psychiatric hospitalizations (discharge diagnosis was Paranoid Schizophrenia) during the previous five years because of these suicide attempts, but continued to experience prolonged episodes of withdrawal and persistently refused to participate in school and work programs. Her most recent admission for psychiatric care resulted after she had severely lacerated her left wrist and right lateral neck region with a broken bottle. She was unable to speak very well or very fluently due to both severe mental retardation and cerebral palsy, but she drew pictures in the admission interview and mimicked behavior which clearly conveyed her desire to kill herself (see Figure 9.1).

Cheryl's psychiatric status presented a complex picture of a schizophrenic, aggressive personality coupled with reactive depression. Yet her depressive features diminished within three days of hospitalization as she responded to a combination of neuroleptic medication, individual psychotherapy, and social role-modeling techniques.

Currently, treatment and management consist of structuring her life both residentially and vocationally so that few, if any, novel or stressful situations occur; role-modeling for self-esteem in order to prevent the negative cycle of interpersonal confusion, anger, and withdrawal; and teaching her, with the help of individual counseling, how to work out any recurring problems. She has had no relapses for nearly three years.

Figure 9.1
Drawings of three mentally retarded patients with depressive disorders

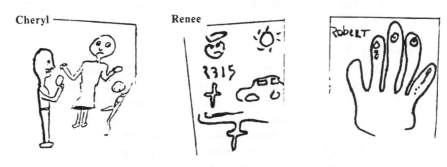

Case vignette 2

Shirley was a 48-year-old severely retarded woman who regularly attended a sheltered workshop and lived in an apartment with off-site staff support. She had previously lived with her parents until their deaths, at which time she was placed in a nursing home for a period of fifteen years. She was then moved into a semi-independent apartment where she received one hour of staff supervision each evening. It was reported that she enjoyed attending workshop and social functions, but that she persistently craved increasing amounts of affection. Her workshop staff then noted an elevation in attention-seeking behaviors when she felt that her needs were not being adequately addressed. Self-abusive behaviors grew frequent, and on two occasions she became violent and destroyed the furniture in her apartment. She began losing weight and her sleep pattern became one of mid-sleep awakening. Shirley was admitted for psychiatric care when, in the midst of a screaming episode, she attempted to amputate her left large toe.

Upon admission, she was noted to display multiple indices of a major unipolar depression, and family history revealed a recurrent depressive disorder in first-degree family members. Her Dexamethasone Suppression Test, which was considered to be valid despite concurrent treatment for a grand mal convulsive disorder (Ruedrich, Wadle, Sallach, Hahn & Menolascino, 1987), was positive. A combined approach of antidepressant medications, individual and group psychotherapy, and active participation in OT and RT helped her to become more accepting in interpersonal transactions, and less withdrawn and bizarre.

Upon discharge, Shirley interacted quite well with others and her previously noted florid and psychotic behaviors were minimal. Yet considering the danger that she could again become despondent without adequate and ongoing emotional support, it was recommended that she receive increased, active, and consistent supervision in both residential and vocational settings, particularly from evening staff. Such support was strongly encouraged since experience has shown that if it is not, a repeated suicide attempt is frequently the result. In this case, however, Shirley was found dead in her bathtub fifteen months after discharge. The possible cause -- a seizure, a volitional act, or an accident -- was never clarified.

Case vignette 3

Joanne was a 44-year-old severely retarded woman with poorly controlled insulin-dependent diabetes mellitus. She had been assessed as legally blind at the age of 39 (diabetic retinopathy), and her emotional adjustment had consistently been one of dysphoria and a quiet, lonely orientation toward the interpersonal world. She had maintained a relatively stable and productive life in a sheltered workshop, which she had attended for over ten years, and with her mother, with whom she lived until two weeks prior to hospitalization. During these two weeks, she resided in a foster home because her mother, due to her own serious somatic illness, could no longer care for Joanne.

Her reaction after placement in the foster home was extremely negative. She became highly aggressive toward her foster parents and to those around her at the workshop, complained of not wanting to live anymore (i.e., "me die," "me go sleep"), and persistently refused to take her insulin. As a result of these behaviors, her aggressiveness increased in frequency and her diabetic status deteriorated rapidly. Upon admission for psychiatric care, she was noted to be seriously hypoglycemic and in an advanced stage of renal failure.

Although Joanne's chronic disorders were long-standing in nature, they were separate from, but exacerbated by, a concurrent psychiatric disorder of severe depression. Themes of loss, abandonment by her mother, and marked irritability, against a personality backdrop of pervasive depression, were noted in the clinical psychiatric assessment. Although she refused assessment for dialysis therapy, she eventually, with the aid of supportive psychotherapy, began to take her insulin. Her depression did abate somewhat, yet she obstinately persisted in wishing to return to live with her infirm and elderly mother. Her foster mother, a nurse, was prepared and able to effectively deal with Joanne's emotional status and serious medical conditions. Yet three months after discharge from psychiatric care, Joanne died from chronic renal failure.

Case vignette 4

Renee was a 34-year-old severely retarded woman who lived in a group home and was employed in a sheltered workshop. She suddenly became combative one afternoon while at home and began fighting and breaking windows. She displayed similar behaviors in the hospital emergency room and again, the following day, in a local gas station, after which she was taken to jail. When she returned to her workshop the next day, she repeatedly displayed aggressive and destructive behaviors and, two days later, overdosed on her neuroleptic medication and was admitted for psychiatric assessment.

In the initial interview it was noted that she continuously slouched over in her chair, had a sad facial expression, and was only passively cooperative. Her mood was depressed, psychomotor activity was very slowed, and she frequently mimicked suicidal gestures, such as finger "stabs" to the chest, choking, etc. The diagnostic challenge involved in Renee's case was to determine whether her recent aggression and suicide attempt were merely manipulative or clear manifestations of a major affective disorder.

Clinical analysis clearly revealed a cyclic bipolar disorder, confirmed by a positive family history of bipolar affective illness. Renee responded well to lithium carbonate therapy and, as she grew less depressed and her behavior became more stable and predictable, she began to look forward to individual and group therapy activities. Both her group home and workshop initiated our recommendations for more tightly structured home, work, and recreational programs at discharge, as well as regularly scheduled appointments for individual counseling and medication monitoring. Renee currently attends an outpatient clinic regularly, understands the need to take her medication on a regular basis, and has learned to relate more directly to supportive individuals in her environment. She has had no further aggressive behaviors or suicidal ideations since her discharge over two years ago.

Case vignette 5

Robert was a severely retarded 28-year-old man who lived in a small group home and was employed in a sheltered work station. He had previously received inpatient care for severe depression and/or chronic symptoms of schizophrenia on at least four occasions. Although he periodically attended a Day Hospital program for milieu and group therapy, he was becoming increasingly frustrated at work and would often walk away from the job or feign illness.

At the request of his housemother, Robert was again admitted for psychiatric care because of crying spells which were increasing in frequency. He was also noted to have both typical and atypical auditory hallucinations; command delusions which repeatedly ordered him to kill himself and instances wherein he would go to the wall, listen intently, and then smile in a knowing fashion. His spontaneous drawings, one of which is reproduced in Figure 9.1, repeatedly reflected the theme of watching eyes. The diagnosis was a depressive episode in a severely retarded individual within the context of chronic paranoid schizophrenia.

Robert was initiated on Norpramine and his auditory hallucinations and suicidal ideation began to subside during the initial ten days of hospitalization. He progressed well during the following week, gradually eliminating all suicidal ideations as the depressive reaction diminished.

165

He eventually agreed to participate actively in a Day Hospital program for ongoing medication monitoring, individual therapy, and group counseling after discharge. Robert has remained emotionally stable within this supportive daily treatment program for two years.

Case vignette 6

Kathy was a severely retarded 25-year-old woman with cerebral palsy who had been residing in a state mental retardation institution for 14 years before moving into a supervised apartment with three other mentally retarded women. She had been referred for outpatient psychiatric care on several previous occasions for depression symptomatology, and had once received inpatient psychiatric treatment because of a serious suicide attempt. She was again admitted for acute psychiatric care because she was increasingly indicating, through both mime and drawings, a wish to kill herself. She cried a great deal, refused to attend her workshop program, spent most of her time alone, and had experienced a distinct decrease in weight during the previous five-month period.

During her initial inpatient hospitalization, she refused **all** treatment and her counselor, advocate, and guardian each agreed with her right to do so. She was subsequently discharged A.M.A. to her apartment, and it was arranged for a community volunteer to visit with her for six hours each week in an attempt to provide outgoing, personalized companionship and emotional support. Nevertheless, she continued to withdraw, her weight decreased at a steady pace, and she persisted in her refusal to attend her sheltered workshop. Community staff felt that she had the right to decide whether or not to go to work, even though it was obvious that a choice not to do so only encouraged increased withdrawal and loneliness. Her counselor also allowed her to choose whether or not to participate in community activities, with similar consequences. As a result, she spent most of her time alone in her apartment and withdrew even more.

At what point does individual choice, in this case the right not to participate, conflict with the need for active intervention? We felt strongly that if Kathy failed to receive energetic treatment and support, she would become more acutely depressed and possibly complete a suicide. Thus, her clinical management consisted of the following steps:

1) Inpatient psychiatric care was initiated which involved daily individual therapy;

2) A direct and concrete approach was taken of **not** offering choices, but rather of convincing Kathy to participate in ongoing treatment programs and leisure time activities;

3) A community counselor was assigned to spend 20 hours per week with her so as to engage her in regularly scheduled community activities -- again, no choice was given;

4) A tricyclic antidepressant was initiated and slowly increased in dosage.

As a result of these initiatives, Kathy began attending her programs on a full-time basis and participated in a number of recreational activities. She made a friend in the mental health therapy group she attended, commented only rarely on negative aspects of herself or others, and presented a markedly more positive affect overall. She dressed neatly and her past subjective complaints of somatic illnesses were no longer in evidence. By the third week of hospitalization she had gained eight pounds and had a perfect record of workshop attendance. After discharge, her community counselor continued to provide approximately ten hours of support per week by assisting her in money management, helping her to plan specific leisure time activities, and ensuring that her diet was adequate.

Professional implications

Diagnostic challenges

The above six case vignettes reflect a range of psychiatric disorders which either directly caused or exacerbated suicidal phenomena; phenomena which could not have been directly addressed apart from an understanding (and treatment) of underlying causes. In Kathy's case, for example, it was determined that she had had a depressive disorder for over two years, although the characteristics of this depressive syndrome were not of sufficient severity to meet the criteria of a major depressive episode. The manifestations of her dysthymic disorder occurred periodically, often around the time of interpersonal crisis, and would last from several days to two weeks. During these depressive periods she would have marked mood swings, lose interest in workshop attendance, and reject recreational opportunities. As her self-esteem diminished, her productivity would drop and she would become tearful and withdrawn. The frequency of these depressive episodes seriously affected her ability to function, and suicidal ideation resulted.

Cheryl, however, presented a more complex diagnostic challenge involving both a previous history of paranoid schizophrenia and allied dysphoria. Stubborn refusal was her reaction to almost all demands placed on her, including attendance at vocational programs and most social functions. Such behavior was more than merely oppositional since she would infringe on the rights of others in order to get her own way. She presented a blunted affect, command delusions, and a persistent history of persecutory behaviors. It appeared that her mental retardation exacerbated her co-existing mental illness, both of which presented major obstacles to the processing of abstract information. Counseling, therefore, had to be direct, concrete, and to the point.

Treatment challenges

In our clinical experience, the most common treatment modalities in the acute care of severe depression in severely retarded persons involves:

1) short-term inpatient care so as to further analyze and manage underlying disorders and to prevent further suicide attempts;
2) intensive individual and group counseling for teaching new ways of venting emotions;
3) renewed engagement in appropriate social interactions through the redirection of maladaptive behaviors;
4) counseling with family and/or service staff members so as to provide an understanding of past and current clinical challenges and to plan for a successful return to previous placement settings;
5) the use of antidepressant medications to treat entrenched depressive disorders.

Treatment of depression in the mentally retarded, when compared with normal IQ groups, tends to be complicated more often by medication side effects. Based on our clinical experience, depressed mentally retarded patients are more prone to confusional states or agitation produced by anticholinergic action. They seem to be more sensitive to the activating influences of antidepressants with adrenergic potentiating properties, which may lead to agitation and tendencies toward overt psychoses, whether organic or functionally mediated.

Such considerations strongly suggest that antidepressant medication should be utilized with more clinical caution in depressed mentally retarded patients than in the general patient population. Similar to our experiences in treating schizophrenia in the mentally retarded with major neuroleptics (Menolascino, Ruedrich, Golden & Wilson, 1985), dosages of the major antidepressants have been between 50% and 75% of what we typically administer to nonretarded individuals with similar types of depressive illness. The newer antidepressants, in which serotonergic activity predominates, may be better alternatives to many of the traditional tricyclic antidepressants, particularly if they are low in anticholinergic side effects.

As shown in Table 9.2, each severely retarded individual presented significant psychiatric problems, and both the suicide ideations and attempts were secondary to these disorders. Appropriate treatment was not simply a matter of controlling acute aspects of presenting clinical problems (e.g., a suicide attempt), but of dealing directly with chronic psychiatric disorders.

Management challenges

An additional dimension involved in caring for depressed mentally retarded patients involves the need in each case to ensure that adequate and ongoing support is provided upon discharge. Most often this means that in order to maintain a stable emotional adjustment, major changes have to be made in the amount of support each person receives. Such recommendations are occasionally met with resistance because they are viewed as movements toward more "restrictive" models of management. The issue, however, is not one of restriction. It is rather a question of the amount of **emotional** support that a severely retarded individual requires, even if he or she may appear to possess acceptable levels of self-help, vocational, and social skills. The cognitive restrictions, frequent absence of language, and at-risk nature of social-adaptive behaviors in the severely retarded makes these individuals prone to the development of psychiatric disorders.

Most of the mentally retarded adults described herein had initially received appropriate staff support, but this was invariably decreased over the twelve- to eighteen-month period prior to hospitalization due to an apparent "stabilization" of behavior. Quiet and passive behavior was, ironically, viewed as a rationale for not providing strong and ongoing support. As a result, these individuals became increasingly lonely and were often left to emotionally fend for themselves. Such a series of events typically led to sharp increases in withdrawn, depressive postures and, eventually, suicide ideations and attempts.

169

As cities and towns begin to integrate more persons with mental retardation into the mainstreams of family and community life, there is an inherent danger that many of these individuals will have difficulty maintaining their emotional well-being. It is unfortunate that the common program guideline for assessing the possibility of independent placement tends to be based solely upon an evaluation of adaptive abilities such as self-care, daily living, and vocational skills. As our case studies demonstrate, however, these placement guidelines often do not appropriately address the totality of the psychological well-being of the severely retarded (Stark, Menolascino, Albarelli & Gray, 1987). The psychiatric at-risk nature of the mentally retarded cannot be overlooked. These individuals very often require more support, not less, if they are to regain and maintain their emotional balance.

Conclusion

Few reports on affective disorders in the mentally retarded have appeared in professional literature, although it is known that the full range of such disorders are found (Duncan, Penrose & Turnbull, 1936; Heaton-Ward, 1977; Herskovitz & Plessett, 1941; Matson, 1982; Matson, Dettling & Senatore, 1980; Reid, 1976; Sovner & Hurley, 1983). Although the affective disorders are rapidly becoming the most treatable of major psychiatric diagnoses, they can also be the most easily missed in the mentally retarded. Thus, when diagnosing mentally retarded persons with minimal or no expressive language, it is important for the clinician to focus more closely on levels of motor activity, sleep and weight patterns, objective changes in affect, detailed family histories, and whatever information can be obtained from other involved individuals. With the severely mentally retarded in particular, we are at risk for under-diagnosis, as well as for the employment of non-specific behavioral approaches to a biologically based disorder.

The current dilemma associated with community placement involves the differentiation between a retarded citizen's ability to live independently relative to functional self-care and his or her need for a high level of ongoing emotional support. It is important, therefore, that communities be equipped to reintegrate the mentally retarded while providing them with the supports necessary to maintain emotional stability. In such circumstances, it often becomes necessary to recommend that a move be made from an isolated apartment to a small group home; that there be increased interpersonal structure in that group home; or that more on-site staff support be consistently and energetically provided.

References

Berman, M.I. (1967). Mental retardation and depression. Mental Retardation, 5, 19-21.

Carlson, G.A. (1979). Affective psychoses in mental retardates. Psychiatric Clinics North America, 2, 499-510.

Diagnostic and statistical manual of mental disorders, Vol. III-R. (1987). Washington, D.C.: American Psychiatric Association.

Duncan, A.C., Penrose, L. & Turnbull, R. (1936). Mental deficiency and manic depressive insanity. Journal of Mental Science, 82, 635-641.

Earl, C.J.C. (1934). The primitive catatonic psychosis of idiocy. British Journal of Medical Psychology, 14, 230-253.

Hasan, M.R. & Mooney, R.P. (1979). Three cases of manic-depressive illness in mentally retarded adults. American Journal of Psychiatry, 136, 1069-1071.

Heaton-Ward, A. (1977). Psychosis in mental handicap. British Journal of Psychiatry, 130, 533.

Herskovitz, H. & Plessett, B.R. (1941). Psychosis in adult mental defectives. Psychiatric Quarterly, 15, 575.

Kaminer, Y., Feinstein, C. & Barett, R.P. (1987). Suicidal behavior in mentally retarded adolescents: An overlooked problem. Child Psychiatry and Human Development. 18, 2, 19-94.

Keegan, D.L., Pettigrew, A. & Parker, Z. (1974). Psychosis in Down's syndrome treated with amitriptyline. Canadian Medicine Association Journal, 110, 1128-1129.

Matson, J.L. (1982). Depression in the mentally retarded: A review. Education and Training of the Mentally Retarded, 17(8), 159-162.

Matson, J.L., Dettling, J. & Senatore, V. (1980). Treating depression of a mentally retarded adult. British Journal of Mental Subnormality, 16, 86-88.

Menolascino, F.J. (1988). Syndromes of depression in persons with severe mental retardation. In: A. Dosen & P. Engelen (Eds.) Depression in the Mentally Retarded: Practical Issues for Diagnosis and Treatment - Proceedings of the International Symposium. Ede, Netherlands: Postacademisch Onderwijs Sociale Wetenschappen.

Menolascino, F.J., Levitas, A. & Gilson, S.F. (1986). Issues in the treatment of mentally retarded patients in the community mental health system. Community Mental Health Journal, 22, 324-327, 1986.

Menolascino, F.J., Ruedrich, S.L., Golden, C.J. & Wilson, J.E. (1985). Diagnosis and pharmacotherapy of schizophrenia in the retarded. Psychopharmacology Bulletin, 21, 316-322.

Parsons, J A., May, J.G. & Menolascino, F.J. (1984). The nature and incidence of mental illness in mentally retarded individuals. In F.J. Menolascino & J.A. Stark (Eds.), Handbook of mental illness in the mentally retarded. New York: Plenum Press.

Pope, H. & Lipinski, J. (1978). Depression in schizophrenia and manic-depressive illness: A reassessment of the specificity of schizophrenic symptoms in the light of current research. Archives of General Psychiatry, 35(7), 811-828.

Psychiatric Aspects of Mental Retardation Newsletter (1982). Suicidal behavior in mentally retarded persons, 1(10), 1-4.

Reid, A.H. (1976). Psychiatric disturbances in the mentally handicapped. Proceedings of the Royal Society of Medicine, 69, 509-512.

Reis, R.K. (1985). DSM-III: Implications of the diagnoses of catatonia and bipolar disorder. American Journal of Psychiatry 142, 1471-1474.

Rollin, H.R. (1946). Personality in mongolism with special reference to the incidence of catatonic psychosis. American Journal of Mental Deficiency 51, 219-237.

Ross, E.D. & Rush, A.J. (1981). Diagnosis and neuroanatomical correlates of depression in brain-damaged patients. Archives of General Psychiatry, 38, 1344-1354.

Ruedrich, S.L., Wadle, C.V., Sallach, H.S., Hahn, R.C. & Menolascino, F.J. (1987). Adrenocortical function and depressive illness in mentally retarded patients. American Journal of Psychiatry, 144(5), 597-602.

Sovner, R. (1986). Limiting factors in the use of DSM-III criteria with mentally ill/mentally retarded persons. Psychopharmacology Bulletin, 22(4), 1055-1059.

Sovner, R., & Hurley, A.D. (1983). Do the mentally retarded suffer from affective illness? Archives of General Psychiatry, 40, 61-67.

Stark, J.A., Menolascino, F.J., Albarelli, M.H. & Gray, V.C. (1987). Mental retardation and mental health: Classification, diagnosis, treatment, services. New York: Springer-Verlag.

Sternlicht, M., Pustel, G. & Deutsch, M. (1970). Suicidal tendencies among institutionalized retardates. Journal of Mental Subnormality, 16, 93-102.

Wallace, J.G. (1983). Affective disorders in the mentally retarded. American Journal of Psychiatry 140, 1539-1540.

Winokur, G. (1978). Mania and depression: Family studies and genetics in relation to treatment. In: Lipton, M., DiMascio, A., and Kellam, F. (Eds.) Psychopharmacology: A Generation of Progress. New York: Raven Press, 1213-1222.

Zlotlow, M. & Kleiner, S. (1965). Catatonic schizophrenia associated with tuberous sclerosis. Psychiatric Quarterly 39, 466-475.

Anton Dosen and Frank J. Menolascino (Eds.) (1990). Depression in mentally retarded children and adults. Leiden, the Netherlands: Logon Publications. ISBN 90-73197-01-5

Chapter 10

Bipolar disorder in persons with developmental disorders: an overview

Robert Sovner, M.D.

Introduction

Bipolar disorder (BP-DIS) is an important differential diagnosis for developmentally disabled persons suffering from depression. In the light of recent advances in treatment (Prien & Gelenberg, 1989; Sachs, 1989), the presence of manic features in a handicapped individual with a psychiatric disorder strongly increases the chance of achieving a complete symptom remission, even for atypical disorders such as rapid cycling illness (Sovner, 1989). However, the recognition of the biphasic nature of the disorder can be a daunting problem.

The detection of diagnostically concordant features of BP-DIS in the developmentally disabled is greatly affected by two phenomena. First, the handicapped person's often undifferentiated and global maladaptive stress responses (e.g., self-injury as an attempt to regulate overarousal) make it difficult to determine if BP-DIS signs and symptoms are present (Carlson, 1979; 1981; Hucker, Day, George & Roth, 1979; Sovner & Hurley, 1983; Sovner, 1986; Sovner & Pary, in press Szymanski & Biederman, 1984).

Second, there is the difficulty in obtaining an adequate history directly from the patient due to impaired communication skills and the ability to think abstractly (Sovner, 1986).

Traditional psychiatric diagnostic tools (mental status examination and clinical history derived form patient self-reports) must be replaced with more relevant methodologies (such as serial objective data collection of rates of maladaptive behavior).

The spectrum of manic syndromes in developmentally disabled persons

Clinical features

In this section, the salient clinical features of BP-DIS in the developmentally disabled are reviewed. The emphasis will be on the phenomenology of mania and how to recognize the spectrum of manic subsyndromes which can be diagnosed in this population, even the presence of other sources of psychopathology, e.g. autism.

Typical manic features can be observed in developmentally disabled persons (Carlson, 1981; Hucker et al, 1979; Reid, 1972). They will most likely be observed in higher functioning patients with good expressive language and an opportunity to function independently.

As in non-handicapped persons, the predominant disturbance in mania is pervasive overactivity (DSM-III-R, 1987). Pacing may be a behavioral equivalent (Rivinus & Harmatz, 1979). Boistrousness or excitment rather than classic euphoria may be the predominant mood state. Manic euphoria may be less infectious than that observed in not handicapped persons or be mistaken for silliness.

Also characteristic are a decreased need for sleep, pressured vocalizations (even in the absence of intelligible speech), and distractibility. The presence of a sleep disorder may only be discerned when the nightly sleep pattern is objectively monitored. However, differentiating insomnia from a decreased need for sleep can be problematic (is the patient trying to sleep, but can't, or just not tired?). Sometimes, the presence of daytime napping suggests that the individual is experiencing insomnia not hyposomnia.

Grandiosity may be present, but it will be commensurate with the handicapped individual's level of functioning. For example, a moderately handicapped manic adult may express grandiosity by requests to get a motor vehicle driver's license. Impaired judgment and disinhibition may present as maladaptive behavior, e.g., teasing, inappropriate sexual behavior, impulsive acts.

In severe mania, grandiose delusions and mood-congruent hallucinations may be present (Taylor & Abrams, 1984). Psychotic phenomena have been reported in developmentally disabled manics (see Hucker et al 1979, and Sovner & Hurley 1983). Some clinicians believe that this population is predisposed to hallucinations (Gordon, 1919; Penrose, 1963).

Table 10.1
DSM-III-R diagnostic criteria for bipolar disorders and behavioral equivalents in the developmentally disabled.

	DSM-III (1987) criteria	Behavioral equivalents in developmentally disabled persons
Mood	Euphoric/elevated/irritable mood (no minimum duration necessary.	Boistrousness or excitement may be the predominant mood state. Self-injury may be associated with irritability.
Symptom criteria:	At least three symptoms must be present if patient has euphoric mood. Four symptoms must be present, if patient only has irritable mood.	Behaviors represent manifestations manic symptoms in developmentally disabled persons.
	(1) inflated self-esteem/ grandosity	Thought content may center around mastery of daily living skills.
	(2) decreased need for sleep	Increased maladaptive behavior at usual bedtime or in early morning. Patient is dressed for work at 5.00 AM.
	(3) more talkative/pressured speech	Increased frequency of vocalization irrespective of whether patient has usual speech.
	(4) flight of ideas/racing thoughts.	Disorganized speech.
	(5) distractibility	Decrease in workshop performance.
	(6) increased goal directed activity/psychomotor agitation	Aggressive behavior and negativism may be present.
	(7) excessive involvement in pleasureable activities	Teasing behavior, fondling others, publicly masturbating.

Table 1 presents Diagnostic and Statistical Manual of Mental Disorders, Third Edition Revised (DSM-III-R) (1987) criteria for mania. In addition, the "behavioral equivalents" which can be observed in the developmentally disabled are also listed. In essence, the clinician must "see past" the developmental disabilities to recognize the patient's manic features (Rivinus & Harmatz, 1979). This is necessary because standard criteria are frequently difficult to apply to developmentally disabled persons, espectially those with hypomania (and therefore manic symptoms of mild severity). For example, a decreased need for sleep may not be apparent unless the patient is disruptive during the night. Also, flights of ideas and pressured speech are difficult to detect in non-verbal individuals or those with poor communication skills. This difficulty in applying DSM-IIIR criteria for mania increases with the increasing severity of the developmental disabilities.

Table 2 lists two sets of proposed criteria for mania. Sovner (1986) attempted to compensate for some of these diagnostic problems by using some behavioral equivalents as diagnostic criteria, e.g., including an increase in the rate of aggression (see discussion to follow). Hucker et al (1979) also attempted to devise more objective criteria. In summary, it is important to note that we lack a set of validated criteria which can be uniformly applied irrespective of the level of the patient's developmental disabilities.

In addition to typical features such as overactivity and sleeplessness, mania in developmentally disabled persons may be present with a variety of maladaptive behaviors. Agression can be a presenting feature, especially when irritability predominates over euphoria (Mc-Cracken & Diamond, 1988; Reid, Swanson, Jain, Spowart & Wright 1987; Singh, 1988; Sovner 1988; 1989). When disinhibition is present, sexual misconduct (e.g., exposing oneself or fondling staff and clients) may be present.

Self-injury has also been reported in developmentally disabled manics (Steingard & Biederman, 1987; Sovner, 1989). A possible explanation is that this represents a "de-arousal" phenomenon, i.e., the affected individual may be attempting to self-regulate an unpleasant mood state. An associated behavior may be self-restraining. Severely handicapped manics can sometimes be observed continuously rocking to and from with their arms tightly wrapped against their chest. Others may wrap themselves in blankets or bulky shirts.

Table 10.2
**Proposed diagnostic criteria for bipolar disorders
in developmentally disabled persons.**

	Hucker et al (1979)	Sovner (1986)
Characteristic mood state	Euphoria or irritability	Elation, irritability or exciteability
Diagnostically concordant behaviors.	Any three of the following must be present.	Any four symptoms must be present. Only three needed if a first-degree relative has has bipolar disorder.
	1. overactivity	1. decreased sleep
	2. increased libido	2. overactivity
	3. pressured speech/flight of of ideas	3. biphasic course
	4. grandiosity (including extravagance)	4. onset/increase in severity of distractibility
	5. reduced sleep	5. increase in rate of frequency of verbalizations.
	6. extreme resentment of restraint	6. onset/increase in severity of aggressiveness.
		7. onset/increase in severity of self-injury.

Mania in the developmentally disabled may also be associated with a transient loss of learned skills (Linter, 1987; McCracken & Diamond, 1988). This may reflect severe cognitive disorganization associated with acute mania (Sovner, 1986).

Hyperthyroidism during manic phases has been reported (Mayer, 1985). In addition, flexion deformities of the fingers has also been described in a few handicapped bipolar patients (Reid et al, 1987).

A diagnostic problem in treating depressed developmentally disabled persons is the difficulty in determining whether or not they have

179

had previous manic episodes. The patient may not be able to give an adequate report and such episodes may have gone unrecognized by caregivers. Consequently, the bipolar nature of the disorder may only become apparent during antidepressant therapy when a manic episode is precipitated. Antidepressant-induced mania in predisposed individuals is a well documented phenomenon (Wehr & Goodwin, 1987). One diagnostic clue suggesting BP-DIS is the presence of hypersomnia and psychomotor retardation which tend to be more common than in unipolar depression (Kupfer, Himmelhoch, Swartzburg, Anderson, Byck & Detre, 1972; Whybrow, Akiskal & McKinney, 1984).

Case Report - induction of mania with antidepressant therapy

The patient was a 36-year-old woman with mild developmental disabilities who presented with "mood swings". A sister had been hospitalized for depression and had made several suicide attempts. She also had a history of periods of "overspending".

The patient was in good health and living in a community residence. The cause of her mental retardation was unknown. At age 22, she became depressed and withdrawn. At age 26, she had been hospitalized for depression and at age 34 had been hospitalized for atypical psychosis. There was no evidence that she had typical manic episodes.

She presented with moderately severe withdrawal, depressed mood, labile affect, somatic complaints, and increased appetite. She had been taking amitriptyline (total tricyclic blood level of 153 ng/ml), lithium carbonate 450 mg x 2/day (blood level of 0.5 mEq/L), and thioridazine 25 mg x 2/day. The diagnosis was felt to be recurrent major depression. Nortriptyline was substituted for the amitriptyline and over a three month period the lithium and thioridazine were tapered off. She initially did well for six months on nortriptyline 100 mg at bedtime (blood level of 148 ng/ml). During the following year, she had periods of increasing dysphoria which may have been related to psychosocial crises.
This culminated in a three week hospitalization for depression. It was thought that beta blocker therapy with atenolol may have precipitated acute depressive symptoms.

However, depressive symptoms returned and attempts to potentiate nortriptyline therapy with lithium carbonate (600 mg/day) and levothyroxine (50 mcg/day) were unsuccesful. She did respond to the addition of methylphenidate 10 mg x 2/day.

She uneventfully remained on this drug regimen for two years. At that time she was hospitalized for 17 days with a diagnosis of atypical psychosis given by the hospital staff. She was exhibiting decreased need for sleep, overactivity, pressured speech, and delusional ideation. This acute episode responded to haloperidol.

It was felt that that she had an acute manic episode and the valproic acid (VPA) derivative, divalproex sodium (DVP), was started and the haloperidol tapered off without a reoccurrence of symptoms. After two months of DVP therapy (VPA blood level of 67 mg/L), depressive symptoms returned and fluoxetine was started. She is now in remission on a combination of DVP and fluoxetine 40 mg/day.

The patient probably had a nortriptyline-induced manic episode. In retrospect, the sister's history of recurrent depression and overspending suggest a family history of BP-DIS. Her previous hospitalization for "atypical psychosis" could have been a misdiagnosed manic episode.

Differential diagnosis

There are a number of psychopathological states and drug side-effects which may be mistaken for mania.

Sedative/hypnotics, e.g., phenobarbital, may produce paradoxical excitement in severe and profoundly handicapped persons (Barron & Sandman, 1985). Discontinuation of drug therapy may be required to insure that the specific sedative agent is not producing a manic-like picture.

Akathisia and tardive akathisia may present with daytime restlessness and difficulty falling asleep (Gualtieri & Sovner, 1989). These extrapyramidal reactions may be mistaken for the signs of mania. The beta blocker treatment of these adverse reactions may be of use in the differential diagnostic process. Tricyclic antidepressants, fluoxetine, and buspirone can all induce an amphetamine-like reaction which may mimic mania.

It may be difficult to differentiate an agitated depression with restlessness, insomnia, and irritability from a manic state, especially when the clinician cannot rely on the patient's self-report to differentiate hyposomnia from insomnia. Also, the pervasive attentional problems associated with restlessness in some severely handicapped adults may appear to be manic unless the absence of a mood change is appreciated.

Reid, Naylor and Day, (1981) have described a clinical picture of overactivity and sleeplessness in severely and profoundly handicapped persons. They could be differentiated from other overactive and hyposomnic individuals who had a more typical mood state associated with mania such as excitement. The latter appeared to respond better to carbamazepine (Reid, 1981).

Recurrent medical conditions may present as maladaptive behavioral problems which seem to have a cyclical nature and are associated with a sleep disturbance. In particular, patients with seasonal allergies may have cyclical agitation, maladaptive behavior, and sleeplessness.

Atypical bipolar syndromes

Clinical features

Atypical bipolar syndromes are particularly problematic when working with developmentally disabled persons. The clinical picture may be quite confusing and the lack of patient's self-report often makes the diagnosis difficult. In addition, these atypical syndromes are frequently resistant to lithium carbonate and may require a noval drug regimen (McElroy, Keck, Pope & Hudson, 1988).

Rapid cycling BP-DIS is defined by a frequency of more than three episodes of affective illness per year (Alarcon, 1985). In some cases, the frequency of episodes is counted in days or weeks. It is highly associated with CNS and/or neuroendocrine dysfunction (Alarcon, 1985) and appears to be related to factors other than those predisposing to BP-DIS (Nurnberger, Guroff, Hamovit & Berrettini, 1988). Rapid cycling may occur spontaneously or be precipitated by thyroid abnormalities, CNS disorders, or antidepressant therapy (Alarcon, 1985). Factors other than a genetic predisposition to BP-DIS are most probably involved in predisposing to this illness (Nurnberger et al, 1988).

In the first systematic study of rapid cycling in the developmentally disabled carried out 15 years ago, Naylor, Donald, Le Poidevin and Reid (1974) reported that lithium carbonate produced a decrease in total number of weeks of illness, but not in the total number of episodes. These results are typical of the partial therapeutic effects usually achieved with lithium carbonate on this condition. Other clinicians have also reported cases of rapid cycling in developmentally disabled persons (Glue, 1989; Linter, 1987; McCracken & Diamond, 1988; Reid, 1972a; Reid & Leonard, 1978; Sovner, 1988; Sovner, in press; Wieseler, Campbell & Sonis, 1988).

BP-DIS should be considered as a differential diagnosis for any patient with periods of overactivity/sleeplessness and withdrawal/underactivity, especially when rates of maladaptive behavior have dramatic exacerbations and remissions which cannot be explained by changes in physical status or environmental conditions. Daily behavioral ratings of activity, sleep, speech, and severity/frequency of maladaptive behavior will be needed to make the diagnosis in severe and profoundly handicapped persons.

Associated with rapid cycling may be state-dependent maladaptive behavior which occurs only during depressed or manic phases. For example, Reid and Leonard (1977) have reported the case of a rapid cycling mildly handicapped 29-year-old woman who had depression-dependent vomiting.

In BP-DIS, mixed type, there is either the simultaneous presence of manic and depressive features or these features rapidly follow each other. This disorder is often treatment-resistant (Prien, Himmelhoch & Kupfer, 1988). BP-DIS, mixed type has been reported in developmentally disabled persons (Naylor et al, 1974, Reid, 1972). In an early survey, Duncan (1936) reported than 13.8 % of his sample of 379 developmentally disabled inpatients suffered from this illness.

Chronic mania is usually a late onset form of BP-DIS in which the individual manifests attenuated manic features (Slater & Roth, 1969). However, chronic mania can be observed in younger developmentally disabled patients (Steingard & Biederman, 1987; Sovner, 1988; 1989). These cases are of particular interest because patients frequently present with longstanding behavioral problems without a recent history of biphasic mood swings.

Case report - chronic mania

The patient was a 24-year-old woman with mild developmental diasabilities and a childhood onset pervasive developmental disorder who presented with chronic overactivity. A maternal aunt had a history of BP-DIS and a second maternal aunt had committed suicide. She was in good health and taking a combination of lithium carbonate (blood level of 1.0 and 1.2 mEq/L) and carbamazepine (blood levels between 8.0 and 8.3 mEq/L). She had mild lithium-induced diabetes insipidus.

The patient was living with her parents. For several years, she had been in a chronic manic state characterized by: overactivity; pressured and perseverative speech; marked distractibility; temper tantrums. These behaviors had only been partially controlled by her drug regimen. She also had history of periods of withdrawal characterized by: increased need for sleep; lack of interest; and suicidal statements.

DVP therapy was initiated and the carbamazepine was tapered off. She became floridly manic, and her symptoms remitted only when her VPA level rose above 100 mg/L. The lithium and carbamazepine were then successfully tapered off. She was also taking nadolol 80 mg per

183

day to control a VPA-induced tremor and modulate overarousal associated with her autistic disorder.

VPA blood levels greater than 100 mg/L may have to be achieved to get a full therapeutic response. It is possible that a genetically determined predisposition to BP-DIS (she had a positive family history) interacted with the pathophysiology of her autistic disorder to produce the clinical picture of chronic mania.

Organic mood syndrome

An organic mood syndrome is an affective disorder in which there is an identifiable physical cause (e.g., steroid induced mania). It is not uncommon to observe chronic states of excitement associated with overactivity, and sleep disturbance in severe and profoundly handicapped residents of developmental centers. Such individuals typically have pervasive CNS dysfunction and treatment-resistant maladaptive behavior (Reid, Ballinger & Heather, 1978, 1984). It seems a reasonable hypothesis that the CNS pathology which produced the patient's developmental disabilities has also affected those limbic system structures which may mediate BP-DIS symptomatology (Snyder, 1988). The partial response of some of these individuals to carbamazepine was reported by Reid et al (1981). In many respects, these cases resemble chronic mania.

Case report - organic mood syndrome

The patient was a 39-year-old man with severe developmental disabilities who presented with chronic self-injurious behavior. A sister had been treated with antidepressant therapy and another sister had taken a drug overdose. The cause of his developmental disabilities was unknown, but presumed to be perinatal brain damage. He also had a history of major motor seizures and unsteady gait. His drug regimen consisted of haloperidol 3 mg/day, benztropine 0.5 mg/day, phenytoin 500 mg/day, and propranolol 20 mg x 2/day.

The patient was living in a community residence. His behavioral problems included; pressured vocalizations; less than four hours of sleep per night; pervasive overactivity; distractibility; and daily angry outbursts. He would begin to punch his head and, if restrained, would be aggressive and destructive. Most of these behaviors had been present since childhood.

A diagnosis of organic mood syndrome, chronic mania was made and he was started on DVP. With a VPA blood level greater than 100 mg/L, his self-injury, overactivity, and decreased sleep remitted. Relapse occurred when his blood level fell below 100 mg/L.

The phenytoin, haloperidol, benzotropine, and propranolol were successfully discontinued. Significant side-effect included a mild pancytopenia and an increase in a chronic unsteady gait which did not require DVP discontinuation.

The virtually lifelong nature of his overactivity and sleep disturbance associated with severe handicaps and seizure disorder were suggestive of an organic mood syndrome. The presence of a positive family history of affective illness may have been a predisposing factor.

Bipolar disorder as a co-morbid state - in association with autism, Down syndrome, Fragile X syndrome and other.

BP-DIS may represent a co-morbid illness superimposed upon another disorder which is associated with pathological behavior (e.g., autism). It may also occur in conjunction with a disorder which can result in developmental disabilities, but does not produce a specific behavioral constellation (e.g., phenylketonuria). These associations have important research as well as clinical implications because the underlying CNS pathophysiology producing the developmental handicaps might alter the vulnerability of affective disorders (Winokur, 1984).

BP-DIS can develop in autistic individuals (Reid, 1980) and there have been a number of recently reported cases (Akkuffo, MacSweeney & Gajwani 1986; Bates & Smeltzer, 1982; Kerebeshian, Burd and Fisher, 1987; Komoto, Usui & Hirata, 1984; Sovner, 1989; Steingard & Biederman, 1987). The onset of a manic episode is often heralded by an increase in behaviors associated with autism, e.g., stereotypic behavior. Caregivers may not realize that the increase in autistic behavior may be a significant diagnostic feature of a psychiatric illness.

These cases are consistent with previous reports suggestive of BP-DIS in association with autism. Rutter, Greenfield and Lockyer (1967) followed up a sample of 24 hyperkinetic children with "infantile autism," who were now at least 13 years old. Four were in a "state varying between hyperkineses and hypokinesis". Wright (1982) in a survey of 1507 developmentally disabled persons who were residents of an English "long stay hospital" found that 41 individuals with "major impairments of social interaction" had an "atypical affective illness."

185

Case report - rapid cycling bipolar disorder in association with autism

The patient was a 53-year-old man with moderate developmental disabilities and an early onset autistic disorder who presented with a sleep disturbance. There was no family history of neuropsychiatric illness.

The patient was in good health and living in in a community residence. At age 22 he was admitted to a state developmental center because of "family difficulties". He returned home after five years and then at the age of 37 was admitted to a state psychiatric inpatient facility when his mother died. One month before his evaluation, he had been discharged to a community living program. He was drug-free, but had a history of treatment with many different neuroleptic agents.

He never made eye-contact, would stare into space or engaged in stereotypic pill rolling, and rarely spoke more than a single word at a time, but his receptive language skills were good. After several months of tracking his behavior, it became clear that he was having biphasic mood swings. His highs were characterized by euphoric mood, pressured verbalizations, irritability, overactivity, decreased sleep, running away from his residence, and aggression. His lows were characterized by withdrawal, fatigue, increase in frequency of self-stimulatory behavior, and depressed mood. Affective phases tended to last from two to three months without intercurrent periods of normothymia.

He was started on DVP (VPA blood level of 87 mg/L) and his affective disorder remitted. He has been in remission for two years. He continues to display the behaviors associated with his autistic disorder. The patient had been considered to be chronically psychotic. The periodicity and affective nature of his behavioral problems had never been recognized.

Depression is generally recognized to develop in persons with Down syndrome, but the occurence of mania has been the subject of debate. Sovner, Hurley and Labrie (1985) proposed that persons with Down syndrome were unable to develop fullblown mania because the neurotransmitter systems which mediate bipolar disorder were affected. This hypothesis was based on their clinical experience and a review of the literature which failed to find a single case of mania, but 28 cases of depression. Since then, other clinicians have supported this hypothesis (Hucker, 1985; Singh, 1988; Singh & Zolese, 1986).

However, four cases of mania in association with Down syndrome have been reported (Cook & Leventhal, 1987; McLaughlin, 1987; Singh & Zolese, 1986, Sovner, in press). Two of the cases were rapid cycling

BP-DIS (Singh & Zolese, 1986; Sovner, in press), and a third was recurrent unipolar mania (Cook & Leventhal, 1987). Sovner (in press) proposed that these cases represent an organic mood syndrome rather than more classical mania.

To date little has been written about the occurrence of affective disorder in persons with Fragile X syndrome. Sovner (1989) has published a case of a VPA-sensitive chronic mania. An association between female carriers of the Fragile X chromosome and chronic affective disorders has also been reported (Reiss, Hagerman, Vinogradov, Abrams & King, 1988).

Case report - chronic mania in a Fragile X adult.

The patient was a 34-year-old man with moderate developmental disabilites and Fragile X syndrome (based upon chromosomal analysis) who presented with a one year history of increasing aggression and loss of functioning. Three of his four brothers had chromosomal evidence of Fragile X syndrome.

The patient was in good health and living in in a community residence. He had been institutionalized from ages 11 to 31. As a child he had been treated with stimulant therapy for hyperactivity. He had been admitted to a psychiatric hospital at age 32 to control his agressive behavior. Treatment had been predominantly with neuroleptics and was largely ineffective.

At the time of his initial assessment, he was taking chlopromazine 200 mg., trifluoperazine 10 mg x 2/day, and benztropine 2 mg. His behavioral problems included agitation, assaultiveness, low frustration tolerance, distractibility, labile affect, and perseverative and bizarre speech (he claimed he was his brother). Orofacial dyskinesia was observed as the trifluoperazine was tapered off.

A diagnosis of organic personality disorder was considered and over an eighteen month period, the chlorpromazine was tapered to 100 mg per day. During this period, his aggressive behavior began to increase and beta blocker therapy was unsuccessfully tried (first with propranolol, which had to be stopped due to hypotension) and then pindolol 60 mg per day.

His clinical status was reassessed (while receiving chlorpromazine 60 mg per day and pindolol 60 mg per day) and he was found to manifest pressured speech, decreased sleep (he would be dressed and ready for work at 6:30 AM), euphoric mood, irritability, sexual aggressiveness at work, and overactivity. It was believed that neuroleptic

187

therapy had masked the severity of these behaviors which were probably present at the time of his initial evaluation.

DVP therapy was started and the pindolol tapered off. There was a clinically signficant decrease in symptom severity with a VPA blood level of 109 mg/L. In particular, sexual behavior and aggression remitted. After ten months of DVP therapy the chlorpromazine was uneventfully discontinued. He displayed no manic behavior or symptoms.

The patient was suffering from a chronic manic illness the symptoms of which were being masked by neuroleptic therapy.

BP-DIS has been reported in association with Klinefelter's syndrome and borderline intellectual function (Sorensen & Nielsen, 1977) and also with homocystinuria (Bracken & Coll, 1985). (In the latter case, a mildly handicapped woman who was overtalkative and hyposomnic was probably misdiagnosed as having schizophrenia.)

Prevalence of bipolar disorders in developmentally disabled persons

At the present time, the prevalence rate of BP-DIS in developmentally disabled persons is unknown. Factors which make epidemiological studies difficult to carry out include:
1. difficulty in diagnosing BP-DIS in non-verbal persons;
2. failing to recognize BP-DIS as a co-morbid state, e.g., development of bipolar disorder in autistic adults;
3. overdiagnosing atypical psychosis by mistaking non-specific stress responses for signs of psychosis;
4. failing to recognize diagnostically relevant signs and symptoms due to the masking effects of psychotropic drug therapy.

Table 3 lists the reported prevalence of BP-DIS in three recent epidemiological studies of psychopathology in developmentally disabled persons. In the Camberwell study (Corbett, 1979) 1.5% were diagnosed to be suffering from BP-DIS. An additional 2.0% had a history consistent with a previous episode of an affective disorder. Corbett (1979) noted that many handicapped persons with psychiatric disorders may have gone uncounted due to difficulties carrying out psychiatric assessments in non-verbal subjects.

Table 10.3
Prevalence studies of bipolar disorder in developmentally disabled adults*

	Aarhus Denmark (Lund, 1985a)	Camberwell England (Corbett, 1979)	Kopparberg Sweden (Gostason, 1985)
Survey site	Danish County	South London district pop. - 175,000 in 1971	Swedish County pop. - 145,000
Methodo-logy	A prospective evaluation of those persons living in Aarhus County and listed as mentally retarded in a Danish national register was carried out. A two stage sampling technique was used.	A prospective evaluation of all persons with DD having a Camberwell address on a specified date and known to any agency was carried out.	A prospective evaluation of those persons identified as having MR by census data was carried out. Subjects for psychiatric interview were selected by stratified sampling technique.
Sample size:	302	402	112
Age range:	20 - 29 y.o. - 32% 30 - 44 y.o. - 37 % 45 - 64 y.o. - 28% over 64 y.o. - 9%	15 - 29 y.o. - 49% 30 - 44 y.o. - 21% over 44 y.o. - 48 %	20 - 29 y.o. - 42% 30 - 39 y.o. - 33% 40 - 49 y.o. - 19% over 49 y.o. - 6%
Sex ratio F/M:	1.00/0.78	no data	1.00/1.49
MR severity	IQ 68 - 85 - 10% 52 - 67 - 25% 36 - 51 - 28% > 36 - 20% unclassif. - 17%	> 50 (mild) - 26% < 50 (severe) - 74%	> 52 (mild) - 44% < 52 (severe) - 56%
Dx Criteria:	DSM-3	ICD-8	DSM-3
Results:			
Depression	(a)	2.0%	0.9% (b)
Bipolar disorder	(a)	1.5%	0.9% (c)
History of depression or bipolar disorder	no data	2.0%	no data

* Adapted from Sovner & Pary, in press.
(a)   Data reported as "affective disorder" with 3.2% prevalance. No breakdown of bipolar disorder vs. major depression.
(b)   Percentage represents one case of atypical depression.
(c)   Percentage represents one case of cyclothymic disorder.

In a Swedish study (Gostason, 1985), a population sample of developmentally disabled persons were evaluated. Only 0.9% (one subject) was diagnosed to have a depressive disorder and another 0.9% was diagnosed to have a cyclothymic disorder.

In a third study carried out in Denmark (Lund, 1985a), a group of 324 handicapped adults (age 20 or older) were selected for assessment and the prevalence rate of "affective disorder" was 3.2%. Unfortunately this category included both mania and depression.

Table 4 describes various inpatient surveys of BP-DIS in developmentally disabled persons which have been carried out. Reid (1972) (based upon assessments of 500 dually diagnosed individuals referred to him from an inpatient/residential population) reported a prevalence rate of 1.2% for manic-depressive psychosis vs 3.2.% for combined schizophrenia and paranoid psychoses). Heaton-Ward (1977), in a survey of four residential facilities, found prevalence rates identical to Reid's findings (1972) for affective disorders and schizophrenia. Glue (1989) evaluated 100 residents of a longstay facility. He found that 12 had an affective disorder and ten of them were rapid cycling. Lund (1985b) examined the admission of developmentally disabled persons to a Danish psychiatric hospital and found that almost twice as many patients (7.0 vs 3.6%) were admitted with "manic depressive" psychosis than with schizophrenia. Wright (1982) in a study of mental illness in developmentally handicapped persons living in institutions found that 2.8% had "typical affective illness" vs 1.7% for schizophrenia and schizoaffective disorder. Other investigators have reported similar affective disorder to psychosis ratios for inpatient admissions of developmentally disabled persons (Day, 1985; Myers, 1986; Parton, Webb and Clarke, 1974).

In summary, the prevalence of BP-DIS in developmentally disabled persons is unknown. In a large scale epidemiological study of psychiatric illness carried out by the United States National Institute for Mental Health, the six-month prevalence rate for mania was 0.5% (Regier et al, 1988). It would be useful to know whether the presence of developmental handicaps influenced the risk of BP-DIS in general and atypical syndromes in particular.

Unfortunately the methodological problems in carrying out psychiatric epidemiological research in the developmentally disabled prevents any meaningful conclusions from being drawn. However, risk factors such as CNS dysfunction, seizure disorders and some causes of developmental handicaps (e.g., autism) may increase the frequency of affective disorders.

Table 10.4
**Prevalence of bipolar disorder in developmentally
disabled persons based on survey data**

Authors	Site	N	Results
Day 1985	Chronic inpatient	357	Survey of residents over age 40, indicated that 4.2% had a cyclothymic or hypomanic disorder.
Glue 1989	Chronic inpatient	100	Survey of residents found than 12 had an affective disorder and ten were rapid cycling.
Heaton-Ward 1977	Chronic inpatient	484	Survey of symptomatic referrals at four facilities for prevalence of bipolar disorder was 2.0%.
Lund 1985b	Acute inpatient	5107	Prevalence of "manic depressive psychosis" in new admissions to Danish psychiatric hospitals was 7.0%.
Myers 1986	Acute inpatient	62	Prevalence of bipolar disorder in admissions to a psychiatric unit was 4.8%
Reid 1972	Inpatient	500	Prevalence rate of "manic-depressive psychosis" was 1.2% for symptomatic referrals.

Treatment of bipolar disorder in the developmentally disabled

At the present time, there are a variety of innovative treatments for acute mania and the prevention of recurrences (see reviews by Prien & Gelenberg, 1989 and Sachs, 1990). This is of particular concern when treating developmentally disabled persons who, as a group, seem very susceptible to atypical and treatment-resistent syndromes. Also, given the fact that it may be very difficult to demonstrate that the patient meets the full symptom criteria for mania, it is particularly helpful to have interventions which can produce a remission and thereby to confirm the original diagnosis. (Demonstrated efficacy is also very helpful in convincing families and caregivers of the usefulness of psychiatric approaches to the management of behavioral problems).

Lithium carbonate can be an effective treatment for BP-DIS in the developmentally disabled (Rivinus & Harmatz, 1979). However, it is less effective in the treatment of atypical syndromes, especially rapid cycling BP-DIS (Naylor et al, 1974). Lithium-induced incontinence can be a significant problem in this population.

Carbamazepine, alone and in combination with lithium, is effective in BP-DIS (Post, 1988). The drug may be useful in lithium non-responders, especially in BP-DIS mixed type (Post, Rubinov, Uhde, Roy-Byrne, Linnolla, Rosoff & Cowdry, 1989).

Calcium channel blockers, in particular verapamil, have been reported to be effective in soms cases of acute mania (Pollack, Rosenbaum & Hyman, 1987; Sachs, 1989). For verapamil, daily between 240 mg and 480 mg may be necessary to achieve a clinically significant response (Pollack et al, 1987).

Clonazepam is useful in the treatment of acute mania (Chouinard, 1985; Chouinard, Young and Annable, 1983). Daily doses as high as 16 mg may be necessary. However, benzodiazepine-induced disinhibition can occur. Its prophylactic effects in BP-DIS are uncertain. Clonidine may have some acute antimanic effects (Sachs, 1989) and has been reported to be effective in the treatment of BP-DIS mixed type (Zubenko, Cohen, Lipinski and Jonas, 1984).

Valproic Acid (VPA) is particularly effective in atypical bipolar syndromes (McElroy et al, 1988; Sovner, 1989; Sovner in press). In such cases blood levels greater than 100 mg/L may be necessary to produce significant clinical results. Chronic mania and rapid cycling disorders seem particularly responsive to this drug (see case reports in this chapter).

Conclusion

The dramatic alterations in mood, energy state, and sleep associated with BP-DIS make it perhaps the most readily identifiable psychiatric illness in developmentally disabled persons. Also, its biphasic nature contributes to a high "signal to noise" ratio so that its state-dependent features stand out against a background of non-specific maladaptive behavior. The often labor-intensive months of behavioral data collection it takes to make this diagnosis is well worth the effort because of the availability of effective interventions.

References

Akuffo, E., MacSweeney, D.A. & Gajwani, A.K. (1986) Multiple pathology in a mentally handicapped individual. British Journal of Psychiatry 149, 377 - 378.

Alarcon, R.D. (1985) Rapid cycling affective disorders; A clinical review. Comprehensive Psychiatry 26 522-540.

Barron, J., Sandman, C.A. (1985) Paradoxical excitement to sedative-hypnotics in mentally retarded clients. American Journal of Mental Deficiency 90, 125-129.

Bates, W.J., & Smeltzer, D.J. (1982) Electroconculsive treatment of psychotic self-injurious behavior in a patient with severe mental retardation. American Journal of Psychiatry 139, 1355-1356.

Bracken, P. & Coll, P. (1985) Homocystinuria and schizophrenia. Journal of Nervous and Mental Disease 173, 51-55.

Carlson, G.A. (1979) Affective psychoses in mental retardates. Psychiatric Clinics of North America 2, 499-510.

Carlson, G.A. (1981) Affective disorder and cognitive immaturity. In: Belmaker, R.H. & Van Praag, H.M. (eds.) Mania: An Evolving Concept. New York: Spectrum Books, pp 281-289.

Chouinard, G. (1985) Antimanic effects of clonazepam. Journal of Clinical Psychiatry 26, (12 suppl.) 7-11.

Chouinard, G., Young, S.N., Annable, L. (1983) Antimanic effect of clonazepam. Biological Psychiatry 18, 451-466.

Cook, E.D. & Leventhal, B.L. (1987) Down's syndrome with mania. British Journal of Psychiatry, 150, 249-250.

Corbett, J.A. (1979) Psychiatric morbidity and mental retardation. In: James, F.E. & Snaith R.P. (eds.) Psychiatric Illness and Mental Handicap. London: Gaskell Press, pp. 11-25.

Day, K. (1985) Psychiatric disorder in the middle-aged and elderly mentally handicapped. British Journal of Psychiatry 147, 660-667.

Diagnostic and Statistical Manual of Mental Disorders, Third Edition - Revised (1987) Washington, D.C.: American Psychiatric Association.

Duncan, A.G. (1936) Mental deficiency and manic-depressive insanity. Journal of Mental Science 82, 635-641.

Glue, P. (1989) Rapid cycling affective disorders in the mentally retarded. Biological Psychiatry 26, 250-256.

Gordon, A. (1919) Psychoses in mental defects. American Journal of Insanity 75, 489 - 499.

Gostason, R (1985). Psychiatric illness among the mentally retarded. A Swedish population study. Acta Psychiatrica Scandinavica 71, (Supplement 318) 1-117.

Gualtieri, C.T., & Sovner, R. (1989) Akathisia and tardive akathisia. Psychiatric Aspects of Mental Retardation Reviews 8, 83-88.

Heaton-Ward, A. (1977) Psychosis in mental handicap. British Journal of Psychiatry 130, 525-533.

Hucker, S.J. (1985) Is mania incompatible with Down's syndrome. British Journal of Psychiatry, 147 93 - 94.

Hucker, S.J., Day, K.A., George, S. & Roth, M. (1979) Psychosis in mentally handicapped adults. In: James, F.E. & Snaith, R.P. (eds.) Psychiatric Illness and Mental Handicap London: Gaskell Press, pp 27-35.

Kerbeshian, J., Burd L., Fisher, W. (1987) Lithium carbonate in the treatment of two patients with infantile autism and atypical bipolar symptomatology. Journal of Clinical Psychopharmacology 7, 401-405.

Komoto, J., Usui, S. & Hirata, J. (1984) Infantile autism and affective disorder. Journal of Autism and Developmental Disorders 14, 81 - 84.

Kupfer, D.J., Himmelhoch, J.M., Swartzburg, M., Anderson, C., Byck, R. & Detre, T.P. (1972) Hypersomnia in manic depressive disease. Diseases of the Nervous System 33, 720 - 724.

Linter, C.M. (1987) Short-cycle manic-depressive psychosis in a mentally handicapped child without family history. British Journal of Psychiatry 151, 554-555.

Lund, J. (1985a) The prevelance of psychiatric morbidity in mentally retarded adults. Acta Psychiatrica Scandinavica, 72, 563-567.

Lund, J. (1985b) Mentally retarded admitted to psychiatric hostitals in Denmark. Acta Psychiatrica Scandinavica, 72, 202-205

McCracken, J.T. & Diamond, R.P. (1988) Bipolar disorder in mentally retarded adolescents. Journal of the American Academy of Child and Adolescent Psychiatry, 27, 494-499.

McElroy, S.L., Keck, P.E. Jr., Pope, H.G. Jr. & Hudson, J.I. (1988) Valproate in the treatment of rapid-cycling bipolar disorder. Journal of Clinical Psychopharmacology, 8, 275-279.

McLaughlin, M. (1997) Bipolar affective disorder in Down's syndrome. British Journal of Psychiatry, 151, 116-117.

Mayer, C. (1985) Mental handicap, psychosis and thyrotoxicosis: A demonstration of the usefulness of an integrated community and hospital service. Journal of Mental Deficiency Research, 29, 275-280.

Myers, B.A. (1986) Psychopathology in hospitalized developmentally disabled individuals. Comprehensive Psychiatry, 27, 115-126.

Naylor, G.J., Donald, J.M., Le Poidevin, D., & Reid, A.H. (1974). A double-blind trial of long-term lithium therapy in mental defectives. British Journal of Psychiatry 124, 52-57.

Nurnberger, J.Jr., Guroff, J.J., Hamovit, J., Berrettine, W., & Gershon, E. (1988) A family study of rapid-cycling bipolar illness. Journal of Affective Disorders, 15, 87-99.

Parton, R.V., Webb, M.G.T. & Clarke J.G. (1974) The psychiatric presentation and identification of mentally handicapped patients. Journal of the Irish Medical Association, 67, 611-615.

Penrose, L.S. (1983) The Biology of Mental Defect, Berg, J.M. & Lang-Brown, H. (revised). London, Sidgwick & Jackson, Ltd.

Pollack, M.H., Rosenbaum, J.F., Hyman, S.E. (1987) Calcium channel blockers in psychiatry. Psychosomatics, 28, 356-361.

Post, R.M. (1988) Effectiveness of carbamazepine in the treatment of bipolar affective disorder. In McElroy, S.L. & Pope, H.G. Jr. (eds.) Use of anticonvulsants in psychiatry: recent advances. Clifton, New Jersey: Oxford Healthcare.

Post, R.M., Rubinow, D.R., Uhde, T.W., Roy-Byrne, P.R., Linnoila, M., Rosoff, A, Cowdry, R. (1989) Dysphoric mania. Archives of General Psychiatry, 46, 353-358.

Prien, R.F., & Gelenberg, A.J. (1989) Alternatives to lithium for preventive treatment of bipolar disorder. American Journal of Psychiatry, 146, 840 - 848.

Prien, R.F., Himmelhoch, J.M. & Kupfer, D.J. (1988) Treatment of mixed mania. Journal of Affective Disorder, 15, 9 -15.

Regier, D.A., Boyd, J.H., Burke, J.S. Jr., Raae, D.S., Myers, J.K., Kramer, M., Robins, L.N., George, L.K., Karno, M., & Locke, B.Z. (1988) One-month prevalence of mental disorder in the United States. Archives of General Psychiatry, 45, 977-986.

Reid, A.H. (1972) Psychoses in adult mental defectives: I. Manic depressive psychosis. British Journal of Psychiatry, 120, 205-212.

Reid, A.H. (1980) Diagnosis of psychiatric disorders in the severely and profoundly retarded patient. Journal of the Royal Society of Medicine, 69, 505-512.

Reid, A.H., Ballinger, B.R., & Heather, B.B. (1978) Behavioral syndromes identified by cluster analysis in a sample of 100 severely and profoundly retarded adults. Psychological Medicine, 8, 399-412.

Reid, A.H., Ballinger, B.R., Heather, B.B., & Melvin, S.J. (1984) The natural history of behavioral symptoms among severely and profoundly mentally retarded patients. British Journal of Psychiatry, 145, 289-293

Reid, A.H. & Leonard, A. (1977) Lithium treatment of cyclic vomiting in a mentally defective patient. British Journal of Psychiatry, 125, 316.

Reid, A.D., Naylor, G.J. & Day, D. (1981) A double-blind placebo controlled, crossover trial of carbamazepine in overactive, severely mentally handicapped patients. Psychological Medicine 11, 109-113.

Reid, A.H., Swanson, J.G., Jain, A.S., Spowart G., & Wright, A.F. (1987) Manic depressive psychosis with mental retardation and flexion deformities: A clinical and cytogenetic study. British Journal of Psychiatry, 150, 92 - 97.

Reiss, A.L., Hagerman, R.J., Vinogradov, S., Abrams, M., & King, R.J. (1988) Psychiatric disability in female carriers of the Fragile X chromosome. Archives of General Psychiatry, 45, 25-30.

Rivinus, T., & Harmatz, J. (1979) Diagnosis and lithium treatment of affective disorder in the retarded: Five case studies. American Journal of Psychiatry 136(4B), 551-554.

Rutter, M., Greenfield, D. & Lockyer, L. (1967) A five to fifteen year follow-up study of infantile psychosis. II. Social and behavioral outcome. British Journal of Psychiatry, 113, 1183-1199.

Sachs, G.S. (1989) Adjuncts and alternatives to lithium therapy for bipolar affective disorder. J. Clinical Psychiatry, 50, (12 supplement) 31-39.

Singh, I. (1988) Down's syndrome with mania. British Journal of Psychiatry, 152, 436 -437.

Singh, I., Zolese, G. (1986) Is mania really incompatible with Down's sydrome? British Journal of Psychiatry, 148, 613-614.

Slater, E. & Roth, M. (1969) Mayer-Gross Slater and Roth Clinical Psychiatry, 3rd ed. Baltimore: Williams and Wilkins, P. 217.

Snyder, S.H. (1988) The New Biology of Mood. New York: Pfizer.

Sorensen, K. & Nielsen, J. (1977) Twenty psychotic males with Klinefelter's syndrome. Acta Psychiatrica Scandinavica, 56, 249-255.

Sovner, R. (1986) Limiting factors in the use of DSM-III criteria with mentally ill/mentally retarded persons. Psychopharmacology Bulletin, 22, 1055-1059.

Sovner, R. (1988) Anticonvulsant drug therapy of neuropsychiatric disorders in mentally retarded persons. In McElroy, S.E., H.G. Pope, Jr. (eds.), Use of anticonvulsants in psychiatry. Recent advances. Clifton, N.J.: Oxford Health Care, 1988.

Sovner, R. (1989) The use of valproate in the treatment of mentally retarded persons with typical and atypical bipolar disorders. Journal of Clinical Psychiatry, 50, (3 supplement) 40-43.

Sovner, R. (in press) Divalproex-responsive rapid cycling bipolar disorder in patient with Down's syndrome: implications for the Down's syndrome - mania hypothesis. Journal of Mental Deficiency Research.

Sovner, R., Hurley A.D. (1983) Do the mentally retarded suffer from affective illness? Archives of General Psychiatry, 40, 61-67.

Sovner, R., Hurley, A.D., Labrie, R. (1985) Is mania incompatible with Drown's syndrome? British Journal of Psychiatry, 46, 319-320.

Sovner, R., & Pary, R.J. (in press) Affective Disorders in developmentally disabled persons. In: Matson, J.L., & Barrett, R.P. (eds.), Psychopathology in the Mentally Retarded, 2nd Edition. Psychological Corporation.

Steingard, R. & Biederman, J. (1987) Lithium responsive manic-like symptoms in two individuals with autism and mental retardation. Journal of the American Acedemy of Child and Adolescent Psychiatry, 26, 932-935.

Szymanski, L.S., & Biederman, J. (1984) Depression and anorexia of persons with Down's syndrome. American Journal of Mental Deficiency, 89, 246-251.

Taylor, M.A. & Abrams, R. (1973) The phenomenology of mania. Archives of General Psychiatry, 29, 520-522.

Wehr, T.A. & Goodwin, F.K. (1987) Can antidepressant cause mania and worsen course of affective illness? Amercian Journal of Psychiatry, 144, 1403-1411.

Whybrow, P.C., Akiskal, H.S. & McKinney, W.T. (1984) Mood Disorders - Towards a New Psychobiology. New York: Plenum Press.

Wieseler, N.A., Campbell, G.J. & Sonis, W. (1988) Ongoing use of an affective rating scale in the treatment of a mentally retarded individual with a rapid-cycling bipolar affective disorder. Research in Developmental Disabilities, 9, 47 - 53.

Winokur, B. (1974) Subnormality and its relation to psychiatry. Lancet, 2, 270-273.

Wright, E.C. (1982) The presentation of mental illness in mentally retarded adults. British Journal of Psychiatry, 141, 496-502.

Zubenko, G.A., Cohen, B.M., Lipinski, J.F., & Jonas, J.M. (1984) Clonidine in the treatment of mania and mixed bipolar disorder. American Journal of Psychiatry, 41, 1616-1618.

Anton Dosen and Frank J. Menolascino (Eds.) (1990). Depression in mentally retarded children and adults. Leiden, the Netherlands: Logon Publications. ISBN 90-73197-01-5

Chapter 11

Diagnostic instruments for depression in the mentally retarded

Steven R. Love, M.A.
Johnny L. Matson, Ph.D.

Introduction

It has become increasingly clear that persons with mental handicaps are susceptible to a variety of psychiatric and mental disorders (Matson & Barrett, 1982; Sigman, 1985; Szymanski & Tanquay, 1980). As Menolascino and Stark (1984) noted, the coexistence of mental disorders and mental retardation is actually quite likely, given that the individual is already handicapped by limitations in intellectual functioning and social adaptation. Because these individuals may react or respond less than optimally to the demands of everyday life, they are "at risk" for the development of psychiatric disorders; an affective reaction, such as depression, may be a presumed result.

Diagnostic issues

Matson (1983) indicates that "the necessity for a separate theoretical model of depression for mentally retarded persons hinges primarily on diagnostic features and is based on one outstanding aspect that separates the group from all others, intellectual impairments" (p. 65). Additionally, the wide range of behaviors and intellectual capabilities of mildly to profoundly mentally retarded persons is invariably great, hence, the symptoms of depression are apt to be varied as well. This fact dictates that assessment and diagnostic methods should be different across mentally retarded subpopulations (Matson, 1983).

Behavioral assessment of depression in the mentally retarded, based on findings drawn from research and clinical practice with nonretarded individuals, has primarily utilized one of three basic systems. These include directly interviewing the person, direct behavioral observations, and obtaining ratings of the person's behavior by knowledgeable informants (Matson & Barrett, 1982). While direct interviews and other's reports of depressed behavior are likely to be of use with mildly or moderately retarded adults and older children (Kazdin, Matson & Senatore, 1983), severely and profoundly retarded children provide a different challenge. Here, rating by knowledgeable others and direct behavioral observations are more likely to be applicable. However, diagnostic assessment of depression in persons with mental retardation must initially draw on the type of behavior characteristic of depression in nonretarded persons.

Two views of depression in mentally retarded persons have been adopted over the years. The first is that mentally retarded persons do not express depression directly; it must be inferred from behaviors and symptoms which "mask" the underlying depressive feelings (Carlson & Cantwell, 1980). Thus, withdrawal, psychophysical complaints, or delinquency might be seen as signs of underlying depression. Such a view would be problematic for a scientific approach since comparison with population norms and statistical analyses of behavior would be very difficult based solely on inferential data. Additionally, according to this view, one might expect increasing numbers of persons with mental retardation to be wrongly labeled as depressed.

The second view, adopted by these authors, holds that depression is manifested along the same lines (same types of operationally defined behaviors) as persons with normal intelligence. Not only is this view more reliable and conservative than the first scientifically, but it helps prevent misdiagnosis of depression. This preferred second view, as Lefkowitz (1980) notes, allows the comparison of rates of behavior on a normative basis, which is the only way that clinicians can avoid selecting persons as deviant based on parental and clinical tolerance levels.

A particularly useful system for diagnosing observable behaviors with a high degree of validity for depression in persons with mental retardation is that of Cytryn, McKnew and Bunny (1980). This system involves an amalgam of behaviors common to three of the four most widely accepted diagnostic criteria for depression: the Diagnostic and Statistical Manual of Mental Disorders - Third Edition (APA,1980), Cytryn and McKnew's (1972) system, Brumback, Dietz-Schmidt and Weinberg's (1977) system, and the criteria of Kovacs and Beck (1977). More specific information on how these diagnoses are conducted will follow.

Diagnosis of depression in mental retardation

At present, only a handful of studies on depression have been undertaken in persons with mental retardation. This research has been discussed with regard to treatment approaches and methodological rigor in other chapters of this book. The focus of this section will be to provide the reader with a review of the various types of instruments used in the diagnosis of depression in the mentally retarded. In the final section of this chapter, specific features of these instruments will be highlighted.

Depression studies in mentally retarded adults

Treatment of a severely depressed 32-year-old borderline to mildly mentally retarded male was undertaken in a case study by Matson, Dettling, and Senatore (1980). Diagnosis of depression was based on DSM-III criteria, self-report of severely depressed affect, verbalizations of threats of suicide, feelings of worthlessness and dissatisfaction, anxiety, observations of loss of sleep, extreme social withdrawal, and flat speech affect. Verbal sequences concerning devaluating self-worth, statements about suicide, or rumination over past events were targeted for treatment in the A-B design. Treatment consisted of continued administration of imipramine (100 mg. T.E.D.) and behavior therapy consisting of "leading and reinforcing positive self-statements, decreasing inappropriate comments and developing a more appropriate lifestyle" (Matson et al., 1980, p. 87). The package was reported effective in increasing the number and length of appropriate comments and eliminating the symptoms of depression. An anecdotal report by the patient of increased social contacts and greater satisfaction with life was also made.

Schloss (1982) assessed the social behavior and verbalizations of depressed, moderately retarded, institutionalized adults. Diagnosis of depression was made using DSM-III criteria for recurrent depression and scores from the Beck Depression Inventory (Beck, Ward, Mendelson & Erbaugh, 1961). Based on criteria established by Miller and Seligman (1973), a cut-off score of nine or above on the Beck was used to differentiate depressed from nondepressed individuals. Eighteen five-minute observations of the nine identified depressed patients showed that the following differences were evident between the depressed group and the nondepressed comparison group: 1) other individuals were more likely to request action from depressed subjects than to make declarative statements; 2) depressed subjects were more likely to gain compliance by exhibiting negative affect; 3) the depressed subjects were more likely to risk requests by exhibiting negative affect; 4) other individuals were more likely to exhibit negative affect when interacting with depressed subjects; 5) staff rather than peers were more likely to interact with depressed mentally retarded adults.

Matson (1982) treated two mildly and two moderately retarded adults by targeting behaviors characteristic of their depression for remediation. Diagnosis of depression was based on several general measures including the Zung Self-Rating Depression Scale (Zung, 1965), the Beck Depression Inventory, and the Minnesota Multiphasic Personality Inventory (MMPI - Hathaway & McKinley, 1967). These three instruments were administered in the manner prescribed by the test authors. However, due to their reading difficulties, all items were read aloud to the subjects. Eight characteristics of depression collected during a structured interview served as target behaviors and further corroborated the depressed affect in the four subjects. These eight behaviors included somatic complaints, number of words spoken, irritability, grooming, negative self-statements, flat affect, eye contact, and speech latency.

Treatment consisted of token reinforcement, instructions, performance feedback, modeling by the therapist, and role playing. The treatment package was effective in changing target behaviors in the desired directions as shown through comparison with eight nondepressed mentally retarded individuals who did not meet criteria for depression based on the Beck, Zung, MMPI, and clinical judgments of target behaviors. Self-report ratings of depression from the Beck and Zung Scales showed a change from severe depression to no depression from pretest to posttest which was maintained at four- and six-month followups.

Reiss and Benson (1985) tested the hypotheses that depression in mildly mentally retarded adults is associated with (a) lower levels of social support and (b) high levels of perceived stigmatization. Social support and perceived stigmatization measures were utilized with 45 mildly mentally retarded individuals assigned to three groups -- depressed, disturbed/nondepressed, and nondisturbed/nondepressed -- based on self- and informant-reports of depression. The Zung Self-Rating Depression Scale (Zung, 1965) served as the self-report measure of depression. One item considered inappropriate for persons with mental retardation ("I still enjoy sex") was omitted. In a previous report (Reiss & Benson, 1984), the researchers found that test-retest reliability for the Zung scores of 32 of the present subjects over a 4-10 week (average 6.2) week period was $r.=.61$, $<.01$.

The items on the informant rating scale of depression were "seems happy" and "cries, seems lonely, and feels worthless." Response alternatives for the items were seldom (0 points), sometimes (1 point), often (2 points), and don't know (treated as missing data). Two work or residential supervisors (non-relatives) identified by the subjects served as the informant raters and the average of these two informant ratings were used. Interrater reliability of this rating scale was $r = .70$, $p < .01$, while the average informant rating score significantly correlated with the Zung total scores, $r = .43$, $p < .02$.

Measures of social support and stigmatization were gathered via the Reiss-Peterson Social Support Scale for Mentally Retarded Adults and a self-report scale for stigmatization. Informant ratings on these two measures were also made. Results of the study indicated that depression was negatively correlated with social support while convincing evidence of an association between depression and perceived stigmatization was not found.

In a follow-up study, Benson, Reiss, Smith, and Lana (1985) again used the Zung Scale and the informant rating scale of depression in assessing whether poor social skills are correlated with depression. Results showed that depression was associated with informant ratings of poor social skills. The authors indicated that further detailed study on the psychosocial correlates of depression in mentally retarded individuals is required based on the findings of these related studies.

Prout and Schaefer (1985) collected self-report measures of depression using standardized unmodified versions of the Depression Adjective Checklist-Level 1 (DACL, Lubin, 1967), the Zung Rating Scale, and the Beck Depression Inventory in 21 mildly mentally retarded adults. Results showed that these 21 subjects scored significantly higher in depression on the Beck and Zung when compared to groups of nonretarded adults who were also administered the three scales. Almost half were reported to score in the clinically significant range of depression on both measures. A failure to find a significant difference in the DACL between persons with mental retardation and those without was hypothesized to be due to the level of abstraction required on the DACL. The subjects with mental retardation may have had more difficulty in responding to a measure that contains only a series of adjectives and not specific symptoms and problems of depression as found on the Beck and Zung (Prout & Schaefer, 1985). Hence, a difference in the measures themselves may have produced these findings.

Significant correlations between the three measures were found however: DACL-Zung, .79; DACL-Beck, .74; Zung-Beck, .73. All correlations were significant at the .001 level. Additionally, based on the recommended clinical cut-off scores for both the Zung Scale (i.e., 40) and the Beck Inventory (i.e. 17), 11 subjects (52%) scored in the clinically significant range on the Zung Scale and 11 scored in the clinically significant range on the Beck Inventory. Ten (48%) scored in the clinically significant range on both measures. The authors reported that "the significant correlations among the measures and the high agreement for clinical significance for two of the measures strongly suggest that mildly mentally retarded adults can reliably report on problems they experience with regard to depression" (p. 221).

Prout & Schaefer's findings are not unlike those of Kazdin, Matson and Senatore (1983) who assessed depression in 110 adults with differing degrees of mental retardation. A number of modified versions of self-report depression instruments and several other informant measures were used. Self-reports included the Beck Depression Inventory, Short Form (Beck et al., 1961), the Zung Self-Rating Depression Scale, and the MMPI depression scale. The various measures were read to the patients individually and a verbal response was then elicited from the patient. Ten Thematic Apperception Test (TAT, Riddle & Rapoport, 1976) cards were used as a projective technique for the assessment of depression where responses to the stories were scored on a 7-point scale (1 = very sad, 7 = very happy). Also used was the self-report version of the Psycho-pathology Instrument for Mentally Retarded Adults (PIMRA, Matson, Kazdin, & Senatore, 1984). Informant measures of depression, the Hamilton Rating Scale for Depression (Hamilton, 1960), and an informant version of the PIMRA were collected from clinicians and ward personnel at inpatient and outpatient facilities.

Results showed that IQ significantly correlated with depression as indicated by Beck and Zung scores -- higher depression scores were associated with lower IQ scores. The Beck Scale was significantly correlated with the Zung and MMPI depression scale scores as well as with one informant measure, the Hamilton scale. A significant positive correlation was found between the Beck and the depression scale of the self-rated PIMRA. The Zung, MMPI-D, and Hamilton scales were correlated with selected measures of depression, but were not consistent with each of the other measures (Kazdin et al., 1983).

Comparisons of depressed versus nondepressed patients based on the Beck, Zung, and Hamilton scales were also made. Categorization of depression or lack thereof was based on cut-off scores for the three scales at the 67th and 33rd percentiles respectively. Findings suggested that high or low scores on these three measures could distinguish among mentally retarded adults on several of the other related measures. Finally, subjects diagnosed as depressed showed greater severity of depression than nondepressed patients on the Beck and Zung scales and were rated as more depressed on the Hamilton Scale in comparison to those without a diagnosis of depression.

Depression studies in mentally retarded children

Frame, Matson, Sonis, Fialkov, and Kazdin (1982) successfully treated a 10-year-old male of borderline mental retardation with major depression through a skills training package involving instructions, modeling, role-play, and performance feedback. Behaviors selected for intervention were inappropriate body position, lack of eye contact, poor speech, and bland affect. The diagnosis of major depression was based on several different convergent measures. Initially, the child met DSM-III criteria for major depression based upon a psychiatric interview. Next the mother rated her child on three different measures: Child Depression Inventory (CDI, Kovacs & Beck, 1977), the Child Behavior Checklist, (CBCL, Achenbach & Edelbrock, 1978, 1979), and the Bellevue Index of Depression (BID, Petti, 1978). The mother's ratings of the child produced criteria considered significant for depression by the authors -- a 27 on the CDI, one and one-half standard deviations above the mean for depression on the CBCL, and the meeting of Weinberg's criteria for depression on the BID (Brumback, Deitz-Schmidt & Weinberg, 1977). An independent rater viewed a videotaped interview of the child and rated his behavior on the CDI (score of 21) and on the Depression Adjective Checklist (Lubin, 1967) where he ranked at the 72nd percentile for depression. The staff of the hospital where the child was an inpatient reported observation of the four target behaviors as further indications of depressed affect.

In the only major study of depression in children with mental retardation, Matson, Barrett and Helsel (1988) matched 31 children with varying degrees of mental retardation on age and sex and compared them with 31 normal children for depression. Parents of the children with mental retardation completed the Child Depression Inventory and the Child Behavior Checklist while children in the normal sample were evaluated at their schools for both self and other ratings on these instruments. Results of ANOVA's run showed a significant main effect for the group on the total CDI score and for two of the factors of the CDI (Factor I-Affective Behavior and Factor IV-Guilt/Irritability) indicating a difference in depression between retarded and nonretarded persons.

Secondary analyses were performed within the mentally retarded group to compare differences between the seven depressed children (scoring at or above one standard deviation from the mean on the CDI total score as well as having a T-score of 60 or greater on the CBCL depression scale) and the 24 nondepressed children. Pearson Product Moment correlations were run with the following results. Total score on the CDI was positively correlated with both CDI Factors II-Image/Ideation and III-Interpersonal Relations ($r = .81$, $p < .01$ and $r = .67$, $p < .05$, respectively). Factor III of the CDI was negatively correlated with CBCL internalizing broad-band ($r = .70$, $p < .05$) and positively correlated with CDI Factor II-Image/Ideation ($r = .69$, $p < .05$), showing that these children were viewed as both clinically and statistically depressed (Matson, Barrett & Helsel, 1988).

T-tests run between the seven depressed mentally retarded children and seven nondepressed (scoring lowest on the CDI total score and CBCL) mentally retarded children showed the former to demonstrate significantly greater depression on all CDI factors ($p < .001$ for Factors I, II and IV, and $p < .01$ for Factor III). CDI total score and CBCL depression subfactor showed significant depression as well ($p < .0001$). It was concluded that "there are marked differences in the level of depressive features between mentally retarded and normal children and between mentally retarded children with and without high measurable levels of depression" (Matson, Barrett & Helsel, 1988).

Diagnostic instruments used in assessing depression in the mentally retarded

Beck Depression Inventory

Of the self-report instruments used for depression with mentally retarded adults, the Beck Depression Inventory along with the Zung Self-Rating Scale are employed most often (Kazdin, Matson & Senatore, 1983; Matson, 1982; Prout & Schaefer, 1985; Schloss, 1982; Senatore, Matson & Kazdin, 1985). The inventory is composed of 21 groups of statements (symptoms or attitudes) of depression which are rated on a 4-point, 0-3 scale as to severity. The patient is required to select the statement that best describes him or her at the time. The higher the score achieved, the more severe the degree of depression.

Internal consistency of the inventory is high. Split-half reliability yielded an r of 0.86 and with a Spearman-Brown correction, the coefficient was 0.93. Validity of the instrument is also good as highly significant relationships between the scores on the inventory and ratings of depression by diagnosticians were found, $r = 0.65$, $p < .01$ in Study I and $r = 0.67$, $p < .01$ in Study II (Beck et al., 1961).

The Beck is relatively easy to read and comprehend, hence, persons with mild retardation may be able to complete the instrument unaided. However, as research has shown, more accurate results may be achieved when modified versions are used where the clinician/researcher reads the statements to the patient and records his or her response (Kazdin et al., 1983; Senatore et al., 1985). Even with such a procedure the tendency for some mentally retarded individuals to provide stereotyped responses or verbal compliance in interviews may be problematic (Sigelman, Budd, Spanhel & Schoenrock, 1981; Sigelman et al., 1980). A true/false screening test and Likert-type test were used by Senatore et al. (1985) to ensure that clients could answer Likert format responses. Additionally, responding on the Beck Inventory has been aided by the use of bar graphs positioned on a wall with increasingly greater heights assigned to the 0-3 Likert scale (Kazdin et al., 1983; Senatore et al., 1985).

A short form of the Beck Inventory is comprised of 13 items (Items 1, 2, 3, 4, 5, 7, 9, 12, 13, 14, 15, 17, and 19 from the original inventory) again rated on a 4-point Likert scale. The 13-item version correlates 0.96 with the longer 21-item scale, and 0.61 with clinicians ratings of depression (Beck et al., 1961). The shorter version has been utilized by Kazdin et al. (1983) and Senatore et al. (1985).

Zung Self-Rating Scale

The Zung Self-Rating Scale has been used to assess and study depression in persons with mental retardation in a number of studies (Benson, Reiss, Smith & Lamadan, 1985; Kazdin, Matson & Senatore, 1983; Matson, 1982; Prout &Schaefer, 1985; Reiss & Benson, 1985; Senatore, Matson & Kazdin, 1985). The scale, composed of 20 items, requires the subject to rate how well the items characterize him or her using four quantitative terms; "a little of the time," "some of the time," "a good part of the time," and "most of the time." The responses are scored 1,2,3, and 4 respectively, depending upon whether the item is worded positively or negatively. Higher scores denote greater depression.

Rehm (1988) reports finding no published reliability data on the internal consistency or test-retest reliability of the Zung Scale. Concurrent validity of the scale is good. Zung, Richards and Short (1965) reported a correlation of .68 with the MMPI-Psychasthenia scale and a correlation of .70 with the Depression scale. Discriminant validity is considered weak.

Depression Adjective Checklists

Created by Lubin (1967), the Depression Adjective Checklists are a set of 7 word lists (Lists A-G) composed of 22 adjectives positive for depression (e.g. gloomy, sad, hopeless) and 10 adjectives negative for depression (e.g. gay, joyous, sunny). The lists were originally created to be used "to measure transient depressive mood, feeling or emotion" (Lubin, 1965, p.57) and, thus, for test-retest purposes on a short-term basis. The respondents check those adjectives which best describe the way they are feeling at that very moment. Originally, lists A-D were complied and administered to a group of severely depressed female patients and a control group of normal females. List E-G were similarly compiled and administered to a group of depressed males and a group of normal males.

Split-half reliabilities for the lists range between 0.82 and 0.93 for normals and between 0.86 and 0.93 for depressed patients. Inter-correlations between the lists are all significant at the .01 level. The smallest correlation between any two lists for females is 0.80, for males 0.83, and for combined groups 0.85 (Lubin, 1965). The author noted that the "high intercorrelations indicate the possible consideration of the lists as equivalent" (p.60).

Validity of the checklists also appears good. When the lists were cross-validated on new groups of normals, nondepressed psychiatric patients, and depressed psychiatric patients, F tests among groups for all lists were significant at the .0005 level. Correlations between all the lists and two measures of depression -- the MMPI-D and the Beck Inventory -- were presented in Lubin's (1965) article. Unfortunately, data were unavailable for several groups. However, correlations between the two scales and all seven lists administered to depressed patients (males and females) were significant at least at the .05 level. Correlations between the MMPI-D scale and Lists A-D given to normal females were significant at the .01 level while correlations between the D-scale and List E-G given to normal males were significant at least at the .05 level. Finally, correlations between the Beck Inventory and Lists A-D given to normal females were significant at the .01 level.

Of the seven lists available in the set of DACL's, Prout and Schaef (1985), in studying depression in the mildly mentally retarded used Checklist Level D, the one reported by Lubin (1967) to have the lowest reading level. Checklist Level A was used by Frame et al. (1982) as a convergent measure of depression (informant-rated) in assessing a 10-year-old borderline mentally retarded boy.

208

Psychopathology instrument for mentally retarded adults

The Psychopathology Instrument for Mentally Retarded Adults (PRIMA) has recently been developed as a screening instrument for assessing seven types of psychopathology in persons with mental retardation (Kazdin, Matson & Senatore, 1983; Matson, Kazdin & Senatore, 1984; Senatore, Matson & Kazdin, 1985). The 57-item instrument is divided into seven subscales of psychopathology: schizophrenia, affective, psychosexual, adjustment, anxiety, somatoform, and personality disorders. Seven or eight items are included for each disorder based upon DSM-III criteria. An additional seven items assess inappropriate mental adjustment. Items are summed to achieve each disorder subscale as well as a total psychopathology score. Both informant and self-report versions have been created, the latter version being modified to include simple sentences and concrete words that can be comprehended by retarded adults (Senatore, Matson & Kazdin, 1985). Responses of "yes" or "no" are rated for each item.

Matson et al. (1984) and Senatore et al. (1985) report adequate reliability for the instrument. Internal consistency for both versions of the PIMRA is acceptable and presented in Senatore et al. (1985). Coefficient alpha for the self-report version was 0.85 and Spearman-Brown split-half reliability was 0.88. For the informant version, coefficient alpha was 0.83 and Spearman-Brown split-half reliability was 0.65. Correlations between individual items and the total score were significant for both versions of the PIMRA with the mean of the item-total correlation for the self-report version, $r = .32$, $ps < .001$ and for the informant version, $r = .35$, $ps < .001$. Both versions indicated adequate test-retest stability with the informant version showing a significantly greater degree of stability over time (Senatore, Matson & Kazdin, 1985).

Recently, Watson, Aman and Singh (1988) assessed 160 mentally retarded adults with both versions of the PIMRA and found the results less robust than that reported in Matson et al (1984) and Senatore et al. (1985). Internal consistency and stability was found to be less than in the originator's studies. Item-total correlations were higher than in the initial reports.

At this time, the PIMRA has not been fully validated. Factors analysis performed on the two versions, however, shows differences in the factor structures (Matson et al., 1984). Self-report inventory factors were labeled as anxiety and social adjustment, while informant-report inventory factors were labeled affective, somatoform, and psychosis. Similar factor structures were found by Watson, Aman and Singh (1988). In their study of the PIMRA self-report inventory, factors included anxiety, social adjustment, identity/reality concern, and one unlabelled factor. Informant-report inventory factors were labelled affective concerns, social adjustment, somatoform difficulty, and one unlabelled factor. Matson et al. (1984) and Senatore et al. (1985) indicate that the differences in factor structures may result because persons with mental retardation may demonstrate difficulty in discriminating the specific form of psychopathology they are experiencing. An affective factor on the informant-rated inventory is promising for the study of depression in the mentally retarded.

Senatore et al. (1985) specifically discussed the use of the affective subscale of the PIMRA as useful in the assessment of depression in mentally retarded adults. Using the same subjects as in Kazdin et al. (1983), subjects were classified as depressed if informant ratings on the affective subscale indicated the presence of sadness plus four or more other symptom criteria, and nondepressed it they did not. Of the 110 subjects in the study, 10 were delineated as depressed and 96 were not. Additionally, these 10 depressed subjects showed higher depression on self-rated instruments for depression (Beck and Zung) and lower social skills performance (Social Performance Survey Schedule, Lowe & Cautela, 1978) than did the nondepressed subjects. When the affective subscale of the self-report PIMRA was used for diagnosis of depression group, differences were not evident.

Hamilton psychiatric rating scale for depression

The Hamilton Scale (Hamilton, 1960) is an informant-rated scale used for persons already diagnosed as having an affective disorder of the depressive type. The scale is composed of 17 variables characteristic of depression (e.g. depressed mood, retardation, agitation, suicide). Ten items (1, 2, 3, 7, 8, 10, 11, 15, 19 and 20) are defined in terms of a series of categories of increasing intensity and rated on a 5-point scale as "absent" (0), "mild or trivial" (1), "moderate" (2, 3), or "severe" (4). Eleven items (4, 5, 6, 9, 12, 13, 14, 16, 17, 18 and 21), in which the quantification of the symptom would be difficult, are simply rated on a 3-point scale as to whether the presence of the symptom is "absent" (0), "slight or doubtful" (2) or "clearly present" (2). The intensity or frequency of the depression variables are to be given equal status by the rater in making judgments. It is recommended that patients be rated by two physicians at the same time to insure interrater reliability. It is also advised that the total score be derived from the score of two independent ratings; if one rater is used, the score should be doubled.

No information on the reliability or validity of the scale is provided in the original report (Hamilton, 1960). Rehm (1988), however, reports adequate internal consistency, excellent interrater reliability, and good concurrent validity for the Hamilton Scale.

Factor analysis of the 17 variables of the Hamilton Scale rated for 49 male patients resulted in four factors best described as "retarded depression," "agitated depression," "some sort of anxiety reaction," and a fourth, unlabeled (Hamilton, 1960, p. 58-59). Rotating factors provided no clearer conceptualization of what specific characteristics of depression are being tapped by the scale. Case histories of patient's scoring high in the four different factors are presented by Hamilton (1960) to provide convergent evidence for the specific factors.

MMPI and MMPI-D scale

The Minnesota Multiphasic Personality Inventory (MMPI, Hathaway & McKinley, 1967) is the most widely used psychological test in the United States (Lubin, Larsen & Matarazzo, 1984). This standardized inventory includes 566 self-reference statements which are subsumed under 10 clinical scales, one of which, Scale 2, is depression. Three scales, the L, F, and K, are used to assess the validity of the respondents answers to the statements. Statements are rated as "true," "false," or "not applicable" to the respondent. Raw scores are then converted to T-scores and scores for each profile are plotted on a profile sheet for analysis.

Dahlstrom, Welsh and Dahlstrom (1975) have reported internal consistency data for a variety of samples with estimates varying considerably, from -.05 to .96. Typical values ranged from .60 to .90. Studies by Graham (1977) and Schwartz (1977) have shown temporal stability of the individual scales of the MMPI to be as reliable as other personality measures. Graham (1987) discussed validity studies for the MMPI, concluding that "it is difficult to make precise conclusions as to the MMPI's validity" (p. 81).

The Depression Scale of the MMPI is composed of 60 items which assess symptomatic depression. Statements address such areas as physical complaints, worry, denial of impulses, and religious fervor (Graham, 1987). Split-half reliabilities for the MMPI-D scale range from .35 to .84 with the median in the low .70s. Test-retest reliability is moderate (Dahlstrom & Welsh, 1960). Three studies have utilized the MMPI in the assessment of depression with mentally retarded adults (Matson, 1982; Kazdin et al., 1983; Senatore et al., 1985). Modified administration procedures were used where the clinician read the statements and the individual rated them.

211

Diagnostic instruments used in assessing depression in mentally retarded children

Bellevue Index of Depression

The Bellevue Index of Depression (BID, Petti, 1978) is a 40-item, semistructured interview modified from an interview initially created by Ling, Oftedal and Weinberg (1970). The interview is appropriate for children ages 6-12. The 40 items are characteristic of adult depression and are delineated into 10 headings: sleep disturbance, somatic complaints, dysphoric mood, self-deprecatory ideas, aggressive behavior, change in school performance, diminished socialization, change in attitude towards school, loss of usual energy, and unusual changes in appetite and/or weight. The items are rated for their absence or degree of severity on a 4-point scale ranging from 0 (absent) to 3 (severe). Patient interviews, parent interviews, and school data are used in making ratings. A child is considered depressed based on Weinberg criteria and if he or she receives a total score of 20 (Petti, 1978).

The BID appears to have concurrent validity. With 73 children rated for depression on the BID, the Weinberg et al. Index of Depressive Symptamology (WIDS) and clinicians judgments, chi-square analyses showed 89% agreement between the BID and WIDS (Petti, 1978). Of the 73 patients, 42 were rated depressed by both scales, while 23 were rated as not depressed (p < .001). Schultz (1981) has reported convergent validity information for the Child Depression Inventory and the BID (r = .65). No reliability data was reported in Petti's original report.

Child Depression Inventory

The Child Depression Inventory (CDI, Kovacs & Beck, 1977) is a 27-item scale completed with both a self- and informant report version. In the latter case, the scale is completed by the child's parent or teacher. The scale is designed for administration to or rating of children from 7 to 17 years of age. It is based on the Beck Depression Inventory and correlated with both global depression (Kovacs & Beck, 1977) and diagnoses of depression (Carlson & Cantwell, 1980). Of the 27 items, each consists of three statements (scored 0, 1 or 2) from which the child chooses the one sentence that best describes him or her during the prior two-week period. The total score is the sum of all the individual items. Friedman and Butler (1979) have found the CDI to be a relatively stable index of depression over a one-month period. Saylor, Finch, Spirito, and Bennett (1980) showed the CDI to have a one week test-retest reliability of .87 for emotionally disturbed children, but only .38 for normal children.

Helsel and Matson (1984) found the split-half correlation to be highly significant with a Spearman-Brown, r = .85, and Guttman split-half, r = .84. Factor analysis in this study resulted in four factors: Affective Behavior, Image/Ideation, Interpersonal Relations, and Guilt/Irratibility.

Child Behavior Checklist

Used by Matson, Barrett and Helsel (1988) because of its depression subscale, the Child Behavior Checklist (CBCL, Achenbach & Edelbrock, 1978, 1979) measures a wide range of psychopathology in children ages 4 to 16. The standardized instrument includes 118 behavior problem items scored on a 3-point scale (e.g., not true, somewhat or sometimes true, or very often true) by the parent. Twenty social competency items are also included in the checklist. Raw scores are converted to T-scores for the three broad-bands (internalizing, externalizing, and social). Separate empirically based norms and scoring procedures for each age group are found. Factor analysis has yielded several subscales including schizoid, depressed, uncommunicative, obsessive-compulsive, somatic complaints, withdrawal, hyperactivity, aggression, and delinquent behaviors. Achenbach (1978) and Achenbach and Edelbrock (1978) reported test-retest reliabilities ranging from .82 to .90. Content, criterion-related, and construct validity have been reported as favorable on the CBCL as well (Frame & Matson, 1987).

In both studies assessing depression in children with mental retardation (Frame et al., 1982; Matson, Barrett & Helsel, 1988), diagnosis of depression was made using information garnered from informant ratings of the children's overt behaviors. The reason for this was largely two-fold. First, the reliability and validity of information given by normal young children in an interview is questionable. This difficulty would invariably be compounded in persons with mental retardation. Second, problems in reading, comprehending, and rating self-report checklists or responding to direct interview questions would also be major obstacles in achieving an accurate assessment of depression in children with mental retardation. Since the parents and teachers are familiar with behaviors exhibited by these children, informant ratings and direct observations of the child are the next best alternatives to self-report. The three instruments discussed above provide the clinician/researcher with ratings of depression as well as other pertinent information regarding the child's behavior. Until a self-report method or instrument can be construed and validated for use with children with mental retardation, the study of depression is limited to checklists and scales used primarily with the normal child population.

Conclusion

There has been considerable progress made in the diagnosis of depression recently. The data related to depression in the mentally retarded is particularly encouraging as research supports the use of several forms of assessment. These include direct interviews, ratings by knowledgeable others, and direct behavioral observations. While these methods are most likely to be viable behavioral assessment procedures with the brightest of the mentally retarded population, developmental factors and severity of mental retardation may limit the possible assessment techniques. Hence, with very young individuals or severely mentally retarded persons, one relies increasingly on ratings by others or direct behavioral observation. The majority of the present research indicates that a multi-method approach is the most effective way of studying and treating depression in mentally retarded individuals. While most studies have used assessment devices initially created for use with persons of normal intelligence, modification of these instruments (e.g., reading the instrument to the subject, changing the wording or using shortened forms of the instruments) has resulted in the ability to identify depression in the mentally retarded. Instruments such as the PIMRA are much needed additions to the armentarium of clinicians concerned with the dual diagnosis of mentally handicapped and behavior-disordered individuals.

Future directions for research should initially be aimed at delineating behaviors that characterize the syndrome. Clinicians and researchers are still relatively ignorant as to how depression is manifested in mentally retarded persons and how these behaviors change across levels of mental retardation (Matson, 1983). Operationally defining behaviors exhibited by depressed mentally retarded individuals is necessary before a theoretical system of diagnosis of depression in this population is possible. Research aimed at the more severely handicapped is required because direct observation plays such a crucial role in the diagnosis of depression; most research has been done with the mildly and moderate mentally retarded. Although our knowledge of diagnosis is minimal at this time, the recent interest in issues of dual diagnosis is promising for future research. As researchers have explored the phenomena of depression in adults, adolescents, and children with normal intelligence, the prospects for fruitful investigation of persons with mental retardation is assured.

References

Achenbach, T.M. (1978). The child behavior profile: 1. Boys aged 6 through 11. Journal of Consulting and Clinical Psychology, 46, 478-488.

Achenbach, T.M., & Edelbrock, C.S. (1978). The classification of child psychotherapy: A review and analysis of empirical efforts. Psychological Bulletin, 85, 1275-1301.

Achenbach, T.M., & Edelbrock, C.S. (1979). The Child Behavior Profile: II. Boys aged 12-16 and girls 6-11 and 12-16. Journal of Consulting and Clinical Psychology, 47, 223-233.

American Psychiatric Association. (1980). Diagnostic and statistical manual of mental disorders. (3rd edition). Washington, D.C.: American Psychiatric Association.

Beck, A.T., Ward, C.H., Mendelson, M., & Erbaugh, M.D. (1961). An inventory for measuring depression. Archives of General Psychiatry, 4, 561-571.

Benson, B.A., Reiss, S., Smith, D., & Laman, D.S. (1985). Psychosocial correlates of depression in mentally retarded adults. II. Poor social skills. American Journal of Mental Deficiency, 89 (6), 657-659.

Brumback, R., Dietz-Schmidt, S. & Weinberg, W. (1977). Depression in children referred to an educational diagnostic center: Diagnosis and treatment and analysis of criteria and literature review. Diseases of the Nervous System, 3B, 529-535.

Carlson, G.A., & Cantwell, D.P. (1980). Unmasking masked depression in children and adolescents. American Journal of Psychiatry, 37, 445-449.

Cytryn, L., & McKnew, D.H. (1972). Proposed classification of childhood depression. American Journal of Psychiatry, 129, 149-155.

Cytryn, L., McKnew, D.H., & Bunney, W. (1980). Diagnosis of depression in children: A reassessment. American Journal of Psychiatry, 137, 22-25.

Dahlstrom, W.G., & Welsh, G.S. (1960). An MMPI hand book: A guide to use in clinical practice and research. Minneapolis: University of Minnesota Press.

Dahlstrom, W.G., Welsh, G.S., & Dahlstrom, L.E. (1975). An MMPI Handbook (Vol. 2) Research applications. Minneapolis: University of Minnesota Press.

Frame, C., & Matson, J.L. (1987). Handbook of assessment in childhood psychopathology. New York: Plenum Press.

Frame, C., Matson, J.L., Sonis, W.A., Fialkov, M.J., & Kazdin, A.E. (1982). Behavioral treatment of depression in a prepubertal child. Journal of Behavior Therapy and Experimental Psychiatry, 13, 239-243.

Friedman, R., & Butler, L. (1979). Development and evaluation of a test battery to assess childhood depression. Unpublished manuscript, Ontario Institute for Studies in Education.

Graham, J.R. (1977). Stability of MMPI configurations in a college setting. Unpublished manuscript. Kent State University: Kent, OH.

Graham, J.R. (1987). The MMPI: A practical guide. New York: Oxford University Press.

Hamilton, M. (1960). A rating scale for depression. Journal of Neurology, Neurosurgery and Psychiatry, 23, 56-62.

Hathaway, S.R., & McKinley, J.C. (1967). Minnesota Multiphasic Personality Inventory: Manual for administration and scoring. New York: Psychological Corporation.

Helsel, W.J., & Matson, J.L. (1984). The assessment of depression in children: The internal structure of the Child Depression Inventory (CDI) and its relationship to the Matson Evaluation of Social Skills with Youngsters (MESSY). Behavior Research and Therapy, 22, 289-298.

Kazdin, A.E., & Matson, J.L., & Senatore, V. (1983). Assessment of depression in the mentally retarded. American Journal of Psychiatry, 140, 1040-1043.

Kovacs, M. & Beck, A. (1977). An empirical-clinical approach toward a definition of childhood depression. In: J. Schulterbrandt & A. Raskin (Eds.), Depression in childhood: Diagnosis, treatment and conceptual models. New York: Haven Press.

Lefkowitz, M.M. (1980). Childhood depression: A reply to Costello. Psychological Bulletin, 87, 191-194.

Ling, W., Oftedal, G., & Weinberg, W. (1970). Depressive illness in childhood presenting as severe headache.

Lowe, B.R., & Cautela, J.R. (1978). A self-report measure of social skill. Behavior Therapy, 9, 535-544.

Lubin, B. (1965). Adjective checklists for measurement of depression. Archives of General Psychiatry, 12, 57-62.

Lubin, B. (1967). The Depression Adjective Check Lists Manual. San Diego: Educational and Industrial Testing Service.

Lubin, B., Larsen, R.M., & Matarazzo, J.D. (1984). Patterns of psychological test use in the United States 1935-1982., American Psychologist, 39, 451-454.

Matson, J.L. (1982). The treatment of behavioral characteristics of depression in the mentally retarded. Behavior Therapy, 13, 209-218.

Matson, J.L. (1983). Depression in the mentally retarded: Toward a conceptual analysis of diagnosis. In: M. Hersen, R. Eisler, & P.M. Miller (Eds.), Progress in behavior modification (Vol. 15). New York: Academic Press.

Matson, J.L., & Barrett, R.P. (1982). Psychopathology in the mentally retarded. New York: Grunne & Stratton.

Matson, J.L., & Barrett, R.P., & Helsel, W.J. (1988). Depression in mentally retarded children. Research in Developmental Disabilities, 9, 39-46.

Matson, J.L., Dettling, J. & Senatore, V. (1980). Treating depression of a mentally retarded adult. British Journal of Mental Subnormality, 16, 86-88.

Matson, J.L., Kazdin, A.E., & Senatore, V. (1984). Psychometric properties of the psychopathology instrument for mentally retarded adults. Applied Research in Mental Retardation, 5, 81-89.

Menolascino, F.J., & Stark, J.A. (1984). Handbook of mental illness in the mentally retarded. Plenum Press.

Miller, W. R., & Seligman, M. E. P. (1973). Depression and the perceptions of reinforcement. Journal of Abnormal Psychology, 82, 62-73.

Petti, T. (1978). Depression in hospitalized child psychiatry patients. American Academy of Child Psychiatry, 17, 49-59.

Prout, H.T., & Schaefer, B.M. (1985). Self reports of depression by community-based mildly mentally retarded adults. American Journal of Mental Deficiency, 90 (2), 220-225.

Rehm, L.P. (1988). Assessment of depression. In: A. Bellack & M. Hersen (Eds.). Behavioral assessment approaches handbook (3rd Edition). Elmsford, New York: Pergamon Press.

Reiss, S., & Benson, B.A. (1984b). Stability and measurement of depression in mentally retarded adults. Paper presented at the annual Gatlinburg Conference on research in mental retardation and developmental disabilities. Gatlinburg, TN.

Reiss, S., & Benson, B.A. (1985). Psychosocial correlates of depression in mentally retarded adults: I. Minimal social support and stigmatization. American Journal of Mental Deficiency, 89 (4), 331-337.

Riddle, K.D. & Rapoport, J.L. (1976). A 2-year follow-up of 72 hyperactive boys. Journal of Nervous and Mental Disorders, 162, 126-134.

217

Saylor, C.F., Finch, A.J., Spirito, A., & Bennett, B. (1980). The Children's Depression Inventory: A systematic evaluation of psychometric properties. Journal of Consulting Psychology, 52, 955-967.

Schloss, P.J. (1982). Verbal interaction patterns of depressed and non-depressed institutionalized mentally retarded adults. Applied Research in Mental Retardation, 3, 1-12.

Schultz, H. (1981, August). Correlates of depression in a clinical sample of children and their mothers. In: L.P. Rehm (Chair), Empirical studies of childhood depression. Symposium presented at the meeting of the American Psychological Association, Los Angeles.

Schwartz, G.F. (1977). An investigation of the stability of single scale and 2-point MMPI code types for psychiatric patients. Unpublished doctoral dissertation. Kent State University: Kent, OH.

Senatore, V., Matson, J.L., & Kazdin, A.E. (1985). An inventory to assess psychopathology of mentally retarded adults. American Journal of Mental Deficiency, 89, 459-466.

Sigelman, C.K., Budd, E.C., Spanhel, C.L., & Schoenrock, C.J. (1981). When in doubt, say yes: Acquiescence in interviews with mentally retarded persons. Mental Retardation, 19, 53-58.

Sigelman, C.K., Schoenrock, C.J., Spanhel, C.L., Hromas, S.G., Winer, J.L., Budd, E.C., & Martin, P.W. (1980). Surveying mentally retarded persons: Responsiveness and response validity in three samples. American Journal of Mental Deficiency, 84, 479-486.

Sigman, M. (1985). Children with emotional disorders and developmental disabilities. Orlando, FL: Grunne & Stratton.

Szymanski, L.S., & Tanquay, P.E. (1980). Emotional disorders of mentally retarded persons. Baltimore: University Park Press.

Watson, J.E., Aman, M.G., & Singh, N.N. (1988). The Psychopathology Instrument for Mentally Retarded Adults: Psychometric characteristics, factor structure, and relationship to subject characteristics. Research in Developmental Disabilities, 9, 277-290.

Zung, W.W.K. (1965). A self-rating depression scale. Archives of General Psychiatry, 12, 63-70.

Zung, W.W.K., Richards, C.B., & Short, M.J. (1965). Self rating depression scale in an outpatient clinic. Archives of General Psychiatry, 13, 508-515.

Anton Dosen and Frank J. Menolascino (Eds.) (1990). Depression in mentally retarded children and adults. Leiden, the Netherlands: Logon Publications. ISBN 90-73197-01-5

Chapter 12

Biochemical findings in mentally retarded persons with depressive disorders

Stephen L. Ruedrich, M.D.

Introduction

Two dilemmas immediately face the researcher or clinician working with mentally retarded persons with affective disorders. The first involves the diagnostic uncertainty inherent in evaluation. The degree of retardation and variability of communicative language necessarily influence the diagnostic criteria that can be utilized (Sovner & Hurley, 1983), and subsequent investigations into the biological correlates of affective disorders in this population can only be as reliable as the diagnoses upon which they are based. Second, and of equal importance, is the potential influence of the mental retardation itself, or its underlying genetic, medical, developmental, or environmental etiology, on any biological aspect of the psychiatric disorder. In previous research in this area, mental retardation as a variable was viewed as monolithic and homogeneous, and little or no attempt was made to tease out its possible influences by either level or etiology of retardation. This unidimensional view obviously influences any conclusions that can be drawn from such research.

Given the above, it is safe to conclude that little data currently exists regarding biological components of affective disorders in mentally retarded persons. The available literature can be divided into two categories -- that dealing with the Hypothalamic-Pituitary-Adrenal (HPA) Axis and the Dexamethasone Suppression Test (DST) in endogenous depression, and all others. This is not unexpected in that this biological variable is also the most widely studied correlate of affective disorders in the nonretarded population, and its applicability to the mentally retarded appears to promise an avenue of fruitful research.

The HPA axis and the DST in affective disorders

By way of review, the HPA axis has been investigated in affectively ill individuals for at least twenty years. Sachar and colleagues (Sachar, Hellman, Roffwarg, Halpern, Fukoshima & Gallagher, 1973) were among the first to report hypercortisolemia in endogenous depression. Utilizing 5 mcg/dl as the benchmark of nonsuppression, Carroll et al. (1981) reported escape from suppression of serum cortisol in approximately 50% of patients with endogenous depression following administration of dexamethasone, a potent steroid. The diagnostic sensitivity of the DST for endogenous depression was low (i.e., 50% false negatives), but reported specificity was quite high (i.e., greater than 95%) in pre-screened patients (Carroll, 1982). Other authors subsequently promoted the DST as a useful marker for predicting response to somatic treatment, confirming successful treatment, and anticipating relapse (Brown & Shuey, 1980; Greden et al., 1980; Targum, 1984).

After an initial flush of success, however, a number of reports appeared that seemed to weaken the previously described specificity, and DST nonsuppression was found to be associated with dementia, schizophrenia, alcoholism, and normal controls (Dewan et al., 1982; Raskind et al., 1982; Stokes et al., 1984; Swartz & Dunner, 1982). A number of medications and medical conditions also appeared to invalidate the DST so that its clinical utility today is questionable (Arana, Baldessarini & Ornsteen, 1985; Carroll et al., 1981; Kraus, Grof & Brown, 1988).

It is interesting to note, however, that none of the major reviews of the DST in populations other than the mentally retarded identifies intelligence or the presence of mental retardation as a potential intervening variable in DST interpretation (Arana, Baldessarini & Ornsteen, 1985; Young, Schwarz & ACP, 1984). The only possible exceptions to this were reports of DST nonsuppression in some demented patients, although no data were given regarding specific levels of cognitive dysfunction and no mention was made of mental retardation (Carroll et al., 1981; Carnes et al., 1983). Because of such limitations, some authors have recently proposed modifications of the DST format by expressing cortisol as a function of serum dexamethasone level (Dexamethasone Suppression Index), while others have recommended additional neuroendocrine tests involving the HPA axis as necessary components of future DST/affective disorder research (Arana et al, 1988; Meller et al., 1988).

HPA axis and DST in depressive mentally retarded persons

Only a handful of authors have investigated the DST with regard to mentally retarded depressed patients. Field et al. (1986) reported on their treatment of a 22-year-old moderately retarded woman with congenital rubella who manifested a behavioral disorder consisting of crying, weight loss, irregular sleep, motor agitation, and screaming outbursts. Her DST was reported as negative, and the authors determined that a diagnosis of unequivocal endogenous depression was not possible in the absence of classic symptoms. The patient was treated with imipramine in a double-blind, placebo-controlled fashion and responded with improvement in eating and sleep patterns as well as decreased crying and screaming.

Szymanski and Biederman (1984) utilized DSM-III (APA, 1980) criteria for identifying depressive disorders in a sample of 155 mentally retarded adults referred for psychiatric evaluation. Of these, fifteen (10%), half of whom had Down's Syndrome, had depressive disorders. The authors provided case study data for three of the depressed Down's patients, and reported DST status for two of these. One patient had a positive (nonsuppressed) DST, which persisted even after apparently adequate treatment. For the other patient, DST was normal.

Pirodsky et al. (1985) divided a group of 39 retarded adults according to the presence or absence of three "primary" behaviors -- aggression, self injury, or severe withdrawal -- and twenty-two "secondary" behaviors consisting of a mixture of DSM-III criteria for Affective Disorder as well as items from the American Association on Mental Deficiency Adaptive Behavior Scale. Five of the 39 were nonsuppressors on the standard overnight DST, which correlated significantly with the demonstration of two or more of the primary behaviors. It was also noted that the individuals with positive DSTs were more likely to manifest secondary behaviors, such as stereotypy, temper tantrums and crying, although these did not reach statistically significant levels. The authors concluded that the DST was potentially diagnostically useful in mentally retarded persons but that, in their sample, few of the classic symptoms of depression were seen in the DST nonsuppressor group. They posited, therefore, that a positive DST in a retarded individual with non-specific behavioral problems, such as assault or self-injury, should be approached with antidepressants rather than antipsychotic medication, as is more often the case.

Sireling (1986) disagreed. He utilized the standard DST protocol in twelve depressed mentally retarded persons, six of whom had a major depressive disorder (MDD) by Research Diagnostic Criteria, and five of whom had definite or probable minor depressive disorders. Only one patient failed to suppress after dexamethasone administration, causing the author to conclude that the DST has little to offer in the differential diagnosis of depression in mentally handicapped patients. Sireling did note, however, that the small sample size may have influenced the outcome of this research.

A significant study conducted by Beckwith et al. (1985) explored the utility of the DST for diagnosing depression in a sample of institutionalized mentally retarded persons. The authors had caregivers rate patients with a check list of depressive symptoms compiled from DSM-III, Research Diagnostic Criteria, the Hamilton Rating Scale for Depression, and the Beck Depression Inventory, which required no verbal response from the patient. A five-point severity scale was constructed for each item, and patients who scored above the group mean were defined as depressed. The authors confirmed the accuracy of ratings with blind interviews, and compared the DST results of 26 high-scoring (depressed) with 31 zero-scoring (non-depressed) individuals. The groups were roughly similar with respect to age, level of retardation, and drug regimen, although they were not specifically matched on these variables. Serum cortisols were drawn at 8:00 a.m, 4:00 p.m., and 10:00 p.m., following the administration of 1 mg. of dexamethasone at 10:00 p.m. the previous night. Using 4 mcg/dl as cut-off, the authors found 21 patients who were DST nonsuppressors. Nonsuppression appeared to particularly discriminate depressed from non-depressed patients in the 8:00 a.m. and 4:00 p.m. sampling times, resulting in a 46% sensitivity of the DST for "depression" -- similar to that reported in nonretarded depressives. Their false positive rate was higher than expected (29%) and was attributed to the 10:00 p.m. administration of dexamethasone (i.e., 1-2 hours earlier than in other studies), causing false positive nonsuppression in the subsequent 10:00 p.m. cortisol sample. It was hypothesized that other nonsuppressors who demonstrated a pattern of "quiet passivity" may have appeared to be cooperative to attendants and, thus, were not identified as depressed according to the rating instrument used in the study. The authors concluded that the DST might offer considerable benefit in the identification of depression in institutionalized retarded patients.

A number of other authors (Beck, Carlson, Russell & Brownfield, 1987; Dosen, 1984; Kazdin, Matson & Senatore, 1983; Matson, 1986; Reynolds, in press; Sovner & Hurley, 1983) have discussed the difficulty of accurately diagnosing affective disorders in retarded patients, especially those with low IQs and poor communicative language. Given this, the reported rates of DST nonsuppression in the affectively ill mentally

222

retarded, in which a diagnosis of MDD or endogenous depression constitutes the independent variable in research, have been called into question. Some authors have utilized the DST **independently** in the nonretarded population by looking at variables, other than diagnosis, which correlated with nonsuppression (Reus, 1982).

Taking this approach, Sandman, Barron, and Parker (1985) administered a standard overnight DST to 28 institutionalized retarded adults, using 4 mcg/dl as the limit for identifying nonsuppression. It was demonstrated that over half (54%) escaped suppression on at least one post-dexamethasone cortisol sample. The subjects had been pre-screened to eliminate known etiologies for false positive nonsuppression, although 11 of the 28 (39%) were receiving anticonvulsants during the study. Eliminating these patients from data analysis still produced a rate of DST nonsuppression greater than 40%, a striking finding in that the patients were not felt to be clinically depressed (i.e., were not chosen on that basis) prior to entry. The authors divided their sample into three groups, based upon zero, one, or two post-dexamethasone levels in the non-suppressor range, and compared the groups on 28 dependent variables including type of handicap, EEG status, medications taken, length of institutionalization, and whether or not depressed, self-injurious, or aggressive behaviors were exhibited. Following discriminate function analysis of the data, the authors suggested that the DST response in their sample might be best explained as an adaptation to institutionalization. Group I, with one elevated post-DST cortisol, had the briefest hospitalizations, lower social and mental ages, normal EEG's, and took more sedative/hypnotic medications. Group II, with two post-DST elevations, were hospitalized longer, had more mood swings and HPA axis disregulation, took sedative/hypnotic medications, and had abnormal EEG's. Finally, Group III, with "normal" HPA axis function, had the longest duration of institutionalization, abnormal EEG's, higher social functioning, and mood swings. The authors concluded that the presence in Group III of mood swings and abnormal EEG's, but normal HPA axis function, might represent the physiological and behavioral costs of enduring institutionalization. They noted that data interpretation was limited by the small sample sizes of some groups, and were uncertain whether a positive DST in their patients was a marker for endogenous depression, or a more general, less specific, stress response.

In similar fashion, Ruedrich, Wadle, Hahn, and Chu (1985) found 3 of 8 retarded adults in a pilot study to have DST nonsuppression, 2 of whom also manifested behavioral disturbances involving anorexia, insomnia, screaming, self-abuse, and crying spells. The authors expanded

223

their sample to investigate 85 institutionalized retarded adults, utilizing the DST independently in data analysis (Ruedrich, Wadle, Sallach, Hahn & Menolascino, 1987). Subjects of both sexes, ranging in age from 18 to 63 years, with all levels of mental retardation and varying degrees of symptomatology were carefully screened to exclude false positive nonsuppression. After data collection, subjects underwent overnight dexamethasone testing, with 8:00 a.m., 4:00 p.m., and midnight cortisol sampling over 48 hours, both pre- and post-dexamethasone (1 mg. orally at 11:00 p.m. on day 1). At the same time, data were collected by raters blind to DST results. Symptoms for which data were gathered included the DSM-III criteria for MDD, as well as a number of other activities and behaviors commonly observed in mentally retarded adults. Thirty-one patients (36%) had at least one elevated baseline serum cortisol, and 20 (24%) demonstrated escape from dexamethasone suppression with a post-dexamethasone cortisol greater than 5 mcg/dl. Baseline hyper-cortisolemia correlated significantly and positively with older age and number of symptoms, and DST nonsuppression was significantly related to age, female sex, level of retardation, and symptomatology. Partial correlations maintained age, level of retardation, and symptomatology, but not sex, as significant. Within the symptoms manifested by nonsupressors, there were a number that fit into the DSM-III criteria for MDD. The authors then retrospectively diagnosed the subjects, using modified DSM-III MDD criteria (i.e., adding crying spells, and requiring only three, not four, symptoms for inclusion), and found that DST nonsuppression correlated significantly with such criteria (sensitivity 41%, specificity 81%). There were also several individual symptoms not associated with MDD that were significantly correlated with nonsuppression (e.g., visual hallucinations, crying spells, laughing, physical aggression, and undress-ing). The authors concluded that the DST is valid when used with retarded persons, that mental retardation is **not** a technical exclusion for the DST in test interpretation, and that retarded persons might manifest some "depressive" symptoms not usually associated with MDD, such as aggression and visual hallucinations. They cautioned that careful pre-screening is mandatory prior to utilizing the DST, but that it can be useful in diagnosing retarded persons with behavioral disorders or psychiatric illnesses which include the above symptoms.

Viewed from a different perspective, these patients raise a fascinat-ing teleological question regarding affective disorders in mentally retarded individuals: Does an individual with profound or severe mental retarda-tion, who has a behavioral disturbance characterized by the signs and symptoms sometimes seen in affectively ill nonretarded persons and an endocrinological abnormality sometimes seen in affective illness, have an affective disorder at all -- or merely a behavioral disturbance associated (causally or non-causally) with the biological finding? These and other areas which appear to produce links among mental retardation, affective disorders, and biological markers constitute important areas for research, and may ultimately produce significant findings relevant to affective illnesses in nonretarded persons.

Additional findings

Biological correlates of affective disorders in mental retardation that do not involve the HPA axis or DST are rare, and reflect the lesser emphasis on investigation into affective disorders and DST in nonretarded populations. Nevertheless, there exists strong evidence for several other biological correlates of affective disorders in adult patients of normal intelligence. For example, a large percentage (25-40%) of individuals with major depression reveal a blunted (i.e., less than expected) increase in thyroid-stimulating hormone following the administration of a standard dose of thyrotropin-releasing hormone (Loosen & Prange, 1982). Interestingly, this group is not generally the same as that having HPA axis abnormalities and DST nonsuppression.

A number of other areas of investigation have produced less striking or more controversial results. These include measurements of neuro-chemical changes of monoamine metabolites (norepinephrine, serotonin, dopamine) in cerebrospinal fluid and urine, alterations in levels and/or transport of the serum electrolytes sodium and calcium across neuronal membranes, neuroradiological abnormalities on CAT or PET brain scanning, neuroendocrine changes in glucose tolerance and growth hormone regulation, and alterations in circadian or other chronobiological rhythms of the above processes. These and other areas of biological investigation in affectively ill patients are comprehensively reviewed by Thase, Frank and Kupfer (1985). A literature review of affective disorders and mental retardation revealed no articles specifically addressing these variables in retarded persons and, in a general overview of these areas in the nonretarded, there was no mention found of intelligence affecting biological variables, test outcomes, or applicability (Kupfer & Thase, 1983).

CSF 5-HIAA and aggression

An additional area of substantial research activity involves the discovery of lower than expected cerebrospinal fluid (CSF) 5-hydroxyindoleacetic acid (5-HIAA) in affectively ill individuals, particularly those with melancholic and delusional features (Asberg et al., 1984). Low levels of 5-HIAA, the major breakdown product of serotonin (5-HT), is thought to indicate decreased CNS 5-HT metabolism. Of further interest is the finding that the lowest CSF 5-HIAA occurred in those depressed patients who had attempted suicide, particularly through violent means (Traskman, Asberg, Bertilsson & Sjostrand, 1981). However, the finding of lowered CSF 5-HIAA in individuals attempting suicide who were **not** depressed and in non-depressed aggressive patients with diagnosed personality disorders led to an alternative hypothesis that low CSF 5-HIAA is associated with aggression rather than (or in addition to) depressive disorders (Brown et al., 1982; van Praag, Plutchik & Conte, 1986).

These are interesting findings in light of the fact that self-injurious behavior is a symptom seen in approximately 10% of institutionalized retarded individuals, and has been causally linked to a variety of potential behavioral and biological etiologies. Theories have included viewing such behavior as a means of maintaining sensory arousal, as a form of communication, as resulting from either the positive or negative reinforcement it engenders, as arising from a disturbed endogenous opiate system resulting in pain insensitivity, or as a possible symptom of an affective or psychotic illness (Rincover, 1986; Rivinus & Harmatz, 1979; Sandman et al., 1983). If this final hypothesis were true, the investigation of neurotransmitter function in depressed retarded persons who exhibit such behavior might provide insight into this complex interrelationship.

Toward this end, a more direct potential link to mental retardation appears to exist in the auto-aggression seen in the Lesch-Nyhan syndrome, an inborn error of metabolism associated with severe mental retardation and self-mutilation. Some Lesch-Nyhan patients demonstrate low levels of CSF 5-HIAA and some have responded to administration of 5-hydroxytryptophan (5-HTP), a precursor of serotonin, with a decrease in self-mutilative behavior (Nyhan, Johnson, Kaufman & Jones, 1980), although negative findings have also been reported in this area (Watts et al., 1982). Other authors have noted a relative decrease in the function of dopaminergic neurons in the brains of Lesch-Nyhan patients at necropsy, attributing auto-aggressive behavior to dopamine supersensitivity (Goldstein, Anderson, Reuben & Dancis, 1985). Whatever the particular biochemical abnormalities responsible for self-mutilative behavior in Lesch-Nyhan patients, there is no clear evidence that this represents a specific psychiatric disorder, such as an affective illness, in these severely retarded individuals.

REM latency

Of further interest is the finding that a much larger portion of endogenously depressed adults, sometimes as many as 75%, demonstrate characteristic changes in the architecture of sleep. Most commonly this involves a shortened latency of Rapid Eye Movement (REM) sleep; that is, the period of time between the onset of sleep and the beginning of the first REM period is decreased, as compared to control subjects or psychiatric patients with primarily non-affective disorders (Kupfer & Thase, 1983). This shortened REM latency may also be associated with increased REM intensity (i.e., increased percentage of sleep time spent in REM sleep), although this is less characteristic than the change in timing and distribution of REM periods.

Nutritional deficiencies

Certain nutritional deficiencies are known to result in psychiatric illness; thiamine deficiency in Wernicke's encephalopathy and Korsakoff's psychosis, and niacin and vitamin B12 deficiencies in dementia, for example. Pathophysiologic theories regarding the connection between nutritional status and psychiatric disorders generally involve postulated deficiencies in the amount or availability of precursors for the synthesis of neurotransmitters implicated in the disorder or, alternately, inadequate amounts of those substances which are necessary co-factors or modulators in neurotransmitter synthesis. Whether such nutritional deficiencies serve a primary etiological role in the pathogenesis of illness or constitute secondary aggravating conditions brought about by the poor nutritional status and/or behavior (e.g., anorexia) seen in the disorder, remains unclear (Abou-Saleh & Coppen, 1986).

Tryptophan (5-HTP) has been implicated in precursor deficiency theories of affective disorders (Coppen & Wood, 1978) and, more recently, folate deficiencies have been reviewed in several psychiatric disorders including schizophrenia, dementia, and depression (Abou-Saleh & Coppen, 1986). Deficits in cholinergic function and decreased activity of choline acetyltransferase, the enzyme responsible for acetylcholine synthesis in the brain, has led to the cholinergic hypothesis of Alzheimer's Disease. This has encouraged some researchers to attempt to enhance acetylcholine activity with dietary supplementation utilizing acetylcholine precursors, although the deficits seen have not necessarily been thought to be due to dietary deficiencies of such precursors (Bartus, Dean, Beer & Lippa, 1982).

While tryptophan, acetylcholine, and folate are not clearly etiologically related to major subtypes of mental retardation, folate is thought to be of benefit to some patients with Fragile X syndrome, a common X-linked genetically based etiology of mental retardation (Abou-Saleh & Coppen, 1986). Males with Fragile X syndrome often have symptoms of infantile autism and pervasive developmental disorder, and heterozygous females, whether mentally retarded or not, have been found to display a higher than expected frequency of schizophrenia spectrum disorders and, to a lesser extent, affective disorders (Reiss, Hagerman, Vinogradors, Abrams & King, 1988). However, there appears to be no clear evidence that either folate deficiency or its supplementation is related to affective illness in these individuals. Clearly, future research will be necessary to delineate the complex interrelationships among nutrition, neuroendocrinologic status, mental retardation, and affective disorders.

Conclusion

A summary of the current state of knowledge in the area of biological correlates of affective disorders in retarded persons will necessarily be brief and raise more questions than it answers. Yet continued research could provide immense diagnostic assistance to clinicians. Biological markers for any psychiatric disorder, including affective disorders, would clearly be useful in the diagnosis of patients who cannot self-report symptoms and for whom accurate diagnosis is often difficult or impossible. It is just such diagnostic difficulty that makes the study of biological correlates in mentally retarded patients with affective disorders so challenging, however, since any biological marker can only be as reliable as the diagnosis upon which it is based. Even so, significant contributions could be made if we extend the previous studies of REM latency, the HPA axis, the thyroid axis, and other biological variables in nonretarded affectively ill individuals into the mentally retarded depressed population. It may be that mentally retarded persons as a group provide a more "pure" research medium in which to conduct such studies as they might represent a more truly biological sample -- the connection between biological variables and symptomatology is more clearly connected and there is less intervening psychosocial overlay or interpretation. If true, investigation involving such biological correlates in retarded persons may be applicable to the work currently being conducted with the nonretarded population, thus providing new insights for all into the biology of these challenging disorders.

References

Abou-Saleh, M.T. & Coppen, A. (1986). The biology of folate in depression: implications for nutritional hypotheses of the psychoses. Journal of Psychiatric Research, 20, 91-101.

American Psychiatric Association (1980). Diagnostic and Statistical Manual of Mental Disorders - Third Edition. Washington, D.C.: American Psychiatric Association Press.

Arana, G.W., Baldessarini, R.J. & Ornsteen M. (1985). The Dexamethasone Suppression Test for diagnosis and prognosis in psychiatry. Archives of General Psychiatry, 42, 1193-1204.

Arana, G.W., Reichlin, S., Workman, R., Haaser, R. & Shader, R.I. (1988). The Dexamethasone Suppression Index: enhancement of DST diagnostic utility for depression by expressing serum cortisol as a function of serum dexamethasone. American Journal of Psychiatry, 145, 707-711.

Asberg, M., Bertilsson, L. Martensson, B., Scalia-Tomba, G., Thoren, P. & Traskman, L. (1984). CSF monoamine metabolites in melancholia. Acta Psychiatrica Scandanavia, 69, 201-219.

Bartus, R.T., Dean, R.L., Beer, R. & Lippa, A.S. (1982). The cholinergic hypothesis of geriatric memory dysfunction. Science, 217, 408-417.

Beck, D.C., Carlson, G.A., Russell, A.T. & Brownfield, F.E. (1987). Use of depression rating instruments in developmentally and educationally delayed adolescents. Journal of the American Academy of Child and Adolescent Psychiatry, 26, 97-100.

Beckwith, B.E., Parker, L., Pawlarczyk, D., Cook, D.I., Schumacher, K.S. & Yearwood, K. (1985). The dexamethasone suppression test in depressed retarded adults: preliminary findings. Biological Psychiatry, 20, 825-831.

Brown, G.I., Ebert, M.H., Goyer, P.F., Jimerson, D.C., Klein, W.J., Bunney, W.E. & Goodwin, F.K. (1982). Aggression, suicide, and serotonin: relationships to CSF amine metabolites. American Journal of Psychiatry, 139, 741-746.

Brown, W.A. & Shuey, I. (1980). Response to dexamethasone and subtype of depression. Archives of General Psychiatry, 37, 747-751.

Carnes, M. Smith, J.C., Kalin, N.H. & Bauwens, S.F. (1983). The Dexamethasone Suppression Test in demented Outpatients with and without depression. Psychiatric Research, 9, 337-344.

Carroll, B.J. (1982). The dexamethasone suppression test for melancholia. British Journal of Psychiatry, 140, 292-304.

Carroll, B.J., Feinterg, M., Greden, J.E., Tarika, J., Albala, A.A., Haskett, R.F., James, N.M., Kronfol, Z., Lohr, N., Steiner, M., de Vigne, J.P. & Young, E. (1981). A specific laboratory test for the diagnosis of melancholia: standardization, validation, and clinical utility. Archives of General Psychiatry, 38, 15-22.

Coppen, A. & Wood, K. (1978). Tryptophan and depressive illness. Psychological Medicine, 8, 49-57.

Dewan, M.J., Pandurangi, A.K., Boucher, M.L., Levy, B.F. & Major, L.F. (1982). Abnormal dexamethasone suppression test results in chronic schizophrenic patients. American Journal of Psychiatry, 139, 1501-1503.

Dosen, A. (1984). Depressive conditions in mentally handicapped children. Acta Paedopsychiatrica, 50, 29-40.

Field, C.J., Aman, M.G., White, A.J. & Vaithianathan, C. (1986). A single-subject study of imipramine in a mentally retarded woman with depressive symptoms. Journal of Mental Deficiency Research, 30, 191-198.

Goldstein, M., Anderson, L.T., Reuben, R. & Dancis, J. (1985). Self-mutilation in Lesch-Nyhan disease is caused by dopaminergic denervation. Lancet, 338-339.

Greden, J.F., Albala, A.A., Haskett, R.F., James, N.M., Goodwin, L., Steiner, M. & Carroll, B.J. (1980). Normalization of dexamethasone suppression test: a laboratory index of recovery from endogenous depression. Biological Psychiatry, 15, 449-458.

Kazdin, A.E., Matson, J.L. & Senatore, V. (1983). Assessment of depression in mentally retarded adults. American Journal of Psychiatry, 140, 1040-1043.

Kraus, R.P., Grof, P. & Brown, G.M. (1988). Drugs and the DST: need for a reappraisal. American Journal of Psychiatry, 145, 666-674.

Kupfer, D.J. & Thase, M.E. (1983). The use of the sleep laboratory in the diagnosis of affective disorders. Psychiatric Clinics of North America, 5, 3-25.

Loosen, P.T. & Prange, J. (1982). The serum thyrotropin response to thyrotropin releasing hormone in psychiatric patients: a review. American Journal of Psychiatry, 139, 405-416.

Matson, J.L. (1986). Treatment outcome research for depression in mentally retarded children and youth: methodological issues. Psychopharmacology Bulletin, 22, 1081-1085.

Meller, W., Kathol, R.G., Jaeckle, R.S., Grambsch, P. & Lopez, J.F. (1988). HPA axis abnormalities in depressed patients with normal response to the DST. American Journal of Psychiatry, 145, 318-324.

Nyhan, W.L., Johnson, H.G., Kaufman, I.A. & Jones, K.L. (1980). Serotonergic approaches to the modification of behavior in the Lesch-Nyhan syndrome. Applied Research in Mental Retardation, 1, 25-40.

Pirodsky, D.M., Gibbs, J.W., Hesse, R.A., Hseih, M.C., Krause, R.B. & Rodriguez, W.H. (1985). Use of the dexamethasone suppression test to detect depressive disorders of mentally retarded individuals. American Journal of Mental Deficiency, 90, 245-252.

Raskind, M., Peskind, E., Rivard, M.F., Vieth, R. & Barnes, R. (1982). Dexamethasone suppression test and cortisol circadian rhythm in primary degenerative dementia. American Journal of Psychiatry, 139, 1468-1471.

Reiss, A.L., Hagerman, R.J., Vinogradors, A., Abrams, M. & King, R.J. (1988). Psychiatric disability in female carriers of the Fragile X chromosome. Archives of General Psychiatry, 45, 25-30.

Reus, V.I. (1982) Pituitary-adrenal disinhibition as the independent variable in the assessment of behavioral symptoms. Biological Psychiatry, 17, 317-326.

Reynolds, W.M. (in press). Depression in persons with mental retardation. In: R. Barrett & J. Matson (Eds.), Advances in Developmental Disorders: A Research Manual, Vol 2. Greenwich, CT: JAI Press.

Rincover, A. (1986). Behavioral research in self-injury and self-stimulation. Psychiatric Clinics of North American, 9, 755-766.

Rivinus, T.M. & Harmatz, J.J. (1979). Diagnosis and lithium treatment of affective disorders in the retarded: five case studies. American Journal of Psychiatry, 136, 551-554.

Ruedrich, S.L., Wadle, C.V., Sallach, H., Hahn, R., & Menolascino, F.J. (1987). Adrenocortical function and depressive illness in mentally retarded patients. American Journal of Psychiatry, 144, 537-602.

Ruedrich, S.L., Wadle, C.U., Hahn, R.K. & Chu, C.C. (1985). Neuroendocrine investigation of depression in mentally retarded patients: a pilot study. Journal of Nervous and Mental Disease, 173, 35-89.

Sachar, E.J., Hellman, I., Roffwarg, H.P., Halpern, F.S., Fukoshima D.K. & Gallagher, T.F. (1973). Disrupted 24-hour patterns of cortisol secretion in psychotic depression. Archives General Psychiatry, 28, 19-24.

Sandman, C.A., Datta, P.C., Barron, J., Hoehler, F.K., Williams, C. & Swanson, J.M. (1983). Naloxone attenuates self-abusive behavior in developmentally disabled clients. Applied Research in Mental Retardation, 4, 5-11.

Sandman, C.A., Barron, J.L. & Parker, L. (1985). Disregulation in hypothalamic-pituitary-adrenal axis in the mentally retarded. Pharmacology, Biochemistry, and Behavior, 13, 21-26.

Sireling, L. (1986). Depression in mentally handicapped patients: diagnostic and neuroendocrine evaluation. British Journal of Psychiatry, 149, 274-278.

Sovner, R. & Hurley, A.D. (1983). Do the mentally retarded suffer from affective illness? Archives of General Psychiatry, 40, 61-67.

Stokes, P.E., Stoll, P.M., Koslow, S.H., Maas, J.W., Davis, J.M., Swann, A.C. & Robins, E. (1984). Pretreatment DST and hypothalamic-pituitary-adrenocortical function in depressed patients and comparison groups. Archives of General Psychiatry, 41, 257-67.

Swartz, C.M. & Dunner, F.J. (1982). Dexamethasone suppression testing in alcoholics. Archives of General Psychiatry, 39, 1309-1312.

Szymanski, L.S. & Biederman, J. (1984). Depression and anorexia nervosa in persons with Down's Syndrome. American Journal of Mental Deficiency, 89, 246-251.

Targum, S.D. (1984). Persistent neuroendocrine dysregulation in major depressive disorder: a marker for early relapse. Biological Psychiatry, 19, 305-318.

Thase, M.E., Frank, E. & Kupfer, D.J. (1985). Biological processes in major depression. In: E. Beckham & W. Leber (Eds.), Handbook of Depression, Treatment, Assessment and Research. Homewood, IL: Dorsey Press.

Traskman, M., Asberg, L., Bertilsson, L. & Sjostrand, L. (1981). Monoamine metabolites in CSF and suicidal behavior. Archives of General Psychiatry, 38, 631-636.

van Praag, H.M., Plutchik, R. & Conte, H. (1986). The serotonin hypothesis of (auto) aggression: critical appraisal of the evidence. Annals of the New York Academy of Sciences, 487, 150-167.

Watts, R.W., Spellacy, E., Gibbs, D.A., Allsop, J., McKeran, R.O. & Slavin, G.E. (1982). Clinical, post-mortem, biochemical and therapeutic observations on the Lesch-Nyhan syndrome with particular reference to the neurological manifestations. Quarterly Journal of Medicine, 201, 43-78.

Young, M., Schwartz, J.S. & the American College of Physicians Health and Public Policy Committee (1984). The Dexamethasone Suppression Test for the detection and management of depression. Annals of Internal Medicine, 100, 307-308.

Anton Dosen and Frank J. Menolascino (Eds.) (1990). Depression in mentally retarded children and adults. Leiden, the Netherlands: Logon Publications. ISBN 90-73197-01-5

Chapter 13

Treatment, care and management - a general overview

Kenneth A. Day, M.D.

Introduction

The aim of this chapter is to provide a general overview of the treatment, care and management of depression in mentally handicapped people. Specific treatments are considered in detail in the chapters which follow.

Assessment and diagnosis

An accurate diagnosis is essential before embarking upon treatment. The diagnostic process and difficulties attendant upon this have already been discussed (see chapters 7, 8, 9 and 10). Assessment should focus on those aspects of symptoms which relate to the illness or have a bearing upon its treatment and the rehabilitation of the patient (Table 1).

The essential features should be encapsulated in a one or two sentence **diagnostic formulation** as in the following examples:

Severe endogenous depression in a mildly mentally handicapped middle aged woman who lives with her parents and has a history of previous depressive and manic episodes which responded well to treatment.

Neurotic depression and anxiety in a moderately mentally handicapped young woman precipitated by concern about her elderly parents' ill health and her own future care.

235

Table 13.1
Assessment of depression

Type	Neurotic/Psychotic Unipolar/Bipolar
Severity	Level, risk of harm to self or others
Other psychiatric symptoms	Problem Behaviour Anxiety, Obsessional.
Precipitating/contributory factors	Presence, Nature and Significance
Past psychiatric history	Number of Episodes, Diagnosis, Hospitalisation, Treatment and Response.
Premorbid personality	Main Features and Relevance to Treatment and Rehabilitation, Personality Disorder.
Other aspects of care	Degree of Mental Handicap Epilepsy and Physical Disabilities Social Functioning Social Circumstances.

Table 13.2
Treatment choices in acute depression
(From Paykel, 1979, with kind permission of the author).

Severity level	First choice	If first choice fails	If second choice fails
severe	ECT	tricyclic	MAO I
moderate	tricyclic	if psychotic: ECT	MAO I
		if neurotic: MAO I	ECT
mild	tricyclic MAO if PH of response	MAO I tricyclic	other drugs ECT in some cases

Table 13.3
Treatment - key decisions

Outpatient or inpatient

Treatment or choice

Additional measures

Rehabilitation and aftercare needs

Consenting status and necessary action

Treatment plan

The treatment of depression in mentally handicapped people is essentially the same as in the general population. Drugs are the mainstay and ECT is indicated in the more severe cases. A systematic approach is essential and a useful schedule has been provided by Paykel (1979) (Table 2). A comprehensive treatment plan should be formulated before treatment commences which includes the management of any associated factors and takes into account any wider or general issues which require further assessment or intervention. The main areas to be addressed are listed in Table 3.

A full explanation of the nature of the illness and the proposed treatment plan and its rationale should be given to the patient and his relatives and carers. Information should include the time lag between commencing drug treatment and the expected response, any dietary restrictions, possible side effects with reassurance that these are reversible, the unlikelihood of dependency developing - a common concern, and whom to contact if there are concerns about the treatment. Relatives and carers have a crucial role to play in ensuring treatment adherence and it is important that their confidence and co-operation is obtained. Suspicion and resistance is sometimes encountered and requires patient and sensitive handling: it stems from the past over-use of sedatives and tranquillisers in institutions (Kirman, 1975) compounded, in some cases, by a failure to accept that the patient is indeed suffering from a mental illness.

Treatment setting

Provided there is good in-home support from the family or other carers and no serious diagnostic problems or anticipated difficulties in implementing the treatment programme, less severe forms of depression can usually be successfully treated on an outpatient basis. Extra support in the form of home-help or care attendant services, community nursing or social work input or day hospital attendance may be required, particularly in the early stages of the illness. Frequent psychiatric review is essential and hospitalisation may become necessary if the patient's conditon deteriorates or other problems arise.

Table 13.4
Indications for inpatient treatment

Severe depression

Diagnostic uncertainty

Inadequate community support/supervision

Major environmental precipitants

Family/carers unable to cope

The indications for inpatient treatment are listed in Table 4. Severe depression where the patient is severely disabled by the illness, or a significant risk of suicide or serious self-neglect is always an indication for inpatient treatment (Kendell, 1983). Electroconvulsive therapy (ECT) is best given as an inpatient treatment to ensure that the necessary precautions are properly observed and to monitor response. Inpatient care is also indicated when a period of intensive observation and investigation is required to establish the diagnosis and when environmental factors have played a significant precipitating or aggravating role in the illness, when it provides an opportunity to effect any necessary changes, or failing this, to assist the patient to better cope with such stresses in the future. Hospitalisation can have a beneficial and sometimes dramatic effect on symptoms (see case 4, chapter 8). In relationship difficulties, for example, a period of separation with controlled access provides valuable breathing space, allowing everyone to settle down and take a more realistic look at their situation and the psychiatrist to obtain a better assessment of precipitating or aggravating circumstances.

Sometimes the decision to admit is dictated more by social factors, for example, when the patient is living alone, where there is concern about the amount or quality of support and supervision available in the community, or when the family or other carers are unable to cope with the additional burden.

Drug treatment

Antidepressant drugs

Antidepressant drugs are the first line treatment in the majority of cases; their efficacy in both affective psychosis and reactive depression is well established. Although there are no specific studies, all the major surveys of depression in mentally handicapped people report a good response to antidepressant medication (Reid, 1972; Hucker et al., 1979; Heaton-Ward, 1977; Carlson, 1979). Administration should follow the same general principles as in the intellectually normal. Monotherapy should be the aim with due regard paid to any complicating factors and the dose titrated according to response and side effects. Snaith et al. (1979) suggest commencing at half the normal dose, postulating that brain damage and abnormalities of the neuroenzymes may modify drug actions and lead to atypical and unexpected responses and a greater variability of side effects. However, whilst this undoubtedly applies to the sedatives and tranquillisers, there are no reports of such reactions with antidepressant medication. Level of handicap has no effect upon response to psychoactive drugs (Freeman, 1970).

Tricyclic and tetracyclic antidepressants, now increasingly referred to as the Monoamine Oxidase Reuptake Inhibiting drugs (MARIs), are the drugs of choice for both types of depression (Paykel, 1979), the newer antidepressants being preferred having fewer side effects. Care should be taken with Maprotiline which is prone to precipitate convulsions (Silverstone and Turner, 1988). Where marked anxiety or agitation is present a drug with sedating properties like Amitriptyline or Mianserin should be used, whilst in retarded depression a drug with stimulating properties like Nortriptyline or Normifensine is indicated (Tyrer, 1979; Paykel, 1979).

Monoamine Oxidase Inhibitors (MAOIs) should be considered as a second line treatment for neurotic depression which has failed to respond to tricyclic antidepressants, and as a third line treatment for endogenous depression which has failed to respond to both tricyclic antidepressants and electroconvulsive therapy (Paykel, 1979). It is now generally agreed that the dangers of this group of drugs have been exaggerated, and that provided proper precautions are taken, they are a safe and valuable therapeutic tool in the anxiety/depression group of illnesses (Tyrer, 1979). Clearly, careful consideration must be given to their use in mentally handicapped people whose ability to understand and observe dietary and other restrictions is impaired to a greater or lesser degree.

The MAOIs are broken down relatively slowly in the body and a single daily dose is all that is required. This is best given at bedtime as it is less likely to be forgotten and the patient is asleep during the peak period for side effects (Paykel, 1979). The MAOIs are broken down more rapidly and a daily divided dose is required. Most mentally handicapped people can manage tablets, for those who can't, the majority of antidepressants are available in a liquid form. In exceptional cases intramuscular preparations may be needed. Compliance is rarely a problem and the risk of overdosing is small. A daily drug dispenser box together with supervisory visits by a community mental handicap nurse helps ensure compliance in those living alone or in group homes. Serum levels are not indicated routinely but are useful in monitoring dosage levels in resistant depression or where there is a risk of serious side effects as, for example, in the presence of severe brain damage.

Under-treatment is a common fault. Having selected the most appropriate drug, administration should be maintained in a sufficient dosage for a sufficient length of time until there can be no doubt, in the event of a non-response, that the drug is ineffective. Only then should it be stopped and alternative therapy considered (Snaith et al., 1979). It may take several weeks before a therapeutic effect is seen with both groups of drugs. Failure to respond is an indication to use a drug of a different class (see Table 2). Very occasionally hypomania may be precipitated: when this occurs the dosage of antidepressant should be reduced and a tranquilliser added.

Antidepressant medication should be continued at the dosage level used in the acute phase for 6-8 months after full recovery (Coppen and Peet, 1979). Studies of both psychotic and neurotic depression have shown relapse rates of 30-50% after early drug withdrawal, which were halved by continuing the treatment for six months (Mindhum, 1973; Paykel et al., 1975; Coppen et al., 1978). Antidepressant drugs should be withdrawn slowly over a number of weeks: severe withdrawal symptoms have been reported following the abrupt cessation of high doses (Paykel, 1979).

Other drugs

A short course of hypnotics may be needed to control distressing sleeplessness in the early stages of the illness. Where anxiety, agitation or other behaviour disturbance is a problem and the sedating effect of the antidepressant used is insufficient, a Phenothiazine should be added. Combined antidepressant and antipsychotic medication is superior

241

to antidepressant medication alone in delusional depression (Silverstone and Turner, 1988).

Electroconvulsive therapy

Electroconvulsive therapy (ECT) is a highly effective and safe treatment for psychotic depression (Greenblatt et al., 1962, 1964; MRC, 1965; West, 1981).
It is the treatment of choice in cases of severe depression with psychomotor retardation and/or nihilistic or paranoid delusions, in depressive stupor, and where is a need for a rapid response because of refusal to eat or drink. It should also be seriously considered as the first line treatment where there is a past history of a similar illness which showed a good response to ECT or failed to respond to drug therapy (Freeman, 1983). ECT is also indicated in psychotic depression which has failed to respond to a course of antidepressant medication, but only after carefully reviewing the diagnosis and the possible reasons for failure to respond to medication, including adequacy of dosage.

There are no specific studies, but surveys (Hucker et al., 1979) and clinical experience indicate that it is effective in psychotic depression in mentally handicapped people. A comprehensive account of the indications for ECT and the standards for administration is given in the Royal College of Psychiatrists' memorandum on the subject (RCPsych., 1977). An initial course of 6-8 treatments at the rate of 2-3 per week by unilateral application to the non-dominant hemishpere should be given, extending as necessary to a maximum of 12-14. A tricyclic antidepressant should also be prescribed and continued for at least six months after the last treatment to reduce the risk of early relapse (Seager and Bird, 1962; Kay et al., 1970). Failure to respond to ECT in the presence of definite psychotic feature occurs in a proportion of cases (Carney et al., 1965; Stromgren, 1973) and has been shown to be related to delay in commencing treatment (Hamilton and White, 1960) and the presence of hypochondrical symptoms, neurotic traits, personality disorder and a fluctuating course (Freeman, 1983).

ECT can be safely given to epileptic patients provided their seizures are well controlled. Reid (1972) has very reasonably urged caution in the use of ECT in mentally handicapped people because of the high prevalence of structural brain abnormality and the possible risk of precipitating epileptic seizures in previously non-epileptic patients. Whilst there are no specific studies in mental handicap, large scale studies in the non-handicapped (Stensrud, 1985) indicate that the risk is minimal. Although a single fit may occur in association with treatment, there is no evidence that persistent epilepsy is precipitated.

Chronic resistant depression

Both acute psychotic and neurotic depression have a relatively good prognosis, but in about 12-15% of cases there is failure to respond to medication and ECT and the illness becomes chronic. This is more likely to occur in unipolar disorders, older patients, females and in the presence of neurotic personality traits. Inadequate or inappropriate treatment has also been found to be a significant factor. The problem is well reviewed by Scott (1988).

Such cases call for a rigorous review of the initial diagnosis and previous treatment with particular attention to possible perpetuating factors including underlying organic disease. Shaw (1977) has proposed the following treatment strategy. Initial withdrwawal of all drugs - which may result in an improvement. A further course of ECT, tricyclic antidepressants of Monoamine Oxidase Inhibitors - if these have not been used recently. ECT should be given by bilateral application because of its greater efficacy and drug dosage pushed to the limit of tolerance and continued for at least a month. If these measures fail, Flupenthixol, which has been shown to have a definite antidepressant effect, should be tried and finally combined tricyclic and MAOI therapy - a sedative tricyclic like Amitriptyline being safer than the relatively non-sedative ones (Tyrer, 1979).

Successes have been reported with other drug combinations, including MAOIs and Tryptophan, tricyclic antidepressants and Tryptophan, MAOIs, Tryptophan and Lithium, and tricyclic antidepressants with Carbamazepine, Triiodothyronine or Methylphenidate. Although Lithium has not been shown unequivocally to have an acute antidepressant effect, Paykel (1979) considers that it is worth trying in resistant bipolar or unipolar depression either alone or in combination with tricyclic antidepressants. A case has been made for stereotactic tractotomy in ultimate therapeutic failures (Barlett et al., 1981).

Counseling, support and cognitive therapy

Contact with the helping professionals, general support and opportunities to ventilate problems and worries have all been shown to improve the well being of both psychotically and neurotically depressed patients. The presence of mental handicap is no bar to their use.
Style and pace, however, must be tailored to the abilities of the individual and the nature of the problem. A pro-active approach is needed as

243

mentally handicapted people are unlikely to spontaneously seek counseling. Situations in which counseling and supportive psychotherapy are particularly valuable include bereavement and domestic and relationship problems. Cognitive therapy (Beck, 1967, 1978) which aims to correct the negative cognitive set of low self image, negative view of life experiences and pessimistic view of the future has been shown to be effective in mild forms of depression, but there have been few studies in severely depressed patients (Fennel and Teasdale, 1982; Bowers, 1990). Its status as a therapeutic intervention is well reviewed by Williams (1984). The extent to which this particular technique can be applied and is valuable in the treatment of depression in mentally handicapped people has yet to be evaluated.

General measures

In addition to specific treatment for depression a full programme of daily activities should be available and the patient encouraged to participate in these. Less taxing and more recreational activities, like art therapy, are best in the early stages, but during recovery patients should be reintroduced, as far as possible, to the types of activities they have been undertaking prior to the illness. At this stage an assessment should be made of social functioning with a view to detecting any areas with potential for improvement and establishing appropriate training programmes. This is particularly important where lack of appropriate social skills has been a major contributory factor to the illness itself. Associated physical disabilities like epilepsy or perceptual defects should also be reviewed and any necessary treatment measures implemented.

Rehabilitation, follow up and aftercare

Discharge and aftercare for hospital inpatients should be properly planned and co-ordinated. This is best carried out at a case conference involving all those with current and future responsibility for care. Rehabilitation and aftercare needs shoud be identified as early in the illness as possible so that appropriate arrangements can be made and undue delay in discharge avoided. Wherever possible the patient should be restored to his former state of mental health before discharge: a premature return home in a fragile mental state can lead to rapid deterioration, readmission and loss of confidence in the treatment programme. After a major illness the patient should be gradually reintroduced into the community through a process of weekend and extended leaves. Some are unable to return to their former placement because they need more support than this can provide or because the previous environment was unsuitable and a major causative factor in the illness (Day, 1985). In these cases careful preparation and a phased introduction to the new placement is essential. All patients should have a routine psychiatric follow-up 2-3 weeks after discharge, at appropriate intervals thereafter and for 2-3 months after discontinuation of medication. Community mental handicap nurses, provided they are appropriately trained experienced, have a valuable role to play in aftercare ensuring treatment compliance, monitoring progress, providing support, guidance and advice and accessing psychiatric intervention when necessary. Relatives and carers should always be informed about signs and symptoms which might indicate a relapse and instructed to seek psychiatric advice accordingly.

Prophylaxis and prevention

The benefits of long term Lithium therapy in the prevention of recurrent attacks of both depressive and manic episodes in bipolar affective illness is well established (Coppen and Peet, 1979) and has been demonstrated in studies in the mentally handicapped (Naylor et al., 1974; Reid and Leonard, 1977; Rivinus and Harmatz, 1979). There is also good evidence that Lithium is effective in preventing or suppressing recurrent depressive episodes in unipolar affective illness (Coppen and Peet, 1979; Glen et al., 1984). Coppen and Peet (1979) suggest that there is a strong case for instituting Lithium prophylactic therapy in patients after their third attack of affective disorder, whilst Kendell (1983) recommends that this should be considered if the pattern of the illness suggests that another incapacitating illness is likely within 2-3 years and after a single manic illness in adolescents and young adults because the chances of a recurring bipolar illness are high. A thorough physical examination and investigations, including renal function tests, should be carried out before commencing, blood levels should be maintained at above 0.6 mmol/l and regularly monitored. Present evidence indicates that Litium prophylaxis therapy should be continued indefinitely. Long term maintenance antidepressant medication has been found to be less effective than Lithium salts (Coppen and Peet, 1979) and there is no evidence to support the use of maintenance ECT as a preventive measure.

The importance of life events in precipitating neurotic depression is well established. Awareness of potential problems and skilled handling at an early stage can sometimes prevent frank illness, but all too often these needs go unmet at crucial periods in the lives of mentally handicapped people (Oswin, 1981). Bereavement, a common cause of reactive depression particularly in middle aged and elderly mentally handicapped people (Day, 1985, 1990), is a good example. The death of a last caring relative brings not only the loss of the last friend but also the loss of home and possessions and often a radical and precipitous change in living circumstances. The emotional problems of mentally handicapped people at this time are all too easily overlooked in the scramble to make arrangements for future care and frequently compounded by well intentioned but mistaken attempts to shield. This is an area which has only just begun to receive attention (Oswin, 1985; McLoughlin, 1986) and which depends crucially upon the awareness and sensitivity of carers and first line professionals. Illness and possibility of death should never be concealed from a mentally handicapped person - this only serves to intensify the shock if death occurs. Attendance at the funeral helps to establish the finality of death and should be encouraged. Skilled counseling should be readily available to help the individual work through his or her grief and to advise and assist other family members. Some of the inevitable devastation which follows could be reduced if mentally handicapped people were introduced to potential new living situations and acclimatised to separation from their parents well before the need arises - although resistance from elderly parents often makes this difficult to achieve.

Many other life events can precipitate a depressive illness in mentally handicapped people including relationship problems, domestic stress, changes of staff or a residential move (Day, 1990). The potential for these to operate has increased considerably with changing patterns of care (Day, 1985). Better education of relatives, carers and professionals would help reduce the risks and facilitate early recognition. The psychiatric aspects of mental handicap should feature prominently in the training of all concerned professionals.

Consent to treatment
Careful consideration must always be given to the consenting status of the patient before treatment is implemented, and appropriate action taken within the framework of prevailing law and practice. Wherever possible, agreement of the next of kin to the treatment proposed should be obtained.

Severe psychotic depression is almost always accompanied by lack of insight and failure to recognise or accept the need for treatment. Mental health legislation in most countries makes provision for compul-

246

sory treatment, with due safeguards to the patient, in these circumstances. In the U.K., for example, a person may be compulsorily detained in hospital and treated under the Mental Health Act 1983 following recommendations by two independent doctors, one of whom must have special expertise, and an application by a specially approved social worker. Treatment may be given for up to three months, after which, if it is to be continued, the patient must either consent or if he refuses or is unable to consent, a second independent medical opinion must be obtained. There is a right of appeal against detention to the managers of the hospital and to the Mental Health Review Tribunal, and the Mental Health Act Commission (Mental Welfare Commission in Scotland) oversees the general care of detained patients.

An added dimension in people with a mental handicap is their capacity to give valid consent to treatment. Valid consent requires that the patient is able to understand the treatment and why it is proposed, its pincipal benefits and risks, the consequences of not recieving the proposed treatment and the availability or otherwise of alternative treatments. Most people functioning in the borderline, mild and moderate handicap ranges are able to give valid consent provided that the explanation and advise is couched in simple terms. The judgement as to whether or not a patient is consenting should relate to the particular treatment at the particular time. Severely mentally handicapped people are unable to give valid consent but this should not deprive them of the opportunity to recieve the treatment they need. In these circumstances the principles of "substitute judgement" and "best interests" are usually applied. The first attempts to arrive at the decision the patient would have made if competent to do so, whilst in the second the decision is based upon the percieved views of the hypothetical average person in the same position as the incapacitated person - this being the most frequently used. The situation remains dynamic, and law and practice varies in different countries.

Service provision
It is essential that mentally handicapped people with a psychiatric illness are treated in services properly geared to meet their needs. The nature of the service provision required is the subject of increasing debate. Whilst there are those who argue from normalisation principles that mentally handicapped people with mental illness should be treated in the generic psychiatric services (Melin, 1988) the majority view is in favour of specialised services and this is reflected in service development throughout the western world (Zarfas, 1988; Day, 1988, Parmen-

247

ter, 1988; Dosen, 1988; Van Walleghem, 1988; Reiss, 1988; Menolascino et al., 1986). The arguments in support of a specialised service have been detailed by Day (1984). They relate to the difficulties of diagnosis, overall pattern of disease and the need to take account of the underlying mental handicap, dependency levels and co-existing physical handicaps in treatment rehabilitation and aftercare. In generic settings where mentally handicapped people would be in the minority and the main emphasis is on the care of non-handicapped patients, there is little opportunity for staff to gain the necesssary experience, knowledge and skills and no opportunity to establish a cadre of experts to teach, train and carry out much needed research.

Table 13.5
Mentally handicapped people with psychiatric needs

---

acute and chronic mentally ill

severely mentally handicapped with behaviour problems

mildly mentally handicapped with maladjustment, emotional problems and social inadequacy

mentally handicapped offenders

brain damaged with epilepsy and associated behaviour problems

elderly mentally handicapped with psychogeriatric problems

Specialised psychiatric services should be comprehensive and include a sufficient number of treatment setting to provide specialised programmes and care for the spectrum of problems presented and to take account of the range of intellectual levels, age and sex (Table 5).

A number of different service models have been developed, ranging from community based services with a small admission facility (Menolascino, 1989; Bouras et al., 1988) to larger campus based units (Day, 1983; Gold et al., 1989). None have been evaluated. Special facilities for rehabilitation and continuing care in the community are also needed as mentally handicapped people with psychiatric or behaviour problems do not always fitt well into regular community facilities. Highly specialised treatment and care settings are required for the small group of dangerous offenders and others who require care in conditions of security. A major barrier to the development of specialised services is the lack of appropriately trained and experienced professionals - particularly a paucity of interested psychiatrists (Zarfas, 1988; Dosen, 1988; Parmenter, 1988; Van Walleghem, 1988). The exception is the U.K. where mental handicap has always been a psychiatric speciality and psychiatrists and nurses working in the field undergo specialist training (Day 1988).

Sovner and Hurley (1987) have provided some useful guidelines where specialised facilities are not available and a mentally handicapped person has to be admitted to a general psychiatric unit. Prior to admission the length of stay and eventual placement after discharge should be firmly established, orientation meetings for the inpatient staff should be set up to acquaint them with the special needs of the patient, a behavioural monitoring programma should be introduced, community staff should continue to be involved and the patient reintroduced to his normal day care programme as soon as possible.

Conclusion

The management of depressive illnesses in mentally handicapped people is essentially the same as it is in the non-handicapped. Specialised services are required staffed by appropriately trained doctors and nurses. There is a need for research into the use of drug therapy, ECT and other treatment techniques in depressed mentally handicapped patients. Better education of families and professional carers would help to facilitate early detection, treatment and prevention.

References

Baker W.A., Scott J. and Eccleston D. (1987). The Newcastle chronic depression study: results of a treatment regime. International Clinical Psychopharmacology, 2, 261 - 272.

Barlett J., Bridges P. and Kelly D. (1981). Contempory indications for psychosurgery. British Journal of Psychiatry, 138, 507 - 511.

Beck A.T. (1967). Depression: clinical, experimental and theoretical aspects. Staple Press. London.

Beck A.T., Rush A.J., Shaw B.F. (1979). Cognitive therapy of depression. New York, Guilford.

Bouras N., Drummond K. Brooks D. and Laws M. (1988). Mental handicap and mental health: a community service. National Unit for Psychiatric Research and Development. London.

Bowers W.A. (1990). Treatment of depressed inpatients. British Journal of Psychiatry, 156, 773 - 778.

Carlson G. (1979). Affective psychosis in mental retardates. Psychiatric clinics of North America, 2, 499 - 510.

Carney M.W.P., Roth M. and Garside R.F. (1965). The diagnosis of depressive syndromes and the prediction of ECT response. British Journal of Psychiatry, 111, 659 - 674.

Coppen A., Montgomery S., Rao V.A.R., Bailey J. and Jorgensen A. (1978). Continuation therapy with Amitriptyline in depression. British Journal of Psychiatry, 133, 28.

Coppen A. and Peet M. (1979). The long term management of patients with with affective disorders. In: E.S. Paykel and A. Coppen (Eds.), Psychopharmacology of Affective Disorders. Oxford University Press, Oxford.

Day K. (1983). A hospital based psychiatric unit for mentally handicapped adults. Mental Handicap, 11, 137 - 140.

Day K. (1984). Service provision for mentally handicapped people with psychiatric problems. In: Care in the Community: Keeping it local. National Association for Mental Health, London.

Day K. (1985). Psychiatric disorder in the middle-aged and elderly mentally handicapped. British Journal of Psychiatry, 147, 660-667.

Day K. (1988). Service for psychiatrically disorded mentally handicapped adults: A U.K. perspective. Australia and New Zealand Journal of Developmental Disabilities, 14, 31-35.

Day K. (1990). Depression in moderately and mildly mentally handicapped people. In: A. Dosen and F.J. Menolascino (Eds). Depression in Mentally Retarded Children and Adults (this volume).

Department of Health (1989). Needs and Responses: Services for Adults with Mental Handicap who are Mentally Ill, who have Behavior Problems or who Offend. HMSO, London.

Dosen A. (1988). Community care for people with mental retardation in the Netherlands. Australia and New Zealand Journal of Developmental Disabilities, 14, 15-18.

Fennel M.V. and Teasdale J.D. (1982). Cognitive therapy with chronic, drug refractory depressed outpatients: a note of caution. Cognitive Therapy and Research, 6, 445-460.

Freeman C.P. (1983). ECT and other physical therapies. In: R.E. Kendell and A.K. Zealley (Eds.) Companion to Psychiatric Studies. Churchill Livingstone, London.

Freeman R.D. (1970). Psychopharmacological approaches and issues. In: F.J. Menolascino (Ed.) Psychiatric Approaches to Mental Retardation. Basic Books, New York and London.

Glen A.I.M., Johnson A.L., and Shepherd M. (1984). Continuation therapy with Lithium and Amitriptyline in unipolar depressive illness. Psychological Medicine, 14, 37-50.

Gold I.M., Wolfson E.S., Lester C.M., Ratey J.J. and Chmievnski H.E. (1989). Developing a unit for mentally retarded mentally ill patients on the grounds of a state hospital. Hospital and Community Psychiatry, 40, 836-840.

Greenblatt M., Grosser G.H. and Wechsler H. (1962). A comparative study of selected antidepressant medications and EST. American Journal of Psychiatry, 119, 144-153.

Greenblatt M., Grosser G.H., Wechsler H. (1964). Differential response of hospitalised depressed patients to somatic therapy. American Journal of Psychiatry, 120, 935-943.

Hamilton M. and White J. (1960). Factors related to the outcome of depression treated with ECT. Journal of Mental Science, 116, 1031-1035.

Heaton-Ward A. (1977). Psychosis in mental handicap. British Journal of Psychiatry, 130, 525-533.

Hucker S.J., Day K.A., George S. and Roth M. (1979). Psychosis in mentally handicapped adults. In: F.E. James and R.P. Snaith (Eds.) Psychiatric Illness and Mental Handicap. Gaskell Press, London.

Kay D.W.K., Fahy T. and Garside R.F. (1970). A seven month double blind trial of Amitriptyline and Diazepam in ECT treated depressed patients. British Journal of Psychiatry, 117, 667-671.

Kendell R.D. (1983). Affective psychoses. In: R.E. Kendell and A.K. Zealley (Eds.) Companion to Psychiatric Studies. Churchill Livingstone, London.

Kirman B. (1975). Drug therapy in mental handicap. British Journal of Psychiatry, 127, 545-549.

Medical Research Council (1965). Clinical trial of the treatment of depressive illness. British Medical Journal, 11, 881-886.

Melin L. (1988). Services and provisions for persons with mental retardation in Sweden. Australia and New Zealand Journal of Developmental Disabilities, 14, 37-42.

Menolascino F.J., Gilson S.F., Levitas A.S. (1986). Issues in the treatment of mentally retarded patients in community mental health systems. Community Mental Health Journal, 22, 314-327.

Menolascino F.J. (1989). Model services for treatment/management of the mentally retarded mentally ill. Community Mental Health Journal, 25, 145-155.

Mindham R.H.S., Howland C. and Shephard M. (1973). An evaluation of continuation of therapy with tricyclic antidepressants in depressive illness. Psychological Medicine, 3, 5-17.

McLoughlin J. (1986). Bereavement in the mentally handicapped. British Journal of Hospital Medicine, 36, 256-260.

Naylor G.J., Donald J.M., Poidevin D. and Reid A.H. (1974). A double blind trial of long term Lithium therapy in mental defectives. British Journal of Psychiatry, 124, 52-57.

Oswin M. (1985). Bereavement and Mentally Handicapped People. Kings Fund, London.

Oswin M. (1985). Bereavement. In: M. Craft, D.J. Bicknell and S. Hollins (Eds.) Mental Handicap. Balliere Tindall, London.

Parmenter T.R. (1988). Analysis of Australian mental health services for people with mental retardation. Australia and New Zealand Journal of Developmental Disabilities, 14, 9-13.

Paykel E.S., Dimascio A., Haskell D. and Prusoff B.A. (1975). Effects of maintenance Amitriptyline and psychotherapy on symptoms of depression. Psychological Medicine, 5, 67-77.

Paykel E.S. (1979). Management of acute depression. In: E.S. Paykel and A. Coppen (Eds.) Psychopharmacology of Affective Disorders. Oxford University Press, Oxford.

Reid A.H. (1972). Psychoses in adult mental defectives I. Manic depressive psychosis. British Journal of Psychiatry, 120, 205-212.

Reid A.H. and Naylor G.J. (1976). Short cycle manic depressive psychosis in mental defectives: a clinical and physiological study. Journal of Mental Deficiency Research, 20, 67-76.

Reid A.H. and Leonard A. (1977). Lithium treatment of cyclical vomiting in a mentally defective patient. British Journal of Psychiatry, 130, 316.

Reid A.H. (1982). The Psychiatry of Mental Handicap. Blackwell Scientific Publications, London.

Reiss S. (1988). Dual diagnosis in the United States. Australia and New Zealand Journal of Developmental Disabilities, 14, 43-48.

Rivinus T.M. and Harmatz J.S. (1979). Diagnosis and Lithium treatment of affective disorder in the retarded: five case studies. American Journal of Psychiatry, 136, 551-554.

Royal College of Psychiatrists (1977). Memorandum on the use of electroconvulsive therapy. British Journal of Psychiatry, 131, 261-272.

Scott J. (1988). Chronic depression. British Journal of Psychiatry, 153, 287-297.

Seager C.P. and Bird R.L. (1962). Imipramine with electrical treatment in depression - controlled trial. Journal of Mental Science, 108, 704-706.

Shaw D.M. (1977). The practical management of affective disorders. British Journal of Psychiatry, 130, 432-451.

Silverstone T. and Turner P. (1988). Drug Treatment in Psychiatry. Routledge, London.

Snaith R.P., James F.E. and Winokur B. (1979). The drug treatment of mental illness and epilepsy in the mentally handicapped patient. In: F.E. James and R.P. Snaith (Eds). Psychiatric Illness and Mental Handicap. Gaskell Press, London.

Sovner R. and Hurley A.D. (1987). Guidelines for the treatment of mentally retarded persons on psychiatric inpatient units. Psychiatric Aspects of Mental Retardation Reviews, 6, 7-14.

Stromgren L.S. (1973). Unilateral versus bilateral electroconvulsive therapy. Acta Psychiatrica Scandinavica Suppl. 240.

Stensrud P.A. (1958). Cerebral complications following 562 convulsion treatments in 893 patients. Acta Psychiatrica Neurologica Scandinavica, 33, 115.

Tyrer P. (1979). Clinical use of Monoamine Oxidase Inhibitors. In: E.S. Paykel and A. Coppen (Eds.). Psychopharmacology of Affective Disorders. Oxford University Press, Oxford.

Van Walleghem M. (1988). Survey of the principal care facilities for people with mental retardation in Belgium. Australia and New Zealand Journal of Developmental Disabilities, 14, 31-35.

West E. (1981). Electroconvulsion therapy in depression: a double blind controlled trial. British Medical Journal, II, 355-357.

Williams J.M.G. (1984). Cognitive behaviour therapy for depression: problems and perspectives. British Journal of Psychiatry, 145, 254-262.

Zarfas D.E. (1988). Mental Health systems for people with mental retardation: a Canadian perspective. Australia and New Zealand Journal of Developmental Disabilities, 14, 3-7.

Anton Dosen and Frank J. Menolascino (Eds.) (1990). Depression in mentally retarded children and adults. Leiden, the Netherlands: Logon Publications. ISBN 90-73197-01-5

Chapter 15

Psychotherapeutic approaches
in the treatment
of depression in mentally retarded children

Anton Dosen, M.D.

Introduction

A number of questions arise when speaking about psychotherapy for mentally retarded children. Most questionable issues are related to the usefulness of psychotherapy for these children because of their low levels of intellectual functioning. Choice of technique and therapeutic goals are also disputable. Some authors (Bicknell, 1979; Rubin, 1983) hesitate regarding the usefulness of psychotherapy in persons with an IQ lower than 50. Others (Monfils & Menolascino, 1984; Szymanski, 1980) believe that intellectual level is an insufficient criterion for determining suitability. These authors feel that any individual who is able to respond to a warm, supportive relationship and possesses a minimal desire to effect change should be considered for individual psychotherapy. Clients at higher levels, who may additionally be capable of using the therapist as a role-model, can learn to recognize and verbally communicate their feelings (Szymanski 1980), while younger children and those at lower developmental levels can utilize play as a tool for communication with the therapist (Corbett 1987, O'Quinn 1988). Family therapy for mentally retarded children with psychiatric disorders may also be recommended (Corbett 1987, O'Quinn 1988) and can be either supportive or directed toward problem solving and achieving insight. Overall, the goal is to help the child develop a sense of personal ability, to be autonomous, caring, and competent according to his or her needs and abilities (O'Quinn 1988).

Despite the growing assumption that all forms of psychotherapy used in child psychiatry are applicable to the treatment of emotional disorders in mentally retarded children, hesitations emerge when one is confronted with the actual practical difficulties involved in treating those children who

255

are severely retarded. Because of their impairments in developmental skills, behavior therapy based on the use of operant techniques has been recommended (Corbett 1987). However, some authors have emphasized that even severely retarded children can benefit from individual psychotherapy if applied from the developmental point of view and if technically adapted to the abilities and developmental needs of the individual child (Bojanin & Ispanovic-Radojkovic, 1988; Dosen, 1984a). In using this approach, the mentally retarded child is seen as a developing organism whose needs and sensitivities vary with his or her developmental level, and whose developmental course is determined in large part by biological substrate and interaction with the environment. The behavioral and intrapsychic problems of the child are thus seen through three dimensions: biological substrate, interaction with surroundings, and developmental course. Keeping the child's developmental needs in mind, a developmentally oriented psychotherapist not only helps the child with present situational and personal conflicts, but actively stimulates psychosocial development by intervening in the child's environmental experiences and influencing those experiences in such a way so as to help with that child's adaptation. Such treatment is aimed at solving intrapsychic problems, such as developmental regressions and fixations, and also strives to help the child to improve motor and psychic functioning, self-concept, social skills, and basic interaction with others.

In this chapter, clinical experiences in treating severely mentally retarded children who have been diagnosed as suffering from depression will be described based on the developmental approach of relationship therapy (Dosen 1984a). Considering depression on the one hand as a disorder of vitality and mood, and on the other hand as a disturbance in psychomotor behavior and thought, it is important to focus therapeutic efforts on **both** aspects. However, as described in the Chapter 4, both of these dimensions are not necessarily involved in all cases of depression. The severity of the illness and the level of emotional and cognitive development play a role. In general, three main aspects of treatment may be distinguished:

A. Treatment of vitality and mood disturbance.
B. Treatment of personal problems.
C. Treatment of impaired interaction with the surrounding milieu.

Treatment of vitality and mood disturbance

Symptoms of disturbed vitality, such as sleeping and eating disorders, severe constipation, loss of day-rhythm, loss of pleasure and energy, and motor retardation may indicate a metabolic rearrangement and neurobio-chemical change in the central nervous system. Mood disorders in such children are also usually quite marked. Such neurophysiological and basic psychological disorders demand acute intervention.

After establishing the diagnosis, specific psychotropic medication, such as antidepressants, may be prescribed. Tricyclic antidepressants, lithium carbonate, carbamazepine and other substances are now being used (Corbett, 1987; O'Quinn, 1988). However, clinicians differ concerning the use of these drugs in mentally retarded children. Diagnostic difficulties involving depression are great and the target symptoms for these drugs are still disputable.

In our clinical practice (see Chapter 7), drugs are prescribed to ameliorate the disturbed processing of internal and external stimuli which cause disruptions in the child's vitality. Such medication helps the child achieve homeostasis and psychobiological adaptation to his or her environment. However, in our opinion it would be wrong to expect medication alone to solve the total problem of any child's affective disorder. In order to help the child, his or her surroundings have to be structured and adapted to individual existential needs. Through a combination of medication and adapted surroundings, the child should attain a certain level of biopsychological adaptation upon which other therapeutic efforts to improve emotional and personality qualities can then be based.

Case History: Child A

A three-year old, severely retarded girl was admitted for severe self-injurious behavior, periodic changes in vitality and mood, agitation, and severe constipation (see Chapter 4). She could not walk or speak, and had no interest in her surroundings or in others. Through biochemical examination, tryptophan malabsorption was found, and a diagnosis of major affective illness was established. Tryptophan and nicotinamide were prescribed to ameliorate serotonin balance in the central nervous system.

However, after several weeks no change in the girl's state was noted. These medications were abandoned and carbomazepine was administered based on the presumption that the child suffered from a mixed manic-depressive condition. Within two weeks her improvement was marked and additional treatment approaches were applied.

The emotional and social developmental levels of the child were noted to be markedly lower than her cognitive level and treatment efforts were directed at discovering what type of stimulation would improve these developmental qualities until they reached the level of her cognitive developmental age. In a constant and stable structured environment the child was encouraged, always by the same therapist, to become familiar with her surroundings and to pay attention to the people and material objects surrounding her. Initially, bodily contact between the child and therapist was the focus, and later, after an improvement in contact had been established, material objects were included in their communication. She was encouraged to use her hands and to realize that she could alter her material surroundings. This therapeutic approach was partially based on relationship therapy and partially on the developmental approach (See Chapter 4).

Treatment of personal problems: Relationship Therapy

Symptoms such as auto-aggression, suicidal ideation, anxiety, low self-esteem, guilt feelings and, in some cases, hallucinations and delusions are viewed as disturbances in an awareness of "self." Treatment consists of psychotherapeutic efforts as well as counseling, support, and assistance, and is aimed at helping these children to strengthen the ego and to experience themselves as playing a role in their surroundings. They are also assisted in solving the problems of the "here and now" and in discovering personal abilities in positive interactions with other people.

Good results have been achieved in treating depressive children with relationship therapy (Dosen 1984a) wherein the developmental characteristics of the individual child are brought into focus. This means that, in addition to psychotherapeutic methods and techniques, the therapist must have the ability to create a simulation of ideal parenting in which the child receives optimal stimulation of various aspects of psychic development. A combination of psychotherapy and developmental stimulation is strongly accentuated.

Theoretically, relationship therapy leans on the psychodynamic and cognitive theories of development and the attachment theory of Bowlby (1977) which states that human beings have an existential need for bonding with others and through this bonding establish a psychological security base from which to explore and master their surroundings. Such exploration and mastery is a condition for further cognitive and personality development.

Relationship therapy is carried out by a day-residential nursing staff under the constant guidance and supervision of a qualified therapist. It begins with attempts to establish a positive affective relationship between the therapist and the child. The therapist searches for a "meeting point" at which the child can be reached. In finding and reaching this point, the therapist tries to "give the child a hand," freeing him or her from isolation, fears, and emotional conflicts. Hand in hand with the therapist, the child is taught to adopt a pleasant attitude in communicating with the therapist and to cope with conflicts in the present situation. The therapist maintains this form of communication as long as is needed to achieve trust and pleasure before introducing other forms of communication or addressing the child on a higher socioemotional level.

Modifications in relationship therapy may be used in treating depressed mentally retarded children depending upon the cognitive level and communication abilities of the individual child. Role-playing appears to be an effective method as does stimulation of verbal communication and expression of feelings in combination with psychopharmacological treatment.

Case History: Child B

An eight-year-old boy functioning at a mildly retarded level was admitted to our clinic for hyperactivity, destructiveness, and aggression toward other children. Psychomotor development was normal. Pregnancy and delivery had been uneventful, although the mother suffered from depression during the boy's first years and, some time later, the father experienced a nervous breakdown. The child's behavior problem began when he entered kindergarten at the age of four. On the basis of his behavior and the family situation, depression was diagnosed (Dosen 1984b).

The child was given individual therapy and empathic attention by a nurse at regular intervals during the day and an affective bond grew rapidly between them. The therapist noted that during physical contact, the child tended to show regressive, baby-like behavior, which led to the decision to introduce role-playing. A clear agreement was made with him that the two would play mother and child. During this role playing, which lasted 30 minutes, he was given diapers, drank from a bottle, cooed like a baby, and clearly showed that he appreciated his role. After two weeks, he no longer wanted to play at being a baby, but preferred to pretend to be a

259

toddler. At the end of the second two weeks, he decided to play the roles of husband, father, and police officer for several months. Thereafter, role-playing no longer interested the boy and he preferred to engage in standard games with the therapist.

During treatment, which lasted six months, he became much more calm and his hyperactivity and aggression disappeared. His fear of failure lessened substantially and, as a result, he concentrated better on task performance. Intelligence testing showed a gain of 20%. Although he had shown no sign of homesickness upon admission, his desire to return home to his mother increased markedly.

Treatment of impaired interaction with the surrounding milieu

Treatment involving interaction with one's surroundings concerns both animate and inanimate objects. The disorders successfully treated in this manner include aggression, destructiveness, negativism, attention deficit disorders, hyperactivity, hypoactivity, passivity, withdrawal, and other adaptation and reaction disorders. These difficulties may partially be seen as learned behavioral patterns occurring in particular circumstances as maladjustment reactions. It is important to analyze the circumstances in which such behaviors occur in order to alter the reaction patterns of persons around the child and avoid a maintenance of behavior. Certain modifications in relationship therapy may be helpful in these circumstances, but behavior modification techniques and cognitive training in handling material objects may be even more effective.

A common feature in these children is that they show a lack of interest in material objects and creativity. Their real performance level is often lower than their potential cognitive ability. In treatment, they should be stimulated to explore and to experience their own power in altering their surroundings in a purposeful way. It is important to stress that the material that makes up their environment has to be cautiously chosen according to the developmental level and the stimulation needs of the individual child. In combining relationships with other persons and with material surroundings, the child is made aware of his or her role in the milieu and in basic social interactions.

Case History: Child C

A ten-year-old severely mentally retarded girl was admitted for severe self-injury, withdrawal, occasional apathy, and eating and sleeping problems. She would sit placidly in her chair for hours and when we attempted to interact with her, she would react with irritated screaming and self-abuse. This behavior began two months prior to admittance and was obviously related to the growing relationship problems between her parents and the depressive state of her mother (see Chapter 4). A diagnosis of depression was established, presumably as a consequence of the loss of parental attention and support.

Treatment was predominately directed at meeting the girl's developmental needs. From the child's history it was obvious that she had suffered severe understimulation all her life and that, due to this unfavorable condition, was predisposed to react with a marked psychic disturbance in conflict situations. She was an only child in a well situated family and her handicap was an enormous burden for both parents. The mother compensated with overprotection and the father escaped in his work. Constant preoccupation with the child exacerbated difficulties in the parental relationship, resulting in severe conflict and depression in the mother. Due to overprotection, the child was understimulated to develop social skills and became overdependent on her mother. By the time she actually needed to seek the mother's attention, self-injury became an effective tool.

During her treatment at the clinic, the girl was initially placed in a structured environment and received the attention of her caregiver at regular times. The primary focus was directed toward finding the means to establish pleasurable communication and to put the child at ease. The therapist discovered that the little girl was pleased when her hands were held and thus expanded the contact by caressing her hands and arms and by moving and playing with them. The child showed more and more interest and pleasure in communicating with the therapist and her apathy and self-injurious behavior gradually diminished.

The next step in treatment was to use the girl's hands in communicating with her material surroundings. Initially sand and water were used, and eventually a more solid material was introduced so as to encourage the child to experience her ability to manipulate and change the objects in her surroundings. This resulted in a gradual increase in her activity and exploration of the environment. Parallel to this approach, efforts were made to change some of her learned negative and maladaptive behavior patterns through behavior modification techniques. The accent was on ignoring negative and rewarding positive behaviors. Aversive techniques were not used.

261

After 4 months of treatment, the symptoms of depression had disappeared and the girl showed an increase in social behavior appropriate to her developmental level.

Discussion

In the case of Child A, a biochemical disorder of the central nervous system was considered, the origin of which was unclear. However, the history of the child let us hypothesize that she had lived in a very stressful situation during the first three years of life. Frequent somatic illnesses and hospital admittance made her adaptation to the environment difficult and disturbed the bonding process with her mother. During this period, the child was viewed as autistic. In a chronic stress situation, this condition might exhaust the psychobiological compensation abilities of the child, leading to disturbances in monoamine. The medication she received probably helped to stabilize this biochemical imbalance, bringing the child to a state in which she was better able to respond to surrounding influences.

Stimulation of the child's socioemotional development was then planned based along developmental lines (see Chapter 4). First, she was helped to adapt to the structure of her milieu through a homeostasis of external stimuli and internal processing. Later, via intensive bodily contact with the therapist, an affective bond was stimulated. After achieving an appropriate bond, material objects were introduced into communication activities between the child and therapist.

In the case of Child B, it was likely that he suffered from a sort of developmental depression since he had never achieved a secure emotional base due to difficulties in attachment development (see Chapter 4). This resulted, initially, in separation anxiety and, later, in extreme anxiety regarding failure, which was probably related to the fear of losing love by making mistakes. Our therapeutic approach attempted to increase his basic security. Regression to a very primitive developmental stage through role-playing helped to rework his burden of existential insecurity and to create a new and secure relationship within a therapeutic setting. This positive relationship made it possible for him to learn other forms of behavior which brought more pleasure and reward.

Child C was diagnosed as suffering from a reactive type of depression. Taking into account the history and current situation of this child, she was certainly at risk for developing a psychic disturbance. The discrepancy between her potential abilities and her performance was striking; her inadequate educational situation and the relationship difficulties between her parents were related. Despite some similarity with the symptoms of Child A, Child C was treated in the first instance by the structuring of her external milieu. Medication was not need during treatment since it was not basic insecurity (like child B) but a sort of deprivation of material surroundings and understimulation which came to the fore as the most obvious problems. The main difficulties in this child lie in her relationship with personal and material surroundings, rather than with biological or interpersonal challenges.

As in all cases, the parents of the above three children were counselled and advised on how to find an adequate attitude and how to provide pedagogical stimulation for their child. They were also involved in the daily life of the ward, practicing therapeutic activities with the child under the supervision of a therapist.

Conclusion

Psychotherapeutic treatment for mentally retarded children is very often combined with other types of intervention such as medication, supportive guidance, and stimulation of various aspects of development. The specificity of development of mentally retarded children demands that treatment be aimed not only at the disturbed psychological aspects, but at ameliorating the total psychophysical condition of the child. In depressed mentally retarded children, a holistic developmental approach such as this has been shown to provide good results.

References

Bicknell, D.J. (1979). Treatment and management of disturbed mentally handicapped patients. In: F.E. James & R.P. Snaith (Eds.): Psychiatric illness and mental handicap. London: Gaskell.

Bojanin, S., Ispanovic-Radojkovic, V. (1988). Treatment of depression in mentally retarded children - a developmental approach. In A. Dosen & P. Engelen (eds): Depression in the Mentally Retarded. Leiden: PAOS.

Bowlby, V. (1977). Attachment and loss - volume 1: attachment. New York: Basic Books.

Corbett, J. (1987). Mental retardation, psychiatric aspects. In M. Rutter & L. Hersov (eds.) Child and Adolescent Psychiatry, London: Blackwell.

Dosen, A. (1948a). Experiences with individual relationship therapy within a therapeutic milieu for retarded children with severe emotional disorders. In J. Berg (ed.), Perspectives and progress in mental retardation - Volume II. Baltimore: University Park Press.

Dosen, A. (1984b). Depressive conditions in mentally retarded children. Acta Paedopsychiat, 59, 29-40.

Dosen, A. (1989). Diagnosis and treatment of mental illness in mentally retarded children: a developmental model. Child Psychiatry and Human Development, 20, 1.

Monfils, N.S. & Menolascino, F.J. (1984). Modified individual and group treatment approaches for the mentally retarded mentally ill. In F.J. Menolascino & J. Stark (eds.) Handbook of Mental Illness in the Mentally Retarded. New York: Plenum Press.

O'Quinn, L. (1988). Medical treatment of psychiatric disorders in the handicapped. In J. Gerring & L. McCarthy (eds.). The Psychiatry of Handicapped Children and Adolescents. Boston: College Hill.

Rubin, R.L. (1983). Bridging the gap through individual counseling and psychotherapy with mentally retarded people. In F. Menolascino & B. McCann (eds.), Mental Health and Mental Retardation. Baltimore: University Park Press.

Szymanski, L. S. (1980). Individual psychotherapy with retarded persons. In L. Szymanski & P. Tanquay (eds.), Emotional Disorders of Mentally Retarded Persons. Baltimore: University Park Press.

Anton Dosen and Frank J. Menolascino (Eds.) (1990). Depression in mentally retarded children and adults. Leiden, the Netherlands: Logon Publications. ISBN 90-73197-01-5

Chapter 15

Treatment of depression in mentally retarded children: a developmental approach

Svetomir Bojanin, M.D.
Veronika Ispanovic-Radojkovic, M.D.

Introduction

Depression in mentally retarded children and adolescents has characteristics specific to age, intellectual level, and social circumstances (i.e., whether they are living within the family unit or in an institutional setting). Depression in such children is not merely an emotional problem, but a problem of cognitive developmental level as well. During depressive withdrawal, one's abilities to judge reality may decrease to such a degree that only internal vegetative sensations can be perceived. Therefore, depression should be understood in terms of emotional as well as cognitive development. In younger children, developmental levels reflect the achieved independence of praxic activities[1], and in older ones, the degree of differentiation between gnostic and praxic functions. This implies an analysis of the child's orientation toward the spatial and temporal qualities of his or her own existential field.

Depression and levels of mental retardation

As one analyzes the level of mental retardation in depressive mentally retarded children, the following facts emerge. The most profoundly retarded achieve only the most elementary forms of praxic activity. The majority of the profoundly retarded do not exceed a level

---

[1] **Praxias** are defined as systems of movements coordinated in functions as a result of an attention (Piaget, 1960). **Apraxias** are defined as the impossibilities of carrying out praxic activities because of lesions in distinct parts of the brain.

of achievement beyond primary circular reactions, and only rarely the secondary circular reactions as defined by Piaget (1947). Left to their own devices, they are unable to discover even the most elementary senses (e.g., vision, hearing, or taste). The level of sensorimotor activities exceeds only slightly that of visceral schemes and remain mutually interchangeable. These children are capable of discovering the certainty of tenderness in a symbiotic relationship only with their mothers. If the mother is unable to handle such a child and rejects him or her, the child falls into a state of emotional absence and loses all interest in sensomotor activities, thereby closing the only path possible for comprehending the world and creatively interacting with it. Consequently, these children are highly irritable, bad tempered, cry often, and are unwilling to engage in any kind of relationship offered to them.

Moderately retarded children are capable of apprehending their environment and mastering it through games and walks. Their sensorimotor activities are more complex, enabling them to develop practognostic[2] functions to some extent. Language, as a symbolic function, is also present, although in an elementary form. These children can be overwhelmed with joy and able to recognize some familiar situation or person or perceive some novelties, but can also become desperate if their expectations for familiar situations fail to materialize or if their current need is not immediately satisfied. Their mood is very unstable. Often overprotected, they remain in a prolonged symbiotic relationship and suffer greatly when placed in an institution. They become depressed, lose the interest they previously had in objects, persons, walking, and games; their activities diminish and they are no longer attracted to exploration of spatial relations. Sometimes, instead of decreased activity, aggressive behavior ensues, presaging the diagnosis of the depression.

Mildly retarded children achieve the level of concrete, logical thinking and a trial-and-error type of problem solving, which makes better comprehension of reality possible (Inhelder, 1963). To some extent, frustrations can be dealt with on a mental level instead of being released through acting-out behavior. An overprotective attitude on the part of caretakers interferes with the development of cognitive functions which often, therefore, remain very fragile. In the population of the mentally retarded individuals generally, violent disruption of the symbiotic relationship is not the only mechanism that triggers depression. Any frustrating environmental event which exceeds the child's comprehensive

---

[2] **Practognostic functions** comprise the functions of praxia and gnosia (Luria, 1973).

capacity can also be provocative. The actual "instruments," such as speech or motor activity, which failed in establishing interaction with the world are abandoned and the child turns toward the more archaic ones, such as aggressive acting-out, in order to merely survive. In some cases, even these mechanisms fail and the child or adolescent attempts suicide.

Depressive mentally retarded children and adolescents are not interested in objects, events, or the surrounding environment. They cease to display any interest in spatial quality in that they no longer perceive even the proximity to or distance from the people around them. Interest is lost even for their own bodies as centers for orientation. The body exists only when it hurts, when it causes discomfort. Even then, they are unable to name these sensations or the corresponding parts of the body. Something aches somewhere and that is all they know. Their life is merely one of existing. Yet they have no interest in the here and now. Nor are they able to anticipate along time and space in terms of the chronology of events. Such states correspond to those described by Minkowsky (1968) in which the individual sinks into despair by losing his or her concept of the future. Depressive mentally retarded children have lost their concept of the self in time and, considering their intellectual abilities and previous experience, this is not surprising. These specific features should be brought to bear on therapeutic measures.

Re-education of psychomotoricity as a psychotherapetic method

The purpose of various kinds of psychotherapy is to reveal to the subject his own individuality, the reality of his relations with others, and some features of the external world which he had previously misjudged. Psychotherapy thus aims at identifying those features of oneself and of others which were previously perceived erroneously or not at all. By so doing, the individual's consciousness expands and he or she is given the opportunity to make more adequate choices.

Speech

The role of speech in psychotherapy is of special interest. It is known that speech is both dependent on and instrumental to the differentiation of gnostic[3] processes. Speech is first perceived in utero

---

[3] Gnostic functions are defined as higher cortical activities comprising reception, coding, and the orage of information. They rely on the secondary (projection-association) areas and the tertiary zones : zones of overlapping) of the posterior parts on the cerebral cortex (Luria, 1973).

as a melody of the human voice (Bojanin & Milekic, 1986). Body language then develops as a sort of nonvoluntary metacommunication, which continues to express authentic attitudes in interpersonal communication during one's entire life. The last to appear is oral speech, the communication carrier within the field of developed consciousness and knowledge. However, words can have the same meaning and communicate the same emotional content, the same messages, only between persons who share the same language, civilization, and even cultural level. Indeed, persons from varying social levels may have difficulties understanding each other as they talk about their desires and dilemmas. Such issues pose a very real question regarding the type of communication one should use in psychotherapeutic procedures (Dosen, 1983).

An even a greater problem is posed with regard to communication between the psychotherapist and the retarded child or adolescent whose verbal abilities are, by definition, insufficiently developed. Some authors would deny the value and even the possibility of pursuing psychotherapy with the mentally retarded. We do not agree with this position; on the contrary, we advocate the necessity of applying a mode of communication inherent to the mentally retarded -- kinesthesia.

Kinesthesia

Movement is the most elementary form of communication. One's first interactions with the world and the first experience of one's own Being-in-the-World take place through kinesthesia. It is rooted in the mother's desire to communicate and exchange love with a child who is unable to understand anything except the fluctuation of muscle tone related to the states of pleasure or discontent. De Ajuriaguerra (1970) spoke of this "tonic dialogue" as the most archaic form of communication, preceding the appearance of the symbolic function.

By means of sensorimotor activity, the child finds its own way in space, recognizes and experiences the safety of familiar circles, learns about the world and reacts to it. By means of psychomotor activity, the child becomes integrated into the social field and, at the same time, is judged by it based on the skill or clumsiness of gait, running, games, drawing, etc. The child develops permanent relationships with space and people by means of movement and muscle tonus. As stated by Montessori (1979), the muscles embody the realization of an individual's life. We would like to emphasize that this realization is spatial and takes place within the context of the social field.

In the method of re-education of psychomotoricity (a term translated from the French), an exchange of feelings is achieved by means of motor activity (de Ajuriaguerra, 1970; Picq & Vayer, 1972). Through motor interaction, the therapist interprets and reveals to the child the world which he or she has abandoned through depressive withdrawal. The therapist uses all those body movements which appear in development and metacommunication. Thus, the treatment of sensomotorically handicapped, intellectually disabled and emotionally disordered children becomes possible in spite of the fact that oral language is insufficiently developed.

To the withdrawn child, the re-education of psychomotricity reveals the pleasure of kinesthesia and a feeling of security, initially in a symbiotic relationship and later in an interpersonal relationship (Stefanovic, Ispanovic-Radojkovic and Bojanin, 1984). The child also discovers the pleasure of novelty through such activity, fascinating and motivating him or her toward further independence. The revelation of one's own Being-in-the-World of others forms the first interpersonal field (Bojanin, Opalic and Ispanovic-Radojkovic, 1982; Bojanin & Ispanovic-Radojkovic, 1981), becoming the basis for the process of socialization and life in the community. The depressive retreat is thus dissolved.

In the re-education of psychomotoricity, a continuous process of summarizing and reintegrating elementary action takes place. New experiences of the surrounding world are recorded in the regions of the central nervous system which enhance development (Menolascino, 1983; Spreen, 1984). In this manner, depressive mentally retarded children gain better insight into the world around them. They are helped to discover various parts of their own bodies, to get to know them, to feel their elbows, for instance, through the hard surface of the table they are leaning on. Such revelations of the details of their particular existential situation, which were not consciously perceived until that moment, helps to strengthen the experience of self (Berges, 1984). The surrounding objects and persons become a part of their own existential field, which is thus gradually discovered, built up, and enlarged.

With regard to profoundly retarded children, re-education helps them to "come out from their own bodies" and discover some sort of pleasure in the world around them. By teaching these children to differentiate the tastes of some foods, simple sounds, smooth and rough surfaces, soft and hard textures, warm and cold temperatures, we provide opportunities to enrich the possibility of choosing from surrounding stimuli. Even on this low level of human experience, the child discovers the decision-making process, which is the central event of human conscious life.

Theoretical basis

Montessori (1979) and Wallon (1956) were the first to point out the importance of sensorimotor and psychomotor activity for a child's psychosocial development. Wallon emphasized that muscle tonus is closely intertwined with the emotional sphere throughout life. This relationship is more obvious in the first months of life when excitement spreads through the muscles of the entire body. Later on, as the child matures and gains more experience, muscle activity becomes more independent and less susceptible to the influence of the emotions. The biological foundation becomes human in the social field only through the interactions between mother and child (Wallon, 1956). The degree of independence achieved is related to the level of psychosocial development and the abundance and steadiness of previous social experiences. In states of regression, caused by an emotionally frustrating event, the emotions and muscle tonus merge again. Sudden emotions inhibit muscle activity. "He became paralyzed with fear" or "She was speechless with joy" are everyday expressions of these states.

The gradual separation of psychological from somatic functions takes place during the whole process of individuation. The vegetative functions, which predominate during the first weeks following birth, gradually lose their priority and the child interacts with the environment mainly at the sensorimotor level.

In the developmental phase, according to Mahler, Pine and Bergman (1975), sensorimotor structures "descend" into a sphere of metacommunication while speech becomes the dominant mode of the child's communication. The presence of another person (mother) is also necessary for intentional movements to appear. Luria (1966) emphasized that the brain alone is not enough for the development of praxic activity. The development of speech follows the same principle.

In disturbed development, the old schemes emerge. Thus, a prolonged symbiotic relationship prevents adequate development of **practognostic** function; the child retains the earlier schemes of behavior. "The proprioceptive schemes dominate over the peripheral sensibility" (Stambak, l'Heriteau, Auzias, Berges and Ajuriaguerra, 1964, p. 493).

With the further maturation of tonic functions and the underlying neural and muscular structures, intentional movements become more refined and precise. The first to mature are the axial paravertebral muscles in craniocaudal direction. The child starts to control his or her upright position, and at the same time practices large joint movements (e.g., the shoulders and hips). Two important crossroads of movement are formed: first the crossing of the cervico-thoracal paravertebral region with the shoulder region, and second, of the lumbo-sacral region with the hip region.

The axial, prevertebral musculature is of special importance since it is an axis around which the upright position, movements of the limbs, and the experience of oneself are centered. One's own existence is realized mostly through body posture, which is also the starting point for activities geared toward the social field. Binswanger (1970) drew attention to the fact that the axis of "absolute orientation" is central for the experience of Being-in-the-World. Wallon (1956), although from a different theoretical position, also noted the importance of the paravertebral musculature, of the axial tonic activities. According to Wallon, the perceived activities of the postural muscles are the sensomotor support of an individual's existential experience and could be formulated as: "I am here in front of you". These activities are the basis for later symbolic functions as well (Ispanovic-Radojkovic, 1986). Postural functions are essential for the affirmation of one's individual existence in the world. The upright or the bent position reveal the person's existential attitude, define one's ethical or even aesthetic values. It is not unusual to say "He stood upright in front of the enemy," or "He bowed his head in front of the tyrant." The custom of bowing to the gods is well known in many religions.

The method of the re-education of psychomotoricity is based on the assumptions of Seguin, which were defined early in the 19th century. Seguin was the first to claim that the treatment of the handicapped should always start and proceed through the experience of posturality (Pelicier & Thuillier, 1980). It is necessary that, during treatment, the child experiences feelings of security and of stability in his or her own basic body posture. Binswanger (1970) also discussed the point of "absolute orientation," and Wallon (1956) wrote about the revelation of social field and the individual's first realization of inter-subjective relations through posturality. In addition, Seguin observed that only the child who experienced security in his or her primary existential position and who mastered his or her own body could have a feeling of confidence, which would serve as a starting point for activity within the world. He also proposed the treatment of spatially orientated senses, that is, of smell, sight, and hearing. Seguin named them the senses of passive and active intelligence, anticipating the role of sensomotoricity in the development of intelligence, as discussed much later by Piaget (1947). The refinement of sense leads to further differentiation of correspondent **gnostic** functions and thus to better conceptual comprehension. It is somewhat peculiar that neither Piaget or Wallon mentioned Seguin as their possible forerunner.

Treatment should use as the point of departure the fact that a depressive child has abandoned the reality of social relations and conceals his or her emotional life. The aim of treatment is to revive interest in social relations and to motivate the child to get more involved. Treatment starts with the basic forms of satisfaction already developed before frustrating events contributed to the occurrence of depressive withdrawal. The first series of exercises revive the experience of total protection issuing from the symbiotic relationship between mother and child. Such symbiosis is the beginning of an individualized existence emerging from the universal. Inside the symbiotic relationship, the child experiences the pleasure of mere kinesthesia, the pleasure of stretching and moving, the pleasure of axial and postural tonic activities.

Separation of the two bodies in the symbiotic unit is the next step in the process of individualization. Distant contact makes the emergence of imitation based on biological functions possible. The imitation becomes more complex and supports the development of mental images as a form of symbolic function (Lacan, 1949; Wallon, 1954).

The next series of exercise is based on the child's predilection for novelty which typically emerge in about the eighth to twelfth month of life. At that time, the child experiences immense pleasure with regard to the shapes of objects, their surfaces, and spatial relations. This new desire coincides with the child's interest in others, but primarily in the mother. Fascination with spatial dimensions exists even before an interest in others develops, with the exception of the mother (Bojanin, 1985).

As the postural functions and the feeling of security consolidate, treatment proceeds to its next phase: spatial games such as building and tearing down, getting in and out, going up and down, etc. The pleasure in movement and imitation experienced previously now develops into the pleasure achieved by manipulations in space which, according to Piaget (1947), are the basis of sensorimotor schemes and ensuing cognitive abilities. Simultaneously, the mutual glances, exchanges of movement, and joint activities during treatment create a microcosm of real life situations that becomes the basic scheme of the child's further socialization.

The seven series: practical schemes of treatment

The following instructions concerning the practice of treatment should be conceived as only a basic scheme, intended primarily to stimulate the therapist's own creative imagination. The exercises are divided into series

272

which are adapted to the age, communicative abilities, and stage of the child's depressive illness. In older and mildly retarded children, the initial phase of re-educative exercises is more easily replaced by verbal analysis of nonverbal behavior, particularly metacommunication.

The **first series** of exercises is anchored in the schemes of very early intimate contact. Children under the age of ten are approached with simple words, carefully modulated as in "baby-talk." Any forced, unnatural behavior could provoke the child's hostility and resistance and is, therefore, to be avoided. The most important thing to remember is that the child should feel accepted and safe in the therapeutic situation.

The therapist takes the child in her arms, holds him on her lap, or places the more communicative child on a facing mattress. A gentle massage of the paravertebral muscles follows. It is performed in cranio-caudal direction: from the neck and shoulders down the thoracic and to the lumbo-sacral region. Light pressure is also applied to the whole surface area of the surrounding muscles. This gentle massage is accompanied by tender verbalizations or humming and by light rocking of the child. The child experiences the fluctuation of muscle tonus during the massage and the kinesthetic sensations of passive movement as a new source of pleasure. A symbiotic relationship with an adult is thus experienced anew. This kind of regression is reversible and is also used in other psychotherapeutic methods. The goal is not the interpretation of the developed transference relationship, but the restoration of a previously undisturbed developmental phase, which becomes the starting point for new achievements. If the child refuses to be touched or exhibits passive resistance, the therapist could imitate his behavior, posture, and movements, or try to engage his attention by some other suitable means.

After a few sessions, when the child has already accepted close contact, the therapist may start to passively move various parts of the child's body: trunk, head, legs or arms, to the left and right, up and down, forwards and backwards, trying to provoke any sign of pleasure in the child. The procedure should be done in front of a big mirror, permitting the child to achieve visual recognition of his own body and movements relative to the therapist's body. The gestures should be accompanied by simple melodic speech adapted to the child's intellectual level, which describe the actions being performed.

During this first series of exercises, the therapist tries to motivate the child to imitate her gestures, posture, and vocalization. For instance, if the child is standing in front of a mirror with his back on the therapist's chest, the therapist can perform slow, wing-like movements with outstretched arms, or can sway her body, raise her arms or legs, or

273

stand on one foot an in imitation of a stork. Using appropriate simple vocalizations, such as the buzzing of a fly or the meowing of a cat, the therapist tries to arouse the child's appetite for imitation. Gradually, the child will start to imitate the therapist, although scantily and for short periods at first. Initially, imitation is done strictly within the symbiotic relationship and takes place simultaneously with the therapist's actions. Later on, the imitation becomes more prolonged, complex, and delayed and the child may even show some initiative. The child will gradually detach himself from the adult model, thus breaking off the symbiotic relationship. These are the first signs that the child is coming out of a depressive state.

In the spheres of vocalization and verbalization, a similar procedure should take place. At first, the therapist plays with sounds, shouting loudly while raising the arms, whispering while lowering them. Later, the sounds of animals familiar to the child can be imitated, adapting the performance to the child's actual state and abilities. Anything that will produce a vocal response can be used, and any kind of response should be encouraged.

In profoundly mentally retarded subjects the massage and passive movements of the whole body should be more intense and frequent, and performed at the beginning of each session. In mildly retarded older children or adolescents, treatment should start with exercises in front of the mirror, followed by suitable conversation. The performed activities and the parts of the body should be described in detail. The child's sorrow could also be described; loss or absence of some dear person or some details from the child's past could be mentioned as well. If the therapist is of the opinion that the child has accepted her and is willing to collaborate, she can proceed to the next phase of the treatment.

The stage of the treatment just described is very important in all depressive children and especially in the mentally retarded. The order of the presented exercises is, however, not strict and is left to the therapist's appraisal of the situation.

The **second series** of exercises resumes the action of the "distant contact phase" (Spitz, 1965). The child's attention is directed toward auditory and visual sensations that accompany the kinesthetic activities.

After a brief massage or a few familiar exercises, the previous imitative activity is transformed into a rhythmic mirror-like activity of two bodies. If the child accepts this, the rhythm may be changed; slowed down or accelerated alternatively. A metronome may also be used, but the most important thing is to follow the kinesthetic activity by appropriately modulated speech. The child is continuously incited to listen to his voice, to look at his movements, and to compare them with his own activity. In this way, the child discovers the pleasure of being seen and heard by the therapist, to move along with her. He discovers the experience of pleasure at the levels of kinesthesia, sight, and hearing. The feeling of pleasure unites the kinesthetic, visual, and auditory sensations into a positive experience of basic trust (Erikson, 1959). This is the first step towards dissolving depression.

The **third series** of exercises is intended to have the child outgrow the symbiotic relationship and to establish independent sensorimotor or psychomotor functioning. The child's and therapist's bodies are no longer in close contact. They are separated in space. The imitation is initially done on command in the presence of the model, as in a mirror. Gradually it becomes an active imitation, the so-called "Imitation Opposition to the Model" (Wallon, 1954). The child opposes his own to the therapist's model. He discovers the pleasure of mutual games, of alternate and opposite action, and finally the pleasure of independent action. He has discovered the pleasure of acting autonomously in relation to someone else. At this stage we may say that the child is coming out of the critical stage of depression. The merged kinesthetic, tactile, visual, and auditory information reveals an experience of the body's integrity, which is to be the basis of the future self-concept. Thus, the center of "Absolute Orientation", of which Binswanger (1970) spoke, is established. We may say that at this moment the child has developed a firm and stable basis for his actions toward the outside world form which he can resist a new onslaught of depression.

The **fourth series** of exercises refers to the development of orientation in time and space. The therapist directs the child to take different positions in relation to her and to surrounding objects: next to or in front of one another, left or right of the chair, under the table, upon the mattress, etc. All these positions are adequately named from the perspective of the child. If the child displays some initiative in exploring the surrounding space, he is encouraged to take over and lead the game. His actions are described and reflected verbally according to their spatial and temporal qualities. For instance: "You are moving slower than I," You just slowed down," "What games did we play before this one?", etc.

The therapist should help the child experience the duration and passage of time during the session. By assigning some pleasurable activities for the next session, she helps the child transcend the present and build up a concept of himself in the future. This gradually lays the foundation for a sense of responsibility.

The **fifth series** of exercises is intended to train the schemes of reversibility through activities like build-and-tear-down, take-and-throw-away, hide-and-seek. They can be performed simultaneously with the fourth series. To illustrate, the therapist first builds a tower, then destroys it, rebuilds it and tries to provoke the child to destroy it. They build it and destroy it several times together. They act in symbiotic manner until the moment comes when the child starts to act independently.

Alternating activities are especially useful in mastering the scheme of reversibility. For example, while the therapist builds a tower, the child demolishes the one previously built. Or, the therapist and child play hide-and-seek, or throw a ball across a screen which is initially transparent (e.g., a volleyball net) and later one that cannot be seen through. Such activities help to consolidate the schemes of object permanency. With children or adolescents on a more advanced practognostic level, such activities can also be performed with the use of didactic materials such as cubes, tiles, and sticks.

The **sixth series** of exercises is aimed at the mastery of the basic schemes of correspondence, seriation, and classification, which form the basis of early logical thinking (Piaget, 1960). Objects or toys familiar to the child, or cubes, tiles, sticks, etc. are grouped and regrouped according to shape, color, or size. For example, the therapist builds up a tower with white or small cubes and the child does the same with the red or big ones. Later on they change the color or size. Thus, the ability to alternate the schemes is also practiced. Developing this ability is very important in depressive subjects, as their schemes are often rigid and they have difficulties changing them.

In the **seventh series** of activities, the practognostic activities already achieved are used in a broader context of social communication. This is the moment to introduce other children into the therapeutic process. The child's attention is now directed toward the existence of other viewpoints, thus encouraging a gradual decentration of thinking processes.
Various games are played (e.g., "snakes and ladders," dominoes, etc.) depending on the developmental level of the child. At first, only the child and the therapist participate in the games, introducing other children later. The leading principle behind these games should always be the child's desire for communication and not the complexity of the games or the skills needed for their performance. Drawing activity is also stimulated.

All the activities are accompanied by appropriate conversation. It can concern the child's daily routine, his feelings, or his relationship to others. Anything the child is capable of noticing or reporting on his own is encouraged. In mildly retarded children, a verbal type of psychotherapy can often be continued at this point in the treatment. For the more retarded, the conversation should be limited to naming the ongoing activities and actual feelings of the child.

Conclusion

In our experience, the results of the re-education of psychomotoricity in mentally retarded depressive children or adolescents are optimal if the sessions are 25-30 minutes long and take place daily or at least three times weekly. In profoundly retarded children, these sensorimotor schemes ought to be continuously stimulated and supported through feeding, toilet, and special re-educative activities. In moderately and mildly retarded children, this initial interpersonal field is enriched through activities in small groups (three to five children). Their socialization is stimulated by the reintegration of schemes of reality already existing in an earlier developmental phase. Treatment of profoundly mentally retarded children should be carried out on a long-term basis with frequent sessions and always using the same timetable. If treatment is discontinued too early, the children are prone to withdraw into the previous depressive state. Medication, such as small doses of tricyclic antidepressants, can be used as an auxiliary therapeutic measure. The counseling of parents by experienced professional psychotherapists or the supervision of special teachers in institutions for the mentally retarded is also desirable. It should help these adults to better comprehend their own roles in the child's development and in reference to his or her actual depressive state. The attitudes of rejection, overprotection or, possibly, cruelty are worked through. The meanings of metacommunication in the relationship with the child are particularly worked through.

In our experience, depressive states will show signs of amelioration after three to six months of treatment through re-education of psychomotorcity.

References

Berges, J. (1984). La psychotherapie et le corps de l'enfant. Psihijatrija danas, 2:177-180.

Binswanger, L. (1970). Discours, Parcours et Freud. Paris: Gallimard.

Bojanin, S. (1982). Neuropsychologiija razvojnog doba; zavod za udzbenike Nastavna Sredsta, Beograd.

Bojanin, S., Opalic, P., Ispanovic-Radojkovic, V. (1982). Pristup i indikacije fenomenolosko-egzistencijalisticke metode u individualnoj psihoterapiji dece i omladine. Psihijatrija danas, Beograd, 4:349-360.

Bojanin, S., Ispanovic-Radojkovic, V. (1981). Psihoterapija neuroza u razvojnom dobu. Psihijatrija danas, Beograd, 1:61-60.

Bojanin, S., Milekic, S. (1986). Prenatal psychology from the aspect of developmental Neuropsychology. Proceedings of the VIII International Congress of the Internal Society of Prenatal Psychology, 21-28. IX. Austris: Bad Gastein.

de Ajuriaguerra, J. (1970). Manual de psychiatrie de l'enfant. Paris: Masson.

Dosen, A. (1983). Psychische Stoornissen bij Zwakzinnige Kinderen. Lisse: Swets & Zeitlinger.

Erikson, E. (1959). Identity and Life-Cycle. New York: Intern. Univ. Press.

Inhelder, B. (1963). LeDiagnostic du Raisonnement chex les debiles mentaux. Neuchatel: Delachaux et Niestle.

Ispanovic-Radojkovic, V. (1986). Nespretno dete-poremecaji praksije u detinjstvu. Beograd: Zavod za udzbenike i nastavna sredstva.

Lacan, J. (1949). Le stade de mirroir comme formateur de la fonction de je telle qu'elle nous est revelee dans l'experience psychoanalitique. Paris: Ecrits.

Luria, A.R. (1966). Higher cortical functions in man. New York: Basic Books.

Luria, A.R. (1973). The working brain: An introduction to neuropsychology. London: Penguin Books.

Mahler, M., Pine, F., Bergman, A. (1975). The psychological birth of the human infant. New York: Basic Books.

Menolascino, F.J. (1983). Developmental interactions of brain impairment and experience. In F. Menolascino et al. (eds). Curative aspects of mental retardation. Baltimore: Paul Brooks.

Minkowsky, E. (1968). Le temps vecu. Neuchatel: Delachaux Niestle.

Montessori, M. (1979). La maison des enfants. Paris: Desclee de Brouwer.

Pelicier, Y., Thuillier, G. (1980). Eduard Seguin: Linstrituteur des idiots. Paris: Economia.

Piaget, J. (1947). La naissance de l'intelligence. Paris: Libraire Armand Colin.

Piaget, J. (1960). Les praxies chez l'enfant. Rev. Neurol., 102, 551-565.

Picq, L., Vayer, P. (1972). Education psychomotrice et arrieration mental. Paris: Dolin.

Spitz, R.A. (1965). The first year of life. Intern. Univ. Press.

Spreen, O., Tupper, D., Risser, A., Tuokko, H. & Edgell, D. (1984). Human developmental neuropsychology. Oxford: Oxford University Press.

Stambak, M., L'Heriteau, D., Auzias, M., Berges, J. & Ajuriaguerra, J. (1964). Les dyspraxies chez l'enfant. Psychiatr. Enf. Paris, 7:381-496.

Stefanovic, T., Ispanovic-Radojkovic, V., Bojanin, S. (1984). Reedukacija psihomotorike kao psihoterapijski metod u detinsjstvu. Psihijatrija danas, Beograd, 2: 193-200.

Wallon, H. (1954). Kinesthesie et image visuelle du carp propre chez l'enfant. Bull Psychol, 3-4:252-263.

Wallon, H. (1956). Importance du mouvement dans le development psychologique de l'enfant. Enfance Paris, 3-4:235-239.

Anton Dosen and Frank J. Menolascino (Eds.) (1990). Depression in mentally retarded children and adults. Leiden, the Netherlands: Logon Publications. ISBN 90-73197-01-5

Chapter 16

Psychotherapy with a depressed mentally retarded adult: an application of pre-therapy

Garry Prouty, M.A.
Melinda Cronwall, M.A.

Introduction

Notwithstanding the complexities of definition, diagnosis, and etiology, (Parsons, May & Menolascino, 1984), successful psychiatric treatment of the severely depressed retarded has been mostly achieved with lithium carbonate (Sovner & Hurley, 1983). However, with the possible exception of Lund (1988), little attention has been given to psychotherapeutics associated with depressed, retarded adults. This paper describes the psychological treatment of a mentally retarded depressed adult (IQ 13) without medications in a custodial setting.

Psychotherapy with the retarded has been viewed with skepticism. Generally, it has been assumed that such persons lack the necessary introspective or verbal capacities for treatment. In addition, assessment instruments tend to lose validity given the more severe levels of retardation. Historically, however, a number of authors (Balthazar & Stevens, 1975; Cowen, 1955; Robinson & Robinson, 1965; Saranson, 1957) have reported numerous case histories describing successful application of several forms of individual and group therapy. Generally, these psychotherapeutic studies lack diagnostic specificity or a focus on depression.

Client-centered psychotherapy

The client-centered approach has traditionally been limited to nonretarded populations. This was due, in part, to Rogers' (1957) opinion that client-centered therapy was not suitable for retarded persons.[1]
Only recently has retardation received significant attention (Badelt, 1988; Hurley & Hurley, 1987; Peters, 1981; Peters, 1986a). This literature, however, mainly reflects the application of Rogers' (1957) theoretical views concerning the therapeutic relationship. This position postulates the relationship as therapeutic if the conditions of unconditional positive regard, empathy, and congruence are experienced by the client. Yet these studies present descriptive case material and not a diagnostic focus or systematic theoretical-methodological expansion relative to the retarded.

Prouty (1988) examined the client-centered theory of psychotherapy and concluded that the major theoretical limitation concerning the retarded centers around Rogers' concept of "psychological contact." Yet Rogers does not define "psychological contact" either conceptually or methodologically, which limits therapists with "contact impaired" clients such as the retarded and austistic, schizophrenic, or depressed/withdrawn. This conceptual and methodological limitation also affects client-centered therapists in their approach to persons experiencing severe organic impairments which impede communicative efforts.

Pre-therapy

Pre-therapy (Prouty & Kubiak, 1988) represents an evolution in client-centered method and theory which has been specifically designed for the treatment of the severely disturbed mentally retarded. Its specific theoretical and clinical goal is to restore or develop "psychological contact" (Rogers, 1957) with withdrawn, isolated, or "out of contact" clients who are not accessible to psychotherapy or habilitation programming (hence the prefix "pre" - therapy).

Pre-therapy is a theory of psychological contact (Leijssen & Roelens, 1988; Peters, 1986b; Prouty, 1987). Its basic structure consists of (1)

---

[1] Ruedrich, S. & Menolascino F., (1984). Dual Diagnosis of Mental Retardation: An Overview. In: F. Menolascino & J. Stark (eds.), Handbook of Mental Illness in the Mentally Retarded. New York: Plenum Press, p 70. These authors attribute considerable professional influence to Rogers' view. They state: "The relative lack of professional concentration of counseling and psychotherapy activities with the mentally retarded reflect the works of Rogers and Dymond, and others who felt that psychotherapy was not indicated or useful for mentally retarded persons with psychiatric disorders because it required high levels of communication, capacity for self-reliance, and other factors inherent in normal intelligence."

contact reflections, (2) contact functions, and (3) contact behaviors. Contact reflections are a set of techniques by which the therapist facilitates contact with the client. Contact functions are a set of psychological functions necessary for therapy to occur (i.e., reality, affective, and communicative contact). Contact behaviors are a set of emergent "outcome" behaviors utilized for research.

Psychological contact is, thus, (a) a set of therapeutic techniques, (b) a set of psychological functions necessary for therapy to occur, and (c) a set of measurable outcome behaviors.

Contact reflections

Essentially, the contact reflections form a common method because they center on pre-expressive, pre-verbal, and primitive aspects of client behavior. They form a common style because they are distinctly literal, duplicative, and concrete. There are five contact reflections (Prouty, 1976): (1) situational (SR), (2) Facial (FR), (3) Word-for-Word (WWR), (4) Body (BR), and (5) Reiterative (RR).

(SR)   The psychological function of situational reflections is the development or restoration of reality contact. These reflections are focused toward the client's immediate environment, situation, or milieu.

(FR)   The psychological function of facial reflections is the development or restoration of affective contact. With these reflections, the therapist verbalizes the implicit affect in the client's face. This helps the client to express "pre-expressive" feelings.

(WWR)   The psychological function of word-for-word reflections is the restoration or development of communicative contact where it is absent or impaired. These reflections develop or restore social speech and help the client to experience self as expressor and communicator.

(BR)   Body reflections are literal or verbal reflections of the client's bizarre body states. These reflections are directed toward "body-sense" and help the client with general "here and now" reality contact.

(RR)   Reiterative reflections are essentially re-contact; utilizing previously successful responses. They assist in the interactive effect of contact and the experiencing process (Gendlin, 1968).

Contact functions

Psychological contact is the first necessary condition of a therapeutic relationship. Rooted in this context, pre-therapy conceptualizes psychological contact as necessary for therapy to occur in severely primitive and regressed clients. Contact functions are described as three levels of functional awareness: (1) reality contact, (2) affective contact, and (3) communicative contact. Reality contact is defined as the literal awareness of people, places, things, and events. Affective contact is described as awareness of mood, feeling, and emotions. Communicative contact is conceptualized as the symbolization of reality and affect to others. Reality, affective, and communicative functions are necessary for therapy to proceed, and as these contact functions are impaired in psychotic retardates, they become the clinical goals in a pre-therapy.

Contact behaviors

As a result of contact reflections and the facilitation of contact functions (reality, affect, communication), a client is more expressive about reality and affective states to other persons. As a consequence, the client is more accessible to psychotherapy or remedial programming (social, vocational, educational).

Contact behaviors are the emergent behavioral manifestation of reality, affective, and communicative contact. Behaviorally, reality contact is the client's verbalization of people, places, things, and events. Affective contact is the client's verbalization of emotions through feeling words (e.g., sad), or through bodily/facial expression. Communicative contact is the client's use of social language in words or sentences. These specific behaviors serve as the basis for scale development and statistical evaluation.

Pre-therapy defines contact reflections, contact functions, and contact behaviors as an interdependent theoretical system.

Case history

The client

Client X was age 21 at the time of treatment, male, and a resident of a custodial institution. He was diagnosed as severely retarded, and was referred to treatment as part of a pilot study designed to assess the effects of pre-therapy. Because of the severity of symptoms, he was not eligible for vocational or educational programing, field trips, or cottage activities. As a result of treatment, symptoms decreased and he exhibited more realistic communication which was confirmed by objective data. The client also became eligible for programmatic services.

The case is significant because the psychological treatment was completed without psychiatric medications, thus allowing for clearer assessment. Medical records indicated that the client had minor cerebral palsy, a history of mood swings, depression, and aggression. Psychiatric medications which had been utilized included Prolixin, Thorazine, Melleril and Vistaril. All psychiatric medications were discontinued at the beginning of pre-therapy.

Stanford-Binet testing reported in 1983 indicated a mental age of 2 years, 4 months with an IQ of 13 and a corresponding diagnosis of profound mental retardation. The client had a history of slow development, sitting up at 14 months and walking at 22 months. The client's parents were of lower socio-economic status. The father was an alcoholic who severely abused and beat the boy during the first five years of his life. This resulted in the parents' divorce and the subsequent placement of the client in a custodial institution. The mother maintained continued interest and remains active with parent advocacy at the institution.

The treatment

The client's presenting symptoms included severe and repeated crying, psychomotor retardation, and obsessive-stereotypic behavior (grass pulling), and mood swings.

Early treatment - Autistic phase: Treatment sessions were 30 minutes, twice weekly. During our first sessions, X would come loping into the room, sit down in a chair, and start driving an imaginary car. He would hold his hands and arms as on a steering wheel (we later introduced a toy steering wheel). He would make clicking noises (turn signals) and engine noises ("Vroom") over and over during the entire session. He would pretend to turn the wheel and bend sideways until he was touching the floor with his hand, shoulder, or arm. Sometimes he would make great crashing noises and say "beep-beep". He drove continually and constantly during our sessions for approximately the first 12 months. There was very little eye contact during this time.

Typical session

T		Hi X
T	(SR)	You're looking at the steering wheel.
T	(SR)	X is sitting in the chair, holding the steering wheel.
T	(SR)	We're both sitting in brown chairs.
C		Vroom
T	(WWR)	Vroom
C		Click, click.
T	(WWR)	Click, click.
T	(SR)	X is turning the steering wheel.

285

T	(BR)	Arms crossing.
T	(BR)	Body bending in chair.
C		Vroom, vroom
T	(WWR)	Vroom, vroom
T	(SR)	Our heads are touching the floor.
T	(BR)	We are bending over.
T	(FR)	You are looking.
T	(SR)	You are looking at the steering wheel. Eee, kruss, sss.
T	(WWR)	Eee, kruss, sss.
T	(SR)	You're making crashing noises. Click, click.
T	(WWR)	Click, click.
T	(SR)	You're making signal noises.
T	(SR)	We're sitting in a big room.
T	(SR)	The sun is shining.
T	(BR)	We're facing each other.
T	(BR)	Your arms are turning.
T	(BR)	Hands on steering wheel.
T	(BR)	You do, I do.
T	(BR)	X is smiling
T	(SR)	X has been driving for a long time.
T	(RR)	Last time we were together, we were in a small room.
T	(FR)	You look sad.
T	(SR)	You are making crashing sounds.
T	(BR)	You do, I do.
C		Vroom, vroom.
T	(WWR)	Vroom, vroom
C		Beep, beep
T	(WWR)	Beep, beep
T	(RR)	Last time we were together, you had a red shirt on.
T	(SR)	Today you have a yellow shirt.
C		Vroom, vroom.
T	(WWR)	Vroom, vroom.
C		Vroom, vroom.
T	(WWR)	Vroom, vroom.

Mid-treatment - Relatedness phase: Gradually he became aware that I was reflecting his verbalizations and body movements. As we started to make contact, he would drive, giving me eye-contact and smiling as I did contact reflections. He would contort his body so his head was on the floor, but he was seated in the chair making driving sounds and actions. He would look to be sure I was doing contact reflections. We

286

spent a lot of time driving, turning corners so that our upper bodies were almost on the floor, while our backsides remained in the chairs. As the driving behavior slowly decreased he would play with cars and other toys. I brought a large unbreakable mirror to the sessions. He would make faces into it and simultaneously watch his image while watching my reflections of his facial expressions. We played with a toy where different shapes fit into holes of the same shape. At first, he played only with the basic toy and had trouble fitting the shapes successfully. He eventually was able to fit the shapes in easily and then became uninterested in the toy altogether. He liked to draw and continue to enjoy playing with cars. His crying behavior was diminishing in the cottage. During all this time I used only pre-therapy contact reflections.

Typical session

T		Hi X
C		Hi Mimi
T	(SR)	You looked at Mindy when you said hi.
T	(SR)	You sit in chair.
T	(SR)	You're looking for the steering wheel.
T	(FR)	You picked up steering wheel.
T	(FR)	You're smiling
		Vroom, vroom
T	(WWR)	Vroom, vroom
T	(FR)	You watch Mindy.
T	(SR)	The big mirror is on the table.
T	(FR)	You stick out your tongue.
T	(RR)	You do, I do.
T	(FT)	You smile when Mindy sticks out her tongue.
T	(SR)	We are both looking in the mirror.
T	(BR)	X and Mindy are sitting next to each other.
T	(SR)	X and Mindy look in the mirror.
T	(FR)	X smiles
T	(FR)	You smile, I smile.
T	(FR)	Your lips are turned down.
T	(SR)	You are looking at X in the mirror.
T	(FR)	X is frowning
C		Here.
T	(WWR)	Here.
T	(WWR)	Now your lips turned up.
T	(FR)	You do, I do.
T	(FR)	X is smiling.
T	(SR)	You pick up the steering wheel.

C		Vroom, vroom.
T	(WWR)	Vroom, vroom.
C		Vroom, vroom.
T	(WWR)	Vroom, vroom.
T	(SR)	You look in mirror.
T	(RR)	You used to drive all the time.
T	(SR)	You pick up the red and blue toy.
T	(SR)	You're turning the toy around in your hands.
T	(SR)	You hand me the toy.
C		Open.
T	(FR)	You look.
T	(FR)	You look at Mindy.
T	(SR)	You want to take the shapes out of the toy.
T	(FR)	You watch.
T	(RR)	Last time we were sitting in the chairs.
T	(RR)	Last time it was raining.
T	(SR)	Today the sun is shining.
T	(RR)	Before, X said, "Open".
C		Here.
T	(WWR)	Here.
T	(SR)	You want the triangle in the hole.
T	(FR)	X smiles
T	(BR)	You do, I do.

Ending treatment - Expressive phase: In the ending phase of therapy, X's driving behavior was extinct as was his crying behavior. He no longer tore up the grass and he was now part of a pre-vocational program.   He went home from our sessions without the aid of staff. During our sessions he was more verbal and more assertive, expressing higher self-esteem.   He would walk around the room and ask questions (basic, but still questions).   He could and would express emotions appropriately and knew when he was happy or sad.   He was able to attend field trips. He would even talk about other people, showing much improved reality contact and social communications.

Typical session

T		Hi X
C		Fine.
T		How are you today?
C		Fine.
T	(WWR)	You're taking off your coat.
T	(SR)	You are looking at Mindy.

C		Hang up?
T	(WWR)	Hang up?
T	(SR)	You want to know what to do with your coat. You can put it over there.
T	(SR)	You put your coat on the chair.
T	(SR)	You're walking across the room.
T	(BR)	You sit down.
T	(SR)	You put your arms on the table.
T	(BR)	You do, I do.
T	(SR)	You reach in the bag.
T	(SR)	X takes out the green car.
C		Vroom, vroom.
T	(WWR)	Vroom, vroom.
T	(SR)	It flies across the room.
T	(FR)	X laughs.
T	(BR)	X stands up.
T	(SR)	X pushes chair back.
T	(SR)	X picks up car.
T	(SR)	You're walking to the candy machine.
T	(SR)	You're rattling the handle.
C		Candy.
T	(WWR)	Candy.
C		Candy (louder).
T	(WWR)	Candy.
T	(SR)	X wants candy.
T	(SR)	No candy now, X.
T	(SR)	You're looking at Mindy.
T	(BR)	You're walking
T	(SR)	You're looking at the stuff on the counter.
C		Plates
T	(WWR)	Plates.
C		Napkins.
T	(WWR)	Napkins.
C		Party?
T	(WWR)	Party.
T	(SR)	You want to know if there is going to be a party?
T	(SR)	Christmas is coming.
C		Santa.
T	(WWR)	Santa.
T	(SR)	Santa comes at Christmas.
T		What are you doing for Christmas?
C		Going home in car.
T	(WWR)	Going home in car.

C		See Mom.
T	(WWR)	See Mom.
T	(RR)	You'll see Mom when you go home for Christmas.
T	(RR)	Before you laughed when you pushed the car off the table.
T	(FR)	You smiled when Mindy says that.
T		Is someone coming to take you back to your house?
C		No.
T		Good-bye X.
C		Good-bye Mimi.

Objective data: pilot study

The client was treated by a para-professional therapist (Associate Degree in Mental Health)[2] who tape recorded each session. All recorded sessions were transcribed, verbatim, to a data sheet for scoring by the therapist and two independent raters who scored contact behaviors. Reality contact was designated as the client's verbalization of people, places things, and events. Affective contact was specified as the verbalization of feeling words or facial/bodily expression. Communicative contact was defined as the expression of socially recognized words.

Table 15.1
Reality contact per minute (200 sessions)

Pre-therapist		Independent rater	Independent rater
1983	.21	.22	.20
1984	1.18	.87	1.15

Communicative contact per minute (200 sessions)

1983	.33	.37	.30
1984	1.82	1.87	1.78

---

[2] The second author has since continued studies and received graduate training in counseling and psychotherapy. She is currently employed as a professional psychotherapist.

The therapist and raters were pre-trained to a competency of .6 correlation with master raters. The data in Table 15.1 represents simple arithmetic averages derived from 100 sessions per year, time corrected over a two-year period. The essential hypothesis was that clients would exhibit a greater frequency of reality, affective, and communicative contact as a function of pre-therapy.

Although a pilot study, this data confirms the therapist's description (expressive phase) that the client was more realistically communicative. Verification by a second independent rater adds validity to this hypothesis. However, the hypothesis concerning increased affective expression, as reported by the therapist, was not supported.

Follow-up

This client received approximately two years of pre-therapy treatment. Clinical impression describes increased ability contact and social communication as well as symptomatic decreases. More objective data also supported the assertion of increased reality contact and social communication. In addition, the client improved sufficiently for placement in a pre-vocational program in the institution.

A four-year follow-up review finds a picture of stabilized and improved adjustment without psychiatric medications. Records indicate the client's continued accessibility to institutional services. He currently participates in vocational, educational, and social-activity programming. Records also indicate some evidence of continued verbal aggression and instances of continued crying. An interview with his mother, reveals impressions such as: "He's improved a lot," "I really think it helped him," "We can bring him home now for longer periods of time without as much stress," "It worked great," and "It helped him see himself." The mother also wished that treatment could have continued longer.

Conclusion

Since psychiatric medications were not utilized during or after the psychological treatment, it was possible to develop a clearer assessment regarding the results of pre-therapy. It seems reasonable to assume that decreased symptomatology and improved realistic communication provided opportunity for programmatic functioning.

The lack of supportive evidence for increased affective expressions seems indirectly confirmed by the fact that the client did not proceed into psychotherapy as it is classically conceived (i.e., the resolution of affective states). This is not uncommon. Some retarded, disturbed clients move into a psychotherapeutic process as a result of pre-therapy, while others do not This is not a direct function of IQ.

In summary, this case history reveals a client with improved adjustment and greater accessibility for institutional programming leading to an improved quality of life which, in turn, is therapeutic.

References

Badelt, I. (1988). Client-centered psychotherapy with mentally handicapped adults. Paper presented at the International Conference on Client-Centered/Experiential Therapy. Catholic University, Leuven, Belgium.

Balthazar, E. & Stevens, H. (1975). The Emotionally Disturbed, Mentally Retarded: A Historical and Contemporary Perspective. New Jersey: Prentice Hall.

Cowen, E.L. (1955). Psychotherapy and play techniques with exceptional children and youth. In W. Cruickshank (ed.), Psychology of Exceptional Children and Youth. New York: Prentice Hall.

Gendlin, E.T. (1968). The experiential response. In E. Hammer (ed.), Use of interpretation in treatment. New York: Grune & Stratton.

Hurley, A.D., & Hurley, F. (1987). Psychotherapy and counseling II: establishing a therapeutic relationship. Psychiatric Aspects of Mental Retardation Reviews, 4(4), 15-20.

Leijssen, M. & Roelens, L. (1988). Herstel van contactfuncties bij zwaar gestoorde patienten door middel van Prouty's pre-therapie. Tijdschrift Klinische Psychologie, 1, februari, 118-127.

Lund, J. (1988). Treatment of depression in mentally retarded adults. In A. Dosen & P. Engelen (eds), Depression in the Mentally Retarded. Netherlands: Organization for Postacademic Studies in the Social Sciences.

Parsons, J., May, J. & Menolascino, F. (1984). The nature and incidence of mental illness in mentally retarded individuals. In F. Menolascino (ed.), Handbook of Mental Illness in the Mentally Retarded. New York: Plenum Press.

Peters, H. (1981). Luisterend helpen: poging tot beter omgaan met de zwakzinnige. Lochem, the Netherlands: De Tijdstroom.

Peters, H. (1986a). Client-centered benaderingswijzen in de zwakzinnigenzorg. In: R. VanBalen, M. Leijssen & G. Lietaer (eds.), Droom en werkelijkheid. Belgie: Acco Press.

Peters, H. (1986b). Prouty's pre-therapie methode en de behandeling van hallucinaties, een verslag. RUIT, 3, 26-34.

Portner, M. (1988). Client-centered therapy with mentally retarded persons. Paper presented at the International Conference on Client-Centered/Experiential Therapy, Catholic University, Leuven, Belgium.

Prouty, G.F. (1976). Pre-therapy: a method of treating pre-expressive psychotic and retarded patients. Psychotherapy: theory, research, and practice, 13, 290-294.

Prouty, G.F. (1987). The development of reality, affect and communication in psychotic retardates. Paper prepared for the International Conference on the Mental Health Aspects of Mental Retardation, University of Illinois at Chicago.

Prouty, G.F. (1988). Evolutions in the person-centered/experiential psychotherapy of schizophrenia & retardation. Paper prepared for publication. International Conference on Client-Centered/Experiential Psychotherapy. Catholic University, Leuven, Belgium.

Prouty, G.F & Kubiak, M. (1988). Pre-therapy with mentally retarded/psychotic clients. Psychiatric Aspects of Mental Retardation Reviews, 7(10) 62-66.

Robinson, H. & Robinson, N. (1965). The Mentally Retarded Child: A Psychological Approach. McGraw Hill: New York.

Rogers, C. (1942). Counseling and pyschotherapy. New York: Houghton-Mifflin.

Rogers, C. (1957). The necessary and sufficient conditions of therapeutic personality change. Journal of Consulting Psychology, 21(2) 95-103.

Saranson, S.B. (1957). Individual psychotherapy with mentally defective individuals. In: C. Stacey & M. Demartino (eds.), Counseling and Psychotherapy with the Mentally Retarded. Glencoe, Illinois: Free Press. (Citation: abridged from S.B. Saranson's "Individual psychotherapy with mentally defective individuals." American Journal of Mental Deficiency, 56, 803-805, 1952).

Sovner, R., & Hurley, A. (1983). Do the mentally retarded suffer from affective illness? Archives of General Psychiatry, 40, 61-67.

Anton Dosen and Frank J. Menolascino (Eds.) (1990). Depression in mentally retarded children and adults. Leiden, the Netherlands: Logon Publications. ISBN 90-73197-01-5

Chapter 17

Symbolic interactional therapy: a treatment intervention for depression in mentally retarded adults

Julie B. Caton, M.S.

Introduction

Despite considerable recent progress in the diagnosis of depression (Kovacs & Beck, 1977; Lefkowitz & Burton, 1978; Matson, 1983), the definition of this disorder, whether relevant to persons with normal intelligence or mental retardation, remains controversial. Essentially, there are two schools of thought regarding the etiology of depression, one of which emphasizes the learning-biologic model (Lewinsohn, 1975) which operationally defines the symptoms and is derived in part from the work of Seligman (1975) on learned helplessness in dogs. The other focuses on the psychodynamic-biological model (Cytryn & McKnew, 1974; Frommer, 1968) which theorizes that internal psychological mechanisms create depressive symptomatology. In this latter group, there is even further disagreement as to whether the depression is overt or masked. According to Glaser (1968), for example, childhood depressive disorders differ from adult syndromes in that children generally "mask" their symptoms in behavioral problems as well as psychoneurotic and psycho-physiologic reactions. This basic difficulty in clearly defining the etiology and characteristics of depression becomes even more complicated when dealing with individuals with mental retardation because of the tremendous variability in symptoms found across chronological ages and degrees of cognitive ability.

Several views of depression relevant to children are considered applicable to the mentally retarded population as well (Carlson & Cantwell, 1980; Kovacs & Beck, 1977). These two positions hold that depression will either (1) appear in symptoms as overt as those found in persons with normal intelligence; or (2) tend to be masked in behaviors and symptoms which substitute for underlying depressive feelings. Symptoms which appear in the overt manifestation of depression include agitated behavior, crying, moodiness, sleep disturbance, somatic complaints, social withdrawal, and self-depreciation. Masked symptoms of depressive equivalents would include temper tantrums, oppositional reactions, school or work phobias, self-destructive behaviors, sexual acting-out, and proneness to accidents.

Regardless of one's accepted explanation for the causes of depression, Symbolic Interactional Therapy (Caton, 1988) constitutes a practical tool for treating this disorder, whether it is conceptualized as overt or masked, or whether one's theoretical orientation is cognitive-behavioral or psychodynamic.

The symbolic interactional technique

Symbolic Interactional Therapy (S.I.T), geared specifically to the adult with mental retardation, combines the techniques of learning in a cognitive-behavioral mode with the fantasy play employed by the psychoanalytic approach. Essentially, the S.I.T. counselor uses symbols, appearing as toys or figurines, as a basis for concrete communication. Within a Rogerian context of a trusting therapeutic relationship, unconditional positive regard, warmth, and empathy (Rogers, 1942, 1951), the therapist introduces interactions or stories through the use of these symbols. Two primary techniques are used; "mutual storytelling" and "instant replay."

Mutual storytelling and instant replay

Mutual storytelling (Gardner, 1970) is a technique often used in play therapy with children and is based primarily upon their fantasies and wishes. For example, the therapist, using a variable script, will elicit a story from the client in a manner similar to the following:

> "Let's make up a story today. You decide who's going to be in it and what's going to happen. (Client chooses figurines from a selection of "symbols"). Now let's begin. 'Once upon a time, there was (turns to the client for the inclusion of a figure or a noun) a _____ who did (waits for an action or a verb) _____.'"

The story thus progresses along this fill-in-the-blank model. For the more advanced client, the counselor might initially suggest that a story needs to have a beginning, a middle, and an end, and even a moral if possible. For the less advanced client, the counselor will be satisfied with the simple movement of two or more figures in a basic interaction. The more nonverbal the client, the more the counselor will fill in the blanks by observing his or her actions, movements, and guttural utterances; in essence making up a story **with** the client by "putting words in the client's mouth" based upon nonverbal cues.

A second modality is the use of "instant replay," which simply involves asking the individual to demonstrate how something concrete actually happened, similar to an instant replay on sports television. If this concept is not understood by the client, the therapist can provide examples and clarify the concept by likening it to "watching a movie of what happened to you yesterday." Most often, instant replay is used in S.I.T. to help the therapist understand the components of a specific "crisis" that recently occurred in the client's life.

The use of instant replay is based entirely on reality. To initiate instant replay, the therapist would simply say, "Show me what happened yesterday when you didn't get on the van for work." A figurine would be assigned to represent the client, as well as any other symbols required to represent the people or equipment (e.g., the van) necessary for understanding the event.

An interesting characteristic of S.I.T. is that there is a meta-level of communication occurring between the "fantasy pole" of mutual storytelling and the "reality pole" of instant replay (see Table 16.1). At this meta-level, the client and the therapist may initially communicate in a manner based entirely on reality and the next minute slide across the continuum towards the fantasy pole, through which the dreams and wishes behind a certain reality are then discussed. In fact, during any given therapy session with any given client, exploration of that individual's thinking and affect can easily shift from the psychodynamic model to the cognitive model with very little trouble. For example, a client may present a story in which the predominate theme is one of a young defective child who is kicked out of her home and forced to live elsewhere, resulting in strong feelings of anger and confusion. Later in the session, the therapist and client can examine a concrete incident through the use of instant replay in which the retarded woman is telephoned by her natural mother and told that she "cannot come for her weekend this month." The therapist can then explore the client's feelings following the phone call, and observe her behavioral reactions to it. By remaining sensitive to the readiness of

297

the client, an interpretation between these two psychological experiences may be made and some alternative (and corrective) solutions can be offered.

Table 16.1
The therapeutic continuum in symbolic interactional therapy

TECHNIQUE - Mutual storytelling   TECHNIQUE - Instant replay

FANTASY POLE -- META-LEVEL --   REALITY POLE

Therapeutic goals: **Therapeutic goals:**

Use projective pole to explore: Use concrete pole to explore:

1. Quality of ego-state; i.e., self-esteem, defenses, sense of self and others	1. Awareness of personal behavior.
2. Wishes and fears.	2. Sense of affect.
3. Locus of control;sense of mastery.	3. Ability to solve problems.

Provide interpretations: **Provide psycho-education:**

1. Indirectly through characters in scenario.	1. Alternative perceptions; Solutions to problems.
2. Link characters with actual events.	2. Affective education.

Assumptions and goals of S.I.T.

Originating out of the classical play therapy model (Axline, 1947; Erikson, 1940; Haworth, 1964; Schaefer & O'Connor, 1983; Winnicott, 1971), Symbolic Interactional Therapy is based on the assumption that the client has a desire to reduce his or her unconscious inner conflicts. It further assumes that people will communicate unconscious material more freely if this takes place in a non-threatening manner, such as talking in the third person and employing the story form. S.I.T. also shares the same goals as play therapy (Harter, 1983), namely, that individuals will use play as an opportunity to manipulate and control a "pretend" environment and that the therapeutic practicing of behavioral and emotional responses will later be used in real life.

Although excellent work has been done with the mentally retarded in the area of play therapy (Leland, 1983; Li, 1981, 1985; Prouty, 1976), S.I.T. goes beyond the pure activity of play and concentrates on extracting its helpful elements and normalizing them for the adult with cognitive impairments. Specifically, it emphasizes concreteness and a high level of structure. Because these developmentally disabled clients are probably functioning at the Piagetian level of cognitive development in the pre-operational or concrete stage (Piaget, 1951, 1952; Piaget & Inhelder, 1969), a heavy reliance on spoken language in therapy tends to be unproductive. Therefore, S.I.T. relies on the use of concrete symbols and interactions. It de-emphasizes insight in exchange for communication through story form and the use of the third person. It has been noted that the cognitive development of this population does not permit free associating (Harter, 1983), thus it is play or "symbolic interaction" which replace free association. Harter points out that the natural mode of expression for people at the concrete level of cognitive development is one of action, and the primary developmental task for these individuals involves the ego's desire for mastery. Furthermore, both children and developmentally disabled adults have a tendency to externalize their conflicts, making play or S.I.T. the modality of choice.

Theories of depression

To understand how a clinician might utilize Symbolic Interactional Therapy in the treatment of depression, one needs a rudimentary understanding of two basic theories of depression. The psychoanalytic theory (Abraham, 1968) holds that individual depression derives from: (1) an attitude of the libido in which hatred predominates; and (2) a suppression of these hostile impulses which are then experienced in a different form (e.g., "People do not love me, they hate me . . . because of my inborn defects."). Freud (1955) viewed depression as the supposed loss of a love object (such as the idealized mother or idealized self, or both) and the feelings of ambivalence and repressed anger regarding that lost love object. To correct this problem, one would need to "uncover" the anger and re-establish a sense of self or love object. S.I.T. encourages the free expression of anger and grief through the element of play, allowing the therapist and client to confront these buried feelings. Once they are uncovered and played out, some sense of "working through" takes place and depression is alleviated.

The cognitive-behavioralist theory of depression is best described by Beck (Kovacs & Beck, 1977) through the conceptualization that a "cognitive triad" underlies depression. Namely, the depressed individual has a negative view of the self, of the world, and of the future. Beck states that the depressed person's cognitive schemata relating to self-assessment consist of seeing oneself as deficient, inadequate, and un-worthy. The depressed person also sees the environment as the cause of failure and defeat, and faces the future with an attitude of hopelessness. Themes of loss and deprivation become paramount. The corrective modality is to restructure the depressed client's negative conceptualization of both the self and the world. This can be effectively done by exploring the client's faulty cognitive processes and the subsequent affect as they are observed and discussed during a S.I.T. instant replay. Dealing with cognitive distortions or perceptions can also be accomplished by working on the meta-level to examine the client's fantasies during any given real life event. Using S.I.T., the therapist is able to provide the client with alternative positive perceptions and an improved world-view. Additional work can be done to build self-esteem and a sense of success in appropri-ately circumscribed areas of the client's life.

Regardless of one's theoretical orientation, it is generally accepted that depression causes troublesome symptoms which need to be alleviated. Using either the fantasy pole or the reality pole, S.I.T. will manifest and make concrete those symptoms through the use of symbols and interac-tions, allowing the client to understand what he or she is doing and why. Combined with a psychoanalytic process of uncovering and ventilation, or a cognitive process of examining and re-educating, S.I.T. will effectively bring about symptom reduction. Only after that occurs can there be a beneficial therapeutic outcome.

Although depression in the mentally retarded has been a subject of recent investigation, prevalence rates are not yet available (Kazdin, Matson, & Senatore, 1983). Yet through direct observation of this population, one can easily detect "defects" and "impairments" which clearly impact a mentally retarded individual's view of the self. A firsthand analysis of the family histories or schooling of the mentally handicapped indicates a high incidence of isolation, rejection, deprivation, and social ostracism (Reiss & Benson, 1984). Suffice it to say, from the theoretical point of view, that mentally retarded clients have legitimate reasons to be depressed. Yet few clinicians have considered treating the depression of the mentally retarded with any other means [modality] except behavioral (Matson, 1982; Schloss, 1982). In fact, only a few professionals over the last quarter century have given credence to the provision of psychotherapy to this special population for any disorder at all (Matson, 1984; Menolascino, 1965; Philips, 1967; Reiss, Levitan & McNally, 1982; Sternlicht, 1965; Symington, 1981).

Three primary purposes of symbolic interactional therapy

There are three primary functions of S.I.T. in treating the depressed mentally retarded client: 1) its use as a diagnostic tool, assessing different aspects of ego functions; 2) as a means to accomplish helpful psycho-dynamic interpretations; and 3) as a psychoeducational device to explore and restructure faulty cognitions and inadequate affective awareness.

S.I.T. as a diagnostic tool

In the initial states of the therapeutic encounter, the clinician has the task of forming a diagnosis and/or conceptualization of the client's problems and personality, and S.I.T. provides a non-threatening arena to do so. During play activity the therapist can function as both a partici-pant and an observer, allowing him or her to assess personality style, behaviors, defense mechanisms, and presenting problems as the client chooses to uncover them. As the session progresses into mutual story-telling or instant replay, the client's ability to express and understand affect can be examined, as can his or her power to comprehend cause and effect.

Stages of affective understanding

For help in forming diagnostic impressions and setting treatment goals, Harter (1983) has outlined four stages through which people

301

progress as they develop an understanding of affect. Stage one suggests that the client has no affective awareness, as is found in most of the profoundly retarded and in some of the severely retarded individuals with whom I have worked. In these cases, one treatment goal would be to begin to identify very basic affect, such as excitement (feeling happy) and boredom (feeling blah or sad). Stage two recognizes that the person does indeed know that feelings exist, but is only able to comprehend one at a time. A client at this age would deny the fact that two feelings might simultaneously occur. A treatment goal would be to examine two or more affective states and to recognize how they can exist near each other in one's daily experience. Stage three suggests that the client is able to think about two or more feelings occurring, but that he or she actually experiences these feelings sequentially rather than simultaneously. A treatment goal, therefore, would be to use the therapeutic encounter, specifically mutual story telling or instant replay, to examine how more than one feeling can exist at the same time. Harter's fourth stage constitutes the conceptualization of two emotions simultaneously experienced. The goal in this instance would be to develop mechanisms with which to cope effectively with their co-existence. To alleviate depression, affect needs to be unleashed, understood, and mastered. Any progress through these affective stages will be helpful in treating depression.

Stages in comprehending cause and effect

Similarly, Selman (1980) suggested four stages of development regarding the intentionality of behavior -- one's ability to understand cause and effect -- which can be used both diagnostically and for goal-planning. Zero level involves a total confusion between the physical and psychological realms, leading the individual to make erroneous causal inferences regarding behavior. At the first level, the individual views people as intentional beings who have some specific motive imputed to their behavior. The second level is arrived at when one realizes that one's motives can be concealed from other people, while at level three he or she becomes aware of mixed or conflicting motives. Finally, at level four, higher order constructs regarding motives as well as the cause and effect of behaviors (e.g., approach-avoidance conflict) are introduced. As the therapist and client progress, these four different levels of understanding behavior can function as bench marks in the treatment process and can aid in setting operational goals and measuring progress. The more advanced the client becomes, the greater his or her capacity grows for coping with life situations and troublesome symptoms.

S.I.T. as a tool for interpretation

The second function of S.I.T. is that of interpretation, a technique derived from the psychoanalytic school of thought. Erik Erikson (1950) suggested that therapeutic interpretation will reveal a unitary theme to the client. This theme is formulated through patterns observed in four aspects of the the therapeutic process: (1) the dominant trend in the patient's story or instant replay; (2) a significant explanation for symptomatology; (3) certain aspects of the client's love and work life; and (4) characteristics which are developing in the relationship between therapist and client.

In her analysis of play therapy, Harter (1983) discovered various interpretative phases which take place in therapy. The first phase of interpretation would be made by the therapist through the characters in a play scenario. If this interpretation was well received, a link would then be made by the therapist between the play character and the client. Ideally, therapy would progress to a third phase wherein the client is found to be thinking along these same lines and makes an indirect personal interpretation through the use of a story. A client might finally offer an interpretation about what is observed and experienced directly, representing the last phase of interpretation. While most of the interpretations produced in S.I.T. occur at the first level, that is, indirectly through story-form by the therapist, they still have a beneficial effect by helping clients to resolve their inner conflicts and to embrace new perceptions about the world around them.

S.I.T. as a psychological tool

The third function of S.I.T. is psychoeducational. Mentally retarded adults will often need guidance in and education about their affective and behavioral lives. Through S.I.T., a client can be taught new affective levels, along the lines of Harter (1983). They can be educated about the more complex causes and effects of behavior, as described by Selman (1980). Finally, they can learn alternative perceptions and solutions regarding their views of self and the world around them, in the best tradition of the cognitive-behavioralists.

Part of the psychoeducational function of S.I.T. is to address the social skills of the mentally retarded client. Research has shown that social skills are often deficient in this population and are correlated to feelings of depression and low self-esteem (Matson, 1982). By using the instant replay-reality pole, the social skills of the client can be assessed and appropriate behaviors and methods of communication can be taught (Matson & Ollendick, 1988). For example, if a client indicates through his S.I.T. interactions that his way of "talking" with a female peer is to

303

kiss and touch her, the counselor can use figurines and movements to play out alternative ways to "be friends" that are more socially acceptable. The therapist should also use what he or she sees occurring during the session itself, between counselor and client, as tools for working on improved social skills.

S.I.T and family therapy

At any point during treatment the counselor might become aware that the client's depression is due in part (or wholly) to pathology in his or her family system. S.I.T. will lend itself nicely to a structural family therapy model (Keith & Whitaker, 1981). Specifically, after working with a developmentally disabled client and family for a few sessions, a S.I.T. interview done with the client can help fine tune the work being done with the family. Such a session can be done individually, or as a subset of the larger family interview. One goal of S.I.T. in this context would be to assess to what degree the mentally retarded client is understanding and retaining the family themes and negotiations. Or the S.I.T. counselor might create an instant replay of a family crisis with the intent of better understanding the client's involvement in it, as well as his or her perceptions and fantasies during this crisis. Finally, S.I.T. could be used to make an interpretation in a concrete, simple, non-threatening way, so that the client's (and family members') awareness of the family system improves.

Conclusion

Diagnosing, making interpretations, and providing psycho-education are all functions of Symbolic Interactional Therapy that can take place at any time during the course of treatment. A clinician might be doing only one of these functions at any given time or all three simultaneously. In addition, S.I.T. can easily be employed as one of several treatment modalities, such as combined individual and family work, or in group sessions for the developmentally disabled. While S.I.T. has been used in numerous settings over the last few years, and its versatility is note-worthy, good empirical research regarding its efficacy has yet to be completed. Nevertheless, whether one feels that depression is due to repressed anger and feelings of loss that need to be uncovered and resolved, or by irrational perceptions about a defective self that needs to be relearned, the techniques incorporated in Symbolic Interactional

Therapy have proven to be an effective means of treating depression in clients with mental retardation.

References

Abraham, K. (1968) Notes on the psychoanalytical investigation and treatment of manic-depressive insanity and allied conditions. In: W. Gaylin (Ed.), The Meaning of Despair. New York: Science House.

Axline, V.M. (1947) Play Therapy. New York: Ballentine Books.

Carlson, G.A. & Cantwell, D.P. (1980) Unmasking masked depression in children and adolescents. American Journal of Psychiatry, 37, 445-449.

Caton, J.B. (1988) Symbolic interactional therapy: A treatment invention for the mentally retarded adult. Psychiatric Aspects of Mental Retardation Reviews, 7, 2, 7-12.

Cytryn, L. & McKnew, D.A. (1974) Factors influencing the changing clinical expression of the depressive process in children. American Journal of Psychiatry, 131, 879-881.

Erikson, E.H. (1940) Studies in the interpretation of play: 1. Clinical observations of play disruptions in young children. Genetic Psychology Monographs, 22, 557-671.

Erickson, E.H. (1950) Childhood and Society. New York: W.W. Norton.

Freud, S. (1955) Beyond the Pleasure Principle. London: Hogarth Press.

Frommer, E. (1968) Depressive illness in childhood. British Journal of Psychiatry, 2, 117-123.

Gardner, R. A. (1970) Therapeutic Communication with Children: The Mutual Storytelling Technique. New York: Jason Aronson.

Glaser, K. (1968) Masked depression in children and adolescents. Annu. Prog. Child Psychiatry Child Dev., 1, 345-355.

Harter, S. (1983) Cognitive-developmental considerations in the conduct of play therapy. In: C. Schaefer & K. O'Connor (Eds.), Handbook of Play Therapy. New York: John Riley.

Haworth, M.R. (1964) Child Psychotherapy: Practice and Theory. New York: Basic Books.

Kazdin, A.E., Matson, J.L. & Senatore, V. (1983) Assessment of depression in mentally retarded adults. American Journal of Psychiatry, 140, 8.

Keith, D.V. & Whitaker, C.A. (1981) Play therapy. A paradigm for work with families. Journal of Marital and Family Therapy, July, 243-254.

Kovacs, M. & Beck, A.T. (1977) An empirical-clinical approach toward a definition of childhood depression. In: J. Schulterbrandt & A. Raskin (Eds.), Depression in Childhood: Diagnosis, Treatment and Conceptual Models. New York: Raven Press.

Lefkowitz, M.M. & Burton, N. (1978) Childhood depression: A critique of the concept. Psychological Bulletin, 85, 716-726.

Leland, H. (1983) Play therapy for mentally retarded and developmentally disabled children. In: C. Schaefer & K. O'Connor (Eds.), Handbook of Play Therapy. New York: John Wiley.

Lewinsohn, P.M. (1975) The behavioral study and treatment of depression. In: M. Hersen, R. Eisler & P. Miller (Eds), Progress in Behavior Modification (Vol 1). New York: Academic Press.

Li, A.K. (1981) Play and the mentally retarded child. Mental Retardation, 19, 3, 121-126.

Li, A.K. (1985) Toward more elaborate pretend play. Mental Retardation, 23, 3, 131-136.

Matson, J.L. (1982) The treatment of behavioral characteristics of depression in the mentally retarded. Behavior Therapy, 13, 209-218.

Matson, J.L. (1983) Depression in the mentally retarded: Toward a conceptual analysis of diagnosis. Progress in Behavior Modification, 15, 57-79.

Matson, J.L. (1984) Psychotherapy with persons who are mentally retarded. Mental Retardation, 22, 4, 170-175.

Matson, J.L. & Ollendick, T.H. (1988) Enhancing Children's Social Skills: Assessment and Training. New York: Pergamon Books.

Menolascino, F.J. (1965) Emotional disturbance and mental retardation. American Journal of Mental Deficiency, 70, 248-256.

Philips, I. (1967) Psychopathology and mental retardation. American Journal of Psychiatry, 124, 1, 29-35.

Piaget, J. (1951) Play, Dreams and Imitation in Childhood. (C. Gattegno & F.M. Hodgson, Trans.). New York: Norton.

Piaget, J. (1952) The Origins of Intelligence in Children. New York: W.W. Norton.

Piaget, J. & Inhelder, B. (1969) The Psychology of the Child. New York: Basic Books.

Prouty, G. (1976) Pre-therapy: A method of treating pre-expressive psychotic and retarded patients. Psychotherapy, theory, research, and practice, 13, 290-294.

Reiss, S. & Benson, B.A. (1984) Awareness of negative social conditions among mentally retarded emotionally disturbed outpatients. American Journal of Psychiatry, 141, 1, 88-90.

Reiss, S., Levitan, G.W. & McNally, R.J. (1982) Emotionally disturbed mentally retarded people: An underserved population. American Psychologist. April, 361-367.

Rogers, C.R. (1942) Counseling and Psychotherapy. Boston: Houghton-Mifflin.

Rogers, C.R. (1951) Client-centered therapy. Boston: Houghton-Mifflin.

Schaefer, C.E. & O'Connor, E.J. (1983) Handbook of Play Therapy. New York: John Wiley & Sons.

Schloss, P.J. (1982) Verbal interaction patterns of depressed and non-depressed institutionalized mentally retarded adults. Applied Research in Mental Retardation, 3, 1-12.

Seligman, M.E.P. (1975) Helplessness: On Depression, Development and Death. San Francisco: Freeman.

Selman, R. (1980) Interpersonal Understanding. New York: Academic Press.

Sternlicht, M. (1965) Psychotherapeutic techniques useful with the mentally retarded: A review and critique. Psychiatric Quarterly, 39, 1, 84-90.

Symington, N. (1981) The psychotherapy of a subnormal patient. British Journal of Medical Psychology, 54, 187-199.

Winnicott, D.W. (1971) Therapeutic Consultation in Child Psychiatry. New York: Basic Books.

Anton Dosen and Frank J. Menolascino (Eds.) (1990). Depression in mentally retarded children and adults. Leiden, the Netherlands: Logon Publications. ISBN 90-73197-01-5

Chapter 18

Behavioral treatment of depression

Betsey A. Benson, Ph.D.

Introduction

Behavioral theories and research have contributed much to the field of mental retardation. Psychological assessment, habilitation, and treatment of persons with mental retardation have all been significantly influenced by behavioral approaches. In the assessment arena, the behavioral approach mandates a focus on observable behaviors that are described in concrete terms. Habilitation plans for teaching self-care skills to persons with mental retardation reflect a behavioral goal and chaining simple behaviors together to form complex motor skills. When intervention is considered for a prolem behavior, a functional analysis is required which results in a description of the antecedents, behaviors, and consequences of behavior and directly links assessment to intervention.

Behavioral approaches to the treatment of depression in persons with mental retardation include the same characteristics. Defining behaviors in observable, concrete terms, linking assessment and intervention, and evaluating treatment results are hallmarks of behavioral treatments of depression. Before examining the treatment literature, first it is necessary to consinder behavioral theories of depression and research on behavioral characteristics of depression.

Behavioral and cognitive behavioral theories of depression

The three most influential behavioral theories of depression are Seligman's learned helplessness theory and its revision (Abramson, Seligman & Teasdale, 1978; Seligman, 1975), Beck's cognitive theory (1967), and Lewinsohn's reinforcement theory (Lewinsohn, Hoberman,

Teri, & Hautzinger, 1985). Each theory has made important contributions to research and treatment of depression (primarily unipolar) for nonretarded persons. The three theories have had varying degrees of impact on the study of depression in persons with mental retardation. According to learned helplessness theory, the perception of a lack of control over environmental outcomes can lead to feelings of helplessness. Learned helplessness was said to provide a model for reactive depression (Seligman, 1975). Cognitive attributions for failure experiences that are stable, internal, and global contribute to helplessness, according to the revised attribution theory (Abramson et al., 1978).

Certainly, a lack of control over events is familiar for many persons with mental retardation who find important life decisions made by others on their behalf. There has been some research to indicate that persons with mental retardation experience helplessness. In two studies, children and adults with mental retardation were more likely to be helpless on questionnaire and behavioral tests than chronological age-matched controls (Floor & Rosen, 1975; Weisz, 1979). In addition, when viewed developmentally, it appeared that children with mental retardation "learned" to be helpless during the early school years (Weisz, 1979). Children with mental retardation were **not** more helpless than age-matched controls at a young age (5 to 7 years), but older children (9 years) with mental retardation were more helpless.

In these studies, helplessness and depression were not linked. A link was established, however, by Reynolds and Miller (1985). They found that adolescents in classes for the educationally mentally handicapped were more depressed on the Reynolds Adolescent Depression Scale and more helpless on the Mastery Orientation Inventory (a questionnaire measure of acadamic helplessness) than age-matched control subjects.

According to Beck's cognitive theory of depression (Beck, 1967), depressed individuals develop a negative cognitive schema and hold negative cognitions about the self, the world, and the future. The cognitive processes of depressed individuals are said to be faulty and contain errors such as overgeneralization (a single event is overblown), arbitrary inferences (conclusions drawn without evidence), and selective abstractions (one element is given undue influence). Cognitive therapy for depression inclused cognitive retraining and graded task assigments (Beck, 1976). There has been little direct application of cognitive therapy with persons with mental retardation, although it has been suggested that the techniques would be beneficial (e.g., Mahoney & Mahoney, 1976).

310

Lewinsohn's reinforcement theory of depression states that the depressed individual has experienced a low level of reinforcement that may be exacerbated by social skill deficits (Lewinsohn et al., 1985). A lack of skill in obtaining reinforcement from others may be a causal or maintaining factor in depression, according to the theory. Research with nonretarded adults has confirmed social skill deficits of depressed individuals (e.g., Youngren & Lewinsohn, 1980). The treatment of depression based on the theory includes scheduling pleasant events (Lewinsohn, Munoz, Youngren, & Zeiss, 1986).

Depression and social skills in persons with mental retardation

Several studies have identified social skill deficits of depressed adults with mental retardation (But, see Matson, Senatore, Kazdin & Helsel, 1983, for failure to find deficits). In an observational study on an inpatient ward, Schloss (1982) indentified five significant differences in social interaction between depressed and nondepressed adults with mental retardation. They were:

1. Other individuals were more likely to make requests to depressed patients than to make declarative statements;
2. Depressed patients gained compliance by exhibiting negative affect;
3. Depressed patients resisted requests by exhibiting negative affect;
4. Other people were more likely to exhibit negative affect when interacting with the depressed patients than with the nondepressed patients; and
5. Staff were more likely than peers to interact with depressed patients.

The results suggest that displays of negative affect are reinforced by persons in the environment and may contribute to the depressed persons's behavior. Schloss also suggested that depressed patients may lack other social behaviors that could be successful in their interactions with others. The results were viewed as consistent with Libet and Lewinsohn's (1973) contention that deficit social skills are a major antecedent to depressive behavior.

Helsel and Matson (1988) found significant correlations between measures of depression and of social skills in adults with mental retardation. The subjects ranged in level of intellectual functioning from severe to mild. Several self-report and informant ratings were used in the correlational study, including the Beck Depression Inventory (Beck,

311

Ward, Mendelson, Mock, & Erbaugh, 1961), the Zung Self-Rating Depression Scale (Zung, 1965), the Psychopathology Instrument for Mentally Retarded Adults (Matson, 1988) and the Hamilton interview rating scale for depression (Hamilton, 1960). Social skills were assessed with self-report and informant versions of the Social Performance Survey Schedule (Matson, Helsel, Bellak, & Senatore, 1983). A measure of receptive vocabulary was also included. The results indicated that depression and poor social skills were significantly correlated. There were no significant associations between depression and age, sex, level of intellectual functioning, or vocabulary.

Social skill deficits could be associated with many types of psychopathology, rather than being characteristic of depression.
The previous studies did not rule out that possibility. A unique associaltion between social skills and depression specifically, rather than psychopathology in general was demonstrated in a study by Benson, Reiss, Smith, & Laman (1985). The subjects were adults with mild mental retardation who either had been referred to an outpatient mentatl health clinic for treatment of emotional problems or were recruited from local vocational training centers. Self-report and informant depression scores were used to divide the clinic subjects into a depressed group and a disturbed/nondepressed group. A third group was identified as nondisturbed/nondepressed. Informants provided ratings of social skills. The study found that depressed subjects were rated significantly lower in social skills that the other two groups, indicating that poor social skills are characteristic of depression and not simply of psychopathology.

Specific social skill deficits demonstrated by depressed adults with mental retardation were identified by Laman and Reiss (1987). Using self-report and informant measures of social skills, social support, and depression they studied forty-five adults with mild mental retardation. Depressed mood based on supervisor ratings of depression was significantly negatively correlated with self-report and informant-rated social support and social skills.

Depressed and nondepressed subjects in the study were found to differ significantly on three of the four factors of the Social Performance Survey Schedule (SPSS) (Matson et al., 1983), Appropriate Social Skills, Assertiveness, and Sociopathic Behavior. When the subjects were divided into High and Low Depressed Mood groups, significant differences between the groups were found for 30 of the 57 SPSS items. Table 18.1 lists the items. It includes behaviors that the depressed mood group performed excessively, as well as items for

312

which behavior deficits existed. The authors point out that several of the questions differentiating the two groups relate to anger and aggressive behavior which corresponds more closely to the depressive symptoms of children and adolescents than of adults. By identifying specific social skill deficits the study suggests target behaviors for social skills training of depressed persons.

Table 18.1
Social skill items differantiating high- and low-depressed mood groups.

Items	T value
Depressed group rated as more often:	
Reacts with more anger than a situations calls for	4.89***
Puts himself/herself down	3.10**
Take advantage of others	2.78**
Threatens others verbally or physically	3.76***
Talks repeatedly about his/her problems and worries	2.54*
Gets into arguments	3.47**
Stays with others too long	2.01 *
Takes or uses things that aren't his/hers without permission	2.14*
Blames others for his/her problems	4.48***
Tells people what (s)he thinks they want to hear	2.34*
Complains	4.60***
Easily becomes angry	5.75***
Tries to manipulate others to do what (s)he wants	2.58*
Allows others to do things for him/her without reciprocating in some way	3.50**
Deceives others for personal gain	3.00**
Depressed group rated as less often:	
Shows enthusiasm for other's good fortune	4.71***
Initiates contact and conversatrion with others	2.36*
Makes other people laugh (with jokes, funny stories etc.)	2.97**
Shows appreciation when someone does something for him/her	2.48*

Demonstrates concern for others' rights	4.29***
Is able to make other people who are anxious or upset feel better by talking to them	3.27**
Asks others how they've been, what they've been up to, etc.	4.81***
Keeps in touch with friends	4.56***
Compliments others on their clothes, hairstyles, etc.	2.52*
Shares responsibility equally with the members of groups (s)he belongs to	6.16***
Takes care of other's property as if it were his/her own	2.72*
Asks whether (s)he can be of help	4.01***
Gets to know people in depth	3.15**
Keeps commitments (s)he makes	2.41*
Tries to help others find solutions to problems they face	2.83**

* $p < .05$.　** $p < .01$.　*** $p < .001$.

From Laman & Reiss (1987), used with permission.

The significant influence of social skill deficits over time was demonstrated in a doctoral dissertation completed by Laman (1988). The investigation was a follow-up of Laman and Reiss (1987) in which the same subjects were studied approximately 20 months later and correlations between Time 1 and Time 2 depression, social skills, and social support were obtained. The study found significant positive correlations between repeated testings of the same measures for the two time periods, indicating some stability over time. In addition, it was found that social skills based on informant report at Time1 was a significant predictor of social support at Time2. Increases in social support frome Time1 to Time2 were greater for persons with better social skills initially. The reverse was not true, however. That is, persons high in social support dod not evidence significant improvement in social skills during the time period studied. It was suggested that individuals with good social skills may be better able to use social skills training for depressed adults with mental retardation.

Social skills training for persons with mental retardation

There has been a great deal of reseach on teaching social skills to persons with mental retardation. The details of this work have relevance for the treatment of depression in persons with mental retardation due to the demonstrated association between depression and poor social skills.

First, we must consider what are social skills and what are appropriate skills to train? A variety of definitions of social skills have been offered. Hersen and Bellack (1977) have suggested the social skills are a person's ability to express both positive and negative feelings in an interpersonal situation without loss of reinforcement. A broader definition is offered by Ladd and Mize (1983) as "an ability to organize cognitions and behaviors into an integrated course of action directed toward culturally acceptable social or interpersonal goals" (p.127). This definition incorporates both cognitions and behaviors and recognizes that cultural factors influence the acceptability of interpersonal goals, and therefore the potential for reinforcement.

When defining social skills for persons with mental retardation, one must keep in mind that **by definition** persons with mental retardation have deficits in adaptive behavior (Grossman, 1983). Adaptive behavior refers to "the individual's effectiveness in meeting the standards of maturation, learning, personal independence, and/or social responsibility that are expected for his/her age level and cultural group" (p.11). Rating scales to measure adaptive behavior assess a person's performance in several areas or domains such as communication, motor skills, daily living skills, and socialization. Social skills overlap with adaptive behavior as defined by these scales and form an integral part of what has been called "social competence" (Brooks-Gunn & Luciano, 1985; Gresham & Elliott, 1987).

Much of the research on social skills training for persons with mental retardation has focused on remediating specific skill deficits observed in everyday life situations, such as: conversation skills (Matson, 1979), loud talking (Matson & Earnheart, 1981), hand waving (Stokes, Baer, & Jackson, 1974), responding to others (Brodsky, 1967), and job interviewing (Kelly & Christoff, 1983). The studies have successfully trained a variety of simple and complex behaviors in individuals who were functioning in the severe to mild range of mental retardation.

The methods of training social skills range in complexity from shaping and simple reinforcement of the target behavior to more complex "packages" containing several behavioral techniques. There is no standard social skills training program, although most approaches include these techniques: instruction; modeling; role playing; feedback; social reinforcement; and homework (Kelly, 1982). **Instruction** is given to provide a rationale for the behaviors to be trained and to identify the focus of the training for that segment of the program. **Modeling** refers to demonstration by the trainer of the appropriate behavior. **Role playing** refers to the supervised practice of the target behavior in an analogue setting and **feedback** is constructive criticism given by the trainer on the verbal and nonverbal aspects of performance. **Social reinforcement** or praise is provided by the trainer for successive approximations to the target behavoir. **Homework** or behavioral assignments may be given to practice the behavior in another setting and to increase generalization of the newly acquired interpersonal skills to the natural environment.

Social skills training is evaluated by observing changes in the performance of the target behavior following training. In addition, follow-up assessment is typically made from several weeks to several months after the conclusion of training to demonstrate that behavior changes are maintained. Finally, information is gathered to indicate that the behavior changes obtained in the therapy setting are performed in the natural environment (generalization). This information may be obtained through direct observations of behavior or through ratings provided by others.

A relatively recent addition to the behavioral treatment literature is the attempt to provide "social validity" data (Kazdin & Matson, 1981). This refers to information that demonstrates the clinical importance of the target behavior and the significance of the behavior change obtained via training.

In the social skills training area, performance standards are developed by assessing individuals who are similar to the subject in many respects, but who are performing adequately. The subject's post-treatment behavior is compared to the criterion provided by the skillful comparison subject. Another method of social validation is provided by obtaining ratings by "expert" others, usually staff or community persons, of the social acceptability of the subject's post-treatment behavior. Social validation of treatment effects has added a new dimension to social skills training research and provides behavioral goals where norms for acceptable functioning are largely lacking.

Behavioral treatment of depression

Three studies have used behavioral interventions to change symptoms of depression in persons with mental retardation. The techniques of behavior change were the same are those used in the social skills training literature, but the target behaviors were those that have been associated with depression. The target behaviors were verbal statements and nonverbal aspects of social interactions.

In the first study, Matson, Dettling, and Senatore (1979) treated a 32-yr old man who was functioning in the borderline to mild range of mental retardation and lived in the community. He had a 10-year history of depression and received imipramine throughout the course of the study. At the start of treatment, the following behaviors were reported: social withdrawal, suicide threats, loss of sleep, flat affect, feelings of worthlessness, and anxiety.

The intervention was called "Independence Training" and included live modeling, praise, self-evaluation, and self-reinforcement. Three types of statements were targeted for change during the intervention (approximately 20 sessions), including negative self-statements, suicide statements, and statements about the past. The intervention goals were to increase positive self-statements, decrease negative statements, and develop a more "appropriate lifestile" (be more sociable.)

The therapist labeled the client's statements as either "positive" or "inappropriate." If the client made a positive statement, the therapist praised him. If an inappropriate statement was made, the client was asked to evaluate the statement. Appropriate responses were modeled by the therapist and the client rehearsed the modeled response. The client was asked to reinforce himself for appropriate statements during the session. Homework assignments were given in which the subject monitored positive statements and kept a weekly tally. He also reported how frequently he participated in enjoyable activities.

Independent observers rated the frequency of the target behaviors during the sessions. The number of inappropriate statements decreased in frequency during treatment and remained at low rates during the post-treatment and follow-up sessions. Staff that worked with the client reported that the frequency of positive statements increased. The client reported that he was participating in more social activities and had a girlfriend.

In the second study, several nonverbal characteristics of social interactions were the targeted behaviors in the behavioral treatment of depression with a 10-year old boy (Frame, Matson, Sonis, Fialkov, &

Kaxdin, 1982). The child was treated in an inpatient setting and was fuctioning in the borderline range of mental retardation. He was admitted to the hospital because of suicidal thoughts and gestures, temper outbursts, and poor school performance. A concerted effort was made to establish the diagnosis of "major depressive disorder" using a psychiatric interview, the mother's ratings of the child on a depression scale and behavior problem checklist, and ratings of a videotaped interview with the child. The child did not receive medication while participating in the study.

Four behaviors were the targets for intervention: inappropriate body posture (turning away, covering face); poor speech quality (few words, long latency to respond); lack of eye contact; and bland affect. Role play situations of typical interactions occurring in the hospital or at home were presented in each session and were videotaped.

Twenty-minute daily sessions were held in which instructions were given in appropriate responding, the therapist modeled appropriate behaviors, role playing was done, and feedback was given on performace. Praise was given for appropriate behavior and edibles were provided at the end of the session for participation. A multiple baseline design was used in which a baseline of the four target behaviors was obtained followed by intervention with body posture and eye contact first (six sessions), then speech quality (five sessions), and finally affect (nine sessions). Follow-up assessment was completed 12 weeks later. The results indicated improvement in each behavior only after the intevention was introduced and the improvements were maintained at follow-up testing. The generalization of the behavior changes to other settings was not evaluated.

In the third intervention study, Matson (1982) reported the treatment of depression with four adults with mental retardation. Two subjects were fuctioning in the mild range and two in the moderate range of mental retardation. None of the subjects was receiving medication during the course of the study. A multiple baseline design across behaviors was used to target both verbal and nonverbal symptoms of depression, including somatic complaints, irritability, number of words spoken, grooming negative self-statements, flat affect, eye contact, and speech latency. The subjects completed the Beck Depression Inventory and the Zung Self-Rating Depression Scale at pre-, post-, and follow-up sessions.

The individual treatment sessions focused on questions pertaining to somatic complaints and negative self-statements. The subject was asked a question, such as "How do you feel today?" Answers con-

318

sidered "appropriate" were neutral or positive in content, whereas "inappropriate" answers were either no response, a negative response, or a somtic complaint. An appropriate response ("I feel OK") earned a token and therapist feedback about the behavior that earned the reward. If an inappropriate response was given (e.g., "Terrible, I shouldn't have to go to work") the Therapist provided feedback and then modeled an appropriate response that the client was asked to repeat. For grooming, feedback was given at the start of the session on several dimensions such as, shoes tied, socks match, hair combed, etc.

Social validation was provided by assessing eight persons with mental retardation who were not depressed on the same target behaviors during individual interviews. The results indicated that all four subjects improved quickly on the target behaviors and at the end of treatment, the four subjects were performing as well or better than the nondepressed subjects. In addition, the treatment gains were maintained at the follow-up assessment period (four to six months later). The subjects also scored in the "nondepressed" range on the self-report depression scales at posttest and follow-up.

The three treatment studies demonstrate the effectiveness of behavioral interventions in changing specific behaviors associated with the syndrome of depression. Both children and adults with mental retardation who were functioning in the moderate to borderline range were successfully treated. The obtained behavior changes were maintained for three to six months. Improvements were noted in the target behaviors as well as in self-reported depression, staff behavior ratings, and, in one instance, participation in social activities.

Some advantages to the use of behavioral interventions are exemplified by these studies. In each case, the intervention was relatively brief and little therapist time was required to achieve significant changes. In addition, the interventions appear to be relatively simple ones that staff could be trained to perform.

The three studies may be viewed as preliminary investigations of the utility if behavioral interventions to improve social skills of depressed persons with mental retardation. The research to date has several limitations. First, attempts to determine the generalization of treatment effects outside of the therapy setting were limited. Unless the behavior changes transfer to real-life settings the improvements in behavior obtained in treatment have limited significance. However, direct observations of the individuals in other environments can be very difficult, costly, and time consuming to obtain as well as being intrusive. reports by familiar observers in their accustomed roles in relation to the client can be useful in tracking progress and generalization of therapeutic gains.

The subjects treated in the three studies were individuals whose intellectual functioning was in the moderate to borderline range. Although this range of intellectual functioning encompasses the majority of persons with mental retardation, the applicabilty of the interventions nonverbal or less capable, depressed individuals has not been demonstrated.

The target behaviors chosen in the studies have face validity as important components of social interaction skills, but no rationale was provided for their selection over other face valid behaviors. Future studies may provide more extensive assessments of the skill deficits (and behavior excesses) of depressed persons with mental retardation. It would be helpful to know if a characteristic social skills profile of depressed persons with mental retardation exists or if particular subgroups of depressed individuals could be indentified who share deficits in certain skill areas.

Other behaviors that could be included in behavioral interventions in the treatment of depression may be identified by comparing the list of target behaviors in the three treatment studies to the Social Performance Survey Schedule (SPSS) items found by Laman and Reiss (1988) to differentiate depressed and nondepressed adults. In doing so, one finds both areas of overlap and of discontinuity. The SPSS items "Complains," "Puts self down," and "Talks about problems and worries" are similar to the target behaviors of negative self-statements and somatic complaints in the studies. However, the list of items from Laman and Reiss (1988) does not contain the nonverbal behaviors included in the intervention studies, such as eye contact, speech latency, body posture, and flat affect (the SPSS contains items on eye contact, but no significant group differences were found). On the other hand, the Laman and Reiss (1988) list does contain several behaviors not targeted in the three studies, such as "Gives compliments," "Ask questions," "Asks is he/she can help," "Tells jokes." These behaviors may be considered more advanced than the target behaviors in the treatment studies or less immediately relevant to depression than those chosen for the interventions.

The treatment studies described above noted the subject's medication status, but no systemmatic study of the efficacy of behavioral interventions and medication has been reported in the mental retardation literature as has been done in research with nonretarded adults (Hersen & Bellack, 1984). Finally, behavioral interventions often receive criticism for focusing on specific behaviors of depressed persons, but not treating the syndrome of depression. Studies have not evaluated the effect of behavioral treatment on other nontarget behaviors, such as vegtative signs of depression.

Table 18.2
Cognitive behavioral schema for research and treatment of depression for persons with mental retardation.

Emotion	Cognition	Behavior	Others
Emotional support	Self-evaluation	Skill performance	Social expression
	Perceptions of control	Communication skills	Rein- forcement
Emotional arousal	Attributions of S,F		Cultural norms

E		
M	Role taking	
P		
A	Discrimination	
T	of situations	
H		
Y	Social problem solving	

Other factors

Premorbid functioning
Developmental level
Severity of depression.

Cognitive behavioral model for research and treatment

The three intervention studies targeted concrete, observable behaviors and changed them through modeling and reinforcement. Improving social skill performance was a productive initial step in research and treatment. However, a broader approach may be warranted for the psychosocial treatment of depression that takes into account theories and research on depression and social skills. Table 2 persents a cognitive-behavioral schema for research and treatment of depression in persons with mental retardation that attempts to incorporate these factors.

The various components of the schema are assumed to be inter-related. Portions of the schema have been researched with persons with mental retardation, whereas other areas have not. The first step is for research to further identify characteristics of depressed persons with mental retardation that differentiate them from nondepressed persons of similar level of fuctioning. The proposed schema suggests some targets for this research.

The learned helplessness and revised attribution theories of depression (Abramson et al., 1978; Seligman, 1975) state that perceptions of control and attributions pertaining to success and failure occupy a central role in the development of depression. In additon, Beck's cognitive theory (1967) suggests that self-evaluation, knowledge of self and/or self-reinforcement play important roles in the etiology and maintenance of depression. These cognitive characteristics have not been examined in the research or treatment of depression for persons with mental retardation, although there has been research on the attribution of succes and failure in persons with mental retardation (e.g., Hoffman & Weiner, 1978; Horai & Guarnaccia, 1975). Future research may examine whether depressed persons with mental retardation exhibit a cognitive style that differs from that of nondepressed persons. Cognitive therapies for depression with mentally retarded persons may be developed that focus on changing attributions and perceptions of control.

Additional cognitive characteristics that may be relevant in the treatment of depression can be identified in the social skills training literature. Role taking ablity, empathy, and knowledge of others are thought to be important skills in social interactions (Van Hasselt, Hersen, Whitehill, & Bellack, 1979). Previous research has reported that persons with mental retardation are deficient in role taking ability (e.g., Leahy, Balla, & Zigler, 1982). Research on depressed persons with mental retardation has not demonstrated significant differences in these cognitive areas in comparison to nondepressed mentally retarded persons. However, a few of the SPSS items that Laman and Reiss (1988) found to discriminate between depressed and nondepressed persons with mental retardation are suggestive of empathy skills, such as, "Shows enthusiams for other's good fortune," and "Demonstrates concern for others rights." Further research is required to determine if these cognitive characteristics are productive areas to pursue in depression research.

Training in social problem solving skills may also be appropriate for depressed persons with mental retardation.

Research has demonstrated that mentally retarded children tend to use fewer stragegies to solve interpersonal problems than nonretarded children matched on chronological age (Smith, 1986). It is possible that depressed persons overuse certain problem solving strategies. Research could evaluate this topic further.

The social skills training literature recognizes that there is no standard and correct behavior that is acceptable in all situations and cultures, but that varying standards of acceptable behavior exist, presumably reinforced by individuals in those situations (Van Hasselt et al., 1979). Socially skillful persons are able to discriminate one situation from another and vary their behavior accordingly. Persons with poor social skills may have difficulty discriminating situational demands and in altering their behavior in response (Ladd & Mize, 1983). Depressed persons with mental retardation may benefit from social skills training to teach alternative behaviors for social interactions as well as specific training in assessing situations.

Standards of acceptable behavior vary from situation to situation and with the individual's developmental level, further complicating the process of identifying norms of acceptable behavior. Howover, developing norms of appropriate social behavior for persons with mental retardation would be helpful in defining the goals of treatment for depression. One approach to this problem is to determine what the socially skillful person does that the nonskilled persons does not do (and vice versa) in interpersonal situations.

Another area for exploration is that of emotions and emotional expression. Depression is considered a mood or affective disorder. As such, emotional expression and, in particular, the expression of negative affect is considered a defining characteristic of the disorder. The expression of negative affect was found to differentiate depressed from nondepressed persons with mental retardation (Schloss, 1982). Research has also found that persons with mental retardation, in general, evidence deficits in emotional awareness and in the recognition of emotions (e.g., Hobson, Ouston, & Lee, 1989; Reed & Clements, 1989). Emotional arousal may indirectly affect interpersonal interactions by interfering with skill performance (e.g., effects of anxiety on preformance). In this way, the emotional arousal of depressed persons may interfere with the performance of interpersonal skills.

A third general area for study is the behavior or skill level of depressed persons. Some of the research on the social skills of depressed persons with mental retardation has been included in previous sections. Much more work is needed in this area. The literature on communication skills also suggests possible topics for future research. Communications skills research has examined the use of gestures, vocalizations, and contact in social interactions of persons with mental retardation and has identified delays and disturbances in their development (Mundy, Seibert, & Hogan, 1985). This work may be extended to depressed persons with mental retardation.

The role of other individuals in the depressed person's environment also requires further study. Schloss' research (1982) and Lewinsohn's work (Lewinsohn et al., 1985) indicate that reinforcement by others is important and may maintain negative affect expression by depressed persons. The treatment studies presented above systemmatically altered negative afffect expression by reinforcing of verbal behaviors by others, social support, in general, has been found to be an important variable in the study depression of nonretarded persons (Billings & Moos, 1985). For persons with mental retardation, depression was found to be associated with low levels of social support (Reiss & Benson, 1985). This factor has definite implications for treatment and prevention of relapse. How may individuals in the depressed person's environment effectively provide social support, without reinforcing negative affect expression?

A treatment model that included these cognitive, behavioral, and emotional factors would also need to incorporate a developmental framework for treatment such that the goals methods of training, and sequencing of training would match the individual's developmental level. The degree of emphasis given to a particular treatment factor and the order in which various elements would be addressed would also require study. Different emphases would be appropriate for individuals of different levels of intellectual funtioning and for persons of varying degrees of severity of depression.

Assessment of premorbid social skill levels would also be important in the development of a treatment plan. One would want to determine if skill deficits and/or performance deficits existed. Increasing the performance of previously acquired skills through pleasant evants scheduling (Lewinsohn et al., 1986), for example, would be appropriate for someone whose skills were currently not being used. Specific skills training, such as leisure skills training (Matson & Matchetti, 1980), could be provided for the individual who had nog acquired the skills.

Conclusion

The cognitive behavioral schema for research and treatment of depression for persons with mental retardation suggests several areas for further investigation as well as areas to direct prevention efforts. A greater understanding of the etiology of depressive disorders may also result from research finding in the areas described above. An immediate need in the research on depression in mental retardation is the development of methods of measuring many of the cognitive, affective, and behavioral components of the schema. The behavioral approach to assessment, along with the more recent cognitive behavioral developments in theory and research, may provide a useful framework for accomplishing these goals.

References

Abramson, L.Y., Seligman, M.E.P., & Teasdale, J.D. (1978). Learned helplessness in humans. Critique and reformulation. Journal of Abnormal Psychology, 87, 49-74.

Beck, A.T. (1967). Depression: Causes and treatment. Philadelphia, PA: University of Pennsylvania Press.

Beck, A.T. (1976). Cognitive therapy and the emotional disorderd. New York, NY: International Universities Press.

Beck, A.T., Ward, C.H., Mendelson, M., Mock J., & Erbaugh, J. (1961). An inventory for measuring depression. Archives of General Psychiatry, 4, 561 - 571.

Benson, B.A., Reiss, S., Smith, D.C., & Laman, D.S. (1985). Psychosocial correlates of depression in mentally retarded adults: II. Poor social skills. American Journal of Mental Deficiency, 89, 657-659.

Billings, A.G., & Moos, R.H. (1985). Life stressors and social resources affect posttreatment outcomes among depressed patients. Journal of Abnormal Psychology, 94, 140 - 153.

Brodsky, G. (1967). The relationship between verbal and nonverbal behaviour change. Behaviour Research and Therapy, 5, 183 -191.

Brooks-Gunn, J., & Luciano, L. (1985). Social competence in young handicapped children: A developmental perspective. In M. Sigman (Ed.,), Children with emotional disorders and developmental disabilities (pp. 45-70). Orlando, FL: Grune & Stratton.

Floor, L., & Rosen, M. (1975). Investigating the phenomenon of helplessness among mentally retarded children. American Journal of Mental Deficiency, 79, 565-572.

Frame, C., Matson, J.L. Sonis, W.A., Fialkov, M.J. & Kazdin, A.E. (1982). Behavioral treatment of depression in a pre-pubertal child. Journal of Behavior Therapy and Experimental Psychiatry, 13, 239-243.

Gresham, F.M., & Elliott, S.N. (1987). The relationship between adaptive behavior and social skills: Issues in definition and assessment. Journal of Special Education, 21, 167-181.

Grossman, H.J. (Ed.) (1983). Classification in mental retardation. Washington, D.C.: American Association on Mental Deficiency.

Hamilton, M. (1960). A rating scale for depression. Journal of Neurology, Neurosurgery and Psychiatry, 23, 56-62.

Helsel, W.J., & Matson, J.L. (1988). The relationship of depression to social skills and intellectual functioning in mentally retarded adults. Journal of Mental Deficiency Research, 32, 411-418.

Hersen, M., & Bellack, A.S. (1977). Assessment of social skills. In A.R. Ciminero, S. Calhoun, & H.E. Adams (Eds.), Handbook for behavioral assessment (pp. 509-554). New York: Wiley.

Hersen, M., & Bellack, A.S. (1984). Effects of social skill training, amitryptylene, and psychotherapy in unipolar depressed women. Behavior Therapy, 15, 21-40.

Hobson, R.P., Ouston, J., & Lee, A. (1989). Recognition of emotion by mentally retarded adolescents and young adults. American Journal on Mental Retardation, 93, 434-443.

Hoffman, J., & Weiner, B. (1978). Effects of attributions for success and failure on the performance of retarded adults. Americal Journal of Mental Deficiency, 82, 449-452.

Horai, J., & Guarnaccia, V.J. (1975). Performance and attributions to ability effort, task, and luck of retarded adults after success or failure feedback. American Journal of Mental Deficiency, 79, 690-694.

Kazdin, A.E., & Matson, J.L. (1981). Social validation in mental retardation. Applied Research in Mental Retardation, 2, 39 - 54.

Kelly, J.A. (1982). Social skills training: A practical guide for interventions. New York: Springer.

Kelly, J.A., & Christoff, K.A. (1983). Job interview training for the mentally retarded. Applied Research in Mental Retardation, 4, 355-368.

Ladd, G.W., & Mize, J. (1983). A cognitive-social learning model of social skills training. Psychological Review, 90, 127-157.

Laman, D.S. (1988). A longitudinal investigation of the relationship among depressed mood, social support, and social skills in mentally retarded adults. Unpublished doctoral dissertation, University of Illinois at Chicago, Chicago, IL.

Laman, D.S., & Reiss, S. (1987). Socail skill deficiencies associated with depressed mood of mentally retarded adults. American Journal of Mental Deficiency, 92, 224-229.

Leahy, R.L., Balla, D., & Zigler, E. (1982). Role taking, self-image, and imitativeness of mentally retarded and nonretarded individuals. American Journal of Mental Deficiency, 86, 372-379.

Lewinsohn, P.M., Hoberman, H., Teri, L., & Hautzinger, M. (1985). An integrative theory of depression. In S. Reiss & R. Bootzin (Eds.), Theoretical issues in behavior therapy (pp. 331-359). Orlando, FL: Academic Press.

Lewinsohn, P.M., Munoz, R.F., Youngren, M.A., & Zeiss, A.M. (1986). Control your depression. New York: Prentice Hall.

Libet, J.M., & Lewinsohn, P.M. (1983). Concept of social skill with specific reference to the behavior of depressed persons. Journal of Consulting and Clinical Psychology, 40, 304-312.

Mahoney, M.J., & Mahoney, K. (1976). Self control techniques with the mentally retarded. Exceptional Children, 42, 338-339.

Matson, J.L. (1979). Decreasing inappropriate verbalizations of a moderately retarded adult by a staff assisted self-control program. Australia Journal of Mental Retardation, 5, 242-245.

Matson, J.L. (1982). The treatment of behavioral charecteristics of depression in the mentally retarded. Behavior therapy, 13, 209-218.

Matson, J.L. (1988). Psychopathology Instrument for Mentally Retarded Adults (PIMRA). Orland Park, IL: International Diagnostics Systems, Inc.

Matson, J.L., Dettling, J., & Senatore, V. (1979). Treating depression of a mentally retarded adult. British Journal of Mental subnormality, 16, 86-88.

Matson, J.L. & Earnheart, T. (1981). Programming treatment effects to the natural environment: A procedure for training institutionalized retarded adults. Behavior Modification, 5, 27 - 37.

Matson, J.L., Helsel, W.J., Bellack, A.S., & Senatore, V. (1983). Development of a rating scale to assess social skill deficits in mentally retarded adults. Applied Research in Mental Retardation, 4, 399-407.

Matson, J.L., Kazdin, A.E., & Senatore, V. (1984). Psychometric properties of the Psychopathology Instrument for Mentally Retarded Adults. Applied Research in Mental Retardation, 5, 81-87.

Matson, J.L. & Marchetti, A. (1980). A comparison of leisure skills training procedures for the mentally retarded. Applied Research in Mental Retardation, 1, 113-122.

Matson, J.L. Senatore, V., Kazdin, A.E., & Helsel, W.T. (1983). Verbal behaviors in depressed and nondepressed mentally retarded persons. Applied Research in Mental Retardation, 4, 79-83.

Mundy, P.C., Seibert, J.M., & Hogan, A.E. (1985). Communication skills in mentally retarded children. In M. Sigman (ed.), Children with emotional disorders and developmental disabilities (pp.45-70). Orlando, FL: Grune & Stratton.

Reed, J., & Clements, J. (1989). Assessing the understanding of emotional states in a population of adolescents and young adults with mental handicaps. Journal of Mental Deficiency Research, 33, 229-233.

Reiss, S., & Benson, B.A. (1985). Psychosocial correlates of depression in mentally retarded adults: I. Minimal social support and stigmatization. American Journal of Mental Deficiency, 89, 331-337.

Reynolds, W.M., & Miller, K.L. (1985). Depression and learned helplessness in mentally retarded and nonmentally retarded adolescents: An initial investigation. Applied Research in Mental Retardation, 6, 295-306.

Seligman, M.E.P. (1975). Helplessness: On depression, development, and death. San Francisco, CA: Freeman.

Schloss, P.J. (1982). Verbal interaction patterns of depressed and nondepressed institutionalized mentally retarded adults. Applied Research in Mental Retardation, 7, 431-442.

Smith, D. (1986). Interpersonal problem-solving skills of retarded and nonretarded children. Applied Research in Mental Retardation, 7, 431-442.

Stokes, T.F., Baer, D.M., & Jackson, R.L. (1974). Programming the generalization of a greeting response in four retarded children. Journal of Applied Behavior Analysis, 7, 599-610.

Van Hasselt, V.A., Hersen, M., Whitehill, M.B., & Bellack, A.S. (1979). Social skill assessment and training for children. An evaluative review. Behavior Research and Therapy, 17, 413-437.

Weisz, J.R. (1979). Preceived control and learned helplessness among mentally retarded and nonretarded children: A developmental analysis. Developmental Psychology, 15, 311-319.

Youngren, M.A., & Lewinsohn, P.M. (1980). The functional reationship between deprssion and problematic interpersonal behavior. Journal of Abnormal Psychology, 89, 333-341.

Zung, W.W.K. (1965). A self-rating depression scale. Archives of General Psychiatry, 22, 63-70.

Anton Dosen and Frank J. Menolascino (Eds.) (1990). Depression in mentally retarded children and adults. Leiden, the Netherlands: Logon Publications. ISBN 90-73197-01-5

Chapter 19

Psychopharmacological approaches to the treatment of depression in the mentally retarded

Jens Lund, M.D.

Introduction

It must be emphasized at the outset that the major problem one faces in treating depression, particularly in the mentally retarded, is the establishment of a reliable diagnosis as a basis for treatment choice (Lund, 1985; Reid, 1972, 1980, 1982; Sovner and Hurley, 1983). For most clinical purposes, the best way of obtaining a useful diagnosis is to describe the disorder systematically. Gelder, Gath & Mayou (1983) have prepared a systematic scheme, outlined below, which is pertinent to this type of description for affective disorders in the mentally retarded.

The severity of the episode is described as mild, moderate, or severe. The type of episode is determined to be depressive, manic, or mixed. Any special features, such as neurotic symptoms, psychotic symptoms, agitation, retardation, or stupor are noted, and the course of the disorder is characterized as either unipolar or bipolar. If the term bipolar is used descriptively, it is logical to restrict it to cases that have had both manic and depressive episodes. However, it has become conventional to record all cases with a manic episode as bipolar, even those with no depressive manifestations. This convention is based on the fact that most manic patients will develop a depressive disorder eventually and, in several important ways, resemble individuals who have had both types of episodes. The predominant etiology is finally noted and encompasses both endogenous and reactive courses.

During the last decade, a number of biological markers have also been presented as indicative of the presence of depression requiring treatment. These include the Dexamethasone Suppression Test (Ruedrich et al., 1985; Sireling, 1986), Reduced REM-Latency Test, and the Thyreotropine Releasing Hormone Test. However, the diagnostic sensitivity and specificity of these tests are very low and cannot, therefore, be recommended as the sole basis for determining whether or not to begin treatment. The diagnostic process must also, aside from a description of psychiatric symptoms, encompass:

1. Social environment - daytime occupation, residence, leisure time activities, family relations, etc.
2. Somatic conditions - additional handicaps, dementia, organic brain disorder, corticosteroid treatment, hypothyroidism, etc.
3. Life events - forced training or education, family contacts, ward shift, departure of staff members, etc.

Table 19.1
Systematic scheme for the description of
affective disorders in the mentally retarded

The episode:

Severity	Mild, Moderate, Severe
Type	Depressive, Manic, Mixed
Special Features	Neurotic Symptoms, Psychotic Symptoms, Agitation, Retardation or Stupor
The course	Unipolar or Bipolar
Etiology	Predominantly Reactive Predominantly Endogenous

When the diagnostic detective work is complete, treatment and management can be planned. The severity of depression, determined according to the symptomatology, should constitute the initial point of reference. Considerable severity is indicated by hallucinations, delusions, biological symptoms, and suicidal behavior. Severe depression is obvi-

332

ously present if the DSM-III-R criteria for major depression are fulfilled. A numerical measure is often more useful, however, and a cutoff point of 4 on the Newcastle Scale can be used as rough guide for separating out the less from the more severe cases. It should also be remembered that an increased prevalence for depressive symptoms is found in epileptic patients with left hemisphere pathology (Perini and Mendius, 1984; Snaith, James and Winokur, 1979).

The treatment of depression

Antidepressants

With the exception of patients for whom electroconvulsive therapy is indicated, tricyclic antidepressants constitute the treatment of choice. The therapeutic effect of tricyclic antidepressants is, in simplified form, thought to depend upon their common property of increasing the availability of catecholamine at central receptor sites by blocking the re-uptake of these transmitters into the presynaptic nerve terminals (Paykel and Coppen, 1979; Rivinus, 1980). The tetracyclic or other, newer antidepressants cannot be recommended in treating the mentally retarded patient mainly because of their inferior effectiveness relative to the tricyclics (Schmidt et al., 1986).

Although a great number of different commercial drugs have been produced, there is no evidence that any drug acts more quickly or more effectively than the rest. The only pharmacological difference in the compounds available is sedative effect. Those with sedative effects (e.g., amitriptyline) are appropriate for the treatment of depressive illness accompanied by anxiety and agitation, and those with effects which are less sedating (e.g., imipramine or nortriptyline) are recommended for retarded depression. The therapeutic efficacy of lithium as an antidepressant is unclarified but certainly no greater than that of tricyclic drugs. However, in obvious cases where tricyclic antidepressants alone fail, lithium as a supplement is certainly worth trying. When persecutory delusions are prominent, a neuroleptic drug (e.g. clopenthixol or fluphenazine) should be added. The use of monoamine oxidase inhibitors is troublesome when treating the mentally retarded, mainly because of its wide range of dangerous interactions with certain drugs and foodstuffs. However, I have seen a few rather successful cases where prolonged milder depressions accompanied by anxiety were cured.

Due to genetic differences, patients will differ widely in the extent to which they absorb and metabolize antidepressants. Ten-fold differences in blood concentrations have been reported after administering identical

333

doses to different people (Pollach and Rosenbaum, 1987). A major improvement in antidepressant drug treatment, and one which should be used as standard procedure is, therefore, the monitoring of plasma concentrations. In addition, tricyclic drugs can, with careful plasma monitoring, be used to treat most patients with mild heart problems.

Table 19.2
Therapeutic indices for standard tricyclic antidepressant drugs

Amitriptylin (Saroten, Tryptizol)	NMOL/L
Nortriptylin	NMOL/L
Total	NMOL/L (430-900 NMOL/L)

Nortriptyline (Noritren, Sensival)	NMOL/L (230-579 NMOL/L)
Clomipramin (Anafranil)	NMOL/L
Desclomipramin	NMOL/L
Total	NMOL/L (250-1000 NMOL/L)

Imipramin (Tofranil, Imiprex)	NMOL/L
Desipramin	NMOL/L
Total	NMOL/L (750-1250 NMOL/L)

Desipramin (Pertofram)	NMOL/L (879- ??? NMOL/L)
Doxepin (Quitaxon,Sinquan)	NMOL/L
Desdoxepin	NMOL/L
Total	NMOL/L (220-900 NMOL/L)

Dosage

The initial dose of an antidepressant should be moderate (Gelder, Gath and Mayou, 1983). For amitriptyline and nortriptyline, for example, 25-50 mg. initially, increased by 25 mg. every second day, is recommended. The effective dose is usually from 75 mg. for individuals advanced in age, to 200 mg. for younger patients. The entire dose can usually be administered at night, so that the side effects of sedation can be used to help the patient sleep, and the impact of any additional side effects are less likely to be noticed. Without plasma monitoring, dosage should not exceed 150-200 mg/day.

If no response is noted after four to five weeks, the physician should examine whether or not the patient has been taking the drugs at the appropriate dose, whether the diagnosis is indeed correct, and to what extent social factors are involved in maintaining depression. A new tricyclic, MAO inhibitor, or ECT can then be considered.

When therapeutic effect has been achieved, medication should be continued at full dosage for at least an additional six weeks. Following this, a reduced dosage should usually be continued for yet another six months. If a relapse occurs when the dosage is reduced, the former amount should be reinstated for another three months before lowering it cautiously for a second time.

Side effects

No systematic research has been carried out in the field of mental retardation concerning the toxic effects of antidepressant drugs (Sprague and Werry, 1971). The troublesome and unwanted autonomic, cardiovascular, neurological, and allergic types of side effects to antidepressants seem to occur with the same frequency and distribution in the mentally retarded as in the nonretarded population.

It is necessary to emphasize to both the patient and non-medical staff that, although side effects will appear quickly, therapeutic effects are likely to be delayed for up to three weeks. Reassurance should be given that most of these side effects are likely to diminish as the drug is continued over time.

Electroconvulsive therapy

It is still a fact that the antidepressive effect of electroconvulsive therapy (ECT) is more effective and acts more quickly than other forms of treatment, particularly in severe cases involving marked weight loss, diurnal variation, and delusions. The use of ECT as a first measure is indicated whenever there is a need to bring about improvement as rapidly

335

as possible due to life threatening dehydration, a high risk of suicide, or depressive stupor. It is important to find out the relevant legal requirements for ECT treatment, however, particularly in cases where treatment without the patient's expressed consent may occur.

If right-handedness can be established with certainty, unilateral electrode placement over the non-dominant right hemisphere should be chosen because of reduced memory loss. In other cases, bilateral electrode placement is preferred for the mentally retarded patient.

There is no need to discontinue tricyclic antidepressants when ECT is given. On the contrary, pharmacological treatment should be maintained, or initiated when ECT is completed. Research has proven that treatment with tricyclic antidepressants or lithium for 6 to 12 months after successful electroconvulsive therapy will prevent the relapses which frequently occur during the first months following ECT.

In view of the high prevalence rate of structural brain abnormality in mentally handicapped persons, many physicians are cautious about using ECT in this population unless indications for doing so are imperative. However, continued damaging effects due to ECT have never been demonstrated.

The treatment of mania

The immediate treatment for mania in the mentally retarded is usually an antipsychotic drug (e.g., haloperidol or clopenthixol), the initial dose of which should be high enough to bring abnormal behavior under rapid control. However, neurological and other side effects set a limit, and dosages of haloperidol which exceed 20 mg/day should not be used. Instead, the combined use of an antipsychotic and an antiepileptic compound (e.g., clobazam, up to 6 mg/day) can be recommended as highly effective.

Practices vary with the therapeutic antimanic use of lithium. It is recommended to begin the use of lithium as soon as acute symptoms are under control, taking care not to use it when the dosage of haloperidol is high. The administration of lithium at an early stage, after tests of renal and thyroid functions have been carried out, has the advantage of shortening the episode, leaving the patient more alert, and diminishing the possibility that a depressive disorder will follow. In cases of moderate mania, lithium can be used alone.

A careful watch should be maintained for symptoms of depressive disorders, particularly when antipsychotic drugs are being administered. A sustained change is likely to require treatment with tricyclic antidepressants.

Preventing relapse with lithium

The unique ability of lithium to prevent recurrence of mania and depression was established by Schou (1983) in Denmark. Although lithium affects a number of cerebral transmitters and enzymes, it is not clear which of the many pharmacological actions explains its therapeutic effects.

The indication to begin prophylactic lithium therapy is usually evident during the second or third episode of either mania or depression, depending upon the length between episodes and the severity of each. Two severe episodes within five years can be used as a guideline for positive indication. A careful routine of management is essential in these cases because of the effects of lithium therapy on the thyroid and kidneys, as well as the toxic effects of excessive dosage. Before administering lithium, a careful physical examination to measure kidney and thyroid functioning should be carried out, including blood pressure, body weight, urine and blood tests.

Treatment should begin and continue with two doses, taken 12 hours apart. For prophylaxis, a lithium level of 0.5 - 0.8 mmol/l in a sample taken 12 hours after a previous dose seems to be adequate for the majority of patients. However, a few may require a level of 0.9 - 1.0 mmol/l and, as treatment continues, such levels should be determined at regular intervals. Blood samples should be taken for electrolytes, urea, creatinine, full blood count, and thyroid functioning every six months. Tricyclic antidepressants can be used as an alternative to lithium in patients with unipolar depressive episodes. Antiepileptic drugs, such as carbamazepine, should be tried in bipolar cases where lithium cannot be tolerated.

The need for the drug should be reviewed once a year. No simple guidelines can be given for the right time to stop lithium, but there should always be compelling reasons for continuing treatment for more than five years without relapse.

Conclusion

The major problem in treating affective disorders in the mentally handicapped is establishing a diagnosis. When a reliable diagnosis is established, psychopharmacological treatment follows standard recommendations. Drug monitoring of tricyclic antidepressants should be routinely used.

References

Adams, G.L., Kivowitz, J. & Ziskind, E. (1970). Manic depressive psychosis, mental retardation, and chromosomal rearrangement. Archives of General Psychiatry, 23, 305-309.

Angst, J. (1983). Patient selection for a long-term lithium treatment in clinical practice. In: H. Dufour, et al. (Eds.) La prediction de la response au lithium. Paris: Masson.

Campbell, M., Fish, B., Korein, J., et al. (1972). Lithium and chlorpromazine: A controlled cross-over study of hyperactive severely disturbed young children. Journal of Autism and Childhood Schizophrenia, 2, 234-263.

Gelder, M., Gath, D. & Mayou, R. Treatment. (1983). Oxford Textbook of Psychiatry. New York: Oxford University Press.

Kirman, B.H. (1975). Drug therapy in mental handicap. British Journal of Psychiatry, 127, 545-549.

Lund, J. (1985). The prevalence of psychiatric morbidity in mentally retarded adults. Acta Psychiatrica Scandinavica, 72, 563-570.

Naylor, G.J., Donald, J.M., Le Poidevin, D. & Reid, A.H. (1974). A double-blind trial of long-term lithium therapy in mental defectives. British Journal of Psychiatry, 124, 52-57.

Paulson, G.W., Rizvi, C.A. & Crane, G.E. (1975). Tardive dyskinesia as a possible sequel of long-term therapy with phenothiazine. Clinical Pediatrics, 10, 953-955.

Paykel, E.S. & Coppen, A. (1979). Psychopharmacology of affective disorders. Oxford: Oxford University Press.

Perini, G. & Mendius, R. (1984). Depression and anxiety in complex partial seizures. Journal of Nervous and Mental Disease, 172, 287-290.

Pollach, M.H. & Rosenbaum, J.F. (1987). Management of antidepressant induced side effects: A practical guide for the clinician. Journal of Clinical Psychiatry, 48, 3-8.

Reid, A.H. (1972). Psychosis in adult mental defectives: Manic depressive psychosis. British Journal of Psychiatry, 120, 205-212.

Reid, A.H. (1980). Diagnosis of psychiatric disorder in the severely and profoundly retarded patient. Journal of the Royal Society of Medicine, 73, 607-609.

Reid, A.H. (1982). The psychiatry of mental handicap. Oxford: Blackwell.

Reid, A.H. & Naylor, G.J. (1976). Short-cycle manic depressive psychosis in mental defectives: A clinical and physiological study. Journal of Mental Deficiency Research, 20, 67-76.

Reid, A.H., Naylor, G.J. & Kay, D.S.G. (1981). A double blind placebo controlled cross-over trial of carbamazepine in overactive severely mentally handicapped patients. Psychological Medicine, 11, 109-113.

Rivinus, T.M. & Hartmatz, J.S. (1979). Diagnosis and lithium treatment of affective disorder in the retarded: Five cases studies. American Journal of Psychiatry, 136, 551-554.

Rivinus, T.M. (1980). Psychopharmacology and the mentally retarded patient. In: L. Szymanski & P. Tanguay (Eds.), Emotional disorders of mentally retarded persons. Baltimore: University Park Press.

Ruederich, S.L., Wadle, C.V., Hahn, R. & Chung-Chou, C. (1985). Neuroendocrine investigation of depression in mentally retarded patients. Journal of Nervous and Mental Disease, 173, 85-89.

Schmidt, L.G., Grohmann, R., Muller-Oerlinghausen, B., Oschenfahrt, H. & Schonhofer, P.S. (1986). Adverse drug reactions to first- and second-generation antidepressants: A critical evaluation of drug surveillance data. British Journal of Psychiatry, 148, 38-43.

Sireling, L. (1986). Depression in mentally handicapped patients: Diagnostic and neuroendocrine evaluation. British Journal of Psychiatry, 149, 274-248.

Snaith, R.P., James, F.E. & Winokur, B. (1979). The drug treatment of mental illness and epilepsy in the mentally handicapped patient. In: F. James & R. Snaith (Eds.), Psychiatric illness and mental handicap. London: Gaskell Press.

Sovner, R. & Hurley, A.D. (1983). Do the mentally retarded suffer from affective illness? Archives of General Psychiatry, 40, 61-67.

Sprague, R.L. & Werry, J.S. (1971). Methodology of psychopharmacological studies with the retarded. In: N. Ellis (Ed.), International Review of Research in Mental Retardation, Vol. 5. New York: Academic Press.

Anton Dosen and Frank J. Menolascino (Eds.) (1990). Depression in mentally retarded children and adults. Leiden, the Netherlands: Logon Publications. ISBN 90-73197-01-5

Chapter 20

Caring for the mental health of the mentally retarded population

Anton Dosen, M.D.
Frank J. Menolascino, M.D.

Introduction

There is no doubt that mentally retarded persons are subject to the same types of mental illness as the general population. In addition, because of specific impairments in the central nervous system and unfavorable developmental and environmental circumstances, mentally retarded persons are at an even greater risk than the general population to develop particular types of psychiatric disorders, including depression of a psychotic and neurotic or reactive type. The concepts of normaliz-ation, integration, and the developmental model have all created an increasing need to establish community-based programs which focus on protecting and improving the mental health of the mentally retarded and, throughout the world, countries are developing mental health care for the mentally retarded in different ways. In Sweden, for example, mentally retarded-mentally ill citizens have the right to be treated by the regular mental health system, yet there is a severe shortage of trained professionals in this field and research is almost nonexistent (Melin, 1987).

In Canada, the mentally retarded-mentally ill are usually served in the psychiatric units of general hospitals for short-term psychotic illnesses. Long-term psychiatric disorders are typically treated in mental retardation facilities and supported by psychiatric consultations. Yet the gap between psychiatric hospitals and mental retardation facilities is wide, and there is little cooperation or understanding between these two service systems (Zarfas, 1987).

The Netherlands has created special units for the acute treatment of behaviorally disturbed, mildy retareded persons. Acute psychiatric

341

problems in the more severely retarded are usually treated in psychiatric hospitals and long-term disorders in institutions for the mentally retarded. Again, the gap between the mental retardation service system and facilities for mental health is striking. There are no special community-based programs, little scientific research, and no special training for professionals who wish to concentrate on caring for the mental health of the mentally retarded. Currently, the construction of special centers for the mental health care of the mentally retarded is being advocated so as to promote mental health in this population and serve as education, training, and research centers for professionals in the field (Dosen, 1978, 1989).

In the United Kingdom, mental retardation is a psychiatric specialty and both psychiatrist and nursing staff undergo a specialist's training. The behaviorally disturbed mentally retarded are cared for in mental handicap hospitals where a body of experienced clinicians is available to provide treatment as well as train other psychiatrists and mental health professionals in this area. In spite of competent training and relatively high level of research, however, there are disagreements regarding the establishment of community-based programs and services (Day, 1987). It has been argued, for example, that the mentally retarded-mentally ill should be served by mainstream psychiatric services, a view that lacks the support of a majority of psychiatrists. Yet recent developments indicate that encouraging work will soon be done in creating solid community=based programs that will further develop the mental health care of Britain's mentally retarded citizens (Bouras & Drummond, 1989).

In the United States, the current challenge is to define and develop programmatic mechanisms which will prevent the institutionalization of the mentally retarded-mentally ill. The array of programs and services that are beining created to facilitate this challenge include models of care and treatment for acute psychiatric disorders, specialized educational and vocational programs, group homes, and supportive services such as day hospitals, counseling, and family support programs. Recent discussions revolve around whether the mentally retarded-mentally ill should be included in separate programs for the dually diagnosed or served through established mental health care programs. The current trend is to provide immediate care for acute psychiatric needs and to follow up with day care through the mental health centers, while mental retardation programs focus on the residential, educational, vocational, and recrational needs of these individuals. Recommendations for the future are to improve these services, to support basic and applied reserach, and to stimulate the training of specialists.

As evidenced in most of these countries, retarded citizens with mental illness tend to fall into the gap which has long separated mental retardation and mental health services. It is gratifying that current trends show a clear tendency to bridge this gap by creating facilities for multidisciplinary care in which mental health and mental retardation services can both make their specific professional contributions. According to The National Strategy Conference on Mental Retardation and Mental Health (Stark, Menolascino, Alberelli and Gray, 1988), the best approach is to treat the acute psychiatric needs of the mentally retarded in psychiatric settings and to meet long-term needs in community programs where secondary support can be provided by the mental health system. For tertiary care, special centers can be organized so as to provide highly specialized diagnostic patient services and state-of-the-art research and training for larger groups of professionals.

A model program

A good example of an effective approach to the mental health challenges of the mentally retarded is the Eastern Nebraska Community Office of Retardation (ENCOR). For the last two decaded ENCOR has been recognized as an outstanding model in the United States for the provision of modern community-based mental retardation services. Examples of such services include the Developmental Maximation Home for the severely retarded-multiply handicapped, integrated pre-school services, crisis assistance services (e.g., respite care), specialized group homes, alternative living units, in-home teachers, work stations in industry, and many other (Casey, McGee, Stark & Menolascino, 1985; Menolascino, 1977, 1989). Each of these models has helped ENCOR demonstrate that innovative services for the mentally retarded can be developed to specifically meet their various needs in a modern, humane, and cost-effective manner.

At any given time, there are approximately 135 persons in the ENCOR system (16% of the total number served) who are identified as having a dual diagnosis of mental retardation and mental illness to such a degree as to require special supports and services. These individuals typically have a wide variety of DSM-III-R (American Psychiatric Association, 1987) acute, sub-acute, and chronic psychiatric disorders.

Table 20.1
Types of mental illness in the ENCOR

Symptoms Cluster	Etiology
1. Tense, overreacts to minimal interpersonal stress; insomnia; fearful of expectations or changes in working or living environments.	Adjustment reaction of adolescence/adulthood
2. Hyperkinetic; increased irritability; excessive focus on self; frequent instances of self-stimulatory (e.g., head banging) and primitive (e.g. pica) behaviors. These and other out-of-control behaviors are noted upon minimal stress.	Organic brain syndrome with transient psychotic reaction
3. Overly dependent, excessively cautious, passive; relatively insensitive to the needs ofothers.	Personality trait disorder
4. Borderline contact with reality; becomes very suspicious/paranoid when under minimal stress.	Personality pattern disorder
5. Hallucinations, bizarre behaviour, distincly out of contact with reality.	Functional psychosis (e.g.,schizophrenia)
6. Unreliable, impulsive; manipulative, demanding; extremely self-centered.	Anti-social personality
7. Diffuse anxious; much procrastination, disturbing thoughts/dreams that significantly interfere with school/work adjustments.	Anxiety disorder
8. Despondent, nihilistic view of life; poor appetite, associated with recent signficant weight loss; persistent insomnia.	Major affective disorder (e.g., depression)

A brief overview of the dually diagnosed individuals served by ENCOR is depicted in Table 20.1, and the following two examples provide a capsule illustration of the wide range of mentally retarded-mentally ill clients served by ENCOR.

Mary is a moderately retarded young adult who lives at home. She has always been shy and hesitant in social situations and is having increasing difficulty adjusting to adult life. As a result she begins to withdraw, loses interest in her usually excellent hygiene, and complains, while pointing to her head, that "Men put bad things in here". She subsequently fails on her job placement in an industry work station.

John, who had been institutionalized most of his life, is now slowly adjusting to a more enriched life in an ENCOR group home. He is severally retarded and periodically displays self-abusive behaviors when directly requested to participate in small group and pre-vocational training acitivities. As he learns to live in more enriched interpersonal and working environments, it is noted that his self-abusive behaviors slowly disappear.

Model service planning

Like all persons, the mentally retarded-mentally ill have personal, emotional, and social needs which require understanding and support. ENCOR has historically served these needs in the mainstream of its service system. A recent survey of the number of mentally retarded persons who present instances of dual diagnosis in the various ENCOR programs shows that these clients can be grouped on three levels:
Level I includes clients who present daily behavioral management problems such as inability to attend to tasks, hyperactivity and aggressive behaviors, etc.
Level II consists of clients who may have several behavioral problems per month, but not daily.
Level III includes clients who present behavioral problems only serveral times throughout the year.

This analysis demonstrates that the planning of services for a population of mentally retareded-mentally ill persons depends not on specific diagnoses, but rather on the type of personnel, supports, and back-up services required. The large majority of Level I and Level II patients are late adolescents and young adults, most of whom currently work in Industrial Training Centers and live in group homes.

Several service challenges can be inferred from the above data:

1. With the mentally retarded-mentally ill dispersed across a rather large geographical area, it is difficult to monitor their programming or the problems which they present to themselves and to others. This is especially true for Level I and Level II patients.

2. The issue of whether these patients should be separated from other patients does not seem to emerge as a basic queston. There are those who are well served in ENCOR settings that congregate clients as well as settings that do not.

3. Staff training is a challenge with this dispersed vocational and residential population. This is further complicated by an average staff turnover rate of 21% every 18 months due mainly to marriages and upward mobility.

4. Some mentally retarded-mentally ill patients appear to be served well, while others seem to present constant "problems". The key factors in this situation appear to center around staffing consistency, staff competency, and staff attitudes.

A small percentage of Level I clients (2 to 4 persons at any given time) present acute psychiatric problems -- aggressive behaviors, self-abusive behaviors, or severe withdrawal. A larger percentage of a mix of Level I and II patients (6 to 15 persons at any give time) present sub-acute psychiatric problems which are usually controlled to a manageable degree, but nevertheless remain in a rather fragile behavioral state. The largest percentage at any given time have chronic psychiatric needs (Level III) which are low in terms of frequency of problems. These patients are in relatively stable condition and primarily require adequate monitoring and responsive back-up servies. Patients at each level present a service challenge that requires specific responses to both residential and day program placement needs. Table 20.2 and the following four points outline a recommended system of services for meeting the special needs of the dually diagnosed.

Table 20.2
Model system of services

Level	Model	Residential pogram	Day program
Level I	Acute Care	2-4 Persons in a psychiatric hospital setting for acute care. Purpose: stabilization. Duration: 2-4 weeks.	Intensive developmental programming, behavioral management and possible neuroleptic medication initiation and adjustment.
Level II	Sub-Acute Care	6-15 Persons in two model group homes; 1:2 staffing with back-up staff available. Purpose: transitional. Duration: 6-12 months. Sub-purpose: practicum training for staff and demonstration of this special model of care.	Separate prevocational programming, either in or out of Industrial Training Centers, with subsequent transition to ITS's or other vocational alternatives.
Level III	Chronic Care	69-75 Persons dispersed in ENCOR's current residential system; 1-3 staffing with back-up staff and liaison monitoring. Duration: long-term.	ITC's, work stations in industry, competitive employment, other structured day programs.

1. Two liaison positions can be created to serve all of Level I, II, and III clients so as to ensure early identification and rapid refferal, and to closely coordinate the transition back to or within an overall system of services. There need be no added cost for these two recommended positions; current advisors can be reassigned with redesigned job descriptions.

2. Two four- to six-bed model group homes can be established for Level I and Level II clients. The majority of these clients will eventually move into other less restrictive residences depending upon the need for supervision. These model group homes serve as facilities for transition from acute care psychiatric hospital settings as well as back-up short-term residential placement options for patients who have become disruptive in other residential settings. These homes should be transitional in nature with a focus on sequential movement into less restrivtive and less costly residential settings. They can also serve as practicum training sites for staff by providing oppurtunities for learning how to effectively manage dually diagnosed clients. No added cost need be incurred if two established group homes are shifted to this proposed model.

3. A model prevocational program for Level I and Level II clients can be set up to demonstrte special treatment and programmatic techniques for patients in cute care of tranistional settings. This model program can be established either in or outside current Industrial Training Centers and can also serve as a practicum training site. It should be considered a short-term program which serves to further stabilize patients prior to subsequent vocational placement.

4. A two- to four-week practicum training program can be established for staff working with the mentally retarded-mentally ill, with periodic follow-up training through community agencies. The needs of this population require practical, hands on pre-service and in-service training. Sites for this special training can be located in the two previously described model group homes and the model prevocational program. Implementation of such a program provied staff with the competencies necessary to serve this population, improves staff turnover rate, and brings improved services to **all** dually diagnosed clients.

Conclusion

The educational, residential, and vocational support requires for the mental health of the mentally retarded must be characterized by stability, constancy, and a spirit of interdependence. Service setttings hould be ones in which consistency in relationships can be fostered so that bonding can be learned. Once a firm, affective bond has been established and feelings of trust and security have grown, a mentally retarded indiviudal can then be motivated to learn new modes of behavior. The challenge for the professoinal caregiver is to lend a hand along the difficult developmental path through fears and emotional conflicts and to break the vicious circle of despair which results from severe behavioral difficulties.

Although there is no easy answer to serving the special needs of this population, there are principes which should be espused from the inception normalization, the developmetnal model, and cost-benefit considerations. The issue is not that service systems for the retarded are "saturated" with a special sub-population of the dually diagnosed, but that at any given time there will exist a relatively small number of mentally retarded-mentally ill persons who require specialized services. The recommendations contained herein can greatly facilitate active provision of the modern services which this challenging population both requires and deserves.

References

American Psychiatric Association (1987). Diagnostic and statistical manual on mental disorders - Third edition - Revised. Washington, D.C.: American Psychiatric Association.

Bouras, N. & Drummond, K. (1989). Community psychiatric service in mental handicap: Six years of experience. London: NVPRD.

Casey, K., McGee, J.J., Stark, J. & Menolascino, F.J. (1985). A community-based service system for the mentally retarded: The ENCOR experience. Lincoln: University of Nebraska Press.

Day, K. (1987, June). Service models in the United Kingdom. Symposium conducted at the meeting of the International research conference on the mental health aspects of mental retardation. Evanston, Illinois.

Dosen, A. (1987, June): Service models in the Netherlands; symposium conducted at the meeting of the International Research Conference on the Mental Health Aspects of Mental Retardation, Evanston, Illinois.

Dosen, A. (1989). Zorg voor geestelijke gezondheid bij geestelijk gehandicapten. Amersfoort: NGBZ.

Melin, L. (1987, June). Service models in Sweden. Symposium conducted at the meeting of the International research conference on the mental health aspects of mental retardation. Evanston, Illinois.

Menolascino, F.J. (1989). Model services for treatment/management of the mentally retarded-mentally ill. Community Mental Health Journal, 25, 145-155.

Menolascino, F.J. (1977). Challenges in mental retardation: progressive ideologies and services. New York: Human Sciences Press.

Stark, J.A., Menolascino, F.J., Alberelli, M.H. & Gray, K.C., (1988). Mental retardation and mental health. New York: Springer-Verlag.

Zarfas, D.E. (1987, June). Service models in Canada. Symposium conducted at the meeting of the International research conference on the mental health aspects of mental retardation. Evanston, Illinois.

Conclusion

Anton Dosen, M.D.
Frank J. Menolascino, M.D.

Ten years ago it was relatively common for mental health clinicians to question the possibility that mentally retarded individuals could develop an affective disorder. Today there is little doubt that depressive states of various etiologies and intensities may occur at all levels of mental retardation in both children and adults, probably in even higher numbers than in the nonretarded population. The fact that this disorder is infrequently detected is due to problems involving recognition and diagnosis rather than low frequency of prevalence. The difficulties with which physicians are faced when discussing the diagnosis of depression in the mentally retared include:

- Questionable reliability of diagnosis: Unique aspects of the manifestation of depression in the mentally retarded can create ambiguity and a disinclination to firmly establish this diagnosis.
- Questions regarding etiology: Can one assume that depression in mentally retarded is caused by the same etiology as in the nonretarded or are there other factors specific to mental retardation which play a role in the onset of this disorder.
- Differing symptomatology: The symptoms of depression at lower levels of mental retardation may be different from those at higher levels which can make diagnosis extremely difficult.
- Questions regarding treatment: Do the same treatment methods come into play for both the mentally retarded and the nonretarded or do the mentally retarded require another treatment approach.

In adressing the questionable reliability of the diagnosis of depression, it becomes obvious that the diagnostician must first accept the fact that depression actually occurs in the mentally retarded before he or she can undertake steps toward its assessment. Yet the occurrence of depression in the mentally retarded is not entirely accepted by all psychiatrists, and a change in attitude regarding the psychopathology of this population is much needed.

Such a change will require a certain elasticity, self-criticism, and creativity on the part of these physicians, who must also have the courage to step outside generally accepted diagnostic systems and

351

criteria. In short, diagnosticians who work with the mentally retarded population have to be aware that they are involved in pioneering work and that in order to recognize a syndrome like depression they must first be convinced that the disorder does occur.

The etiology of depression in the general population is typically discussed in broad terms. Professionals in the field of mental retardation believe that depression in the mentally handicapped may be caused by the same etiology as in the nonretarded, but that there are factors unique to the retarded - biological, organic, psychosocial, and developmental - which may also play an etiological role. Scientific insight into relationships among each of these factors and depression itself is scarce, and the mechanisms of onset are rather unclear. One of the reasons for this lack of concise understanding concerns our current knowledge regarding the specific socio-emotional development of mentally retarded individuals. Despite growing scientific interest in the emotional and social development of the cognitively normal child, there has been little investigation into the development of the mentally retarded child. Current insight into the roles that developmental problems may play in the onset of depression assumes that the same mechanisms are important etiological factors for both. However, because of the delayed developmental progress of the mentally retarded, its link with depression is complex and difficult to recognize and, in instances of combined developmental problems, a single clinical picture may be colored by symptoms of other syndromes, making the diagnosis of depression in this population extremely challenging.

The symptomatology of depression in the mentally retarded, dependent as it is upon cognitive level, age, and expressive ability of the individual under assessment, may also differ from that found in nonretarded individuals. It is important to remember that individuals with severe or profound retardation tend to exhibit more primitive symptoms, whereas persons at mild or moderate levels exhibit symptoms similar to those seen in nonretarded persons. The fact that the severely and profoundly retarded may show identical symptoms for different psychopathologies makes diagnosis in these instances even more challenging. Thus a symptom, as such, provides little support for the diagnosis of depression and must be related to other findings based on holistic case histories and examinations. While symptoms alone do not serve as clear diagnostic criteria, however, they may provide clues for further target-directed assessment.

Various diagnostic tools are currently being developed to aid in this assessment, yet the results have so far failed to provide much support. There have been a number of attempts to develop rating scales, but they have all faced similar problems of low reliability in cases involving severe retardation. Biochemical tests for depression are promising, but their reliability for establishing a clinical diagnosis remains questionable. Neurophysiological assessment is in full development, but the results are not yet sufficient to lend support to the diagnostic process.

Although all forms of depression are known to occur in the mentally retarded, questions remain as to whether these individuals can develop a specific form of depression caused and colored by their unique lives and developmental problems.

In principle, the treatment of depression in the mentally retarded involves the same therapeutic forms as those used for the nonretarded population. While psychotherapeutic, medical, and other types of therapy are all applicable, each needs to be adapted to the developmental level, organic substrate, and communication capabilities of the mentally retarded patient. When applied without modification, such treatment methods usually fail to provide satisfactory effects. Psychopharmacological adjuncts may result in improvement, but there is great uncertainty concerning specificity, dosage, therapeutic blood levels, and the sensitivity of mentally retarded persons to side effects.

Although research into the occurrence of depression in the mentally retarded is developing, it is not progressing as rapidly as one would wish. Clinical research is needed in epidemiology, diagnosis, prevalence, treatment, and prevention. One of the reasons for the current paucity of research can be attributed to the diagnostic problems already addressed.

Widely accepted systems, such as DSM-III-R, are often insufficient for diagnosing the more severely retarded, who are not only unable to express their emotional state but may exhibit symptoms which simply do not emerge in nonretarded persons. One task for investigators in this field is to discover the ways in which existing diagnostic criteria can be adapted for use with mentally retarded patients. Until then, one must remain cautious when applying otherwise widely accepted diagnostic criteria to mentally retarded patients.

New strategies concerning the treatment of depression in the mentally retarded are encouraging, but in most cases researchers describe single case studies without outlining their basic philosophy or systemizing their methodology of treatment. In addition, such treatment strategies are intimately related to the initial diagnoses of depression and thus require that diagnostic criteria be included as a basic consideration. Since it is presumable that factors which are not particularly relevant in the nonretarded play a role in the onset of depression in the mentally retarded, one can assume that in addition to existing treatment methods there are other possibilities for treating depression in retarded individuals. These possibilities should be explored.

Further work in the prevention of depression in the mentally retarded is much needed. It should be directed towards both early detection of emotional disturbances and early counseling and guidance of parents and other caregivers concerning adequate social and emotional stimulation and the pedagogical approach that is compatible with the mentally retarded person.

Understanding the nature and underlying causes of mental illness is only the beginning of the care for mental health. Regardless of the types or intensity of disturbed behavior, the fundamental objective of care should be to break through whatever avoidant, self-injurious, disruptive or destructive behaviors might exist, and to respectfully move the person into a state of human interdependence and optimal social reintegration. In order to accomplish this, specialised service models are required, offering a range of medical, psychiatric, educational, vocational and residential services. The task of professional caregivers is to discover and put into practice personal and social change strategies to help clients lead a satisfying life within their families and communities. To accomplish this task, professionals need adequate training that enables them to recognize and respond to the mental health needs of the mentally retarded.

Most authors of this volume have accentuated the need for further scientific enquiry in the field of depression in the mentally retarded. Many chapters offer indications as to the possible direction and topics of further research.

We hope that this book will serve its purpose in both areas, practice as well as research, so that it will help practitioners in their daily work and stimulate researchers to extend and improve the knowledge now available.

Subject index

A

affective disorder 17, 26, 27, 40, 45, 50, 55, 67, 76, 82, 115-117, 119, 127, 131, 134, 141, 152-154, 156, 158, 160, 164, 184, 186, 189, 190, 191, 193, 195-198, 210, 220, 221, 225, 245, 253, 257, 323, 339, 344, 351

aftercare 237, 244, 245, 248

aggression 15, 21, 41, 48, 96, 102, 104, 115, 118, 119, 121, 125, 132, 164, 178, 186, 187, 213, 221, 224, 226, 229, 232, 258-260, 285, 291

agitation 45, 115, 116, 118, 119, 129, 132, 133, 138, 157, 168, 177, 178, 182, 187, 210, 221, 240, 241, 257, 331-333

akathisia 181, 194

aloneness 98-100, 103-106, 109

Alzheimer's disease 28, 228

anaclitic depression 40, 68, 79

anhedonia 45, 116, 118, 119

anxiety 13, 20, 23-25, 27, 45, 49, 66-69, 74, 83, 88, 89, 92, 95, 97, 107, 109, 115, 116, 118, 119, 132, 133, 142, 144, 145, 148, 149, 150, 201, 209, 211, 235, 236, 240, 241, 258, 262, 317, 324, 333, 338, 344

attachment 69, 74, 77, 78, 82, 85, 87-89, 92-94, 96, 124, 258, 262, 263

attention deficit 260

authoritarian 99, 100, 105, 106

autism 11, 16, 20, 21, 24, 29, 34, 73, 176, 183-186, 188, 190, 195, 198, 228, 262, 285, 338

B

Beck Depression Inventory 46, 137, 201-204, 206, 212, 222, 311, 318

behavioral assessment 92, 199, 214, 218, 326

behavioral treatment 216, 309, 316, 317, 320, 326

Bellevue Index of Depression 205, 212

bereavement 147, 153, 243, 245, 252

beta blocker 180, 181, 187

biochemical balance 119

biological marker 228

bipolar disorder (BP-DIS) 154, 157, 158, 165, 172, 175, 176, 179, 180-186, 188, 189, 190, 191, 192, 195, 196, 198

bizarre behavior 24

buspirone 181

C

carbamazepine   119, 120, 181, 183, 184, 197, 200, 243, 257, 337, 339
catatonia   134, 154, 158, 172
Child Behavior Checklist (CBC)   205, 206, 213
Child Depression Inventory (CDI)   205, 206, 212, 217
chronic depression   253
chronic mania   183, 184, 187, 192
chronic resistant depression   243
classification   11, 12, 33, 37-39, 50, 54, 57, 61, 71, 78, 129, 152, 172, 215, 276, 326
client-centered   282, 292, 293, 307
clonazepam   192, 193
clopenthixol   333, 336
cognitive therapy   48, 92, 243, 244, 250, 251, 310, 325
cognitive-behavioral   296, 322
communication skills   55, 135, 175, 178, 324, 329
community placement   20, 161, 170
compulsory   246
constipation   115, 118, 119, 121, 122, 257
counseling   91, 102, 147, 162, 165, 166, 168, 243, 246, 258, 264, 277, 282, 290, 292, 293, 307, 342

D

death   17, 37, 40, 47, 85, 86, 97-102, 104, 106, 109, 115, 116, 118, 119, 134, 135, 144, 146, 147, 150, 159, 245, 246, 307, 329
dementia   23, 26-28, 141, 220, 227, 231, 332
dependent personality   83, 89, 91
depressed mood   69, 93, 110, 129, 132, 133, 138, 145, 148, 155, 180, 186, 210, 312, 313, 328
Depression Adjective Checklist   203, 205
depressive personality   82, 92
deprivation   29, 41, 43, 46, 68, 88, 89, 92, 96, 263, 300, 301
desipramine   334
destructiveness   115, 116, 118, 119, 121, 259, 260
developmental contingency   13
developmental depression   74, 124, 262
developmental stage   68, 262
Dexamethasone Suppression Test (DST)   44, 45, 136, 139, 140, 143, 148, 151, 153, 154, 158, 163, 219-225, 229-233, 331
diagnostic overshadowing   137, 154
differential diagnosis   26, 140, 147, 156, 158, 175, 181, 182, 222

distractibility   157, 176, 177, 179, 183, 184, 187

dosage   140, 167, 241-243, 335-337, 353

Down syndrome   12, 76, 79, 85, 101, 105, 131, 136, 141, 151, 185, 186, 221

doxepin   334

drug combinations   28, 243

drug treatment   238, 240, 253, 334, 339

DSM-III   11, 24, 37-39, 54, 59, 61, 114, 116, 117, 120, 139, 154-156, 172, 176, 177, 178, 197, 201, 205, 209, 221, 222, 224, 333, 343, 353

dual diagnosis   32, 51, 57, 59, 99, 190, 214, 253, 282, 342, 343, 345-348

divalproex sodium (DVP)   181, 183-187

E

Eastern Nebraska Community Office of Retardation (ENCOR)   22, 343-347, 349

electroconvulsive therapy (ECT)   45-47, 136, 140, 142, 144, 237-239, 240, 242, 243, 245, 249-251, 253, 335, 336

emotional development   34, 65, 67, 72, 75, 94, 95, 110, 122, 125, 352

emotional fragility   97, 98

emotional support   163, 166, 169, 170

encopresis   121, 122

endogenous depression   129, 140, 219-221, 223, 230, 235, 240

enuresis   121, 122

epidemiology   38, 50, 57, 76, 114, 128, 131, 144, 188, 190, 353

epilepsy   236, 242, 244, 248, 260, 333, 339

etiology   38, 43, 45, 46, 96, 122, 124, 219, 228, 281, 295, 322, 325, 331, 332, 344, 351, 352, 354

excessive expectations   19-21

existential anxiety   66-68, 97

existential paradigm   97, 109

external locus of control   97

F

family history   38, 54, 131, 136, 139, 142, 143, 148, 156, 161, 163, 165, 181, 184, 185, 195

family therapy   46, 255, 304, 306

follow-up   127, 197, 203, 219, 245, 291, 314, 316-319, 348

Fragile X syndrome   185-187, 228

357

G

Goldberg Clinical Interview Schedule 137
grandiosity 84, 143, 158, 176, 179
guilt 37, 52, 67, 69, 88, 123, 124, 129, 132, 133, 138, 144, 159, 205, 213, 258

H

haloperidol 181, 184, 336
Hamilton Rating Scale for Depression 137, 204, 222
hemisphere 49, 76, 77, 155, 333, 336
homocystinuria 188, 193
hopelessness 37, 54, 68, 99, 106, 134, 155, 300
Hypothalamic-Pituitary-Adrenal (HPA) 219-221, 223, 225, 228, 231, 232
hyperactivity 13, 87, 96, 115, 116, 118, 119, 121-123, 187, 213, 259, 260, 345
hypersomnia 104, 180, 195
hyperthyroidism 179
hypochondriasis 132, 133, 144
hypomania 127, 178, 241
hysterical 132, 134, 148, 149

I

ICD-9 37, 50, 54
imipramine 126, 201, 221, 230, 253, 317, 333
individuation 65, 66, 72-74, 84, 88, 89, 91, 270
insomnia 103, 145, 176, 181, 223, 344
irritability 45, 58, 87, 90, 93, 94, 96, 105, 115, 116, 118, 119, 132, 133, 135, 146, 149, 157, 158, 164, 177-179, 181, 186, 187, 202, 205, 318, 344

K

kinesthesia 268, 269, 272, 275
Klinefelter's syndrome 188

L

learned helplessness 63, 75, 82, 85, 91, 92, 95, 295, 309, 310, 322, 329
Lesch-Nyhan syndrome 226, 233
life events 123, 144, 245, 246, 332
lithium 119, 120, 135, 143, 154, 165, 180, 182, 183, 192, 195-198, 231, 243, 245, 251-253, 257, 281, 333, 336-339
low self-esteem 15, 17, 69, 75, 89, 114-116, 118, 119, 122, 258, 303

M

major affective disorder 115-117, 164, 344
mania 127, 129, 131, 135, 140, 151, 155, 157-159, 173, 176, 178-181, 183, 184, 186, 187, 190, 192-194, 196-198, 336, 337
manic depressive 49, 129, 131, 143, 151-154, 171, 190, 191, 195, 197, 252, 338
Mastery Orientation Inventory 310
meaninglessness 98, 103
medication 21, 86, 90, 119, 120, 124, 136, 137, 140, 142-144, 162, 164, 165, 166, 168, 221, 240-243, 245, 257, 262, 263, 277, 318, 320, 335
melancholia 77, 129, 229, 230
mental health care 36, 38, 92, 341, 342
metacommunication 98, 268-270, 273, 277
mild retardation 17-19, 53, 72, 85, 114, 115, 123, 259, 266, 273, 274, 277
Minnesota Multiphasic Personality Inventory (MMPI) 202, 211
moderate retardation 13, 16, 17, 20, 53, 54, 70, 72, 118, 200-202, 221, 266, 328, 345
monoamine metabolites 225, 229, 232
Monoamine Oxidase Inhibitors (MAOIs) 44, 47, 237, 240, 241, 243, 253, 333, 335
Montgomery-Asberg Depression Rating Scale 46
motor retardation 69, 257
Mutual Storytelling 296-298, 301, 305
myelinization 64-66

N

neuroendocrine 152, 154, 155, 182, 220, 225, 232, 339
nicotinamide 119, 120, 126, 257
normalization 91, 93, 230, 341, 348
nutritional deficiencies 227

O

object-loss 88, 89
observation 94, 114, 117, 121, 136, 138, 143, 150, 205, 214, 239, 301
obsessional behavior 132, 148
onset of depression 68, 74, 76, 122, 352, 353
organic brain syndrome 26, 27, 344
organic mood syndrome 184-186
organic psychosis 155
overprotection 20, 99, 105, 106, 266

P

paranoid   22-24, 129, 132, 134, 140, 142, 144, 157, 160, 161, 165, 168,
190, 242, 344
phenothiazine   241, 338
plasma monitoring   334, 335
play therapy   296, 299, 303, 305-307
practognostic function   270
pre-therapy   281, 282, 284, 285, 287, 291-293, 306
precipitating factors   140, 146
predisposing personality   148
Present State Examination   59
prevalence   22, 33, 46, 49, 51, 55-59, 61, 76, 93, 113, 114, 119, 122,
125, 130, 131, 144, 153, 188-191, 242, 301, 333, 336, 338, 351, 353,
354
prevention   26, 44, 192, 245, 249, 324, 325, 353, 354
profound retardation   28, 31, 54, 57, 71, 72, 114, 115, 118, 119, 123,
196, 200, 265, 269, 277, 302, 338, 352
prophylactic   192, 245, 337
psychomotor retardation   45, 114, 116, 129, 133, 136, 138, 142-144, 157,
180, 242, 285
psychomotoricity   267, 269, 271, 277
Psychopathology Instrument for Mentally Retarded Adults (PIMRA)   204,
209, 210, 214, 218, 311, 328, 329
psychopharmacological   37, 251, 259, 331, 337, 353
psychotherapy   19, 25, 46, 92, 102, 109-111, 119, 124, 162-164, 215, 243,
252, 255, 256, 258, 264, 267, 268, 277, 281, 282, 284, 290, 291-293,
301, 305-307, 326
psychotic depression   36, 129, 131, 134-136, 138-140, 142, 147, 148, 150,
154, 232, 242, 246

R

rapid cycling   135, 141, 152, 175, 182, 183, 185, 186, 190, 192-194, 198
rapid eye movement   140, 227
reactive depression   102, 105, 114, 120, 140, 144, 147, 162, 240, 245,
310
regression   11, 16, 114, 121, 134, 157, 262, 270, 273
rehabilitation   235-237, 244, 248
reinforcement theory   309, 310
relationship therapy   119, 124, 126, 256, 258-260, 264
relocation syndrome   147
REM latency   227, 228, 331